SUPERNATURAL SURVIVORS: A COUNSELLOR'S GHOST STORY

BY

LOUISA MARSH

www.authorsonline.co.uk

An Authors OnLine Book

Text Copyright © Louisa Marsh 2010

Cover design by Matthew Swann ©

All rights reserved. No part of this publication may be reproduced, stored in a retrieval system, or transmitted in any form or by any means, electronic, mechanical, photocopy, recording or otherwise, without prior written permission of the copyright owner. Nor can it be circulated in any form of binding or cover other than that in which it is published and without similar condition including this condition being imposed on a subsequent purchaser.

British Library Cataloguing Publication Data.
A catalogue record for this book is available from the British Library

ISBN 978-07552-0640-7

Authors OnLine Ltd
19 The Cinques
Gamlingay, Sandy
Bedfordshire SG19 3NU
England

This book is also available in e-book format, details of which are available at www.authorsonline.co.uk

For Steve...and all the dogs that see rainbows...

CONTENTS

Part One – Mind, Body or Spirit? 1

Introduction – Origins of Post Traumatic Stress – Hysteria, War & Abuse – 'Ghosts' Emerging – Flashbacks & Perceptual Memories – Visual, Auditory & Other Sensory Disturbances – Triggers & Timing – Abused Children, Haunted Adults – The Body – Brain, Bonding & Biology – Haunted Clients; Leonie, Gita & Jennifer – The Devil? – Or Dissociation? – The Three Faces of Eve – Sybil – When Rabbit Howls

Part Two – The Dog That Saw a Rainbow: The Haunting of Steve 41

Ten Years Later – The Universal Appeal of the Supernatural – Steve's Background – Encounters 2006 – Night Ghosts – 'John' – Ghosts Hurt or Hurting – Projection onto an Apparition – Projective Identification – Physical Ghosts – As For Me – Exorcism, An Obvious Answer? – Banishment – The Psychologist's Report – Death on the Railways – Re-Encounters 2007 – Electric Entities – A Pivotal Night – Prophets, Pareidolia & More Projection – A Spiritualist's Perception – The Nature of an Essence – How Do We Know We Are Dead? – Ghostly Motivation – Further Encounters 2008 – Scents and Sensations – A Colleague's Report – Voices – Outstanding Questions – Counsellors in Conversation

Part Three – Psychic or Psychotic? 158

Belief & Desire – Group Belief – Science & Spirituality – Mysticism & Mental Health – Temporal Lobe Epilepsy – Schizophrenia – Spirit Possession – Energies, Auras & Vibrations – Under Psychic Attack – How Healing Works – Facing Demons – Three Psychics – Doris Stokes – Sally Morgan – Michele Knight

Part Four – Tilting the Mirror 216

Implications; Why This Person, Why This Problem? Why Now? – A Ghost in the Therapy Room – Challenges for the Counsellor – Spiders, Spooks & Spaceships – Anything Else Out There? – Thoughts & Reflections – Where to From Here? Supernatural Evolution – On the Unknown

Part Five – The End of the Rainbow 242

Encounters 2009 – Final Thoughts

Afterword 262

Bibliography 263

PART ONE

MIND, BODY OR SPIRIT?

Introduction

In some way, I had already started to notice the ghosts. During the 1990s I was employed as a counsellor at the local Rape Crisis Centre. My therapeutic work was undertaken mainly with female adult survivors of childhood sexual abuse. Over the five or so years I spent there, I gradually began to observe that the impact of these women's experiences appeared to go much deeper than the legacy of physical, emotional and mental effects that appear predominately in many contemporary studies on this issue. At the time many of my clients were reporting seeing, hearing and sensing phenomena that they were interpreting as originating either from supernatural or paranormal sources, or it seemed that they simply felt that they were going 'mad.' Either way, it felt like some women were literally being 'haunted.'

Part one of this work comprises a brief summary of some of the conclusions I came to at the time, when I considered the evidence that severe levels of anxiety, stress and the effects of trauma were manifesting in symptoms such as flashbacks, psychosomatic bodily sensations and perceptual disturbances, which were sometimes being interpreted by survivors as paranormal experiences. Some client examples briefly illustrate my discoveries. I was also concerned with studying how traumatic experiences may be 'forgotten' or 'repressed' through dissociation and I also include the biographies of three sexual abuse survivors who have a strong dissociative disordered identity diagnosis and how hints of supernatural myth and apparent activity seems to pervade the lives of some abuse survivors generally. This section of the book is quite academic and illustrates theory which seemed to fit in with my learning and belief systems at this point in my life. My purpose in writing part one, therefore, was to essentially challenge the notion of the existence of ghosts and argue that haunting events take place in the psyche and as part of the brain's processing. These experiences basically remain valid experiences for some individuals, perhaps as one consequence of trauma resulting in disturbances in sensory perception. I claimed at the time that the experience of being haunted by ghosts focussed around how the person affected may choose to interpret such experiences, perhaps as a defence or re-routed way of coping.

A decade later and having changed my client group to counselling university students, I began to question whether my findings around haunting events and issues pertaining to the existence of ghosts did indeed manifest all in the mind as I had believed. I began to wonder if some physical and perceptual disturbances were in fact a product of genuine supernatural phenomena.

This transition occurred when my partner, Steve, started to be regularly haunted by an apparition and this experience is explored extensively in part two. Here I share a personal story of a haunting which affected us both and subsequently I detail my own thoughts and reactions to the situation from the perspective of being in a personal relationship, whilst endeavouring to include some observations as a therapist. My aim has been to write what happened to my partner and illustrate the process both he and I went through during this disturbing period of time in our lives.

Less academic and considerably more emotional in content, this main section of the book includes the facts about what happened within the environment and part consists of extracts from a diary I kept over the years when we were affected by the events. Steve also contributes. My diary entries record an unfolding of experience and detail my thoughts and emotional responses. Like stopping at stations, I pause occasionally for contemplation; to observe the view, to ground myself and to take on the theoretical viewpoints of other passengers. Essentially my story is not only about my observations on my research into paranormal phenomena and my search for a rational explanation but is partly a reflection on my own journey, particularly towards the end of the book.

I have also made reference to literary and fictional accounts of the supernatural in order to illustrate various points and try to enrich the reading experience. Additionally it was important to ascertain the reactions and viewpoints of some of my partner's colleagues who were also affected by what was happening, either directly or indirectly.

For part three, owing to the haunting my research became more specific to issues around psychic and spiritual phenomena in a wider social context. I take a general look at issues surrounding belief systems, scientific and mystical viewpoints which include spirit possession, links between mental health and supernatural experiences and I explore the life and works of three famous psychics. In part four, I continue to think about the implications for me, as a partner to someone who is being haunted and in the context of how this may affect my work as a counsellor. I also sought out and reflected on therapists who shared their own experiences when counselling 'haunted' or psychic clients. Some counsellors are also psychic themselves and I reflect on how this impacts the work in the therapy room and the relationship with the client.

We pick up the final part of Steve's ghost story in part five.

Throughout the book I have used the terms ghost, apparition, phantom and entity interchangeably. I have also changed the names of everyone mentioned, whether they are a therapist, client, colleague, or the ghost in question.

Whether you are a therapeutic practitioner who is a believer or non believer in the supernatural, I hope you find this book interesting and enjoy reading it.

Origins of Post Traumatic Stress

'I have memories that I can touch and make me wake up screaming. I'm haunted all day and all night.' From 'The Woman Who Walked Into Doors' by Roddy Doyle.

This book is largely about a man who becomes haunted. That man is my partner Steve, with whom I began a relationship in 2005. His story is described in part two, along with my reactions, some research and a gradual unfolding of events over the following years. Some of this comprises extracts from my diary, where I detail my responses as a partner but of course it is also hard to ignore the fact that I work as a counsellor. My experience as a therapist, my views and theoretical knowledge permeate and colour my reactions to Steve's situation.

Let us begin with what I felt I knew prior to Steve coming into my life and well before the 'haunting' of him began. During the 1990s I was a therapist working at the local Rape Crisis Centre and whilst studying for my master's degree in counselling, I had become fascinated by the symptoms of post traumatic stress and the process of memory retrieval for clients who were sexually abused in childhood. Some of these symptoms of PTSD and memories leaked out via perceptual disturbances that I felt could be interpreted by some survivors as supernatural or paranormal phenomena. My dissertation was concerned with this topic and as a result of this study, I concluded that whilst I could not comment on the existence of supernatural entities, I did strongly suspect that most experiences of haunting had a psychological explanation, even if this was not clear. I wondered whether neurobiological activity or dissociated split off areas of the personality could be the answer, or that physical or mental health issues held the key. It may be that a multitude of other reasons that could be aligned with many theories that have kept psychological researchers enthralled and stimulated over the centuries could 'explain ghosts.' In other words, following a certain amount of reading and a few years of experience working closely with traumatised clients in particular, I became more or less convinced that haunting occurs 'within the mind.'

So that is where I was at that point in my life as a single woman in my thirties, as someone who happened to work as a counsellor and as someone who simply didn't believe in ghosts.

What follows is something of what I had learned at the time and comprises a brief and simplistic overview of some of the physical, psychological and emotional effects of post traumatic stress disorder. The effects of trauma, I felt, seemed to be particularly significant when it comes to providing a psychological and perhaps physical environment that could induce perceptions of supernatural activity. I also include this as it provides a foundation for the later consideration I give to the way Steve experiences his own supernatural phenomena.

Hysteria

In order to provide a solid foundation to a potential haunting experience, therefore, it is important to firstly consider the effects of post traumatic stress, which may lead a person to believe that they are being truly 'haunted.'

Many specialists in trauma work, for example Judith Herman who wrote the classic book *'Trauma and Recovery'* in 1992, have considered three different types of psychological trauma and the links between them. The first is hysteria, placed into the public awareness by French neurologist Jean Martin Charcot in the mid 1800s. Charcot was motivated by a desire to *'demonstrate the superiority of a secular over a religious conceptual framework'* and thereby placing *'secular enlightenment over reactionary superstition.'* Herman goes on to cite that *'Charcot's formulations of hysteria offered a scientific explanation for phenomena such as demonic possession states, witchcraft, exorcism and religious ecstasy....Charcot and his followers also entered into acrimonious debates on contemporary mystical phenomena, including cases of stigmatics, apparitions, and faith healing.'* Interest in the occult which was running concurrently with explorations in psychoanalysis in the nineteenth century is further explored in part two.

Hysteria was also studied extensively by Freud and Breuer in the second half of the nineteenth century. A disorder that has ever since been associated with women, possibly originating within the uterus, was at the time associated with ventures into unknown territory and described by a historian cited in Herman as comprising *'dramatic medical metaphor for everything that men found mysterious or unmanageable in the opposite sex.'* Related to the *'domain of hypnotists and popular healers,'* and potentially linking women with alternative or occult practices whilst also labelling them as potential *'malingerers,'* women struggled with the effects of physical paralysis or convulsions, sensory and memory loss. These symptoms Charcot eventually found to be psychological in origin and he claimed that they could mostly be relieved through the use of hypnosis. He claimed that *'formulations of hysteria offered a scientific explanation for phenomena such as demonic possession states, witchcraft, exorcism, and religious ecstasy.'* His studies also incorporated links with 'paranormal' phenomena which included *'cases of stigmatics, apparitions and faith healing'* (Herman). Other eminent followers or rivals in the psychoanalytic professions, significantly Janet, Freud and Breuer went on between them to develop the theory that such conditions were traumatic in origin – *'unbearable emotional reactions to traumatic events produced an altered state of consciousness, which in term induced the hysterical symptoms.'* It was suggested that the repression of traumatic events occurring in childhood triggered a specific condition, *'hysteria'* in adulthood. Freud in particular claimed that memories were not forgotten per se but remained repressed until accessed, perhaps through dreams into conscious awareness and so *'talking treatments'* were beginning to be developed.

Freud theorised that symptoms of hysteria diminished once memories were recalled into consciousness. Significantly, he began to discover that the source of the symptoms of hysteria in his female patients appeared to be incidents of childhood sexual abuse. He said, *'At the bottom of every case of hysteria there are one or more occurrences of premature sexual experience, occurrences which belong to the earliest years of childhood'* (1962). As most therapists are now aware, Freud was increasingly risking ostracism from his profession owing to his discoveries on childhood sexual abuse in women which were producing such dramatic symptoms. Becoming increasingly appalled at his findings and the implications, this resulted in him famously retracting this theory. The sheer number of cases of hysteria in women presenting – even as Freud noted, in 'respectable' bourgeois families - was overwhelming and indicated an unpalatable truth, that premature sexual experience was extremely rife and created vast amounts of trauma. Freud succumbed to societal pressure in the face of such challenges and retreated from his original aetiology on hysteria. Abused women were, for the moment, condemned to accusations of fantasy, resulting in silence. Any findings on hysterical conditions, therefore, were once more relegated to the realms of the occult, the unknown and the unexplained.

War

The second trauma examined by Herman is battle fatigue or 'shell shock.' Some eighty years following the end of the First World War and subsequent evidence from the Second World War, Vietnam, Afghanistan and Iraq, few people would now dispute the evidence of post traumatic stress experienced by some combatants. Van der Kolk, who has written extensively on the subject of PTSD (1996), traces the history of warfare and its impact. He notes that *'Confined and rendered helpless, subjected to constant threat of annihilation, and forced to witness the mutilation and death of their comrades without any hope of reprieve, many soldiers began to act like hysterical women. They screamed and wept uncontrollably. They froze and could not move. They became mute and unresponsive. They lost their memory and their capacity to feel.'* Psychological treatments, from the culture of shaming and punishment for cowardice to electric shock and drug use, suffering soldiers were initially berated and abused. War poet and survivor Siegfried Sassoon famously struggled with life long symptoms with nightmares, nerves and the *'haunting of those who had not been so fortunate'* (Herman).

Interest in the long term psychological distress in combatants faded after the First World War, although it revived following the second. Thorough investigations, however, were not carried out until Vietnam in the 1970s. Talking treatments started to impact upon the acceptance of counselling as a viable healing process. It was recognised that all soldiers could potentially experience stress and not just a handful who were somehow weaker than others, were 'lacking in moral fibre' or indeed were suffering from any type of hysteria coined by Freud et al.

Abuse

The third stressor which can lead to post traumatic stress is sexual and domestic violence. Several theorists have compared the psychological effects of childhood sexual abuse with combat neuroses. *'Not until the women's liberation movement of the 1970s was it recognised that the most common post traumatic disorders are those not of men in war but of women in civilian life'* (Herman 2001).

In 1972, following an extensive study of the effects of sexual violence, *'Rape Trauma Syndrome'* was eventually recognised, alongside symptoms such as *'Insomnia, nausea, startle responses and nightmares, as well as dissociative and numbing symptoms and they commented that some of the victim's symptoms resembled those previously described in combat veterans'* (Herman). This discovery led to a re-emergence and in depth studies of psychological traumas following sexual attacks on women and children. During the 1980s prominent theorists such as Herman and Rose concluded that the psychological effects of rape, childhood sexual abuse and domestic violence were basically the same as combat traumas experienced by war veterans. *'Hysteria, combat neurosis, rape response syndrome, post traumatic stress disorder are one'* (Rose 1999).

Hysterical women, war torn veterans, abuse survivors. Are those affected by these issues likely to be at an increased risk of persecution by supernatural forces – if indeed such forces exist – or do such experiences exist only within the mind as a result of these varied traumas? I am left wondering whether there is a possibility of a new category *'Psychic Trauma Syndrome'* perhaps relevant for people who are repeatedly haunted by supernatural phenomena or those 'psychics' who are subject to extreme material that others cannot perceive. I am left with the question of whether psychic activity creates stress or would stress perpetrate perception of psychic phenomena? For now, let us discover more about post traumatic stress generally; what it involves and how it may be experienced.

'Ghosts' Emerging

'You couldn't just incorporate what had happened into your life experience. It didn't digest. Your mind kept coming back to it, pawing it lightly like a kitten with a ball of string until eventually of course, you went crazy or got to a place where it was impossible for you to function.' From 'It' by Stephen King.

Van der Hart, Nijenhuis and Steele inform us that *'Trauma essentially means 'wound,' injury or shock'* and that the term 'psychic trauma' was introduced by a German neurologist, Eulenburg in 1878. Such feelings will usually dissipate over time and are experienced as a temporary disturbance within the personality until complete integration of the stressful event has taken place. Much has been researched and written about post traumatic stress in recent years and its existence is no longer in dispute. It was finally included as a new category in DSM 3 in 1980. Significantly, however, symptoms of post traumatic stress vary for everyone, even if the triggering event is the same, and Rothschild (2000) raises that clinical studies indicated that only about twenty percent of people may go on to suffer from post traumatic stress disorder following a traumatising event. Research demonstrates that traumatisation in childhood in particular may comprise a high risk factor of the development of complex PTSD in adults. Herman emphasises the important point that *'Traumatic life events, like other misfortunes, are especially merciless to those who are already troubled.'* Rothschild explores additional factors that may influence this minority of sufferers and their ability to better protect themselves, for example: *'Preparation from stress (where possible), successful flight or fight responses, developmental history, belief systems, prior experience, internal resources and support (from family, community, and social networks).'* All of these influences, therefore, need to be borne in mind when we consider all of the examples illustrated throughout this book of our 'haunted' cases – from the abused clients and dissociative women cited below, Steve in part two and the psychics whose autobiographies are explored in part three.

It is stated in DSM 4 that post traumatic stress disorder *'may be especially severe or long lasting when the stressor is of human design (e.g. torture or rape). The likelihood of developing this disorder may increase as the intensity of and physical proximity of the stressor increases.'* Situations where humans inflict immeasurable distress on one another, which we can see time and again occur in examples that include war, terrorism, torture, domestic violence and various forms of childhood abuse. Judith Herman in her book *'Trauma and Recovery'* (2001) concurs and raises that whilst disasters are natural, atrocities are man made forces. She suggests that if stressors are of non human origin, for example natural disasters, then perhaps longer term symptoms of PTSD may be less likely. For me, this argument raises the question of whether an encounter with a supernatural entity would be classed as a 'human' or a 'non human' stressor. Experiences of severe supernatural haunting, whether this presents as a one off event or repeating random occurrences as in Steve's case, coupled with a combination of unpredictability and expectation when the ghost visits, of course causes a degree of stress. The ghost, or stressor, as we will see, does indeed continually hold 'physical proximity' to Steve. DSM 4 also raises that *'unexpectedly witnessing a dead body or body parts'* can be a stressor triggering anxiety problems and I am aware that this may lead to the question of whether a ghost can be labelled as 'a dead body or body part.' Given these descriptors, I am curious to know if ongoing haunting may indeed hold its place in triggering an experience of acute anxiety, stress disorder, or brief psychotic episodes; however its origin may be categorised.

Whilst experiencing traumatic responses, our view of the world is disrupted. Our perception of safety, balance, control and the order of things are broken down and the client needs support in order to re-build; psychologically and sometimes physically, what has been lost. What we are learning here is that traumatised reactions may be more likely if the event is inflicted by another person, if threat of death or injury are present, if the survivor has a problematic background and also, if events are *'Intense, sudden, uncontrollable, unpredictable and extremely negative'* (Van der Hart et al). If a person is 'wounded, injured or shocked' by an unpredictable supernatural event, or by repeated experiences of haunting, then once again I am left with the question of how likely are they to begin to experience symptoms of trauma or severe stress?

I am not suggesting that Steve himself was tortured in the sense of the repeated traumatic attacks that are inflicted upon individuals and communities all over the world; however, I am confident that he was traumatised in his own way and that some of his responses, for example those of hopelessness, helplessness and despair bear similarities. The perceptions of the world he inhabited were smashed and his belief systems knocked off balance as we see later when we look at his story.

Later on, therefore, I take into consideration how responses to seeing a ghost may differ in accordance with the individual's background, belief system, attitude, life circumstances and support network. Additionally I reflect upon the possibility of Steve's experience being triggered owing to a significant life transition.

Flashbacks and Perceptual Memories

'And anyway how can we tell if what we're seeing is real? Reality seems to go out the window when perception comes in the door' From 'Human Croquet' by Kate Atkinson.

I have learned during the course of my therapeutic work that traumatic memories can be severe, wide reaching and life affecting. They differ from cognitive recalling, the reminiscing of 'ordinary' memories. Memories of any traumatic event, but to use childhood sexual abuse as a sound example, may not always be remembered at will but can make themselves felt, seen, heard or even smelled as dissociated *experiential* states - post traumatic effects which disturb the senses causing *'temporary sensory hallucinations'* (Maltz 1991). Many theorists recognise that in addition to re-experiencing taking the form of nightmares, intrusive thoughts and images, flashbacks in particular are a common effect of post traumatic stress. Flashbacks embody an experiential re-living of the original abuse. Goleman (1997) states that *'A childhood memory can suddenly take possession of consciousness with so lively an emotion that we feel wholly transported back to the original situation.'* Maltz agrees, describing flashbacks as *'An intense flood of feelings, sensations and memories rush forward as the original sexual abuse is re-created in the present moment.'* One survivor cited in Hall and Lloyd (1993) adds that *'It was like being inside a videotape with every detail and colour very vivid with the addition of smell.'* Another client, quoted in Sanford (1991) describes her flashbacks as *'Home movies in Technicolor with Dolby sound'* as she awakes suddenly, every night exactly forty five minutes after going to bed. This is how long it took her mother to fall asleep which would signal her male relatives entering her bedroom to rape her. In later years she was re-experiencing a conditioned, automatic response.

Gallagher (1991) lists the following bodily and somatic complaints which can be evident in various survivors: *'Physical exhaustion, nightmares, flashbacks, eating disorders, alcoholism, drug addiction, dissociation, anger, rage, sexual problems, emotional and physical freezing, numb extremities, severe pain without organic basis, generalised fear, choice of a life mate who physically abuses, sense of guilt and shame or unworthiness, grief, terror.'*

Much has been written on the subject and the above examples provide a mere snapshot. An abundance of literature on childhood sexual abuse details numerous further examples of memories leaking out in mental, emotional, physical and behavioural ways.

Visual, Auditory and Other Sensory Disturbances

'The eye was watching him from the door...only when he was sure there was no eye did he start to relax.' From 'Regeneration' by Pat Barker.

In her autobiography *'Am I Not a Person'* (1998) abuse survivor Sylvia Hurt is constantly haunted by images of her abusers. The sense of being 'haunted' is a repeating theme throughout her book. Flashbacks, agoraphobia, somatic complaints and other strong mental and physical sensations persecute her throughout her life as memories of her abusers follow her. *'Their eyes, their piercing eyes from the past were always there to haunt me. I couldn't talk about my pain to anyone.'* She sees her father's face in the mirror, triggering a level of distress that causes her to claw her face until it bleeds. Bass and Davis (1988), and Hall and Lloyd (1993) raise, however, that sensory memories do not have to be visual as in the case of women who are visually impaired, were raped face down, or had pillows or blindfolds used by the perpetrator. Other senses can provide equally important clues for the hyper-tuned survivor.

In adulthood, another survivor Pennachia (1994) periodically smells sweat, dirt and blood, having bled during all of the childhood rapes perpetrated by her uncle. Other examples of sensory disturbance include the smell of alcohol or tobacco used by an adult abuser. My own clients have also frequently described a sensory taste of semen or the smell of blood, the latter particularly common with violent or pre-verbal abuse inflicted upon a small child. Auditory hallucinations may include examples such as dripping taps, footsteps, birds singing, any sound, in fact that took place during sexual abuse and is re-created in the client's present. Triggers to sensation and memory can, however, also be more subtle. For example, feelings may be triggered by a look, a touch, a posture, or a voice, perhaps by a partner. Anything entering her senses at the time of the abuse, particularly if she fixed on them during dissociation, can trigger a strong emotional response later. I examine dissociation in more depth in due course.

When we consider all this, it may be that we can begin to accept that flashbacks and such intense intrusive sensory perceptions may be mistaken for supernatural activity. Maltz (1991) informs us that *'Automatic reactions may seem like an external threat, an outside force that is intent on inflicting harm.'* In part two, we see how Steve smells petrol and there is actually an odour of sulphur prevalent in the warehouse when the ghost appears. He perceives the ghost or at least some of its body parts as real and solid phenomena in addition to hearing it speak to him. There are strong indications that Steve is digging up a long buried memory of some sort of event that is triggering him physically, emotionally and in a way in which all of his senses are becoming involved.

I am aware that not only is there a need to raise the question of what is happening to this person, but also, why is this happening to this person and why is it happening now?

Triggers and Timing

'The things we have tried to forget and put behind us would stir again and that sense of fear, of furtive unrest, struggling at length to blind unreasoning panic...might in some manner unforeseen become a living companion, as it had been before.' From 'Rebecca' by Daphne Du Maurier.

Triggers and timing are highly significant when it comes to asking these questions. Of course we all recall events, feelings and behaviour when we are reminded of them by people, situations or environmental conditions. A trigger may not even be obvious; we may ask of ourselves, 'Why on earth did I think of that now?' Such occurrences are regular, however, and we may just dismiss them as reminders quite naturally without giving them much thought. We may sometimes have more poignant thoughts of earlier times when we are undertaking activities such as visits to the seaside, placing flowers in a graveyard, encounter smells for example of baking, spot someone we have not seen for a long time or strangers who remind us of someone else. We can then become momentarily transported back to the events or feelings generated by the trigger. I was certainly aware of such issues when I was working specifically with survivors of child abuse and I was taking note of social and trauma history, in addition to exploring present life circumstances and any recent change. This is where the volume can get turned up and the triggers can cause significant amounts of distress and emotional disturbance.

Maltz (1991) raises that *'The trigger can be almost anything, an object, a touch, a movement, a smell, a setting, a sensation, a physical characteristic, or a feeling such as fear, abandonment or anxiety.'* Not only may day to day situations provide significant triggers but major life transitions can activate memories, which in turn can be experienced in a variety of ways through such disturbances of perception. For abuse survivors recovering memories, triggers can cause quite violent reactions. For example, incest survivor Marilyn Van Derbur's memories are fully triggered and intensified by her own child reaching the age of five, the age that Marilyn herself was when her father began to abuse her. During her recovery process, she goes on to describe further triggers to powerful sensory remembering: *'I wasn't remembering the memories and feelings, I was living them. When memories and feelings are split off and stuffed deep within the body, it is necessary to disgorge them and feel them as if they are happening in real time. This was not a voluntary decision. When the memories are triggered by a child's age, a medical procedure, a sexual experience, sound or smell, the memories and feelings are instantly felt and no amount of willing them away or decision to "just get over it" will work'* (2004).

Another survivor, Williams (1991) says of her experience: *'On one hand I had no memory of the abuse but, on the other hand pieces of the abuse were part of my everyday life. Fear of the dark, fear of opening my mouth for the dentist, disgust with the smell of beer on someone's breath are but a few of the pieces of the abuse that I remembered.'*

Transitions and events that cause triggers, however, do not have to be negative. I have noticed in my work with students who are enjoying their experience of higher education that those who access the counselling service on the transition to university frequently ask something along the lines of – 'Why am I remembering and feeling all of this stuff from the past when I am finally so happy and settled and life is good here?' I guess a simplistic answer would be 'Because you are now in a place where your mind and body are safe and strong enough to deal with it.' As we see later on, Steve becomes haunted when he leaves his wife and feels happier in life. We have since agreed that had he not made this life change and had continued to feel unhappy, angry, physically and emotionally tense and generally 'closed down,' we believe that it could have been unlikely that he would have suddenly 'opened up' and begun to be persecuted by a supernatural entity.

Survivors may endeavour to avoid triggers, believing that their reactions are part of an external threat, rather than an internalised feeling. This of course can be frightening and instil in survivors a sense of life being beyond their control.

Abused Children, Haunted Adults

'My father's house isn't haunted. I am haunted. I don't see things as they are.' From 'My Father's House' by Sylvia Fraser.

Imagine a typically frightened child – scared of the dark, scared of the bogyman under the bed, scared of ghosts. This can be a free floating undefined anxiety. We see later on in part two during my interview with my therapist that indeed her own anxieties as a child were rooted not in *'guns and violence'* but in being *'scared of the unknown, scared of ghosts, scared of the supernatural'* and *'something not OK in my room.'* Parsons (2001) cites the Freudian idea that the unconscious or *'psychic reality is a particular form of existence not to be confused with material reality.'*

The child who cannot sleep through terror may therefore tell her father that she is afraid of burglars, nuclear war or death – or anything to get her needs met in terms of getting him to recognise her existential internalised fears. The father, however, meets her only in terms of reassurance – that there are no burglars, no wars and she is not yet old or sick enough to die: *'In order to see that there was something to be afraid of, and then to think about what might be, he would have had to negate his ordinary way of thinking,'* (Parsons).

When a child is being sexually abused, such fears become solid, grounded and existing – often beyond the child's comprehension and imagination - impossible to articulate, particularly if the abuse occurred pre-verbally. As an abused child Sylvia Fraser tells us that *'I cry when my mother puts me to bed. I didn't used to be afraid of the dark but now I know that demons and monsters hide in the cubby holes by my bed. I'm afraid one will jump out at me and rub dirty dirty up against me.'*

The abuse experience is transformed into one the child can more easily communicate whether this is a monster, a bogyman, or perhaps a strong sense of presence at the foot of the bed. To illustrate this further, let us consider briefly the stories of two women who are undoubtedly haunted. These 'supernatural' examples, however, are rooted in abuse and how the mind responds to such trauma. I am feeling that it is important to consider such issues in order to fully explore how many people may come to believe themselves to be haunted – haunted in their mind's eye and as a natural response to childhood trauma. Once we have come to grips with the possibility that disturbances in perception may lead people to believing that the 'hauntings' they experience are phenomena external to the activities of their own minds, we can go on to explore the 'ghost' described in part two with raised awareness and hopefully proceed with a more open mind.

I am now going to take a look at two autobiographies, both of them being favourite books of mine when it came to learning about work with abuse survivors, the effects on them of their experiences and their strategies for survival. Both women cited here were repeatedly sexually molested by their fathers throughout their childhood. '*My Father's House,*' published in 1989, details the childhood, teens and gradual retrieval of sexual abuse memories in adulthood by author Sylvia Fraser. In one sense she does literally live in a haunted house – the house where the abuse is taking place and experiences herself to be haunted in mind whilst being repeatedly abused in body. She therefore projects her terror onto her home. '*I feared the house we shared, which by guilty association became the house that knew. In my imagination, monsters prowled its cubby holes – my monstrous secret, my monstrous other self, turned into something outside me that I could fear.*' This is an important point. Do our inner responses enable us to project onto external sources and create tangible things to fear – monsters, ghosts, demons, supernatural entities that are perhaps more understandable, easier to articulate and therefore 'easier' to bear?

In order to cope with what is happening to her as a child, Sylvia literally split her personality into two. '*Thus somewhere around the age of seven I acquired another self with memories and experiences separate from mine, whose existence was unknown to me. My loss of memory was retroactive. I did not remember my daddy ever having touched me sexually. I did not remember ever seeing my daddy naked. In future, whenever my daddy approached me sexually I turned into my other self, and afterwards I did not remember anything that had happened.*' Thus one part of Sylvia functions well in society, achieves academically and allows herself to love her father. The split is quite a definite one. '*Only my head went to college,*' she says, '*my severed head.*' The other part, the body part, quite separately holds the traumas of the abuse and the memories that are at this point fully repressed. Hints of memories of abuse, however, began to 'leak' out over time. Sylvia goes on to explain that it feels as if the two aspects of herself become 'psychically attuned' and that the traumatised self '*telegraphed messages to me through the dreams we shared. She leaked emotion to me through the body we shared.*' So through this comment we begin to see why some individuals, particularly those who have been traumatised, may begin to believe they are being actually haunted by an external entity over which they have no conscious control. Another unseen person seems to be haunting Sylvia as she grows up. She says: '*Imagine this: imagine you discover that for many years another person intimately shared your life without your knowing it. Oh, you had your suspicions – the indented pillow beside you, the toothpaste with a thumbprint that wasn't yours. Now it all fits, you know its true, but during all that time you never actually saw this person.*' We can begin to see that, in one very real sense Sylvia is indeed haunted, by her abusing father and by her own reactions to and interpretations of the abuse.

There are several themes which emerge in cases of abused children and are important to bear in mind as they repeatedly re-occur in other examples cited in this book. Firstly, in Sylvia's history, there exists a faith blueprint in the background as one of her grandmothers is fanatically religious. Secondly, trauma comes down the family as two young sisters of her mother die from disease and Sylvia's mother in her own youth discovers the body of her own father hanged. Possibly as a reaction to this her mother, consciously or unconsciously through the process of selective sight, chooses not to see or acknowledge the abuse of her daughter by her husband. Finally, already vulnerable owing to the ongoing abuse, Sylvia is further sexually molested – by a boy in the cinema and by the lodger, Mr Brown. Interestingly, like Eve White whose story is told later, Sylvia is also pressurised by her mother to kiss a corpse – the dead body of her grandmother. Sylvia understandably reacts with the utmost unspeakable horror and seems aware of some sort of need to dissociate as a coping strategy, underlining a need for such a response in order to survive the ordeal. *'I know as sure as anything in my life, that if I am forced to kiss Other Grandmother's corpse, I will go somewhere far away inside myself and never come back.'* I go on to examine dissociative responses in more detail later on.

Themes of splitting and dissociation are significant and we can see how dissociative individuals begin to suspect that all that occurs in real solid conscious physical life is, apparently, not as it seems. For now let us perceive Sylvia as clearly mentally disturbed and, it could be argued, prone to a view of reality that seems to be of a 'paranormal' nature: *'the world inside my head becomes more real than the physical world; feelings more real than facts; thoughts more real than spoken words; my unconscious mind more real than my conscious mind; the visionary world of dreams more real than the waking world.'*

My second example of a 'haunted' survivor of abuse is that of former American beauty queen, Marilyn Van Derbur who wrote *'Miss America by Day'* published in 2004. Marilyn was sexually abused by her father from the age of five until she was in her late teens. Like Sylvia Fraser, she represses memories of the abuse and begins to retrieve them in adulthood. Also similarly to Sylvia, she copes by splitting herself into two very distinct parts – a 'day' child and a 'night' child, compartmentalising an inaccessible part which holds the pain and humiliation of acts happening to her over which she has no control and the other part that is able to function 'normally' and go out and 'be somebody.' She creates a separate self as a way to survive the abuse being perpetrated by her father and is also, therefore, able to give herself permission to continue to love him.

She is also able to forget the abuse, compartmentalising this safely away from the 'day' child and achieving psychological protection away from destructive memory. Driven by a constant state of high anxiety and terror caused by the constant need for unconscious repression, Marilyn achieves absolutely everything she tries out for, becoming highly skilled in a variety of activities at school and college. Once she wins the Miss America title in 1958 and her life changes forever, she functions 'as if' she holds confidence whilst in a state of terror at the thought of the vast amounts of public speaking she is expected to undertake in her new high profile role.

It is interesting to note that both Sylvia and Marilyn become high achievers. In the book *'The Haunted Self'* (2006) which is concerned with effects of trauma and dissociation, Van der Hart, Nijenhuis and Steele refer to an 'Apparently Normal' part of the personality (ANP) and the 'Emotional Personality' (EP) which holds the traumatic responses of fight, flight or hyper-vigilance. The ANP gets on with maintaining a level of functioning in the world, denying painful memory and representing logic and rationality. For Sylvia and Marilyn this comprises a high degree of apparent success. The emotional part meanwhile remains suppressed, denied and distorted for both women until leaking out and coming into sharper focus during adulthood. Put very simply it may be that given this blueprint it could be the experiencing EP that perceives a ghost and the logical ANP that denies its existence.

Not only are survivors such as Sylvia and Marilyn haunted through the gradual retrieval of memories via the senses but they also experience physical and bodily clues.

The Body

The rank stench of those bodies haunts me still
And I remember things I'd best forget.'
From 'The Rank Stench of Those Bodies Haunts Me Still' by Siegfried Sassoon.

Today, numerous autobiographies are readily available and openly displayed on book shelves in shops and libraries, written by abuse survivors detailing their appalling experiences and outlining their coping strategies which contributed to their survival. One factor that many have in common is descriptions of how the legacy of child abuse makes itself felt well into adulthood. Not only are such memories experienced emotionally, mentally and perceptually, but they may also manifest themselves through the ongoing physical sensations felt within the body. Sanford (1991) acknowledges that the body stores memories of violent trauma or abuse, also raising that unaccessed memories stored in the body can lead to health and medical problems. She describes the body as *'A museum filled with artefacts from childhood. Trauma is stored in the time of the body until the day it is expressed and resolved.'* Boadella (1987) cited in Smith (1993) agrees that *'Tension patterns are held in the body'* and *'Can be looked on as a person's frozen history.'* The body thereby *'Remembers sensations and pain and reacts accordingly.'* In his book *'Child Abuse Trauma,'* (1992) John Briere writes more specifically that somatic complaints can include: *'headaches, stomach pain, nausea, sleep disturbance, anorexia, asthma, shortness of breath, chronic muscle tension, muscle spasms, elevated blood pressure and other physical complaints without known biological cause.'*

Abuse survivor Sylvia Fraser cites such an example in her autobiography, describing how she is led into conscious memories of her previously forgotten childhood sexual abuse via clues from her body, as she experiences extreme episodes of violent physical memories. *'Spasms pass though me, powerful, involuntary - my pelvis contracts leaving my legs limp. My shoulders scrunch up to my ears, my arms press against my sides with the wrists hung out like chicken wings, my head bends back so far I fear my neck will snap, my jaws open wider than possible and I start to gag and sob, unable to close my mouth - lockjaw in reverse. These spasms do not feel random. They are the convulsions of a child being raped though the mouth.'*

Marilyn Van Derbur also describes her physical reactions which remain with her throughout her life. She experiences an excruciating tightening of the body, a rigid posture, intense muscle pain, constipation and a refusal to 'allow in' that which was inevitably going to be forced on her small child's body by a more powerful father. Periods of total physical paralysis plague her in adulthood. She says: *'Many times, we place our pain and disease where our violations occurred... we need to get out of our heads and into our bodies because our bodies have memories. Our bodies have their own stories to tell...the second my father first opened my body, my reaction was to try to close my body tight. This started a muscular holding pattern that I would invoke thousands of times until my buttocks, arms and legs lost their ability to release the chronic muscular contractions. Living with this body torment and chronic insomnia have been the two most difficult parts of my recovery.'*

Society interprets this bodily trauma as a natural regal pose which is ideally suited to Marilyn's role as America's crowned beauty. It is also possible to comprehend how this condition may be interpreted as severely repeating states of 'hysteria.' Of course such extreme bodily responses leading to treatment from Freud and his contemporaries may have perpetrated a diagnosis of the patient holding fantasies around sexual incest. Marilyn herself confirms that *'I would go into a kind of craziness – what Freud would call "hysteria."'*

Freud himself (1962) cited in Haaken, stated that hysteria is a condition where *'The mind makes use of the body to communicate the incommunicable.'* The body will retain and try to communicate the truth of the experiences inflicted upon it as the trauma exceeds any language that can describe it, particularly if the abuse was pre-verbal and therefore remains linguistically inaccessible. One client of mine, for example, was rescued from her parents when she was six months old, having been starved, neglected and sexually and physically abused in a variety of ways. Despite holding no cognitive memories of these experiences, she continues to have sensations of burning, drowning and suffocating, particularly during times of stress. Sanford has likewise counselled survivors with repetitive throat infections or dental problems directly related to strangulation or oral abuse as children. Similarly, survivors experiencing panic attacks or asthma may have been suffocated, dominated or restricted in some way.

Pennacchia (1994) in her own diary detailing gradual memory retrieval, receives various disturbing hints of a past she cannot fully remember. Her physical reactions include fits of crying, hyperventilation, and self harm through heavy smoking and consuming large amounts of sugar. Her experiences commence with the sudden feeling of having a tube pushed into her vagina, a burning sensation in her stomach and waking with her arms locked as if tied. These body experiences are swiftly followed by conscious memories of rape by her uncle. In the company of her therapist she also regresses, gagging in the therapy room, physically becoming five years old as her adult body lives out the memory of violation in childhood. Her body posture and breathing changes as the estrangement from her own body diminishes. During therapy her body jerks and she says, *'My whole insides crumpled and reformed.'*

Distressing as this is to comprehend, again these issues need to be addressed before we go on to consider Steve's bodily reactions and the repeated facial scarring he experiences when attacked physically by his 'ghost,' described in part two of this book.

Brain, Bonding and Biology

'Thus bad begins and worse remains behind.' From 'Hamlet' by William Shakespeare.

In addition to bodily trauma, I felt that the early environment and the impact on the brain is worth taking into consideration, again with the aim of exploring every possible angle when it comes to exploring my main 'ghost' story in part two, which is why I have included this section here. It also provides a foundation when I go on to consider the possibility that babies may be 'born psychic' or whether these skills – if there are such skills – can be developed later on in life. Let us briefly consider the impact on the environment and how the care received by the new born may or may not influence how that individual experiences the world later.

I decided that it is well beyond the scope of this book to explain brain function and its responses to shock and trauma in depth, nor did this seem necessary, however, it was interesting for me to note that the responses to trauma do occur within the same area of the brain as mystical experiences.

Many people are familiar with the somewhat vague interpretations of the brain holding both 'left' and 'right' areas and functions, although in neuroscientific terms this description is somewhat overly simple and outdated. When I was training on an art therapy skills course, however, I certainly became aware of the ongoing instruction to get into my 'right brain' before I could start effectively creating images. The 'right brain' or 'survival brain' is concerned with emotional and sensory memory, whether this is verbal or non verbal and instinctive responses when it comes to survival. Put simply it is the creative or emotional side. Along with the mid brain section including the amygdala, the hypothalamus and the hippocampus these form the limbic system. The creation of basic emotion such as rage, shame and terror occurs in this area and provides a link to the brain's higher structures which instruct the body functions *'The limbic system's most fundamental purpose is to generate and modulate primal emotions such as fear aggressiveness and rage'* (Newberg, D'Aquili and Rause).

The limbic system regulates the Autonomic Nervous System which is responsible for mostly unconscious natural functions, and includes the basic flight, fight or freeze responses to trauma. Reacting to stimulus, logic and reason are deactivated until response mechanisms have been triggered. It is the limbic system that is also responsible for states such as déjà vu, (paramnesia), sensory hallucinations, out of body experiences and religious or spiritual states. It is therefore of little surprise to learn from Newberg et al that the limbic system itself has been referred to as the *'Transmitter to God.'* From the supernatural viewpoint, exactly what this 'transmitter' may be transmitting remains debateable and I go on to explore this further in part three.

This 'right brain' part continues to develop and is dominant during childhood and teens. The neocrotex, the 'left brain' or rational part which carries on with daily life functioning and which often holds no conscious memory of early trauma, does not come into full maturity until the age of about twenty. If children are psychic, then it is within the limbic system that such activity takes place and it may be logical to suppose that once the rational part of the brain fully matures, psychic activity experienced in childhood and teens may cease.

From the moment of birth, the tiny child, flooded with stimuli, needs to learn, with the aid of its carers, how to regulate emotional responses – those of *'bonding and attachment, upset and regulation, stimulus and attunement'* (Rothschild), to both the environment and the emotional reactions she is experiencing within herself. There is a powerful argument which lies in the supposition that if the attachment is severed or disrupted through neglect, abuse, absence or death of the baby/toddlers carer, then a predisposition for traumatic stress may be in place *'Failures of attachment can contribute to an individual's vulnerability to developing PTSD'* (Rothschild).

Similarly to Sylvia Fraser's mother, Marilyn Van Derbur's mother also seems to be aware on some level of the abuse taking place under her roof but she remains avoidant and in denial. *'Psychological orphaning'* (Van Derbur) caused by the disbelief or lack of appropriate support from the non abusing parent is abusive in itself and the early environment is of course highly significant when we consider how an abused child may experience and subsequently work through - or fail to adequately work through - her emotional and physical legacy of issues.

Other studies born out through study of war or from the accounts of holocaust survivors illustrate that trauma can, however, still be activated for adults who experience stressors but who have had secure attachments in infancy. It is evident, however, that healing can occur more easily if the traumatised person has access to a trusted supportive other. I have observed time and again during my work with rape and abuse survivors that those who are responded to with sensitivity, care and common sense from empathic others will often move on from their acute distress more readily than those who are disbelieved, isolated, victimised or simply misunderstood. More widely, it is evident that negation, denial and disbelief of the client's experience, whatever those issues are that are being presented, will potentially have a damaging effect upon the client. The experience of seeing a ghost, of course, whether perceived by a child or by an adult, is frequently denied.

An honest and poignantly written book, *'Ghosts from the Nursery'* (1997) by Karr-Morse and Wiley further illustrates how children are impacted by their environment and how the care, or lack of care from the adults around them from gestation and birth influence how the child's capacity to empathise, to think in a focussed way and to create a template of personal expectations in relation to the world around them, develops. It is raised that *'even before birth the brain is shaped by stimulation from the environment, as biological and neurobiological elements in the babies' brain whilst in the womb are affected by the emotional state of the mother. After birth, development is an interactive process between the baby's physiology and his or her environment.'*

Karr Morse and Wiley continue to inform us that whilst genetics provide a blueprint for a baby's personality, it is stimulation via senses, sounds, smells, touch, contact and environmental factors that ultimately generates the building of the specific areas that regulate the visual, auditory and other senses. It follows that some of these potentialities are thwarted if the environment or contact with primary caregivers is absent, abusive or becomes untrustworthy. The first two years after birth comprise the most vigorous point of brain growth for the baby. It is whilst the brain is developing at this escalating rate that any trauma, whether severe, long term, repeated or a one off event, can potentially alter the make up of the brain itself – and if severe enough these changes can be permanent. The ANS and emotional brain part can remain over stimulated as a result of continual traumatic experiences. Trauma itself then, can have a physical impact upon the brain. Herman tells us that changes can occur in the endocrine, autonomic and central nervous systems, also altering its structure and function. Van Derbur says, *'Research has now confirmed what I always believed to be true. Years of trauma change children's brain chemistry. Our brains become hardwired differently.'* Quoting Dr Bruce Perry she adds, *'If trauma continues, the neural thermostat becomes stuck on high.'*

Following birth, if the bond between mother and baby is severed, neglected, or abused, which Karr-Morse and Wiley refer to as *'breaking the web of trust,'* then this can have a potential for decreasing the child's capacity to develop empathic relationships with others and they may be at greater risk of perpetrating criminal or violent behaviour in later life. Other factors such as birth complications causing cognitive impairment and subsequent environmental forces encountered during developmental stages of life, for example during school and/or occupational failures can also of course, have an impact. Karr-Morse and Wiley raise that abused children, once beginning the process of socialisation within the nursery or school environment, may show signs of depression, limited interest in their surroundings and a suspicion of hostile intent in others even in the absence of any such cruel motivation. This behaviour often triggers peer rejection which can result in perpetuating a cycle of feeling and action. Longer term mental health issues become an increasing likelihood.

Let us pause to consider some fictional examples from literature. We can find many examples in fairy tales of children being poverty stricken, orphaned, abandoned, threatened, starved, enslaved and rejected. Snow White, experiencing a major life trauma with the death of her father and surviving an attempted murder by her stepmother provides one such sound example. Cinderella is forced to work in the kitchens by her stepmother and stepsisters again following the death of her father. From the moment she is born, Rapunzel is locked away in a tower with no human contact other than her imprisoner. And so on. Loves first kiss provides the redemption required by these young women and 'happily ever after' comprises heterosexual love and marriage with no trace of longer term mental or physical ill health despite their ordeals. Fairy tales do provide a wealth of psychoanalytic material about severed attachments, abuse, gender stereotyping and avoidance, among other rich themes.

Popular children's author Roald Dahl frequently wrote of abused children. James, in *'James and the Giant Peach'* (1961) tells the story of a little boy who lives an idyllic life until the age of four when his parents are killed horribly (by a rhinoceros in fact) and he is entrapped and abused by two powerful aunts. Charlie, in *'Charlie and the Chocolate Factory'* (1967) is considerably more fortunate in that he is loved, despite having to survive in an environment that allows him and his undernourished family to gradually starve near to death. Dahl's character *'Matilda'* from the book of the same name (1997) also has to be an interesting example of a neglected child, subjected to scapegoating and verbal put downs. Surviving through the discovery of books and school Matilda somewhat interestingly develops a telekinetic ability which, when triggered by strong emotions of fear, rage or stress, enables her to wreak her revenge on her abusers and ensure her survival. Her skills wane once they are no longer needed but obviously assist her at a significant point in her young life. Matilda's case, albeit a fictional one, provides us with a hint that certain children, given the appropriate conditions can indeed develop some sort of psychic powers which can assist them in their life struggles. We will be examining this theme further in part three of this book when we explore non fictional examples of children who are, apparently, psychic.

Despite the fact that some fictional abused children may hold magical powers, like Matilda or J K Rowling's popular character Harry Potter, either because they are born with them, or like Cinderella have helpful magic bestowed on them, our fairy tale princesses along with these other children in the real world would be more than likely to grow up highly psychologically and emotionally disturbed given their early traumatic experiences. Our other fictional children, with the exception of Matilda's unloving parents and Harry's 'muggle' relatives, however, may hold some hope that recovery is possible – because they all led relatively stable lives before the age of two, when the brain development is at its most significant and potentially most vulnerable to negative environmental influences. These children later all also receive healing from a secondary attachment source, whether human or magical. In fiction, children, orphans et al may get what they need following abuse and neglect, but non fictional cases do not end in any such unlikely 'reality' nor pertain to the myth of a child's 'natural resilience' and incapacity to be affected by negative events including that of extreme early trauma. Books such as these appealed to me when I was a child as they focus on courage, resourcefulness and survival. The young reader holds faith in an eventual happy ending when problems are solved, the good are rewarded and the bad justly punished. As an adult, however, I am discomforted by such reading matter – with the adult state comes an increase in awareness of the reality and horrors of childhood abuse.

Haunted Clients

'I was still afraid of walking home alone at night, shadows, dark bushes, even the dark upstairs when I went to my room alone. But these fears did not stem from my personal experience; rather our culture, the real dangers of our world, seep into our minds at an early age. We learn fear even before we know how much there truly is to fear.' From 'I Never Told Anyone. Writings by Women Survivors of Child Sexual Abuse'. Editors Bass and Thornton.

In order to root these observations in my own experience as a counsellor, below are a few examples of 'haunted clients' which pulls together some of the themes I have explored so far.

Leonie

Leonie, aged fourteen and recently raped by a teacher, attended just one session of counselling with me. Her parents prevented her from attending any more as they 'did not want to pamper to her craziness' and they seemed resentful of any change or perceived interference from external support. Leonie was continually haunted by a figure at the foot of her bed and disembodied hands floating above her face, particularly at night. A single session, however, showed Leonie that her 'madness,' comprising her visions, ghosts and voices were a natural post traumatic effect of the rape she had suffered. Leonie acknowledged the significance of the acceptance of her experience by another person.

Gita

Another of my clients, Gita, attended many sessions of counselling and felt that sharing her experiences was helpful. She was highly distressed with visual images of fires in the walls and sparks around her bed. This may have been indicative of cigarettes used by the abuser and perhaps she had dissociated during the abuse and focused on the fireplace.   She did, however, continue with her belief that her disturbances were from external, supernatural sources over which she had no control. She was eventually referred by her GP into psychiatry for treatment of psychosis. This saddened me, although I need to recognise that a diagnosis of mental illness may be appropriate on occasion. Herman raises the significant point that *'many develop the belief that their abusers have absolute or even supernatural powers, can read their thoughts, and can control their lives entirely.'* A general sense of disempowerment is rife when working with abuse survivors and the need to enable a client to regain a sense of power is paramount when working with this client group.

Jennifer

Jennifer, whose case is illustrated below in slightly more detail, is interesting in that she held a firm belief that her abuser would, literally, 'haunt her from the grave.' Jennifer's story is illustrative of some of the themes mentioned when taking into consideration the legacy of childhood sexual abuse and how in some cases, the blurring between post traumatic stress reactions and a perception of haunting by supernatural entities is present. Her particular case perhaps served to fuel my assumption that all haunting is a product of disturbances within the mind.

Jennifer was a client in her mid thirties, white, heterosexual, single with one small child. She talked a lot and at great speed. Her feelings tumbled out out as she detailed a turbulent childhood, with a violent alcoholic stepfather and a mother who was trapped in a pattern of continually leaving the family home and later returning. Jennifer had a single memory of child abuse when her stepfather raped her while he was drunk. Jennifer could not remember how old she was. Her only specific memory was of the smell of whiskey on his breath and being treated by her mother for vaginal injuries the following day. Her mother minimised her distress and told Jennifer that she had had 'an accident.'

Jennifer's stepfather had been a professional and religious man who kept his alcoholism and violent side well hidden from the community. He had died ten years before. Jennifer did have some positive memories of him as a good parent, yet described him as 'two people' owing to the trauma of what he had done to her.

Jennifer felt that the happiest time of her life was 'now' and she could not understand why she was suddenly falling apart for no apparent reason. She had been cast in the role of strong survivor out of all her five brothers and sisters who were all affected by various abuse experiences. Their perception was that Jennifer had emerged as the most 'untouched' one. Following her stepfather's death, she had told her siblings of the abuse incident but despite their own issues, they had refused to believe her. The subject was dropped.

Just prior to entering therapy, Jennifer felt calm, happy, was in a caring relationship with a fiancé, with her family around her and a lot to look forward to. She had, however, recently begun to experience severe effects of post traumatic stress. Jennifer's distress manifested itself in periods of lethargy and she started to dissociate, once laying for two hours in front of an open fire and burning her leg very badly without noticing. She shut herself away to cry on her own. She felt dirty, had to wash after sex and could not bear to touch male genitalia. She suffered from an unexpected stabbing pain in her vagina which could not be explained by the medical profession. Jennifer also went through a brief phase of cutting herself, to let feelings of 'filth' out of her body.

Only now was it psychologically safe enough for the feelings to be confronted and hence Jennifer was feeling 'flooded' by intrusive sensations that included nightmares, depression and hallucinations. She saw the shadow of a man at the foot of her bed and familiar feelings of abandonment and invasion of space would periodically return to haunt her. She was convinced that this was the returning entity of her dead stepfather; that he was indeed 'haunting her.'

During the course of therapy it became evident that Jennifer's disturbance had escalated once her own daughter reached the age of eight. Jennifer was experiencing periods of dangerous dissociative episodes, extreme depression and distress when flashbacks were triggered by sexual activity. She also vomited if she came into contact with the smell of whiskey.

Memories of being abandoned returned to haunt Jennifer whenever her boyfriends left her and she always had problems recovering from the break up of intimate relationships. This appeared to be linked with the emotion she had felt in childhood each time her mother left. She eventually acknowledged in counselling that her present relationship with her fiancé was negative and she split up with him during the counselling process. She felt trapped by her impending marriage and the sexual side felt wrong. She directly likened his behaviour to abuse. We reflected that physical touching was being experienced as an intrusion and bed did not feel like a safe place for Jennifer to be. The memories of loneliness, being controlled and being forced into sexual intimacy were influential in her admitting to herself that her relationship was not the perfect one she had tried to make herself believe it was. Jennifer's memories, leaking out through the clues of dissociation, inactivity, depression, flashbacks and nightmares, were a signal for her to change her situation.

The themes apparent in this case include taking into consideration Jennifer's early history with issues of severed attachment and abandonment by her mother, the effects from the trauma of the rape by her stepfather and her resulting coping strategies. These comprise amnesiac and dissociative states, psychosomatic responses and self harm. She is triggered into strong reactive stress at the times when she is particularly vulnerable, for example by further experiences of abandonment. Negation, denial and minimisation by her immediate family have a damaging impact on Jennifer which leads her to a complex presentation of her trauma. A lack of control in her present and the pending life transition as she is being pressurised into marriage further serve to disempower her. Significantly, Jennifer can see a ghost - she is indeed repeatedly haunted by the image of a frightening and powerful man standing with threat at the foot of her bed. In this sense she experiences a strong sense that her abuser is still 'alive.' He is present in some form as an ongoing manifestation of her own internal feelings which were remaining beyond her awareness in terms of being processed and integrated.

Whilst some of Jennifer's presenting issues were symptomatic of supernatural phenomena, was she actually being haunted by a ghost? I think not, if we are to take into account the arguments and reflections that I am exploring in part one of this book. It is highly likely that Jennifer, the clients like her and those who are now recognised to dissociate as a natural response to extreme trauma, are experiencing an inner turmoil which makes itself felt in a variety of interesting and disturbing ways. These effects are clearly experienced as sometimes being external to the self and are in fact, born out of projections from the psyche onto the external environment. For any such cases, ghosts may clearly exist as 'all in the mind.'

The Devil?

'Devil n. an evil spirit, (The Devil) the supreme spirit of evil; a cruel or annoying person; a person of mischievous energy or cleverness; (colloquial) a difficult person or problem.' From 'The Oxford English Dictionary'.

Through the two autobiographical accounts by Fraser and Van Derbur, along with similar accounts by abuse survivors, we can begin to learn how children cope with abuse by splitting themselves off, in Sylvia's and Marilyn's cases, by separating out into two very distinct halves. The link with the supernatural and demonic possession is never very far away. Herman raises the point that: *'Survivors routinely describe themselves as outside the compact of ordinary human relationship, as supernatural creatures of non-human life forms. They think of themselves as witches, vampires, whores, dogs, rats or snakes.'* She goes on to cite a survivor who tells us that: *'I used to have seizures. I'd go numb, my mouth would move, I'd hear voices and I'd feel like my body was burning up. I thought I was possessed by the devil.'*

Sylvia Fraser has severe convulsions along with continual imagery of giving birth to a demon. She links this with some sort of satanic presence and quite accurately observes that: *'In a more superstitious society, I might have been diagnosed as a child possessed by the devil. What in fact, I had been possessed by was daddy's forked instrument – the devil in man.'* Anxiety clearly plays a large part with survivors inducing images and sensations of *'guilt induced visions of being persecuted by a devil or demon, or of being tortured in hell'* (Van der Hart, Nijenhuis and Steele). In her biography of author and abuse survivor Virginia Woolf, Louise De Salvo (1989) raises that among her many ongoing symptoms as a result of sexual molestation in childhood, Virginia experienced herself as *'Being pursued by something animal'* and questioning her boundaries *'Was the animal separate from her, or did it come out from her?'*

Freud himself was convinced that man's nature was basically destructive and that the id could be construed as a 'beast within man' or a primitive devilish force that needs to be tamed by the ego. Cited in Herman, he also described symptoms of trauma as *'signs of daemonic force at work'* and De Salvo raises the myth that men are not fully in control of their sexual instincts and behaviours and in particular the *'Victorian belief in male sexuality as pure aggression, as demonic possession.'*

Male sexuality therefore, along with the impact of trauma, resulting symptoms of 'hysteria' whether found in women or shell shocked soldiers, seemed for the psychologists and writers of the time indicative of mysterious forces which lie outside of the self, sometimes including that of demonic activity at work. It is only later, with the implementation of serious studies in neurobiology and mental health, that other alternatives were beginning to emerge as viable 'answers' to such perceptions and distresses.

Herman concurs and comments of Sylvia Fraser that *'In earlier times, Fraser notes, she might well have been diagnosed as a classic hysteric. Today she would be diagnosed with multiple personality disorder.'* She comments that generally survivors will still attract diagnoses of somatisation disorder, borderline personality disorder and multiple personality/dissociative identity disorder which will still attract negative labels that once would have been clustered under the term of 'hysteria' – a term that still haunts and impedes individuals, particularly women, today. I will now explore the splitting off into separate personalities, which again will provide some foundation and thought in preparation for our main 'ghost' story in part two of this book.

Or Dissociation?

'I can sing the singing. I can think the thinking. (Suddenly savage) But you're not going to catch me feeling the feeling. No sir.' From 'The Singing Detective' by Dennis Potter.

Although there are varied mental health reasons as to why someone may perceive themselves to be haunted by a ghost, I am intending to emphasise Dissociative Identity Disorder as a major trigger to such perceptions and resulting beliefs. This is mostly owing to the fact that I researched the subject in detail as part of a master's degree course in addition to having worked therapeutically with a number of dissociated clients during the course of my career in counselling so far. It did seem to me that dissociative states appeared to provide a likely and logical answer to events such as voice hearing, disturbances in sensory perception and unremembered events such as the movement of objects. For affected people, an alternate reality can literally be created. Haaken (1998) raises that interest in dissociation re-emerged in the 1980s, possibly as a reaction to the work of Freud with his perceived *'deafness to hysterical patients.'* DSM 4 now term dissociative disorders as *'A disruption in the usually integrated functions of consciousness, memory, identity, or perception of the environment. The disturbance may be sudden or gradual, transient or chronic.'*

Dissociation itself occurs on a continuum. Many of us dissociate relatively frequently at low level on a day to day basis. We mislay objects, we daydream, we enter rooms only to forget what we came in to fetch. When we engage in creative processes or become moved momentarily by art, nature or during sex, we may journey off into our own little world. We may fantasise, lose track of time, forget our way, or slip momentarily in concentration which can result in minor accidents. Anxiety may also play its part in milder forms of dissociative experiencing when we panic, or 'space out.' In more severe cases we may disown or split off our emotions, partially or entirely. Therapeutic writing on this subject often further illustrates this concept by using a quote from Charles Dickens's novel *'Hard Times'* in which Mrs Gradgrind is so out of touch with her own feelings that as she lies dying she can only murmur, *'I think there's a pain somewhere in the room...but I couldn't positively say that I have got it'* (1985). More extreme still, we may have 'out of body' experiences. We may also access spiritual or deeper unconscious dimensions of the self during episodes of dissociation. Anything that moves us out of a sense of the here and now, therefore, may be counted as a dissociative state.

In their book *'The Haunted Self'* authors Van der Hart, Nijenhuis and Steele further normalise dissociative episodes, raising that such sensations may be owing to alternative physical or mental health reasons, not necessarily resulting from serious forms of dissociative disorders and they caution us that: *'...it can be difficult to assess whether or not a phenomenon is a manifestation of structural dissociation, that is, a dissociative symptom, or whether it is something else. For example, abnormal levels of forgetfulness may be a manifestation of dementia, a brain tumour, exhaustion, intoxication, or structural dissociation. Similarly, a different sense of self may be due to major depression, exhaustion, intoxication, or structural dissociation. The proof that symptoms are manifestations of structural dissociation like in demonstrating that one part of the personality recalls a memory or has experiences that another part does not.'*

Dissociative Identity Disorder, formally known as Multiple Personality Disorder, is a far more defined state than either these ordinary behaviours or physical causes suggest. DID is now recognised as symptomatic of post traumatic stress and is frequently associated with severe physical or sexual trauma in childhood, having strong connections with the effects of ritual abuse and satanic occult crimes in particular. Jones Wood (1998) also raises a significant point that psychological splitting may occur not only during abuse but also in the absence of a nurturing parent or guardian as we have explored. Whilst trauma may not cause dissociative activity itself, it may certainly heighten it.

So what purpose does dissociation serve and how does it happen? The answer lies in self preservation. Extreme threats to ourselves and resulting anxiety may generally be kept from conscious awareness as a defence. Goleman (1997) terms this *'Protective filters.'* Broadbent (1958) cited in Goleman (1997) suggests that a filter controls what we let into our conscious awareness. This filter changes via the focus in the child's attention. In much the same way we can tune into what one person is saying in a crowd. The abused child may similarly 'tune out' of the horror that is happening to her and perhaps focus on something else. This may go some way to explain how some survivors may not remember the abuse itself but feelings can be triggered later by other sights, sounds or images. One of my clients, for example, can remember in exact detail the pattern in the bedroom curtains, but cannot recall of the identity of the man who was abusing her. Goleman (1997) reiterates that: *'Dissociation occurs when the abused child succeeds mentally in disappearing completely from the scene of the ordeal...and that which has not been consciously experienced of the trauma cannot be remembered. There, is, however, probably at least one other (dissociated) part of the personality that has wholly or partly experienced the event, and is therefore fully aware of what has happened.'* Goleman goes on to state that involuntary or unconscious 'pain leaks out,' via a survivor's body, dreams, or perceptual disturbances, as we have already observed.

Most importantly, this psychological removal from emotion, a lack of reactive responses and a filtered sense of detachment, numbing and dissociation can now be regarded as natural and adaptive coping mechanisms on the part of the child to combat the horror of abuse. Briere (1992) confirms that dissociation is *'A defence or disruption in the normally occurring connection among feelings, thoughts, behaviour and memories, consciously or unconsciously invoked in order to reduce psychological distress.'* Putnam (1989) agrees and lists among the 'survival benefits of dissociation' a need to *'escape from the constraints of reality (for example 'its just a dream') to provide a container for traumatic memories and affects outside of conscious awareness, the 'alteration or detachment of sense of self' (no longer/ out of body) and finally Analgesia, or numbness, no pain.'* Minimisation, denial and rationalisation may also form responses to abuse inflicted in childhood. Thus much abuse may remain 'forgotten,' unacknowledged and undisclosed. Courtois (1991) also raises that the more violent the abuse, the greater the likelihood of repression as a means of coping with the memories. Habitual dissociation can result in a sense of fragmentation, loss of personal history and can become a problem when it occurs unconsciously, repetitively and with little control.

As we have observed, therefore, as part of her survival technique, it follows that a child may dissociate or 'switch off' during an abuse experience. Flight or fight responses are unavailable as the child's choices are eliminated and only the mind is able to 'freeze' or 'fly' in an attempt to escape the horror, which leaves a dissociative space. Gil (1990) suggests that multiplicity occurs when another personality steps into this gap left by the fragmented part of personality which has departed through dissociation. This personality she terms an 'alter' and an alter may be partial or whole, perhaps having one major specific characteristic or emotion. Rigid boundaries between parts can be created. Some can even actually be seen, as separate and individual as we see when we go on to examine the biographies of DID patients below.

These parts or alters are, however, all manifestations of an individual person albeit with separate ways of communicating. Often only one alter is present at any one time in the here and now, or they can manifest themselves in groups. Assagioli (1993) raises that emotional states can exist independently of one another, for example, one alter can experience joy while another is suffering. They may transcend gender and need not be human, for example Ganaway (1989 cited in Haaken) suggests that at the extreme end of the continuum, alters can manifest themselves as *'demons, angels, sages, lobsters, chickens, tigers, a gorilla, a uniform and god to name a few.'* Haaken likewise raises that alters may appear from different galaxies. I would add possibly from different dimensions, and it is bearing all of this in mind that I can now start to understand how people with DID may begin to believe themselves to be 'haunted.'

Diagnosed cases of DID are rising. An entry in DSM 4 theorises potential causes for this increase; firstly owing to the raised awareness of the condition in mental health professionals and secondly owing to the fact that some cases may be misdiagnosed, as particular patients can be highly suggestible. It is interesting to contemplate examples of possible misdiagnosis and there is the potential to make some tentative links with such instances later on in part three, when I consider the argument that some cases of DID are misrepresented and that patients could, in fact, be psychic or attuned to spiritual presence. Dean (1998) states that alters are indeed *'entities in the astral eager to step into a vacant body.'* When they are refused entry they will leave to seek host bodies elsewhere. In contrast with many other theorists, Dean perceives that alters are external biblical demons in search of forgiveness. We have a deeper look at this possibility in part three when I undertake a more detailed and fascinating exploration of the work of spiritual possession and healing.

Possessed or not, it can become difficult for dissociative individuals to differentiate between internal and external reality. Dissociative symptoms can be concerned with effects such as uncontrollable auditory, visual or olfactory hallucinations which may intrude upon life to an excessive level. DSM 4 goes on to point out that *'An identity that is not in control may nonetheless gain access to consciousness by producing auditory or visual hallucinations (e.g. a voice giving instructions').* It is symptoms such as these which may lead some of those affected to assume that they are perceiving supernatural phenomena and I will be considering this further in due course.

Whilst DID is also not attributed to the common experience of fantasy playmates encountered by children, hallucinations clearly can form a significant component of dissociative states and may often present in the form of a child. As we have already seen, in the book *'The Haunted Self'* by Van der Hart, Nijenhuis and Steele, the authors divide the personality into 'EP' (Emotional Personality) and 'ANP' (Apparently Normal Personality). There is usually present a main shareholder of the personality and the 'child' who holds the trauma. Van der Hart et al raise that child EPs are more numerous that ANPs and in fact that DID patients at times *'may literally experience themselves as actual children.'* My client Melinda would frequently see herself either in dreams or as part of a waking state as a completely separate child part. She would act out behaviours as a toddler, talking in a childlike voice to her husband and putting her hair in plaits. She would have no memory of these episodes later. We also witness an example of this sort of behaviour below, when we explore the details of Mrs White's story in the biography *'The Three Faces of Eve'*.

Van der Hart et al illustrate that *'Various ANPs and EPs may have strong investment in the belief that they are separate persons.'* Routing this ANP/EP split in further examples, such powerful divisions are particularly evident when we consider the functioning parts of Sylvia Fraser, who can leave home to successfully perform at college, and Marilyn Van Derbur, who can achieve at virtually everything she attempts. Neither woman remembers their abuse until later in life, although both are aware of memories leaking out and negative effects in terms of mental higher thinking, emotional experiencing and behaviour. Narrative memory is not possible for such cases and life is 'relived' rather than 'retold' via these intrusive visual images and sensations. There may be present an observing EP and an experiencing one, with an ANP enabling the 'ordinary' functioning of the personality. The observing part may be that which watches the body being abused, the part that can become detached. For example, abused Celie in Alice Walker's novel *'The Colour Purple'* (2000) is able to become a tree whilst she is being beaten. *'It all I can do not to cry. I make myself wood. I say to myself, Celie, you a tree.'* Van der Hart et al cite the case of Lisette, a twenty seven year old patient who, chronically traumatised as a child, has an EP who 'Watches from above' as she undergoes resuscitation during a hospital stay to undergo surgery. Losing consciousness, Lisette is revived to the EP's belief that she has died and now exists as a ghost. This is a persevering supposition as she observes the treatment of her body from an elevated position.

Van der Hart, Nijenhuis and Steele also cite the example of a clearly unintegrated client, Lena, whose EP cannot comprehend that if Lena commits suicide, then the EP would also perish, as they share the same body. This EP's aim was to free herself from Lena, who she experienced as inhibiting and curtailing the EP's freedom to do as she wished. We see a similar example in the case of Eve/the Woman below and not only how ANPs and EPs may be unaware of each other's needs and prohibit impulses associated with specific EP needs but also how the EP's vision, focus and behaviour may be very limited – for example how one part holds the urge to party, to be sexual, to be rageful etc.

In the book *'The Haunted Self'*, the authors raise that parts may become more avoidant of each other and this then emphasises the divide. Integration, however, seems to be the goal of many psychological interventions. We can see in the biographical examples cited below that Eve achieves this, as does Sybil, however, for the Troops for Truddi Chase, learning to live with each 'part' remains a satisfactory aim. One of my own clients, Isabel, described feeling misunderstood by her psychiatric team, saying, *'They tell me I'm the pie and my alters are slices, but I try and tell them that I'm a slice too. I am not the pie.'*

As abuse focussed counsellors we need to become familiar with both mild and extreme effects of DID, eliminate dissociative disorders as any form of psychosis and recognise that dissociation can be a natural defence mechanism employed by traumatised children. At some point, however, defences from traumatic memory may start to falter and the effects of DID may become problematic later in life.

The next part of this book is concerned with classic biographical and autobiographical literature that has been written on this subject; examples of women who have become dissociated on a multiple level. Again, we can bear in mind that prior to any firm diagnosis the individuals discussed here may at first have perceived themselves to be 'haunted' by forces external to themselves. Starting with the '*Three Faces of Eve,*' this is an early work on the subject written from the viewpoint of the psychiatrists providing treatment to a patient who has three personalities. Secondly '*Sybil*' who has sixteen alters, and finally '*When Rabbit Howls,*' the story of a woman who has over ninety identities to contend with.

The Three Faces of Eve

'Many students of the occult confidently inform us that our patient is 'obsessed with discarnate spirits.' From 'The Three Faces of Eve'.

The first work to be published on the subject of alters was *'The Three Faces of Eve'* written by Corbett Thigpen and Hervey Cleckley and published in 1957. It tells the story of Eve White, her alter Eve Black and finally the introduction of a third, named Jane, who links the two more dominant separate personalities of Eve.

Dated now and written in a style I would describe as 'quaint' I found *'The Three Faces of Eve'* highly interesting to read and almost poetic in style. The dissociative split seems quite simplistic, occurring between an introverted and extroverted personality and a third who provides a bridging link between them. Written by the medics involved with Eve White, an accompanying commentary on therapeutic ponderings and techniques when it comes to treating Eve unfolds and the narration flows over the reader like water.

Eve White suffers from blinding headaches, visual disturbances associated with migraines and blackouts and she presents to the medical and psychiatric professions as physically delicate. A *'neat colourless'* woman of twenty five, who is married and the mother of one young child, it emerges that she engages in violent confrontations with her husband, forces the ending of her marriage and indulges in purchasing expensive clothes, events of which she has no memory. Eve White presents as meek during the contact with her doctors but her husband reports that she flies into extreme rages. Forgetfulness and memory loss plague Mrs White as she purchases the uncharacteristic items of clothing and has rows with her husband she later claims not to remember. This is interpreted by the medics as *'material slightly alien or extraneous, as lacking a little in some dimension of reality, not quite like-but little like-elements from a weirdly incompatible and disturbing dream.'*

Other opinions on Eve's case are linked considerably more directly with supernatural causes. The two doctors and authors of the book reflect on how *'Many students of the occult confidently inform us that our patient is 'obsessed with discarnate spirits. One such correspondent urges that static electricity be applied to her body in order to drive these invaders out.'* Voodoo spells and astrological reasons are also put forward as reasons for Mrs White's case and those similar. The authors also cite an example as a *'counsellor from a suburb of Los Angeles rebuked us for 'metaphysical illiteracy.'* He said, *"Your patient ...can easily be relieved of her possessing entities through exorcism by a competent spiritualist, preferably by one who has had experience in this particular field. One half of the mental patients in our mental institutions suffering from schizophrenia can also be cured. I have studied this subject for many years and know whereof I speak."'*

In distress Mrs White reports hearing voices which she interprets as 'madness.' Her doctor acknowledges that auditory hallucinations indeed indicate a state of psychosis although later reflects that most patients who report voice hearing tend not to be alarmed by the experience and that *'almost uniformly the patients assume that the voices are real. They insist that the sound comes to them by radio, by radar, by telephonic projective radioactivity, by invisible waves playing upon an intrapsychic ectoplasm etc. The psychotic schizophrenic almost never regards the hallucinations as an indication of mental disorder. No one can convince him that they are not objectively real.'*

The possibility of both spirit possession and schizophrenia are explored later in this book and we begin to see how differing opinions and interpretations on patients such as Mrs White are offered by medics, psychics and members of the public alike. During the sessions with Mrs White, the doctor notices how she changes completely in posture, tone and manner as the second personality, that of Eve Black, transcends the first. Whereas Eve White presents as meek, timid and passive, the sparky Eve Black encompasses the opposite personal qualities, expressing pity and derision of her alter's life choices and behaviour. Whilst Eve Black has access to Eve White's memories, thoughts and feelings - *'She shared the factual data of Eve White's memory and verbally knew her thoughts, but she perceived her emotional reactions and values only as an outsider'* - which she finds 'boring,' Eve White has at this point no knowledge of Eve Black's existence.

Eve Black has no marriage and no child. Headaches and blackouts experienced by Eve White would indicate that Eve Black was likely to be present, the other aspect of the self 'getting in.' Hangovers, rages, outrageous clothes – all these belong to Eve Black. When the medics raise the possibility that if Eve White is institutionalised, Eve Black would have to share the experience, treatment is agreed to by both of the patient's alters.

Thigpen and Cleckley quite naturally raise the issue of dual personality. *'It has been presumed for many years that so called dual personalities arise through the dissociation of an originally integrated entity of functioning and experience.'* They go on to comment that many people suppress traits and tendencies that may lead to unrewarding behaviour, that some speak of leading 'double life' or of hypocritical behaviour which all naturally lead to *'the development of secondary personality....as coming about through the mobilisation, organisation and eventually the emergence of what has been thus discarded or dissociated from consciousness.'* It follows that they and many similarly affected patients will go on to reflect on the novel published in 1886 *'Dr Jekyll and Mr Hyde'* by Robert Louis Stevenson and it is mentioned in the case of Eve: *'The concept of an evil and criminal presence or spirit gaining ascendancy in a hitherto benevolent and honourable person can scarcely be presented without arousing in the human heart some echoes or stealthy overtones of witchcraft and demonology. Instead of a theological devil or some lesser vile and supernatural spirit entering and possessing the body, we find in Mr Hyde its seizure and operation by forces of human evil.'* This fictional book has clearly entered public awareness, triggered some stereotyping of a good and evil split in personality and mention of it crops up a lot in discussions on dissociative conditions.

It is noticeable that hysteria continues to haunt the 1950s as a viable explanation for Eve's behaviour. The medics initially collude with such a diagnosis, providing observation on 'hysterical dissociation' in order to categorise conditions that cannot be classified by epilepsy or brain disorders and they make links with witchcraft and possession by the devil. The latter having been somewhat 'respected' through religious models in the past, the doctors do acknowledge that such conditions are now written off as 'imaginary illnesses' or that the afflicted are 'malingering.' They observe that: *'Hysterical manifestations, though formerly respected as major afflictions and interpreted with awe in terms of devil possession and witchcraft, have come to be regarded by many as imaginary illnesses, or as little more than dramatic and deceitful "putting on".'* They continue *'Every physician knows that many hysterical patients are notoriously suggestible and dramatic'* and observes that over enthusiastic medics may have been taken in by *'some of the most bizarre performances attributed at first to poltergeists – astonishing and apparently supernatural feats of levitation, teleportation and necromancy, that in our times have convinced learned men they were dealing with ectoplasmic spirits of the dead – have been produced by naïve girls with hysteria responding co-operatively, and perhaps unconsciously, in situations that grew progressively more histrionic and unbelievable.'* Dr Edith Fiore, a psychologist whose work on spirit possession is cited in part three, would no doubt, however, have perceived Eve Black to be a possessing spirit rather than Eve White to be a hysterical malingerer. Many references are indeed made to Eve Black as a 'manifestation,' a term commonly associated with spiritual presence and other supernatural terminology. This is persistently evident throughout *'The Three Faces of Eve.'*

Hospitalisation, psychotherapy and sessions of hypnosis are deemed to be the treatments of choice for Eve's case with the aim of *'rapprochement'* or enabling the two aspects of Eve to become aware of each other. The goal for Eve therefore is to *'promote reciprocal recognition and eventual reintegration.'*

A significant point in Eve's story is that there appears to be a lack of any particularly traumatic childhood experience, either repressed or any that emerge into conscious awareness during the narration of Eve's dissociation and treatment. Eve's condition, however, would no doubt have escalated throughout her childhood owing to the confusion caused by unremembered wrongdoings of her more mischievous alter, Black, with White having to take the subsequent physical punishment for causes of which she has no recall. I also suspect that during the 'banshee scream' at Eve's point of integration between her alters and her cry of *'Mother...! Oh mother...! Don't make me...Don't...I can't do it! I can't!'* presents us with more than a strong hint that all has not been well in the family.

A new 'entity' or 'personality manifestation' calling herself 'Jane' emerges as a *'capable and intelligent functioning entity.'* Linked to the past, the Eves are not aware of her as she is described as *'a disparate entity, another being whose experience remained apart from that of the others.'* The doctor refers to her as an 'intruder' and makes his patient aware of her presence.

The woman's integration occurs dramatically when Jane retrieves a lost memory of being forced by her mother to touch the face of a dead grandparent, lying in the coffin. This deeply traumatised her. *'Who was it that screamed again this afternoon in the doctor's office? A few days later our patient said,"It seems to me I can remember hearing someone scream. After I got home I could not be sure whether it was I or not".* She identifies in the most part with Jane and misses the two Eves. She recognises and loves Eve White's child as her own, adopts Eve's White's name and realises she can't possibly wear the overly sexy red dress that Eve Black frequently wore. The doctors do question whether the trauma of the funeral incident was enough to cause such a drastic splitting in their patient, or whether this was the result of an accumulation of 'emotional forces' present since birth. They are certainly doubtful as to whether this one incident was enough to trigger the extremity of Eve's disorder. They speculate that Eve's reaction to death *'might have motivated her special and extraordinary efforts to be good and to avoid what she had been taught was bad or evil. This may have been the beginning of a pattern of unusually meticulous conformity and restraint.'*

Eve White, Eve Black and Jane ultimately attain a *'beautiful integration'* and here the story ends.

Sybil

'The classic true story of a woman possessed by sixteen personalities.' From 'Sybil'.

'*Sybil,*' written in 1973 by Flora Rheta Schreiber, details the story of Sybil Dorsett, a young woman who is continually beset by problems involving gaps in memories and the loss of whole days. Sybil experiences her emotional state as *'some terrible, nameless thing having to do with time and memory'* and as *'this black shadow that followed her everywhere.'* Similar to Eve's childhood experiences, when an EP indulges in behaviours that cannot be accounted for by the ANP, Sybil tells us that *'All her life people had said that she had done things she hadn't done.'* As a child Sybil experiences intense physical abuse by a highly mentally disturbed mother. Consequently, as a result of her dissociation, Sybil has to live with a terrible *'this is where I came in'* feeling, with no continuity of time or memory of what may have gone before. She says: *'People she had never seen before would insist that they knew her. She would go on a picnic and have a vague sense of having been there before. A dress that she had not bought would be hanging in her closet. She would begin a painting and return to the studio to find that it had been completed by someone else – in a style not hers. Sleep was a nightmare. She just couldn't be sure about sleep. Often it seemed as if she were sleeping by day as well as by night. Often too, there was no dividing line between the time of going to bed at night and waking up in the morning. Many were the occasions of waking up without going to sleep, of going to sleep to wake up not the next morning, but at some unrecognisable time.'*

Sybil is described by her psychiatrist, Dr Wilbur, as being inflicted with *'Grande Hysterie'* and goes on to explain that *'The kind of 'grande hysterie' from which Sybil Dorsett suffered, not only with multiple personalities but with a variety of psychosomatic illnesses and disturbances in the five senses was as grave as it was rare.'*

Sybil knows nothing of the existence of her other dissociated 'parts' – sixteen of them. Dr Wilbur quickly diagnoses multiple personality, openly questioning the possibility of genetic links or physical predisposition. She believes trauma to be at the root of Sybil's splitting. We see how the concept of the good/evil divide of 'split personality' has integrated into public awareness when, like Eve White, Sybil enquires, *'Then I'm like Dr Jekyll and Mr Hyde?'* Her doctor reassures her that most splits hold the same moral and ethical codes and that the split between good and evil is not clear and evident, unlike this work of fiction.

For me, a pivotal moment in Sybil's story occurs when she is at school. Sybil 'wakes up' to find she is in a classroom that is not familiar, being taught by a teacher who is not hers. In front of her on the desk lies a notebook with work she does not recognise. She had believed herself to be a member of the third form but it seems she is now in the fifth. Any memories of her time spent in the fourth grade have been completely erased. She cannot understand the academic work but, it seems, she has previously always been an A grade student. Now her talents are uneven, some days she can perform in subjects such as maths and music, at other times her ability is wiped out. The children in her class, some of whom are familiar, are physically bigger. Sybil herself has grown and her clothes are strange to her. She understandably feels terror and panic as she has to re-learn the script of her life. At home things are also different; rooms are painted, her grandfather is changed and deteriorating in health, her collection of dolls has grown. *'You're just not yourself today,'* Sybil's mother observes. Having to hold her bewildering secret and hide her resulting confusion at home and school, Sybil is lost. *'You knew it yesterday,'* the teacher berates her in exasperation. *'Yesterday? Sybil was silent. For her – she was beginning to know it now – yesterday was never. Things had taken place that she was supposed to have done or learned of which she had no knowledge.'* This is a deeply shocking situation, unimaginable.

Sybil grows older and the image of the 'hysterical' young woman is evident. *'During the later spring of 1935, Sybil faces a new terror, brought on by the vulnerability of puberty. The terror centred around hysterical conversion symptoms that were part of her then undiagnosed illness. For hysteria – 'grande' or otherwise – is an illness resulting from emotional conflict and is generally characterised by immaturity, dependency, and the use of the defence mechanisms not only of dissociation but also of conversion. Hysteria is classically manifested by dramatic physical symptoms involving the voluntary muscles or the organs of special senses. During the process of conversion, unconscious impulses are transmuted into bodily symptoms. Instead of being experienced consciously, the emotional conflict is thus expressed physically.'*

Furthermore, the author observes that *'Hysterics flourish in a naïve social milieu and even better in an environment bedecked with the fire and brimstone of a fundamentalist faith.'* Sybil's grandfather is indeed described as a religious 'hysteric' and we can see how powerful an influence a religious blueprint can be. Sybil's religious roots are described as *'hysteria'* in themselves and *'she pondered whether both Freud and the Church could be right at the same time.'* Rather like the 'haunted' sensations of a supernatural presence experienced by Sylvia Fraser, Sybil also describes feelings of being stalked by Satan *'as a living breathing presence…fearing that he would creep in at night, she had also feared that nothing she could do would or could keep him from 'getting her.'*

Sybil is unsupported by her family. As she is not able to attain rescue from external sources, she has to seek within herself to gain resources to ensure her survival and the result is a dissociative state: *'…being a multiple personality was the ultimate rescue. By dividing into different selves, defences against not only an intolerable but also a dangerous reality, Sybil had found a modus operandi for survival. Grave as her illness was, it had originated as a protective device.'*

Dr Wilbur dismisses any suggestion that Sybil is being haunted by any paranormal source. *'It's not possession Sybil,'* the doctor declared emphatically.

'Not some invasion from without. It comes from within, and it can be explained not by the supernatural but in very natural terms.'

Similarly to Eve, the goal for Sybil's treatment is that of integration – the need to return memories and behaviours to the 'waking Sybil.' Unlike the case of Eve, however, Dr Wilbur picks up the root of trauma which triggered the original split when Sybil was aged three and a half. Significantly Dr Wilbur also recognises the 'selves' as necessary defences resulting from the abuse. *'Sybil's mind and body were possessed by these others – not invading spirits, not dybbuks from without, but proliferating parts of the original child.'* These parts vary in age and experience. *'As had already become apparent, these other people within Sybil had different religious attitudes and different tastes in books. They also had different body images. Their reactions to sex were not the same.'*

At the point where Sybil is ready to have contact with her other selves she achieves an ability to actually visually see one of her other parts, two year old Ruthie, not as a hallucination which could be indicative of psychosis but as a *'visual impression'* in *'the mind's eye.'* One could argue that, in some sense, she could be seeing an apparition, that of a dissociated part of herself, a visible image of an inner child part from the past.

Sybil does achieve a way of living with her parts becoming integrated, however, she does retain a sense that they *'Function as autonomous entities'* but with herself as manager. She concludes that *'The others talked to me sometimes, especially at the end, but I ran things.'*

When Rabbit Howls

'Mental health,' Stanley sighed, 'the inexact science.' From 'When Rabbit Howls.'

Published in 1988, The Troops for Truddi Chase's story, *'When Rabbit Howls'* is a particularly traumatic one. The woman known as Truddi Chase herself has not been present since the age of two when she was pre-verbally raped by her stepfather. She has in fact been described by her other multiples as being 'asleep' since this time and that *'Her place was taken by a succession of persons.'* The purpose of such persons is to protect Truddi from the effects of the trauma, to experience specific and separate emotions resulting from the original abuse and also to *'deal with various stages of the life cycle.'* For the Troops, remembering the events as a whole would have been unendurable.

Like Eve and Sybil, clues to her condition encompass blank periods of time. Physically, headaches occur which, unlike those experienced by Eve White, *'don't hurt'* and seem to *'come from forty miles away'* but she *'senses a pounding.'* *'They're strange headaches, she said. 'they hurt but they don't hurt.'* The woman makes many references to 'us' and 'we' and she typically experiences distress and confusion at the concept of time. The Troop's medics observe differing styles of handwriting, vocal inflection, accent, facial and body posture and other physical and psychological variances between the personalities. Each medic seems to have a breakthrough shocking moment. For the main protagonist, Stanley, it comprises the moment when the woman begins to speak in the voice of a very small child: *'Rabbit was a very young and unevolved child who held the pain for almost the entire Troop Formation....He would also understand how the woman, when she was present, and unbeknownst to herself, was only a conduit for other Troop members.'*

We witness the progression as over ninety personalities make themselves felt or known. These transcend gender and age and vary in how they present, even physically to the woman's therapist. Handwriting, intelligence levels, posture, demeanour, voice, accent, even eye colour are observed to change as each part breaks through. The focus of the therapy and therefore the book's narrative is concerned with memories and the gradual retrieval of memories. For me, as in the other books on the subject, I am aware that this process does seem to embody a sense of the supernatural in the language used, for example the parts are clearly composed of separate 'entities' at different ages and once more a specific 'presence' is prevalent. In this respect, the woman is indeed haunted: *'Two unseen children were about to make her "acutely aware" not of their ages, or physical characteristics, but rather their human emotions...The presence beside her was as real as the music. It cried and wiped its nose with the back of its hand. Another presence wiped its eyes with the hem of the woman's skirt. She managed to determine that neither could be flesh and blood, but only the materialism in the form of two unseen entities.'* The woman can physically see some of her parts, others are sensed. In one case, she is actually able to perceive a child part playing with a doll on the rug. This doll is then laid on the woman's lap.

Typically, the woman cannot remember much of her childhood. *'Why couldn't she remember school or birthdays or more than one or two flashes of Christmas holidays? Why couldn't she remember more precisely the family?'* Also, similarly to Sybil, there is a fanatical religious family member, a Catholic grandmother, exerting an influential background.

The medics treating the woman become aware of *'a break with reality'* as the woman hallucinates and hears voices. Stanley observes: *'The trouble with multiplicity... was that to an outsider it did sound "crazy"...What must it be like for a multiple to start making comparisons between the world he or she lived in and what society said was the norm? Especially when everything being experienced was real to the multiple and so unreal to everyone around them?'* We pick up on this theme in part three when I detail the autobiographies of three psychics – who each have contact with their 'reality' of perceiving and communicating with spirits. This reality is generally denied by the 'norms' of society.

The taping equipment which Stanley uses when he and the woman are in session continually goes 'haywire.' The woman cannot, it seems, wear a watch without it breaking. Nor can she drive a car without technical problems occurring which are inexplicable to any investigating mechanic. Electrical malfunctions abound: *'...the question arose immediately as to what was wrong with the stereo, the radios, the television set, and every light bulb in her house. Next she had to ask why, if she were in anyone else's house too long, their lights began to flicker, their stereo started to crackle.'* During his testing, Stanley also notes a high energy output from different independent personalities and he observes that all generate interference with electrical appliances when strong emotions are experienced or suppressed. *'When one of them tries to repress an emotion like anger or rage, it just heightens the energy level, like built up electricity with no outlet.'* Together the medical team reflect on this strange impact on electrical charges and conclude that *'If the Troops can interfere with electrical appliances they can interfere with the energy in your brain.'* Electrical faults are a significant theme when I consider the presence of supernatural entities later on when I am faced with the 'actual' haunting of Steve and it is interesting to note that such malfunctions exist in the case of this DID patient.

During her therapy, the woman has a revelation; a memory of snakes raining down on her when at the age of six she is lowered into a well by her abuser. This is a pivotal memory which unlocks much pain and triggers positive therapeutic movement. The small child part 'dies' at this point. Some of the other child parts are also 'dead' as a result of traumatic abuse beyond their ability to cope mentally and only their 'essences' remain. These are the echoes of their traumatic experiencing. We can see how the alters perceive each other as separate entities in this exchange between some of these parts. *'Lamb Chop had been rattled since the last session. First, hearing the "dead essence" of Olivia II in the well, then seeing Olivia I's child mirror image, and finally having the "dead essence" of the other child emerging almost on top of her...it had been a lot to handle.*

'They're so different from me' Lamb Chop sobbed in spite of the yellow gumdrop Mean Joe had given her. 'What's wrong with them?' 'They're dead,' Mean Joe told her.

'I was scared. Am I dead, too?

'No, you're not dead, and everybody's scared.'

'Even you Mean Joe?'

Especially me, and I'm supposed to be the strong one.'

The essence of such 'dead' parts, are perceived by the 'living' parts as 'ghosts.' *'Action by the dead ones now, if there was any at all, was only a "remainder," a ghostly automation.'* Some parts communicate willingly with each other, some are reluctant, whilst others remain 'unevidenced' via less direct thought transference. Integration itself again seems to be a recommended outcome, despite the fact that many dissociative people seem to go on to lead successfully functioning lives without fully achieving this. Van der Hart, Nijenhuis and Steele suggest that *'fusion of the parts'* leads to a *'higher level mental efficiency.'* Unlike Sybil and Eve, however, the woman does not achieve a full integration. *'...for as long as she lived, she would experience only through others, never precisely on her own.*

As long as she lived, the others would always be there.' As Stanley learns, for the woman who was known as Truddi Chase, it is too late. The 'core' of the woman is dead and the parts, the 'Troops for the Woman' communicate through the 'shell.'

With death, of course, comes the notion of ghosts. So finally let us consider a suggestion that there may even be a paranormal dimension to DID. Stanley describes a medium as *'someone who communes with spirits'* and therefore is doing consciously what the woman is doing unconsciously. Interestingly and certainly open minded on the subject, he also questions a link between intelligence and psychic ability: *'Extreme intelligence, the paranormal; one is usually the foundation for the other,'* and he goes on to question *'Could your client have been a gifted child, perhaps one that nobody recognised, because multiples hide or fragment this creative, extreme intelligence? Does your client indicate, as most gifted children do, familiarity with the paranormal, and, quite possibly, does that disturb your professional aplomb?'*

Another client described in the book, Jeannie, does indeed not only combat the same kind of electrical problems the woman experiences but she also holds a further secret, that of extra-sensory perception and psychic ability, in addition to working through a life affected by DID. Jeannie's biggest problems are thereby centred on trying to hide not only a gifted mind but extra-sensory perception and she is aware of social prejudice and ignorance, which she finds problematic when it comes to supernatural phenomena. *'People, Jeannie had told Stanley bitterly, ran from the notion of multiplicity, but they bolted outright at the idea of anything to do with the paranormal.'* Could it be that people who see ghosts then, could be abnormally intelligent or gifted, or are experiencing unremembered events from the past or who are simply neurologically or mentally unwell? Stanley also makes links with social attitudes towards people who have displayed such conditions throughout history - which have veered between the revering of saints and the burning of witches.

In the *'Troops for Truddi Chase,'* therefore, a further depth to DID is posed and this question is asked: *'Are we seeing into the realm of what modern persons call psychic phenomena, or are we viewing the vestiges of past lives? Perhaps we are peering into a world of which we cannot conceive, and are privileged to go beyond our senses into the world of the spiritual.'*

All of these possibilities need to be born in mind when we consider the events described in part two.

******

To conclude this first part then, I was aware that at the commencement of my relationship with Steve and his subsequent 'haunting,' I had begun to formulate my own opinions on supernatural phenomena, despite never having been particularly interested in such matters. These views I had gathered over time were owing to my own history as a sceptic; then they had further developed during my observations and work with clients. Finally I pulled together certain themes on 'haunting' for my research into the topics for my master's degree. The knowledge, learning and assumptions I was carrying at that point in time therefore seemed to involve considering the potential impact of:

- Attachment issues – neglect, severed, abusive
- Early abuse issues which may trigger resulting long term disturbances of perception in adulthood
- Stress and anxiety owing to a change in life circumstances
- Resulting neurological changes in the brain from any of the above
- Psychosomatic symptoms
- Dissociation which occurs on a continuum in terms of severity
- Feelings of loss of control – a sense of actual or perceived persecution from sources external to the self
- The impact of responses from significant others
- A sense that haunting could easily be occurring but is essentially 'all in the mind'
- A general belief that ghosts in the 'paranormal' sense of the word do not exist, owing to the influences of some or all of the above

It is also important to bear in mind whilst reading part two, the possible influences of religious blueprints, life transitions and stressors, electrical activity, a sense of presence and a sense that feelings seem to be detached and disowned.

So, having explored why 'supernatural' experiences may be perceived via the disturbed perceptions of the mind, the psychosomatic reaction of the body and the coping strategies afforded by dissociative identity disorder, I was left with the question – what of those people who claim to be haunted, to see ghosts quite clearly, but who have not suffered any such experiences? And are people more likely to develop psychic ability if they have been abused in some way during childhood? Parts two and three go on to explore these issues.

PART TWO

THE DOG THAT SAW A RAINBOW: THE HAUNTING OF STEVE

Ten Years Later

'There wasn't a lot of bullshit in my heaven.' From 'The Lovely Bones' by Alice Sebold.

A new client comes to see you. He is male, white, middle aged and in steady employment. He says, *'Hello, my name is John. There have been some problems in my family. My daughter got pregnant and I was so upset and angry with her, I threw her out of our home. Now I'm sorry and I want her to come back, but I don't know where she is. I need help finding her, but no-one seems to want to listen to me. I feel very depressed about this. Can you help me?'*

Of course you can. Following the usual assessment procedures, it seems you are left with a manageable presenting problem. You can support John in his feelings of distress whilst he endeavours to sort out his personal issues.

Your perspective will change, however, once you realise that John has been dead for some years.

But ghosts do not exist. Or do they? Gestalt therapist, Fritz Perls, is attributed with saying *'Everything before a "but" is bullshit.'* In the second part of this writing, I am not seeking to discredit or disprove anything undertaken in the work I have produced so far. I still firmly believe that in the context of trauma, particularly that of childhood sexual abuse, the research I explored surrounding psychosomatic reactions, disturbances in perception and dissociation experienced by the survivors with whom I worked and which were perceived by them to be of a paranormal nature, holds a great deal of value.

At the time I wrote that I could not comment on the existence of ghosts. Ten years on I have undergone a period of transition. I began a relationship with my partner, Steve, who moved in with me in October 2005. I also developed my career, changing my client group so I am now undertaking mostly brief focal therapy work with students in the local university. Although sexual abuse and extreme trauma still present from time to time, issues from this client group are now more wide ranging and accounts of haunting have considerably lessened. I am aware of my own parallel process, moving from working with sexual abuse survivors into a university environment and how at this point in my life I am seeking to try to educate myself further and broaden my viewpoints with regard to the subject of haunting.

What I have certainly not chosen to do, is to use accounts of 'factual' haunting as detailed by individuals from 'ghost' books, the internet or other sources claiming to be an authority on the subject. Despite the numerous amateur researchers who have put forward copious theories and are clearly working hard in their ongoing investigations and practical experimentations with affected public and environments, writers such as Lee (2007) raise that the lack of *'Tangible, tabulated evidence'* and the fact that *'Ghost stories are also purely anecdotal and seem to be very personal experiences'* remain the reason many people do not believe in the existence of paranormal activity.

In my opinion, whilst these personal and reported stories may be interesting, no amount of reading such material, which can be so subjective, really influences the viewpoint of the reader. The existence of ghosts may only be 'believed' either through religious, spiritual or cultural influences, or if they have actually been perceived through the senses by the individual, or in much rarer cases, by a group. Indeed, if a ghost is encountered, as in my partner's case, it is interesting to note that in many people, a reactive need for rationalisation of the experience continues unabated and our belief – certainly mine as I write this - is still not absolute.

Additionally I am aware of the many anomalies and contradictions that arise in these recorded experiences which serve to add to my confusion. I have, however, made reference to one book *'The Complete Book of Ghosts'* (Roland 2007) which I did find useful when doing general research around the topic and I have included some references to Roland's arguments. A 'complete' work on the supernatural felt positive, albeit realistically unachievable and I was hopeful that it would save me from hours of futile anecdotal reading about ghostly encounters. I am left, however, with the strong awareness that anything more than speculation is impossible and, whilst many researchers and authors theorise about the nature of the supernatural and how the lives of the living are impacted, these accounts vary to a great degree. My sense in reading these stories and accounts which are accessible to all, is that it would serve little purpose as 'proof' that ghosts either exist or that they do not. The aim of this section of the work is not to attempt to provide definitive proof in the existence and activity of the paranormal – I leave that to the plentiful individuals and groups who specialise in such investigations all over the world - but I intend to continue to question whether ghosts exist in the psyche, or as phenomena within the environment, or whether there may be other explanations in view of what has occurred in my personal life experience.

One general agreement from reading these accounts, however, and researching the 'evidence' appears to be that 'discarnate' spirits do have a presence which can be felt in a variety of ways by living people and that these phantom visitations differ in terms of their nature, behaviour and appearance and I will be exploring this in more depth later.

The Universal Appeal of the Supernatural

'Everyone has a ghost story' Steve.

Much has been written about ghosts over the centuries. They exist in folklore, are mentioned in religious contexts and are generally speculated upon whether 'believed' or not through anecdotal personal experience. If a group of people are gathered in one area, it seems that many will have a supernatural story to tell, pertaining to be from their own experience, from someone known to them, or they are keen to share and theorise about something they have read or watched on television. Through this activity we are merely continuing a culture that has been perpetuating for thousands of years. In bygone ages stories generally would have originated through family and community groups gathering around a fire. Visitors from neighbouring villages would enrich and embroider these tales before passing them on.

Jesus himself was highly creative in communicating his messages to his disciples and the wider population. As an authority as the Son of God, through the use of the Holy Ghost, he drew great crowds and triggered a great many differing reactions from worship through to rejection. He communicated lively stories and parables to illustrate his points. Even when he performed miracles, however, there were those who doubted him, who tried to find alternative or rational explanations for what they had witnessed. Many people who see or hear a ghost will likewise protect themselves. Culture changes with time and details may alter as the impact of scientific progress infiltrates the collective consciousness. Today, television sets have replaced fires and fewer people report sighting angels but are possibly more likely to encounter aliens, be a part of abduction by a UFO and even claim to undergo experimentation. However, one thing remains constant – people tell ghost stories to other people, who listen. Narrative is a significant way of learning, exploring, speculating and inciting emotional responses in the listener. Whilst Tim Bond in his article *'Naked Narrative: real research?'* (CPR Vol 2 no 2 June 2002) questions whether narrative can be viewed as valid research from a therapeutic viewpoint, he does conclude that: *'Narratives of client work, often presented as case studies, are the raw material for the generation of therapeutic propositions and practice'* and that: *'The systematic use of narrative opens up the possibility of studying lived experience more directly and creates new challenges in how to communicate new insight to readers.'* He underlines the significance of emotional reaction to narrative further by raising that the process *'depends not on a dispassionate consideration of "facts" but the evocative qualities of the narrative and its capacity to incite the empathy and critical reflection of the reader.'* In other words, the emotional responses of the listener are highly significant. Hairs may rise on the back of our necks and shivers may creep up and down our spines as we are thrilled or afraid to hear. Ghost stories in particular capture the imagination and evoke strong responses at times.

Life after death themes seems to stimulate an interest universally. Perhaps the desire to listen to the subjective stories of the supernatural catches our very human and basic need for an afterlife. I have certainly become aware that tales of the supernatural seem to appeal to many people, whatever their social background, education, ethnic origin or spiritual upbringing. Dr Edith Fiore (1987) says, *'Library shelves full of books about spirits attest to the lasting appeal of the hope that personality does survive death.'* Not only do we now have stories passed by word of mouth and access to books, but we also have popular films and television documentaries. Ghosts hold a certain fascination through literature, film and media interest. Examples include the 1984 comedy *'Ghostbusters'* – a whimsical tale of a group of men trying to eliminate persecutory spirits through use of equipment and physical force, animation such as the 1995 film *'Casper the Friendly Ghost,'* which to my mind, is a somewhat horrific story about a murdered child, or more traditional supernatural films, from the laughable 'B' movies of the 1950s to the heavier material of landmark horror such as *'The Exorcist'* (1973). Finally we are presented with a steady stream of allegedly 'reality based' contemporary documentary series, among them such delights as *'Ghost Hunters,' 'Ghost Whisperer,' 'Medium,'* or *'Britain's Most Haunted.'* It has become interesting for me to notice how often I refer to films, how they obviously have an impact on our modern lives and imagination and how their depiction of supernatural events can be used as effective illustrations when I am considering my life issues. It feels almost as if film and literature not only have made such subjects increasingly accessible and acceptable in mainstream entertainment but they can also provide significant frames of reference when illustrating universal themes, despite the fictional aspect of them.

Regardless of our sources, all of these supernatural themes for the most part ignite a sense of energy, fear, excitement and indeed, hope for some sort of afterlife. Debbie Charles, in her article *'Real Feelings'* published in CPJ (October 2003, Vol 14 no 8) also raises the interesting idea that films serve an important purpose as they have the potential to *'bypass the intellect, and possibly our defences, and go straight to our feelings.'* This can be useful when keeping myself open to my fears, defences and increasing fascination with supernatural issues that my intellect, my reasoning and rational 'left brained' parts argue cannot possibly be holding any real truth.

What follows then, is the narration of my own subjective story through the sharing of my own lived experience. I have illustrated my points with film, fiction and with some theoretical input and reflection. I am understandably limited in production of data and quantifiable 'proof' and I am aware that this may make me vulnerable to negative judgement, derision and even personal attack. I was heartened, however, when in February 2008 I attended a lecture given by Sir Richard Bowlby, son of the late renowned psychologist Sir John Bowlby. Quoting his father, Richard told his audience: *'never be afraid to extrapolate from a sample of one.'* Obviously I cannot speak for the thousands of people who claim to have encountered ghosts, nor can I verify or disprove their experiences of supernatural visitations. All I can do here is narrate the events that happened to my partner, Steve. What follows, therefore, is the story of my *'sample of one.'*

Steve's Background

'I was deprived
I never had the unhappy childhood
necessary for greatness.
The worst things that happened
were shopping with mother
unfinished homework
and the ghost beneath the bed' From 'The Portrait of the Artist' by Steve Turner.

My partner Steve was born in 1948 to a working class family. His father, Dan, had various jobs, including a stint for a few years working on the railways in the 1950s. Dan's major line of work, however, was as a long distance lorry driver, which frequently took him away from home for lengthy periods of time. It was during one of these trips in the early 1960s that he died suddenly from a heart attack at the age of fifty two. Steve was sixteen years old at the time. Steve's mother passed away much later, in the early 1990s. Steve was the only boy born into a family of six sisters and was the only longed for son. One sister directly elder to him died at the age of eleven months. I did raise the possibility with Steve of his mother becoming depressed, postnatally or otherwise and thereby physically or emotionally inaccessible to him at any time as he was growing up. The need for the mother to tune into the baby's needs and soothe or elevate the child's emotional state is highly significant to the healthy development of that child. Depressed or emotionally unavailable mothers may have more damaging implications for the young child than a physical absence. Steve feels, however, that whilst his mother would have experienced a natural bereavement response associated with such a loss, he has no sense of any issues around delayed or complex grief which may have rendered his mother emotionally unavailable. Of course, however, he was very young at the time of this event.

Whilst his father was frequently physically absent during much of his childhood, his mother was not. Steve tells me he feels sure that he had a secure primary attachment figure in her and she, as was traditional at the time, remained at home full time to care for her growing family. As far as he remembers, he experienced consistent, loving and attentive parenting from her. Steve also feels he had plenty of secondary attachment carers; namely his father despite his lengthy absences, and of whom Steve holds some valuable positive memories, and the sisters, grandparents and numerous aunts and uncles in a large and lively family. There was also a strong sense of community typical of the time and now sadly dissipated in modern society. Most importantly, Steve knew he was loved, describing his childhood as poor but happy. From the viewpoint of attachment theory, it is difficult to foster any interpretation that Steve's very early childhood experiences had much bearing on the issues that occurred in his adulthood, although it is of course important to bear his childhood history in mind throughout our exploration of his later supernatural perceptions and psychological reactions.

The family moved around the local area, changing rented accommodation frequently. In fact they had moved a total of eight times before Steve left home at the age of fourteen. Important to a secure development, however, he consistently attended the same school which provided stability and friendship. To this day he still maintains strong connections with boys from his childhood. On the whole, however, Steve was a mature and independent child who enjoyed the company of older people and hated the confines of the educational system. He was clearly bright and intelligent but did not fully reach any academic potential in an environment he experienced as restrictive.

Throughout his childhood he had some episodes of physical illness comprising bouts of pneumonia, pleurisy and a mild form of polio which meant that he had some lengthy periods of non attendance at school. Like most children who dislike school, he often played up on this to extend his frequent absences! During these illnesses, Steve tells me that he felt as if his hands were swelling up to frightening proportions and his mother was somewhat concerned about Steve's reporting of interaction with 'little people' gallivanting playfully at the foot of his bed. These are, however, not unusual hallucinations for a child in high fever and do not appear to hint at supernatural experiencing.

Steve took the opportunity to leave school at the age of fourteen to become an apprentice and this involved leaving home, living both abroad and in other areas of England before settling back in the small town of his birth as a young adult. As an apprentice Steve did encounter some bullying from other lads who habitually resented the presence of the new boy and played this out for a while. On one occasion Steve's father intervened and Steve was moved to work elsewhere.

Other than this, it is apparent that Steve was not beaten, neglected or traumatised at any stage of his childhood development. He was certainly something of a rebel and a fighter himself, developing sound defensive and coping mechanisms. Nor was he sexually abused. He did, however, begin sexual relations early, at the age of fourteen, losing his virginity to a seventeen year old girl, an experience with full consent he describes as 'highly pleasurable.' It is interesting to me to note, however, that this young woman had moved in with the already overcrowded family temporarily as a refuge from her own father, who was, in Steve's words 'taking too much interest in her.' Sexual abuse therefore throws a shadow even in this situation and whilst today social services or the police may or may not intervene in this situation if they had become aware of it, in those days certainly no-one batted an eyelid. Following a few further casual relationships, Steve married at the age of nineteen and was a father to a son by twenty.

During his early twenties and having explored his spiritual side via various religions, Steve became a practising Mormon, a faith founded in America in 1830 by Joseph Smith. Steve's involvement with the church lasted for a few years. He describes his religious motivation as follows: **'I found it very stabilising. I found the whole thing about that church fascinating. The fact is, I did a lot of searching when I was a teenager and like a lot of people that sort of age I was exploring whether there was any truth in religion. I went through quite a few of the religions. Mormon/Latter Day Saints were the ones that hit home to me and it seemed like a good religion to take on board. It was a very full religion where people believe in all parts of the Bible, all parts of religion and went by what was termed as "spirit". You talked and you got answers back from the spirit and there were a lot of things happening with the church that I felt guided by – the upper spiritual side. And I found that it just fulfilled everything that I wanted from a church. And the people there were brilliant, absolutely beautiful; it was just like being at home – lots of brothers and sisters.'**

Steve later left the faith as it was causing tension with his non religious wife owing to the fact that Steve was spending a lot of time away from the family to undertake the sermons and visits to parishioners required. Steve then described himself as an atheist once he had left the Mormon Church, his interest and belief in the faith having diminished. He explained his reasons for this life change as follows: **'I think it was a case of throwing off the old and putting the new on. Well, if I can't believe in it then I don't want to believe in it at all. If there's truth and I've found truth in that one religion, then it hasn't helped me stay on that path when I was doing the right thing. So it was like, if I can't do this, I can't believe in it and I don't want to believe in it because if there's truth in it then I've given it up, therefore I don't want any part of it.'** Steve's rejection appeared to be absolute. During his time as a church goer, Steve acknowledged that there was a supernatural side to his faith but he then chose to no longer believe in the existence of ghosts, along with God, thereafter.

The only experience which he describes as being anywhere near supernatural occurred about a year after his father's death and before Steve became a practising Mormon. He would have been about seventeen at the time. He was with a girlfriend during the dark early hours of the morning in the local park. The couple were sitting together on a bench, and Steve tells me that he remembered sensing a sudden strong odour of petrol, a smell he associated with his father who as a lorry driver, mechanic and amateur drag racer frequently smelled of oil and petrol fumes. Acting upon a sudden uneasy feeling, Steve had a sense of his father's presence, which he interpreted as a warning of some form of pending danger. He then saw the figure of a very tall man approaching him and his girlfriend from some distance away. Steve chose to act upon his sense of foreboding and left the place before this man came any nearer. He has never felt able to explain from where the petrol scent or the uneasy feeling emanated but feels that the sensations he experienced were linked with protection in a time of pending danger. Steve explains: **'It was very early morning, about four or five a.m. Because it was summertime there was an early fog off the ground – a very strange atmosphere. So then seeing this figure, getting this smell, when you're in the middle of a park – it was a massive park – there is no way I could get the smell of petrol, no way at all...Getting the smell of petrol made my awareness heighten. Looking up and seeing this figure approaching us I just had a feeling of dread, so I just said to my girlfriend ,"Let's go."**

Steve's long marriage was initially happy but then degenerated into a volatile and often discontented state in more recent years. Steve and his wife finally parted in 2005 and he began a relationship with me later on that same year. At this point Steve was fifty five years old and I was forty one. Steve had had a variety of jobs but at this point he had been working the night shift at a large warehouse for a period of six years. He was happy there and felt that this was the best job he had experienced, if not financially, then certainly in terms of quality of life and compatibility with the environment, the working conditions and sound relationships with most of his colleagues.

These are the basic facts around Steve's life history. If a counsellor were to be assessing him, it would also be ethical to note that Steve does not take drugs, is not on medication and drinks alcohol in moderation. The final issue to mention regarding Steve's background concerns his eldest sister, Lily, who died from heart failure in the mid 1990s. She was said to be psychic. This is a significant point which re-emerges later on.

Encounters 2006

'Encounter: v. meet by chance; be faced with. n. a chance meeting; a battle' From 'The Oxford English Dictionary.'

Steve's shift as a stock handler starts at 9.30pm and continues until about six in the morning. His work is located within a large warehouse full of clothes hung on carousels which the workers sort, hand pick and box ready for delivery to customers. The night shift comprises a small team of less than thirty people, all known to each other and relatively trusted. They are spaced out over several open plan floors and there can be some lone or pair working. During the winter months, however, and in preparation for the Christmas period, a temporary intake of agency workers swells the team to at least twice the size. The team then returns to its core number in the spring. This is a factor that is taken into account later in my story. In this highly secure environment, there is no plausible way that any intruder could possibly enter the premises undetected by the security officers or the electronic detection system that is in place. Workers are randomly searched upon leaving the premises at the conclusion of the shift to prevent theft of work property or misconduct, for example carrying banned items such as mobile phones.

It was 26 March 2006, a Sunday evening. Steve was working alone when he witnessed a man, probably in his fifties with greying hair and dressed in dark blue, running through the premises shouting *'Help me! Help me!'* The man then ran out through the fire door and Steve followed to ask if he could help, wondering who the stranger was. The man had, however, disappeared. Steve descended to the floor below to inform the team leader of this strange man's presence. Whilst Steve and his colleague stood in the stairwell they then both heard the fire door suddenly slam on the floor above them. They looked at other, puzzled by the peculiar incident. Steve tells me that his initial reaction was to wonder to himself *'Who is that idiot messing about?'* and to gain an impression that the man was either a colleague who had passed through the area too rapidly to be fully recognised, or was one of the security guards, possibly a new member of staff. It certainly did not occur to him at this point that the stranger was any form of apparition or anything less than 'real.'

Steve went on to describe the incident, saying: **'There was hardly anybody in, it was a proportion of the shift, it was Sunday so say there were about twelve of us in. I was put on the top floor by myself, so I know there was nobody else up there. I was binning in an H** (an H being a specific work area that the warehouse is divided up into) **and then in the H opposite I could see this person. He was very solid, very solid...well his legs really, I didn't see much else, just his legs – the rest of him was obscured by the hanging clothes. I came out of the H wondering where he had gone, asking him, shouting at him "What's wrong?" I thought that it was a new security guard that we'd never seen before because I didn't recognise his voice and I knew the person that was on duty that night – I talk to all of the security guards. I went downstairs and I said, "I think one of the security guards is having problems – he seems to have run by me but didn't see me and he's gone through the fire doors."** Michael (one of the team leaders) **said that there shouldn't be anyone on the floors yet because security is timed work. So we went to have a look and we went right down to the bottom of the fire tower – its three floors – and as soon as we got to the bottom the door on the top floor opened and shut. The fire doors are big heavy things, they don't blow open – they are solid because they have to stop draughts and things, so both of us ran up there and there was** *nobody on the floor, absolutely nobody. And then Michael said "There's somebody messing about," and I said "Obviously." So it was like, a question at that time of "Who is messing about?" rather than "What is that?" Either there was somebody messing about or a security guard who was new had lost his way. I think Michael did phone and say, "There's one of your security guards on the floor," and they replied, "No there's not," so it wasn't a security guard.'*

Discussing this event the following morning with Steve, I felt that the possibilities included someone accessing the building and playing some sort of trick. We know, however, that this is absolutely impossible, given the tight security of the working environment. Steve pondered: **'When the time passed and you think well, there's no explanation, you think well, what did I see then? It was solid, it was tangible – I mean I can't say I didn't see it because I know for sure that I did see him. You know, your brain's saying well, what is it and then you're saying well, it wasn't real, it was a ghost. Then you sort of start saying, Oh how daft.'**

It seemed to me that the most likely explanation was that Steve had dozed off for a few minutes and imagined or dreamed the episode. I also considered the fact that it had possibly been a hypnagogic hallucination. These can occur in the state between sleeping and waking and I have on occasion experienced these myself, in addition to episodes of somnambulism, particularly when I have been experiencing stress. We felt satisfied with this likely explanation and we subsequently forgot all about it.

Dreams, nightmares, night terrors and nocturnal hallucinations are obviously the stuff of darkness – associated with deep feelings of unease, when most of us are asleep or in the process of falling asleep. The Freudian view of dreams as *'the royal road to the unconscious,'* perhaps holds a sinister feel when we reflect upon dreams and their potential function and meaning. Cushway and Sewall (1992) in their work on dreams note the contrast between Freud's interpretation with the Jungian idea that *'...the dream is a normal, creative expression of the unconscious, rather than Freud's perception of the dream as a disturbed mental activity.'* Gestalt psychotherapist Fritz Perls put forward the theory that *'All dream objects or characters are split off portions of the self that need re-integrating into the personality. Nightmares are an extreme form of this split. Thus we attempt to push away our worst fears and feelings and they come back in our dreams, in the form of nightmare creatures or objects to haunt us.'* I have certainly used Perls's method of working with dreams effectively, both when making sense of my own dream experiences, and also in client work. It may be that Steve's nightmarish man may be some sort of projective split and we look at this possibility in more detail later on. More recently, Ernest Hartmann, in his book *'The Nightmare'* (1987) takes a more normalising stance and has concluded from his investigations that *'...although nightmares can be a symptom of psychological disturbance, they are not necessarily a pathological symptom. In fact... frequent nightmares may occur in relatively healthy but sensitive people.'* Cushway and Sewall also raise the significant point that *'Nightmares increase with certain illnesses, stress, fevers, anxiety, depression, schizophrenia, or traumatic stress disorders and with certain medication.'* Perhaps Steve was merely overtired or slightly unwell at the time of his 'visitation.' Let us now, however, go on to briefly consider how nocturnal incidents and perceptions may be interpreted as being supernatural in nature.

Night Ghosts

'It came in a night time vision as others slept. Suddenly, fear gripped me; I trembled and shook with terror, as a spirit passed before my face - my hair stood up on end!' Job 4 vs 13-15

Some years ago, my grandmother died suddenly at Christmas and I was feeling shocked and devastated by her passing. Four nights later I was in bed and somewhat bizarrely I witnessed her emerging from the wardrobe. She spoke to me and I never remembered what she said but I experienced a sense of comfort which greatly sustained me and allowed me to fully access the healthy grieving process that followed. I always assumed that this experience comprised a hypnagogic hallucination which can occur in the period between sleep and wakefulness. I thought I had been awake when in fact I must have been in a stage between consciousness and sleep. At the time it never occurred to me that I may have met with any sort of spiritual presence connected with my grandmother or that she had somehow managed to visit me following her death in a time when she was needed to aid me in my emotional distress. Interestingly, quite recently after this, I recited the incident to a peer counsellor as part of an experiential triad exercise for the master's degree course I was studying. I sensed that the counsellor struggled to hold and contain the experience and in the feedback session afterwards, she admitted as much. This further underlines for me the importance of a counsellor's need to offer belief. Obviously significant in issues surrounding extreme abuse and torture, as I explored in part one, when working with the paranormal as counsellors we surely need to similarly bracket our own internalised belief and cultural systems and endeavour to believe our client's experiences. Belief issues are explored further in part three.

It seemed likely that Steve may have had a similar vision induced by a parasomniac episode. DSM 4 describes parasomnia as *'disorders characterised by abnormal behavioural or physiological events occurring in association with sleep, specific sleep stages, or sleep-wake transitions.'* These disorders are linked with the autonomic nervous system, motor system or cognitive processes during sleep wake transitions.

Hypnagogic hallucinations are not uncommon. These trigger the experiencing of vivid images on at the onset of sleep with the sense of being awake. Hypnopompic hallucinations are the opposite, experienced when the individual is in the process of waking up. One client of mine, a young man, cited an interesting experience when he had a strong vision of his best friend who had committed suicide the week previously. *'It seemed too real to be a dream,'* my client told me. *'We were together in a white room and I was able to ask him why he had done what he'd done. We had a real conversation. My friend told me that "It was not that bad." "Easy for you to say," I replied. I was able to be angry with him, to say goodbye, to get some closure. It was just too real an encounter to be any old dream. I don't believe in ghosts but now I don't really know what to think.'*

More extreme forms of parasomnia occur when we consider the issue of 'Night Terrors,' also known as 'Sleep Terrors,' or 'Pavor Nocturnus.' Night Terrors occur when the individual will experience intense anxiety, often waking up crying or screaming, but without recalling any dream content in full. These truly horrifying experiences can predominantly affect children. Cushway and Sewall do raise the interesting point that *'For children, the boundaries between reality and imagination, or waking and dreaming, are far less fixed than for adults…'* The Night Terror Resource Centre cites that fifteen percent of children between the ages of three and twelve are affected, in addition to both male and female adults. Night terrors differ from nightmares, occurring in deep wave as opposed to REM sleep. It is the feeling of fear itself which has an impact on the sufferer. Nightmares occur during REM sleep and also leave the individual feeling terrified, but the frightening images associated with nightmares can often be remembered.

REM sleep is a phase comprising twenty percent of sleep time and involves dreaming with rapid breathing, an increase in heart rate and blood pressure. During the deeper wave sleep it can be difficult to rouse the sufferer back into conscious awareness for some minutes. Screaming, sweating, rapid heart rate, choking, experiencing extreme feelings of fear or threat to self are characteristic of the night terror state. Many sufferers awake in a highly confused condition and have been unaware of the disturbance caused to others by their intense arousal. Night terrors embody emotional states to a degree more intense than nightmares.

The stages of sleep consist of four phases plus the REM component. Phase one comprises a light sleep, during which the sleeper is easy to wake, may experience a jerking of the muscles and sensations of falling, which many people on occasion report. Fifty percent of sleep time occurs in phase two, when brain activity becomes slower but includes periods of rapid movement. Phase three is the first stage of deeper sleep with phase four as the second stage and the sleeper is hard to wake. This phase is significant for a good quality of refreshing sleep. It is during the phase four periods that night terrors occur. The REM sleep occurs occasionally throughout the night alternating with REM sleep about eighty to one hundred minutes (DSM 4). Sleep paralysis can form part of a night terror experience or occur as an independent phenomenon. This distressing state literally disables the sleeper who awakes suddenly to find they cannot move their limbs for a period of time. Sleep paralysis occurs in phase one of sleep whereas night terrors are experienced in phase four.

Unlike more conventional nightmares, during a night terror, images of threat symbolic to the sufferer may be felt to be actually present in the room, for example snakes, spiders, people or other threatening archetypes meaningful to the individual or the culture to which they belong. Hallucinatory or hypnologic sleep paralysis may also go to the extreme length of taking on the form of a creature or person which will sit on the victim's chest, causing difficulty in breathing or a sense of strangulation. A friend of mine cited an experience when she witnessed a white ghostly face floating above her and a sense of constriction in her chest area. She tells me, however, that whilst in a state of terror, she was fully aware that this was all due to disturbances of her mind and nothing to do with any external source of haunting. Other people are not so able to bracket such experiences and may project meanings into these episodes, becoming convinced of supernatural sources as a result.

The Night Terrors Resource Centre cites that *'Different cultures throughout time have interpreted Hallucinatory Sleep Paralysis as different spirits or events.'* The following common archetypes are then listed as:

- *'Ancestral ghosts – South East Asians*
- *Hag – Irish and Scottish*
- *Cats – Chinese*
- *Spectral foxes – Japanese*
- *Djinn – Arabs*
- *Guilt – Romans and the Egyptians*
- *Witchcraft – Mexicans*
- *Vampires – Europeans*
- *Demons – mediaeval Europe '* (2007).

Here we have a clear example of archetypes – whether taking on the form and persona of the hook nosed warty old woman or witch that seems to haunt the night terror sufferer in the UK or the more mystical animals and entities of the East. For the traditionally Christian, angels 'haunt' the Bible along with visions of saints and visitations by God. Jesus is mistaken for a phantom when he walks on water. *'But when they saw something walking along beside them they screamed in terror, thinking it was a ghost'* (Mark 6:49), and following his death and resurrection, *'But the whole group was terribly frightened, thinking they were seeing a ghost'* (Luke 24:37). Psychologist Carl Jung who developed the idea of archetypes, himself suffered from extremely vivid hypnagogic hallucinations and describes waking and witnessing a vivid image of Christ, simultaneously beautiful and terrifying. It is interesting to note that people not only encounter angels but now are more likely to see or even find themselves fully included in experiences surrounding aliens and UFO abduction. This seems to indicate a significant change in culture in the West, perhaps as we become more scientific and less spiritual in our outlook. Interestingly, in contemporary American culture, the collective agreement of the archetype seems to appear as the long limbed, slant eyed, a-sexual space alien. Later we note that Steve's colleague Bernie cites alien abduction as a potential cause for his own supernatural experience, albeit with a degree of humour.

Genetics have been cited as a possible trigger to night terrors and other sleep disorders. Sleepeducation.com (2007) cites that sleep terrors appear to have a strong family link with members perhaps experiencing similar problems. Other medically based theories suggest that psychologically adults may have a history of bipolar disorder, depression, anxiety and stress. Physical triggers may include sleep deprivation, migraine, fever, head injury, thyroid imbalance, menstrual or stomach problems, stroke, medication, alcohol or drug use. Charles Dickens's character Scrooge *(The Christmas Carol)* initially refuses to believe that he is being persecuted supernaturally and cites indigestion as a possible cause for the visitation of the ghost of his former partner, Marley, on the seventh anniversary of Marley's demise. Scrooge informs the apparition that *'You may be an undigested bit of beef, a blot of mustard, a crumb of cheese, a fragment of underdone potato. There's more of gravy that of grave about you, whatever you are,'* (1985).

Environments may also have an impact, for example sleeping in a strange location, whilst travelling or when disturbance is owing to a change in noise or light levels. It remains more uncertain as to why children in particular experience this condition.

It seems hardly surprising that owing to the extremity of the reaction and the intensity of the images recalled by the sufferer, for some people night terrors were – and still are in certain cultures or religions - believed to be indicative of the presence of demons or of some sort of ghostly 'possession.' This may be one interpretation as traditionally, in the Christian religion in particular, demons and ghosts in general are viewed as evil entities that use the souls of the dead to try to corrupt others, their function being to persuade people to follow a less righteous path.

For now, finding it unlikely and being unable to detect any signs of obvious demonic possession in my partner, I was at this point assuming that his experience of the running man had been some form of momentary sleep disturbance. This was despite the fact that Steve had never encountered anything of the sort or dropped off to sleep during the many years he had worked on night shifts. Night or late shift workers, however, are likely to suffer from fatigue, health problems and even premature death. These employees are simply working against nature; not gaining much needed natural sunlight and not allowing the body to catch up with the production of the hormone melatonin which is produced when darkness naturally falls. For Steve, having worked most of his life on night and shift work, this is nothing new. He is well aware of the toughness of the implications, telling me that: **'When you are working through the night, once or twice you hit a brick wall, about three o'clock so if you don't carry on**

working, you just lose the will to work and you just feel like sitting down and going to sleep. It's a case of pushing yourself through to carry on, to make sure you get through it.' It is also well documented that sleep deprivation can be a significant trigger with regard to the experiencing of hallucinations and it is whilst in such vulnerable states that an individual may be prone to anxiety, depression and when buried memories may emerge. In the book by Van der Hart, Nijenhuis and Steele *'The Haunted Self'* (2006) we are informed that: *'Dreaded memories that are awakened by strong reminders haunt survivors, especially when they have exhausted their emotional and physical resources. And unfortunately, many survivors live their lives on the edge of exhaustion and thus are more prone to the intrusion of traumatic memories.'*

Perhaps Steve was merely sleep deprived, emotionally and physically shattered which had rendered him vulnerable to disturbances in perception. This seemed like a logical explanation. I realised later that I had a lot to learn.

'John'

'Haunt: v. linger in the mind of; (esp. of a ghost) repeatedly visit (a person or place) n. a place often visited by a particular person.' From 'The Oxford English Dictionary.'

Some weeks later the apparition of the man re-appeared, once more running through the area where Steve was working. He was shouting 'Help me, Dan, help me.' The name Dan immediately resonated with Steve as this was his own father's name. As we know, Dan had died suddenly when Steve was a sixteen year old teenager. This time Steve identified that it was the same man, dressed in the dark blue of a 1950s British Rail uniform. Steve was aware that his father was also employed for a while on the railway, in the exact location of Steve's present working environment. We believe the sidings existed and were subsequently demolished in the spot where the warehouse has been built.

The man in uniform then started to appear to Steve about once a week and visiting increasingly frequently but on random nights over the next two or three months. According to Steve he was *'real and solid'* and it had been easy to mistake him for a living human person. Steve began to question his own sanity. He said: **'I think it was a case of am I actually going mad here, because it was only me that was having this happen to me. There was nobody else. I spoke to a number of people and they were saying they've not seen anybody so I was wondering, well, why is it happening to me? And I can remember thinking have I got pressure on my brain? Am I seeing something that's not there because of something that's inside my body? I thought it was me.'**

During his increasing number of appearances to Steve, this bizarre railwayman began to display increasing amounts of agitation and anger and began to berate Steve in rage, shouting at him, *'You aren't helping me.'* He also addressed Steve as Dan, clearly believing that Steve was his deceased father – a man the angry railwayman had once known. At one point, mustering all of his courage, shock and persistent disbelief of what was happening, Steve was able to have a dialogue with the railwayman, asking him who he was and what he wanted. He learned that the man was called 'John' and he wanted Steve to contact the daughter who John had thrown out of home *'two days before'* for getting pregnant. John then turned to go, Steve says *'as if going through a curtain.'* This communication was useful – Steve had clearly encountered an apparition on a mission. We now had a name, a reason for the unfinished business that was keeping John present in the warehouse, a sense of the task that he wanted Steve to accomplish but also a puzzlement around what the statement 'two days before' may mean…two days before…what?

Or was it so useful? I became aware on reflection that once 'it' has a name, then 'it' stops being an 'it' and has become a 'him' and 'he' has become 'John.' This thing is now personalised and has an identity. In many ways it now feels like there is no going back from here and 'it' will be John from now on. This shift from a vagueness – a sense of a tired mind playing tricks to something concrete, could have implications for my partner and me; perhaps on our faith or lack of faith, our belief or not in the supernatural and ultimately our view of the world and the wider universe.

Over a period of time on the occasions when he became visible to Steve, John was becoming increasingly verbally aggressive. He was clearly frustrated at Steve's inaction regarding contacting his daughter. Of course, the task itself was impossible for Steve to undertake, even if had chosen to attempt it. We had no way of knowing who the daughter may be or even, given the possible time scale by Steve's dating of John's uniform, if she would still be alive herself. Furthermore the possibility of tracking her down to inform her that her long dead dad was seeking forgiveness was disturbing, somewhat tragic and frankly, laughable.

Steve continued to question the incidents and talked of his perception of the apparition as similar to having a three way mirror in front of him. He can adjust the mirror to see what is behind or to one side, but move them too much and the image changes or disappears. Catch a glimpse in the moment. He says: **'I thought at the time, it was all in my head, am I speaking to myself and am I answering myself and afterwards it was like, well did that really happen? It's something that's not reality so you can't put it down to what it was or wasn't and it was like saying, hold on a minute, what happened there? I remember feeling very cold but then it was like having somebody in front of you in a mirror and the mirror tilts one way and he disappears and then he comes back again – it was like that constantly. It was like him kind of not fidgeting but going in and out constantly whilst** *he was talking to me. It's like, a mirror turning sideways and then just going and then coming back.'*

Then strange physical marks began to appear on Steve's face. These were lengthy welts which faded into scratches, about four or five lines of them very close together. It looked to me like very fine marks you may make with a razor, and they were certainly far too fine and too meticulous to be caused by fingernails or any sort of tool or weapon. To me it almost looked like someone was trying to literally cut off Steve's face. They went round his forehead to his jaw line, always on the right side. The marks would last a day or two then fade. These scratches became increasingly vivid and at its height were occurring two or three times a week. Welts upon welts, scratches upon scratches, we began to worry that this would lead to permanent scarring. Steve would get the marks irrespective of whether he actually saw John but Steve always felt his presence. Steve says it felt like he was 'being brushed' and sometimes he felt a slight burning sensation. The scratches were also physically sore. In time on the recurring occasions that he was marked, the scratches would begin to bleed more profusely, require medical attention from a first-aider working on the shift, but then appear to heal up unfeasibly rapidly. Self harm, psychosomatic symptoms and dissociation were possibilities that Steve did not dismiss, as we see in his comments here: *'I didn't altogether feel like it was a ghost at this point; I was still thinking, am I standing here by myself talking to myself, is there anybody around – am I going mad – is it a part of insanity that causes this – is it pressure on my brain, whatever, and the mark on my face the first time I remember feeling, it was like feeling lashed, whipped. It was very strong the first time and I remember thinking possibly, this is what a brain can do – stigmata. You know, nobody can say the person's brain isn't making these marks – so I was still putting it down to the fact it could still be me that's making a mark on my face. I was even going through a period of thinking I was blacking out – doing it without knowing. Is somebody looking at me whilst I'm in a daze, doing it to myself and that was a fear as well, somebody might walk by and see me marking myself saying I'm doing it myself without me knowing it.'*

Significantly though, sometimes the marks began to appear on Steve's face in front of his colleagues. Steve was much relieved by this, explaining: *'It was a big relief. I suppose it was like a present, a vindication – it's like me being able to ask, "Have I been hit?" and they'd look at my face and say, "Oh my God, I can see it travelling around your face!" Then that was me being able to say, "It's not me," – it's like, just being vindicated I think.'* There is more on this issue later on in this book when I describe these continuing events in my diary.

These physical attacks on Steve were the most upsetting and disturbing aspect of the 'haunting' and the event that recurred the most throughout the whole experience. It seemed that Steve was literally being chosen for persecution and branding. We can see from the photograph (page 155) that the marks on Steve's face still clearly show three days after an attack when this picture was taken. They always comprise several fine scratches close together on the right side of his face.

As a therapist I did, of course, firstly wonder if this could be some sort of psychosomatic reaction to Steve's emotional life. Symptoms which can be traced to no obvious physical cause but may be sourced from emotional and psychological processes rather than illness or injury can be classed in this way. Freud famously researched psychosomatic conditions which influenced his theories around repression and the unconscious mind. His legacy includes the negative label 'hysteria' that lingers in modern culture and which was discussed in part one. Secondly, I considered the possibility that Steve was inflicting the scratches upon his own face during episodes of dissociation or splitting, again which have been explored in part one, in the context of coping strategies and reactions to trauma. Thirdly, I was left with the unpleasant option that for whatever reason, Steve was lying about the whole situation. The idea of fabrication I quickly dismissed, owing to witnessing the level of genuine emotional distress Steve was experiencing and the nature of the strange physical scarring. Owing to its peculiarity and consistency the scarring simply did not look like it was being inflicted deliberately as it would have taken time, patience and a steady hand with a specific tool to have been self inflicted. It was also a highly speedy process, the scars apparently appearing spontaneously and in front of witnesses. I was also aware that this was all causing disruption to Steve's life at work and I knew that Steve did not want to lose his job, be labelled as mentally ill or as a 'hysteric.' Nor did he wish to damage his credibility as a hard working and conscientious employee who was hoping to be promoted. Any motivation for lying or attention seeking just did not seem plausible.

Considering that none of these theories were carrying any real weight at the present time, I was left to consider the challenging possibility that some sort of supernatural entity was violently attacking my partner whilst he was at work and on a fairly regular basis. I was then also left with questions about whether ghosts, if there are such things, can indeed be physically dangerous.

Ghosts Hurt or Hurting

'So, if you wonder what happens when a ghost gets mad, it pretty much depends on the ghost. If he was a jerk when he was alive, he'll be a jerk when he's dead. The jerk probably can't hurt you. But, he might try.' From the 'McPike Mansion' Website.

Are ghosts capable of hurting the living? Perhaps it may also be worth asking the question – can living people cause harm to a ghost? Let us consider a few fictional examples of ghosts – who are hurting or causing hurt – and who are attempting to get their needs met from living people. Consider the narrative of the unfortunate Mr Lockwood, Heathcliff's new tenant in Emily Bronte's novel *'Wuthering*

Heights,' as he describes his horror and panic reactions at the encounter with the child ghost Cathy lost on the moor. Assuming at first that this experience is the result of either a nightmare or of auditory disturbance caused by a branch tapping the pane during a storm, Lockwood stretches his arm through the window only to be seized, horrifyingly, by an icy hand and to hear a child's voice: *'Let me in. Let me in! ...I'm come home, I'd lost my way on the moor!' As it spoke, I discerned, obscurely, a child's face looking through the window – terror made me cruel: and, finding it useless to attempt to shake the creature off, I pulled its wrist onto the broken pane, and rubbed it to and fro till the blood ran down and soaked the bedclothes...'* (1976).

More up to date, Christopher Eccleston's character Charles, in the 2001 film *'The Others,'* returns to his family as the ghost of the soldier he was, lost in the Second World War. *'Sometimes I bleed,'* his inactive and highly depressed ghost informs us. So the ghost Cathy bleeds and the dead Charles likewise is able to shed blood.

It does, however, seem highly unlikely that ghosts can actually bleed in the way of living flesh, or if so, that despite such an abundance of gore left on Lockwood's bedclothes, that they can really be treated as having the physical qualities of living people.

There is, however, no question in that it seems many discarnate entities are in a state of emotional 'stuckness' or pain, which seems to be a theme not only in novels and plays, but is also firmly indicated in more serious accounts of haunting and ghostly manifestations. I will be examining this issue further later on.

I have not been able to find many examples of ghosts being actively physically violent towards their living counterparts albeit many can be noisy, volatile and may cause disruption to objects and environments. Poltergeists, German for 'Noisy ghost' are known for their physical force; being mischievous or downright vindictive with a habit of moving or throwing items at a living recipient. Their activity is probably the most obvious example, along with the occasional incident in which people are tripped or have doors closed and locked on them by unseen forces. For my research Steve's colleague Bernie provided an example of his own haunting experience. He describes the extreme physicality of how he is pinioned and helpless in addition to feeling the malevolence of his particular ghost, which he senses is a male who is highly vindictive: *'As I walked up the stairs I felt myself being dragged back and pinned down in the hall. I could not move off the floor. I remember a swirling mass around my head and sensed that it was a male who was doing this as I sensed anger and rage. The scariest part was that something was effortlessly pinning me down and I was completely helpless. Two months later I was sitting on the couch when I saw out of the corner of my eye something move. Again I felt pinned down and unable to move. I saw a swirling mass that seemed to be taunting me and showing me its power. It was the realisation that I had not imagined the first occasion that made this one absolutely terrifying. I remember screaming at this thing to let me go. I was a nervous wreck.'* Bernie's fear and helplessness also underlines his physical powerlessness during these incidents although he later jokes that *'My wife thinks I was abducted by aliens but rejected and thrown back!'*

The McPike Mansion in Illinois claims to be at the present time, *'One of the most extensively investigated haunted sites in America,'* and has a website devoted to a place where physical violence has recently been recorded. Former owner and resident ghost, Henry McPike, was known for beating his wife and servants and an example is cited of one of the women investigators feeling a blow across her face which left a red 'slap' type mark. Unpleasant, but an example of a relatively milder form of abuse, and this did remind me at the time of reading of Steve's facial scarring.

One far more extreme case of physical bodily harm inflicted by a spiritual entity, however, has to be the Japanese legend of the Kuchisake-onna. She is the spirit of a young girl whose beauty was mutilated by her jealous Samurai husband or lover. The unfortunate woman had her mouth slit from ear to ear. A masked ghost, she wanders in the fog haunting men, women and children and having removed her veil she poses them the question 'Am I beautiful?' (Watashi Kirei?) Those brave enough to reply in the affirmative she releases but for those horrified by the vision of her face she kills if they are male, or disfigures if female, thereby dooming the latter to also take on the role of a Kuchisake-onna. Stories of such a ghost still roaming and persecuting the living were evident in South Korea as recently as 2004.

Perhaps ghosts may cause harm to the living through less physical means - by emotional manipulation, for example. Perhaps such ghosts are lonely or still carrying the jealousies, rages and even feelings of strong love they experienced in life which may motivate them to cause significant harm. They may simply want the living to join them in the after world. A classic example of this occurs in Noel Coward's (1941) comic play *'Blithe Spirit'* which encapsulates these themes when Charles's first wife Elvira, who died young, is conjured up from the 'other side' during a séance. Upon her arrival she complains that she has been interrupted whilst playing backgammon with Genghis Khan. Elvira initially stakes an emotional claim on Charles and wants him to join her in the afterlife; however, she then proceeds to harass and persecute him and we see the negative reality of the relationship's history emerge. At first only Charles can see and hear Elvira and reasons cited for his experience by others include hysteria, cold draughts, hallucinations, alcohol and *'something wrong with the brain.'* Elvira succeeds in killing Charles' second wife, Ruth, after tampering with the car intended to be driven by Charles. Once Ruth, now dead, is also conjured up we can see through this peculiar ménage a trois the true nature of the tensions and resentments, as the two spirits of the wives destroy the room around Charles at the conclusion of the play. Of course, this is fiction, but it illustrates some of the themes that I explore and develop later.

Expert on spirit possession, Dr Edith Fiore in her book *'The Unquiet Dead'*

(1987) informs us that a tactile ghost is not unusual and that a light ghostly touching is to be expected. She advises: *'Don't be alarmed. Remember they cannot harm you. It could be a loved one trying to let you know he or she is there. Notice how often living people touch each other, even giving friendly punches at times.'*

If, however, as in Steve's case, it is not a loved one who is attacking him causing the pain and scarring, then we are at this point suspecting that our case does not fit with the stereotype of the phantom that is not motivated to harm. Let us also consider some extremes illustrated in film. *'The Entity'* (1983) allegedly based on actual events, tells the story of a woman who is repeatedly raped by an invisible supernatural force. This initially begins with her feeling a slap to the face and a rape incident which is passed off as a bad dream; however, repeated attacks swiftly escalate in intensity with the woman, Carla, suffering bruising and other physical signs of severe sexual assault. Carla's car is also taken over by an unseen entity, her son is prevented from movement and electrocuted by the supernatural force and the windows of a house violently smash. In the classic 1973 film *'The Exorcist,'* which was in fact voted the most frightening film of all time, we witness twelve year old Regan being possessed by the devil. Her body is profoundly abused and contorted whilst she self mutilates. Speaking in demonic voices she is verbally abusive and the bed violently shakes.

If we are going to take any notice of the cinematic experience, we know that some malevolent ghosts do hurt us and they can even kill.

Projection onto an Apparition

'Daddy's flown across the ocean
Leaving just a memory
A snapshot in the family album
Daddy what else did you leave for me
Daddy what d'ya leave behind for me' From 'The Thin Ice' by Roger Waters.

Now I am going to take a risk and pause to consider the situation as it stands at the moment from something of a therapeutic viewpoint. If I am to detach myself from the partner role and begin to reflect on Steve from an observing therapeutic stance I would of course, be wondering why Steve may be projecting emotionally from an internal focus to an external one – onto that of a perceived apparition. Maybe we see ghosts when we are literally feeling haunted, as was explored in part one. But why could Steve be seeing a ghost now at this point in his life and what could he be projecting onto this 'object' and beyond himself? Considering projection generally in its simplest form, when difficulty with ownership of our own feelings is present, projection of our material onto external sources may occur. This may include examples such as a situation, other people, the weather, the government, a racial minority or – I am now wondering - maybe even onto something as inexplicable as a ghost. Casement (1994) raises that the person who is projecting is disowning some undesirable aspect of themselves as a defence and Rosenfeld likewise describes the process as people *'ridding themselves of unwanted parts,'* (1971 in Casement). What is occurring is literally our own emotional content being attributed onto something else; perhaps when one individual is claiming, 'You are the reason I am feeling my pain/madness.' Selwyn (1994) further clarifies that projection is: *'A process whereby we attribute to other people thoughts, feelings, beliefs and attitudes which we do not acknowledge as our own,'* and Van der Hart, Nijunhuis and Steele likewise evaluate that: *'There are times when emotions become overwhelming and intolerable… Individuals prone to vehement emotions may employ maladaptive mental coping strategies such as profound denial, disavowal, projection and splitting,'* (2006).

This process is illustrated when I remember that some years ago I had an external clinical supervisor with whom I didn't feel any particular connection. I remember leaving the sessions feeling uncontained and anxious, but justifying my feelings by convincing myself that such repeated discomfort indicated an emergence from my comfort zone and must somehow be of psychological value for me. What I remember most of all, however, were my responses to the supervisor's home, the environment where supervision was taking place. It was a large Victorian house, with many rooms, high ceilings, hefty key holed doors, a musty smell and an oppressive atmosphere. There, I felt unsafe and under threat. I remember telling my therapist at the time that this house felt like it was 'full of dead people.' Clearly, I was projecting onto the house emotions I could not readily articulate to the supervisor herself around feeling stifled, restricted, unsafe and simply not receiving what I needed. I struggled on for a year or more before acknowledging that the supervisory relationship simply was not working for me and comprised a felt sense of dead energy. I subsequently left. As I reflect now, maybe I could have been picking up something else of course – a psychic sense of a lingering entity; a deceased presence or two, but somehow I doubt it.

Whilst I was pondering on my projections in this example and likely reasons for my experience, it is clearly not so easy to organise or make so much sense of the supernatural. Projection, however, does seem to be a real possibility when we think of Steve's ghost. Let us imagine that Steve cannot safely express the intensity of his emotions – feelings he may be holding unconsciously as 'unacceptable.' We are bearing in mind that he was lonely in his marriage and split off part of himself by living a relatively separate and even secretive life from his wife. This involved experiencing a combination of strong emotional reactions comprising rage, frustration, guilt and hurt. This results in anxiety, low mood and an escalating atmosphere of mistrust between himself and his wife over the years. He then undergoes the traumatic end of this long relationship, triggering a strong emotional response. He also meets me. Van der Hart et al add that beginning a new relationship may have an impact: *'Attachment also evokes trauma related stimuli such as feelings, unfulfilled wishes and needs, and memories, all of which survivors have tried to avoid.'*

We can observe how Steve, potentially in a state of trauma following the break down of his long term relationship, may indeed be susceptible to a degree of stress, although symptoms other than perception of the apparition of the railwayman do not appear to be present. I do wonder if it is possible that the loss of his marriage may be triggering grief and memories of a long dead parent. Images of this man, seen in uniform in a working role connected with his father may be provoking an out of context childhood memory during the present time in his life. Perhaps the random attacks and visions of John comprise some sort of repeating flashback. Rothschild raises that: *'Individuals with PTSD suffer inundation of images, sensations and behavioural impulses (implicit memory) disconnected from context, concepts and understanding (explicit memory)'* and that such experiences: *'involve the recall of implicit memory of a traumatic event in the absence of explicit memory, so that the references necessary to make sense of the memory to put it in perspective are lacking,'* (2000).

Given the possibility of the *'disavowal of threatening material'* (Ogden), I can further consider that if much of this were to do with Steve's father, then we are left with the question of why Steve is not seeing an apparition of his father himself? John is older than Dan was when he passed away and his appearance is physically different. Whilst he may be connected with Dan on some level, this apparition is not presenting as Dan himself. The unconscious, however, is not known for its logic. Steve's father abandoned the family, firstly by being absent through his work and then by dying unexpectedly and prematurely, away from home. For Steve, aged just sixteen at the time, there was no closure, no goodbye. Now of course, Steve has in effect, abandoned his own family and lost friends, through leaving. Interrupted attachments can perhaps do strange things to the psyche and linger long term within the unconscious, only to emerge later in the most unexpected of ways.

If Steve, in a state of stress, cannot explain or articulate a repressed sense of rage, despair and depression, could he then be projecting this onto something that defies any logical explanation? Has Steve somehow been thrown back into an earlier development stage? Is he accessing some memory either of his father or of another man from his past?

Is the reporting of seeing a ghost a safe place for Steve to deposit an unwanted or unaccessed part of anger, rage, violence and sense of 'lostness?' Is this either stemming from the loss of his relationship with his wife or through some sort of delayed complex grieving process linked with the death of his father? As we know, there are no timetables for emotion and a number of feelings may manifest themselves years after a loss or stressful event. The depressed, isolated part is being impacted by the termination of the relationship with his wife, his home, some of his friends and the other losses associated with the end of a marriage – feelings that cannot be readily honestly and congruently shared with his new partner, his only adult child or remaining attachments. By attributing unwanted parts onto an apparition and thereby ridding himself of these perhaps re-establishes him as visible and unique, but at the same time illustrates a state of vulnerability that serves a function, conscious or unconscious of attracting attention. For Steve, something of an alpha male who can be quite confrontational at times, the receiving of negative attention is as much a familiar pattern as positive affirmation.

So far so good; we can imagine that Steve is splitting off his feelings of despair and depression and projecting them onto the ghost, perhaps coupled with a dissociated or psychosomatic reaction with regard to the marks on his face. I felt a need to enter a little deeper, however, when we also take into consideration the following. Sometimes Steve would hear a voice and not see John at all. On a couple of occasions, colleagues also claimed to feel or hear something, albeit undefined, when Steve could hear a voice quite clearly. Steve would also be overwhelmed by feelings of despair and depression - awful feelings - and on two occasions he had to go off by himself and weep. Although Steve was becoming increasingly distressed and disturbed by all of this experience, he told me that it seemed as if he was feeling *'someone else's'* emotions which did not feel remotely like his own. He acknowledges openly that severe feelings of depression, overwhelming despair and being tearful are totally alien to the way he usually functions emotionally.

This reminded me immediately of the more complex issue of projective identification, often prevalent in the counselling room as a form of communication between therapist and client.

It is not unreasonable to speculate that Steve has been unable to contain these feelings and like many children and clients subsequently in therapy, displaces these split off feelings onto another source. He therefore may be experiencing what he currently cannot bear to feel; however, instead of projecting onto a therapist or significant other, this split off emotional part is being projected via a hallucination in the form of a phantom. It is also worth considering that in somewhat dramatic form he could be splitting off the angry part of himself and projecting onto an image or memory of an actual living person from his past. John's physical appearance and uniform may echo a person or incident from his childhood – possibly an abuse incident? This co-incidentally only occurs at night whilst Steve is battling with the state of exhaustion that night workers have to contend with until the early hours of the morning.

Projective Identification

'Harry had given a cry of pain: his scar had burned again as something flashed across his mind like a bright light on water. He saw a large shadow and felt a fury that was not his own pound through his body, violent and brief as an electric shock.' From 'Harry Potter & the Deathly Hallows' by J K Rowling.

I am aware that projective identification involves an interaction that is person to person (projector and recipient) and not person to spirit. I recognise that by exploring this particular theoretical route, I could again be pushing my luck in therapeutic terms. But as a counsellor observing what is going on with Steve, I am inevitably going to be reminded of projective concepts and it seems worthwhile recording some of my further thinking here.

Melanie Klein introduced the concept of projective identification in her research on 'bad objects' becoming split off and projected onto another person or object. Interestingly, she cited this as feeling like a sense of 'visitors' within the body. For me, currently feeling especially sensitised and attuned to a sense of the supernatural, this has echoes of spirit possession which, in fact, we explore in part three of this book. For now, however, reflecting from a therapeutic stance, Wilfred Bion who also wrote extensively on the subject, simply states that projective identification is *'Like having a thought that is not one's own'* (Ogden). The sense of 'alien' feelings or thoughts deposited into the individual crops up in *'When Rabbit Howls'* explored in part one, when the dissociative woman informs us that *'She recognised the anger in herself at times, it was not hers.'*

Unlike simple projection, projective identification is more complex and involves the projector not fully disavowing his projected material. The recipient is left with the feelings and this can naturally produce quite uncomfortable sensations. Ogden raises that *'It is unsettling to imagine experiencing feelings and thinking thoughts that are in an important sense not entirely one's own,'* particularly as the unwanted or undesirable part is *'deposited in another person in a powerfully controlling way.'*

Unlike other forms of projection, there needs to be this interaction between the projector and a recipient. Ogden further illustrates that *'The recipient is pressured to think, feel and behave in a manner congruent with the ejected feelings.'* Thus the recipient can be manipulated into feelings and action that are misattributed, for example Steve is being led into violent reactions of despair. Feeling the ability to resist such manipulation is important in the therapy room. Most counsellors, particularly when less experienced, will identify how easily it can be to become drawn into the client's material and feel impelled to respond in accordance with a client's projected need. Examples of behavioural action comprises the counsellor who acts out in accordance with a client's projected needs by feeling compelled to extend sessions in time or frequency, reduce the cost of sessions or in one interesting case I came across from one particular counsellor, in allowing herself to be psychologically repeatedly 'seduced' by the client buying her coffee prior to the commencement of every session. Ultimately, however, it remains the counsellor's task to contain the feelings of the clients he or she counsels. For Steve, a non therapist who is going about his nightly work and is being randomly attacked and intimidated, of course, no such onerous task exists and all we have to go on are ways of considering his personal survival strategies.

A depressive implosion of despair and some rage are the feelings for Steve that do not seem to fit and he experiences as alien. Selwyn raises that projective identification occurs outside of our awareness and, quite often, though not always, is indeed to do with feelings of anger. Anger, bottled up, re-routed, perhaps ancient material being projected onto objects (people, ghosts?) in the present. I am aware and confused by the fact, however, that the healthy expression of anger for Steve has never presented itself as much of a problem. He has never appeared to have had much trouble in expressing it, being somewhat volatile and passionate by nature. It is the depression which interests me – an emotion that feels alien to Steve but may be how his grief for his father, for his wife, for an accumulation of losses - is making itself felt. This is of course taking up a lot of energy, particularly if Steve is trying to suppress it and particularly if he is maintaining the task of keeping me as his new partner, happy. Selwyn says: *'The energy which I have used to suppress my feelings is a psychic one. The stronger my feelings, the greater the psychic force which I used to project them outwards. I may become irrational and uncontrolled and my behaviour may be awesome and shocking to myself and others.'* Seeing a ghost is of course irrational, most unexpected and shocking and may trigger alien behavioural responses.

So the fact that Steve may be splitting off an unwanted part of his psychical process and projecting it onto an apparition is one likelihood. But I also consider a second, unnerving possibility - that a phantom is projecting its feelings onto Steve. So who is really the projector and who the recipient? What came first – John's depression and rage or Steve's and to whom does the anger belong? DSM 4 suggests that *'Not infrequently, the individual induces the very feelings in others that were first mistakenly believed to be there, making it difficult to clarify who did what to whom first.'* It may be that Steve is feeling the pain, rage and frustration of John, who, if he did indeed exist and if his conflict with his brother and estrangement from his pregnant daughter is to be believed, is inducing Steve to feel his own emotional content - sensations of aggression, pain and the unbearable wandering with unresolved issues for a lengthy period of time with no-one to help. Clearly in Steve's case, the feelings induced within him are experienced by him as being totally alien, separate and in his own words, *'nothing to do with me.'*

If it is the case that the phantom is projecting onto Steve, strange as it is to think about and inflammatory to counselling theory, I do wonder what feelings Steve (or brother Dan, if that is who he is perceived by John to be) is inciting within John. We discuss the possibility of strong emotion being more directly communicated to recipients – often mediums and psychics - in part three. Later on we do also begin to become aware of John's likely agenda.

Steve and I have speculated long and hard on these potential explanations. But somehow, it seems doubtful that any of these events seem to fit with the peculiar and extreme nature of what is happening to Steve.

Further reflections for me at this point, however, not only involved reasons for projection onto a hallucination, thinking about who was feeling what emotional content and why, but I also found myself bringing into question whether Steve has fully disowned his spiritual side. Perhaps he isn't allowing himself to re-contact God but is in touch with the part that represents the 'Devil?' Who or what else is available for Steve? Does this experience comprise some sort of re-accessing of a spiritual world which is currently needed by Steve as a link with a time when he experienced himself as a 'better' person? As a therapist I was fascinated by the possibilities of what was occurring for Steve in his mental and possible projective state of mind. I was also aware of coping through launching into action regarding my encouragement of and participation in the exorcisms which are described shortly, the commencement of my extensive research and the building up of my 'pro atheist' and close minded defences regarding spiritual issues for a while. As a partner I was feeling concerned and I wanted to help, to rescue, for the problem to end.

To return to the present circumstances, as John got increasingly frustrated, clothes began to be flung around and to fall unexpectedly from the carousels. The carousels themselves were somehow thrown at Steve, once actually striking him on the head. This ghost, if that is what it is, seems to be one that can cause harm. Other colleagues began to be affected by the physical disruption and on one occasion three colleagues fetched Steve to witness one of the work cranes being driven on its own. Steve described this incident: **'We kind of said, well, what's happening there – it must be a fault – it must be driving itself. We tried to find a reason why it was actually doing it by itself – especially a group of us – saying well, it can't actually happen because if it's a ghost, as I understood it can't actually touch anything. It doesn't feel anything so how can it make a machine work? Because you have to press buttons to make it work. But then again it was throwing things around in the warehouse. But your only point of knowledge about ghosts is what you see on films and read in books and apparently their force field can throw things around – that's as much as you know. But actually having something as solid as thumbs to press and make a machine go we don't know. So its like, did that really happen? Was it a malfunction in the machine?'**

Possessing fingers and thumbs or not, clearly this ghost, if that is what it is, has a great deal of physical ability and a degree of bodily presence and strength. Steve also emphasises that John was 'real and solid,' not a fading or translucent apparition and he would normally appear about five feet behind Steve. So I will now go on to explore how ghosts may 'look'.

Physical Ghosts

'Look at my hands! Look at my feet! You can see that it is I, myself. Touch me and make sure that I am not a ghost. For ghosts don't have bodies, as you see that I do!' Luke 24 vs 39

The issue of how ghosts appear to us visually, in 'physical' form is an interesting one. The Egyptian Book of the Dead depicts deceased people as possessing souls which are an exact duplicate of their physical bodies, including the clothing they wore. This makes identification comparatively easy and such apparitions can therefore be categorised by their witnesses into those who belong to various historical bygone ages and those who are more contemporary. I include John in the latter category since, owing to Steve being able to date his uniform he was clearly living within the last fifty to eighty years. A reference made in Wikipedia (2007) questions the logic of ghosts wearing clothes; however, given their supposed spiritual nature: *'suggesting that the basis of what a ghost is said to look like and consist of is quite dependent on preconceptions made by society.'* Of course, a common and childish preconception is of a ghost wearing a white sheet, moaning a lot and rattling chains! A type typically found in the popular *'Scooby Doo'* animated series of the 1970s when such phantoms are inevitably unmasked at the end, by the pesky 'meddling kids' who foil the plot.

'Real' ghosts, however, are very different to this stereotype. Townsend (2007) categorises ghosts that have traditionally been haunting for centuries, fuel legends, may even be cited in guidebooks and are clearly identifiable, into 'Classic' cases. These can be discernable from 'Modern' cases. It seems that once we have identified our apparitions by their clothing and thereby divided our ghosts into ancient and contemporary types, we can then further separate them into sub groups of those who appear as faded and translucent beings and those who seem solid and have a more colourful and relatively healthy appearance. Appearing as a mist may also hold roots in the fact that in colder climates a person's breath may be clearly visible and some cultures would traditionally interpret this as the soul making its presence felt. A further division may then be made, between those ghosts that interact with the living whether by watching us and being clearly aware of our presence or even speaking directly to people and those who ignore or seem unaware of us.

Those ancient or 'Classic' ghosts who appear en masse in troops, armies, or in organised historical groups may appear in a fragmented and comparatively fragile countenance, but it seems they may not overly interact with the modern living person. It is easy to find examples of figures who have existed in history and continue to carry out their specific roles either in groups or, quite often, alone. Roman armies marching, monks, nuns and horsemen, aristocratic and lowlier ladies, gentlemen and children in numerous guises abound in supernatural accounts.

Oliver Lodge (1851 to 1940) was a physicist whose scientific contributions and inventions included the spark plug, wireless telegraph, valves and tuners, among other significant developments. In addition to these achievements Lodge was an eminent researcher on the paranormal and author of over forty books on the subject. He became convinced of the possibility of life after death, albeit this may have been influenced by the death of his son during the First World War in 1915. Such a tragic bereavement may of course have firmly established in Lodge a clear and natural desire for an afterlife. Subsequently he developed the 'Stone Tape Theory' which claims that ghosts are *'emotional energy recorded in matter,'* (Roland). It seems that often this 'matter' may comprise the physical environment itself, hence possibly perpetrating the common notion of the 'haunted house,' although Lodge appears to take this idea further when he argues that: *'The original tragedy has been literally photographed on its material surroundings, nay even on the ether itself; by reason of the intensity of emotion felt by those who enacted it; and thenceforth in certain persons an hallucinatory effect is experienced corresponding to such an impression,'* (Roland).

According to this view, 'Ghosts,' therefore, are merely a type of residual echo from traumatic events linked with the past. These events in conjunction with the emotional content are replayed by phantom protagonists who are unaware of being watched by the living and therefore do not interact. Such 'residual' apparitions are often described as being 'translucent.' Somewhat elusive, these apparitions may disappear into rooms which then turn out to be empty, pass through walls or emerge unexpectedly outdoors. They can be transparent or have various body parts missing owing to floor and road levels having been changed over time. Thus an apparition may appear only beyond the knee. Apparitions seemingly undertake quite a common activity of walking through walls where none used to be or ascending stairs which are no longer in existence. Accounts recall legions of Roman soldiers sighted trooping through areas with their legs invisible beneath the floor boards, the most famous example having being witnessed by a worker at The Treasurer's House in York (Lee). Stories of moaning victims and headless apparitions around the Tower of London, historical site of incarceration, torture and execution, are also plentiful.

The battlefields of Edge Hill (1642) and Flodden Field (1513) have long been cited as examples where ghostly battles can be seen to be re-enacted. In France during and following the two World Wars numerous spectral images of soldiers have been reported, providing excellent examples of such activity in times when fear of imminent violent death and post traumatic stress must have been at an all time collective high. War poet Wilfred Owen, highly influenced by the death of numerous peers, writes of an encounter in the afterlife between soldiers on opposing sides, in his poem *'Strange Meeting:'*

'I am the enemy you killed, my friend
I knew you in this dark: for so you frowned
Yesterday through me as you jabbed and killed,' (1984).

It seems that historical and popular literature and culture have concluded that ghosts are returning individual or groups of spirits; the dead souls of people somehow trapped within their ancient or more recent histories. They are doomed to re-play out their actions and this can be witnessed by those who are sensitive enough. Why these actions seem to comprise mere glimpses of brief activity, however, rather than whole scenes remains theoretically problematic.

Such glimpses into activities of the past are known as retrocognition, a term developed by Frederic Myers (1843-1901). Another psychologist and keen investigator of the paranormal world, Myers was a co-founder of the Society for Psychical Research, contemporary of Oliver Lodge and also a prolific writer and researcher. Like Lodge, Myers was spectacularly convinced of the actuality of some sort of afterlife. Myers wrote extensively of the 'subliminal mind' or 'real ego' separate from the body and providing just a small fraction of conscious awareness. Myers therefore was questioning the reasoning behind the existence and activity of the subconscious with its rich bank of thoughts, memories and creative processes if ultimately it were to die altogether and serve no real purpose. Survivalafterdeath.org (2007) cites Myers' reasoning: *'As the powers which he claimed for the subliminal self did not degenerate during the course of evolution and serve no purpose in this life they are obviously destined for a future existence.'*

Retrocognition also includes the psychic phenomena of psychometry (touching an object and acquiring information about the previous owner/s) and past life regression. In retrocognitive techniques, gainful insight is acquired through contact with historical objects or events by the individual, who can then perceive scenes from the past which may incorporate sounds, smells or directly affecting the other senses. Visions, hallucinations, a sense of displacement from time and action replays may all be a factor during the retrocognitive experience.

If we consider the 'recording in matter' idea, it seems logical then, that such ghosts follow a pre-determined pattern of behaviour and action. Townsend (2007) raises that in order for the theory of recordings to be viable; they must not vary in any way. Whilst these ghosts will not change over time, they may fade as any 'tape' will gradually perish.

Whilst I find the Stone Tape theory and investigations involving retrocognition somewhat reassuring in the apparent provision of some sort of logical explanation, it seems we become unstuck when we consider our 'solid' ghost of the present in terms of the wide variety of interpersonal qualities displayed by John. John can communicate with Steve, appearing in a variety of postures – notably either running or standing still - and displaying behaviours that are physically and it seems, psychologically violent. We know that John is a volatile ghost who operates solo, his communication and behaviour have been erratic and therefore not conducive to the idea that his presence lies in any sort of repetitive recording. He is interactive and not passive. When considering John as a 'Modern' case which implies that he has literally only been sighted in more recent times and makes active exchanges with one individual, it seems that we have a different kind of ghost on our hands.

Steve, of course, at first mistook John as a real person. Roland (2007) cites examples of people perceiving this latter category of ghosts, the 'Moderns,' to be as whole and living as we are. In his *'Complete Book of Ghosts,'* he writes of a contemporary woman feeling concerned at the pale and ill looking demeanour of a man sitting next to her on an aeroplane. He disappeared once she called upon the flight attendant to assist him and his vanishing was also witnessed by the staff member. Numerous other examples abound and can be easily accessed through anecdotal and fictional literature, film and by talking to random people who are willing to share experiences. In the (1991) film *'Truly Madly Deeply'* we cannot obtain a ghost much more 'real' and solid than Jamie who returns from the dead to reunite with his lover, Nina. He moans that he feels constantly chilly, he catches a cold, and he complains and bickers with Nina. He is depressed and annoying. He moves her stuff, brings his dead mates round to watch videos and they form an orchestra. He disrupts Nina's life and friendships. In other words, he displays all of the human traits he possessed when he was alive.

Such ghosts, however, are not confined to contemporary times. Roland also gives examples that on historical sites, for example at Versailles, the base of Marie Antoinette and the French Revolution, various ghosts have appeared; presenting so realistically that tourists are led to believe that actors dressed in period costume are adding to the atmosphere. It turns out, however, that no such people donning these roles are employed on the sites. There is of course, a rational explanation to these incidents, as visitors do frequently dress up when visiting these areas. So it seems that some confusion may lie between who is living and who is not, as these ghosts are clearly perceived as real people going about their business and not fitting the stereotype of the more ethereal and possibly malevolent spiritual being. It may be that these apparitions are only found out to be ghosts in retrospect.

Continuing on the theme of interaction, an interesting variety of ghostly encounters seem to have made themselves felt following the devastating tsunami in Thailand on Boxing Day in 2004. A news item reports on the web that local people, who have a cultural tendency to be highly superstitious, still today have to contend with reports of numerous ghosts being either heard or sighted in the area. One example includes a taxi driver who, taking a young couple to the airport and being convinced enough by the demeanour and conversation to assume that they were alive, turned around to find them de-materialised from the back seat of his cab. Another story is of a woman roaming the beaches crying for her lost child (2007). She is more elusive to the naked eye but can certainly be heard in her distress. Bar manager and survivor of the tsunami Napaporn Phroyrungthong says: *'I believe in ghosts and I always will. (The tsunami) happened so quickly, the foreigners didn't know what happened and they all think they are still on the beach. They all think they are still on holiday.'*

Phantom figures are, therefore, believed by some paranormal experts to be trapped in a pattern in which their final actions continue to be carried out in a repetitive loop, echoing time and space and whose presence can be picked up by those who are in tune with such activity. I will also be returning to the significant issue around ghosts remaining unaware of their own deaths which may be keeping them trapped in their patterns.

Mental health workers are, quite naturally, claiming that such clairvoyant and clairaudient accounts are a result of mass trauma, with tragedies such as the terror attacks in New York on 9/11 and natural disasters such as the tsunami and earthquakes being obvious examples: *'This is a type of mass hallucination that is a clue to the trauma being suffered by people who are missing so many dead people, and seeing so many dead people and only talking about dead people,'* (Piyamanotham 2007). Some time ago and certainly when I was researching the theories around trauma reactions described in part one, I would certainly have agreed with this view.

On one occasion that Steve encountered John, Steve became aware that he was being watched through the glass partition in one of the fire doors. Living people being silently watched by phantoms appears as a recurring theme when exploring the subject. Jamie in *'Truly Madly Deeply'* tells Nina that being dead *'was like standing behind a glass wall while everyone got on with missing me.'* This seems to indicate inaccessibility between two worlds; an inability for true communication as we would recognise it to take place and this understandably leaves the living with a sense of confusion and fear.

Steve describes this silent but intrinsically threatening watching through the glass as the most frightening appearance by John so far: **'It was something that was going to hurt me. I knew it was wicked. I could see in its face, in its expression. It was studying me and waiting for a chance to...it was horrible. It was a point of, I think, the truth hitting home, that there was something happening to me, rather than it trying to get my attention for help or whatever. It was a case of "I'm going to get you." I could see it in his face.'** Steve later described it somewhat humorously, perhaps as a coping strategy, as the *'Here's Johnny'* moment in the film *'The Shining,'* (1980) based on the Stephen King book of the same name. Johnny is the character played by Jack Nicolson who famously tries to axe down his family, having been progressively and negatively influenced by the supernatural elements present in his accommodation.

John appeared a total of three times on this night and everything – the activity and frequency of John's presence – appeared to be reaching a climax.

As For Me…

'You can't snort the universe' Steve

So clearly, this ongoing situation was having an impact on me, as Steve's partner. I was of course feeling deeply concerned. As a therapist I was now starting to consider the state of his mental health. As a human being I was fearful and fascinated by what I was hearing. I was in therapy myself at the time and carefully discussing the events with my own counsellor. This process included taking particular note of my responses whilst considering the blueprint of my own background and exploring my past perceptions on supernatural matters.

My parents are atheists and my father worked in a scientific background until his retirement. For me, growing up there was no significant exposure to religion apart from school assemblies and nor did I experience anything I remember that could be described as specifically supernatural. There was not much room for

God or ghosts in our family home or in our heads. Given this blueprint, I found an advantage later when I entered the therapy profession, in that I have always felt myself to be open to the religious or spiritual experiences of others, whilst holding onto what I would have described as a healthy unbiased open mindedness. Any interest I had in supernatural phenomena and the client's experiencing, I carefully considered and eventually found expression in my work described in part one of this book. My own reactions during this time, therefore, marked a trail through maybe what can be perceived as an obvious therapeutic route. I had known Steve for ten years before we became a couple. I believed that Steve may have been somewhat traumatised by the life transition he had undergone by leaving a long relationship which had at times, during my observation, been abusive and unsafe. Steve's wife had been known to attack Steve physically and emotionally, which had certainly negatively affected his stress levels and lowered his self esteem. During his gradually disintegrating marriage he had also experienced periods of sleep deprivation which can cause hallucinations. Steve, however, through my personal observation of him seems to be what Jung would describe as a robust, extraverted type: *'The extraverted attitude is characterised by an outward flowing of libido, and interest in events, in people and in things, a relationship with them and a dependence on them...the extraverted type is sociable and confident in unfamiliar surroundings. He or she is generally on good terms with the world, and even when disagreeing can still be described as relating to it, for instead of withdrawing they prefer to argue and quarrel, or try to shape it according to their own patterns,'* Fordham (1964).

Steve would agree that he certainly deals with situations very assertively – using aggression and confrontation if necessary, although quick to forgive and move on; preferring not to dwell on any distressing life incidents. Although hating and avoiding the conventions of school, Steve remembers his schoolmates with fondness and has put much of his past into perspective. Whilst having worked through healthy grief reactions for the losses in his life, he certainly feels he has never suffered from any degree of depression or particular anxiety. His pragmatism and practicality in these issues are qualities which attracted me to him – he was, and still is, able to keep me firmly grounded in the times when I can retreat into my own head or suffer from my own low moods or states of insecurity.

Living with me, Steve tells me that he feels he has 'mellowed,' and it is observable that he has lessened his defences. His colleagues have also noticed some change in him and fed this back. He has relaxed into a new relationship whereas previously he was wound up like a tightly coiled spring and could fall into rage relatively easily. By the time John appeared during March and April, Steve had been living with me for six months and we had settled into a secure and loving routine as a new couple. He did, however, in a recent conversation raise the possibility that he feels he has now got in touch with his inner child, and become emotionally more open and we wonder if this has impacted on him being able to somehow 'let John in.'

As we have seen, I was reflecting, however, on the possibility that Steve had somehow shut off some trauma from his conscious awareness and that this may be manifesting itself in the peculiar sightings of the British Rail man. I did wonder if his grief for his long dead father may be being triggered by his life change in a highly potent and somewhat unusual way. As we know, there are no timetables for emotions and delayed or complex grief may manifest itself years after a loss or stressful event. The interesting fact was that the main emotional content of the situation – John's behaviour and emotions and Steve's reactions to having this enforced contact with John - was clearly anger. Steve at this point in this life was working through his rage, loss and guilt following his traumatic marriage and break-up. It seemed to make sense, therefore, if I was open to the possibility, that he was somehow re-routing his rage and experiencing a disturbed perception coupled with a dissociated or psychosomatic reaction with regard to the marks on his face.

Despite the apparent benefits Steve has experienced in his life transition, living with a therapist can be a challenge in itself. This amusing quote from the comedian Billy Connelly, married to psychologist Pamela Stephenson, has been used as part of his act: *'My wife…who's a very clever person…considers me a work in progress.' Billy confided furiously to subsequent audiences. 'I was perfectly sane when all this started, but now I'm completely fucked up. I've got abandonment issues! If I say, 'No I haven't!' she says,"See you're in denial!" You just can't win,'* (2002).

Whilst writing in 2006, I asked Steve how, if at all, he felt that the experience with the ghost had affected our relationship. He felt it had not, or if anything it had 'made us stronger.' On reflection my thoughts on this follow the person centred route – I had been offering Steve unconditional support in a non judgemental way, providing empathy (as far as possible given the uniqueness of the experience he was describing to me) and being emotionally congruent. The latter condition of worth (Rogers, 1995) I felt was evident in my transparent reactions of shock, anxiety, curiosity, but as time went on, the main feeling I was experiencing was also increasingly of rage. I was becoming very angry with John and with his invasiveness into our lives. Also I am aware that understandably I like to be in control of my life and this was something that was occurring to someone I cared deeply about and could neither be explained nor rectified.

I confided in a couple of friends about what was happening and their reactions varied; from an unquestioning complete belief in the paranormal and the afterlife and that John was indeed a ghost, to outright scepticism, to a sharing of my confusion and sense of powerlessness in how to provide appropriate support. One thing I noted in all of these conversations was that there seems to be universal interest in talking about or listening to a good ghost story. 'How's the ghost?' began to be a regular conversation opener on the phone, via e-mail or when meeting up. To talk or not to talk? There have been times when I have felt the need to reflect on what was happening with Steve either with my support or with

Steve himself. Obviously I am an advocate of talking as a helpful therapeutic intervention – but often Steve has not wanted to be reminded or raise the subject of the pain and fear he was undergoing. If Steve had been a client of mine in a therapeutic alliance, I would of course have been more respectful of his wish, whilst gently probing or challenging, or simply raising awareness of his choice to avoid. In a personal relationship, however, it becomes harder to reign in my own desires and quell the urge to satisfy my own needs and curiosity.

During the writing of this work I have experienced anxiety and many feelings of unease particularly when alone, despite having lived comfortably by myself for over fifteen years before Steve moved in with me. My vivid dreams, hypnagogic hallucinations and so Steve tells me, occasions of screaming in the night that I do not remember, have all understandably escalated with the exploration of such disturbing material. I have felt in turn reassured by the idea that death may not be totally the end of everything but also terror at the thought of this. The threat of death and a sense of fragility of life have been all around for me and I have also become aware of the need to take a break from the writing in order to ground myself. Psychosomatically I have had headaches, stomach pain and physical tension linked with anger and fear.

Other emotional reactions during all of this have comprised helplessness and powerlessness, similar to my experiences working alongside abuse survivors. Whilst I can endeavour to understand as far as possible the short and longer term psychological effects of rape, childhood sexual abuse and torture and I am used to strong counter transference during my sessions with clients, trying to tolerate the bizarre unknowns with Steve's situation was a new feeling.

Exorcism – An Obvious Answer?

'Exorcise: v. drive out (an evil spirit) by prayer; free (a person or place) of an evil spirit.' From 'The Oxford English Dictionary.'

Steve's own defences were ceasing to be helpful to him. He was employing a need to be alone following an 'attack,' he was displaying aggression with both colleagues and towards the entity itself and he was aware that the resulting feelings of depression and despair seemed to be somehow split off from his own sense of himself. All of this was becoming problematic for him, in addition to the fearful experiencing of the actual haunting. Ultimately, it felt like there needed to be a way to eliminate the trigger itself to all of Steve's emotional and behavioural issues. Exorcism. An effective exorcism.

During the time when the haunting had escalated to such frightening and disturbing proportions, the Human Resources manager at the warehouse, Kate, arranged for us to hold an exorcism with an Anglican priest. I am aware that the subject of exorcisms, unless one works closely in certain religious professions, does not tend to come up regularly in day to day discourse. Most people, however, have heard of them. From discussion with others who knew of my situation and who suggested this as a potential solution, I would conclude that for many people, the perception is that an exorcism will 'work.' Of course they do. We are brought up with childhood stories that hold the promise that good will always prevail and vanquish evil, even if severe losses and sacrifices are sustained along the way. Later on in life we are instilled with moral codes, the hope and the knowledge that even if we are not experts in solving our own problems there are higher powers that will ultimately succeed and right will prevail. I am reminded of the horror film *'The Exorcist'* here. The priests endeavour to drive out a very present and malevolent devil from a little girl and whilst ultimately they succeed, they perish as a result. The film illustrates an extreme example of an exorcism ritual. It was perhaps inevitable that it was such an image I held in mind when I was invited to attend the procedure and I did wonder on some level whether any drama or crisis situation would unfold in front of my eyes. I was perhaps holding onto an unconscious desire for it to do so – for the possibility of an afterlife to manifest itself beyond question in some form or another and with my personal involvement. All this had to be appealing on some level.

The exorcism would take place at the warehouse during the daytime, between shifts to minimise disruption and when no workers would be present. Four of us were involved, Steve, myself supporting him, the priest and Kate. The priest was a pleasant man and I was aware of feeling surprised at his youth. We walked to the areas where Steve had felt most affected or had actually seen or heard John. I was given the job of carrying the holy water and was grateful to be given something useful to do, whilst the priest sprinkled this around, carefully and sensibly avoiding anything electrical! He was offering up prayers taken from exerts in the Bible, mostly with a theme of acknowledging the potential continuing restlessness of souls of people who may have died suddenly or violently in the area. During this process I journeyed through a variety of emotions, ranging from anxiety and a degree of apprehension, to feeling deeply moved. The whole process lasted about three quarters of an hour as we walked and paused to pray in each place.

This was the first time I had been inside the warehouse. My immediate impressions of the place were that I would have difficulty working there myself. The place is vast, spreading over three floors and completely open plan. Floors and gangways are made from an open grid metal and one can see down to all levels. Steve has described the structure as 'a study in meccano' referring to the child's nuts and bolts construction toy invented in the twentieth century and still popular. Apparently it has been known for workers to experience vertigo when looking down from the top floor. Numerous clothes in polythene wrappers on carousels and other hanging devices flank the narrow gangways like a fashion addict's retail dream. Harsh strip lighting beams brightly overhead and there are no windows. I was immediately struck by the claustrophobia of the area despite its vastness and in particular by the loud hum, the 'buzz' of the electrics. Coupled with the amount of plastic covering the garments I was aware of a continual sense of electrical static in the atmosphere and I felt fearful of touching anything in case I received a mild shock. I can imagine that whilst the three to four hundred people working on the day shift could move around comfortably and remain in contact with each other, the small night shift could easily be entirely swallowed up and concealed by the racks of carousels and hangars, each worker becoming isolated from another.

There is one area called T86 which is flanked on each side by children's clothes - little girls' clothes - newborn up the age of three. Steve has had his worst experiences with John there and he refused to enter it, feeling physically nauseous and mentally anxious. The priest and I, therefore, went there alone to administer more prayers and to continue to sprinkle the holy water whilst Kate waited with Steve. Walking back afterwards, following the priest across the gangway to rejoin them, I became aware of a strong sensation of being followed, but I felt unwilling to look round behind me. Having reflected on my reluctance here I have considered the following motivations for my lack of action. Firstly, I was aware of an understandable fear, given the circumstances, of actually seeing anything terrifying lurking behind me. Secondly, my own pride in not wishing to appear in any way vulnerable, either to myself or to the group, was present and this is linked in with feelings I have been aware of since being a small child. Better to maintain one's dignity and turn the other cheek than to react emotionally or risk losing my personal power. There has been a process of unlearning this pattern during my years in therapy and experiencing a sharing of vulnerability and emotional fragility which may previously have remained hidden. Thirdly I was aware of my strong need to protect Steve, not wanting him to sense that there was anything amiss. Steve then also thought he had heard something when we got onto the stairs; he turned, paused and Kate asked if he was OK. I guess we were all feeling somewhat hyper-alert and open to startle responses.

Following the visit by the priest things went quiet. Of course, we wondered if this religious based ritual exorcism had worked and this posed the question of Steve and I potentially needing to question our faith beliefs (or lost beliefs) and opinions. Steve, however, proffers this opinion on the subject: **'To be honest, I just took on board that there wasn't any kind of power behind it. It just felt like it was going through motions. The priest didn't believe what I was saying – it was a case of, this person wants reassurance and there's nothing in this place. It's a reassurance of – look I'm doing this, now he'll be alright - I was definitely being humoured.'**

There were of course, also implications for the employing firm. Was this a problem person or a person with a problem? In Kate, Steve had been fortunate enough to approach a manager who had some sympathy for his plight and was taking on board health and safety implications as far as possible. She herself described herself as feeling typically 'intrigued' by the whole situation and confesses that: *'In one way I would have liked to have the experience, however, seeing how upset Steve was initially and even more so as time went on, then it's probably not a positive thing to hope for.'* Ambivalent herself, she did state she believed that *'Steve has had experiences real to him but unless I see a ghost myself I'm finding it hard to believe in them.'* She goes on to question: *'Sometimes I think there are ghosts but then I think it through and don't think it's possible just by taking into account all the people that have ever lived - can they now be ghosts? Or is it that not everyone becomes a ghost? I believe there is something more than we as humans understand at the moment. But I'm unsure about ghosts specifically.'* Kate owned that she had no idea how to proceed. Employment protocol and procedure does not generally include advice on how to deal with supernatural activity at work. Interestingly, some time later Kate did discover a website article in the magazine of the Chartered Institute of the Personnel and Development (*'How to…make a ghost redundant'* 09/11/2007) that was devoted to the subject of workplace haunting! This feature raises the possibility that ghosts can be found trapped in buildings owing to cracked or damaged energy lines which has prevented their travel. This is turn triggers strong emotions such as fear, rage or frustration for the affected entity. A 'haunting' will then make itself felt in the workplace. The workers themselves will be influenced by over active imaginations, over indulgence in caffeine and a general twitchiness once rumours of a haunting become known. It is suggested in the article that the workers be initially brought together in an informal team meeting, experiences compared and then a medium or exorcist brought in if the haunting does seem to hold some weight. *'Because if a large part of the workforce believes the building is haunted, then they are also likely to believe in the things that purportedly get rid of ghosts, and will then feel a lot better after such a process. And that makes perfect psychological sense.'* Kate was presumably hopeful that an exorcism would work, either owing to the phantom actually being banished, or as a mentally reassuring and calming process for Steve. The firm were seen to be taking action. At this point, however, Steve was isolated with his 'ghost' and his word was being taken on trust by management.

Despite the initial apparent success of the exorcism, in due course John re-commenced his disruptive activity and the priest was, a few weeks later, recalled to do a 'stronger' exorcism, but again this had no effect. The same group attended. This time, however, my sense was that of hopelessness and frustration and I felt certain that these ritualistic attempts would neither prove protective nor effective. Again I had a sense of the small group of us being watched, but I put this down to my general unease with being in a strange place that felt deeply alien to the comfort and comparative sense of safety afforded by the offices and therapy rooms which I am used to in my own working life. I was also aware of the very practical issue of the security guards being present and aware of our activity as they carried out their duties elsewhere in the huge building. Steve reiterated that: **'The first priest brought another priest in with him who I found** *out later didn't believe in ghosts – didn't believe in spirits and I think he thought it was me who was actually doing it. He said it in a meeting afterwards. He spoke out about it. If he didn't believe, how can he take part? Your belief is that you are doing something, that you are cleansing something, you are cleansing an area, but if you didn't believe it there was no power there and it was pointless.'*

At this point, Steve felt unable to work in certain areas, was periodically feeling physically unwell and deeply afraid. It was a shock to him to be feeling so vulnerable and so unable to engage any practical techniques himself to move the situation on. Being consistently attacked, carrying scars and feeling deep despair were obviously having a profoundly debilitating effect on my partner.

Banishment

'Banish: v. condemn to exile; dismiss from one's presence or thoughts' From 'The Oxford English Dictionary.'

Autumn was approaching. Throughout the spring and several months on from the apparition's first encounter with my partner, the situation was now reaching a climax in frequency and intensity. John was, however, finally banished on a night he appeared to Steve expressing extreme levels of rage. Steve was able to master himself enough to get in touch with his own anger and in a state of aggression he told John to *'fuck off.'* At this point, it is interesting to note the common advice on how to communicate with the dead. Most psychics and others advise us to calmly ask the ghost its purpose and assume that the apparition will co-operate. Many people on hearing his story have raised the need to find out who John is and what he wants with Steve. They don't tend to advocate Steve's somewhat more direct and aggressive approach! Clearly Steve broke the rules here. It is important to note that on all of the occasions Steve was confronted by John, it was highly unexpected and shocking. Steve would go into the natural trauma responses of freeze, flight, or in this final case, fight. He had demonstrated all of these during his encounters with John. Consider the impossibility of a child calmly asking the motivation of the man who is raping her. To speak to a randomly attacking ghost seems almost as difficult. Whilst some regulated aggression may be desirable in some situations, for example through sport, film and playing computer games, clearly the communication between John and Steve is uncontrolled and comprises random attacks and responses. In their book *'The Haunted Self'* authors Van der Hart et al observe that: *'There is perhaps nothing more threatening for chronically traumatised patients than inconsistency, unpredictability and uncertainty.'* The authors continue to say that patients will: *'Invest much time and effort in unnecessary defensive actions'* and that reflective thinking *'is impossible when the patient is not safe, or does not perceive physical, emotional, or relational safety issues. Relational or emotional threats that do not include physical violence may be less obvious to the therapist than physical threats, but are no less of an impediment to the patient, such as an emotionally abusive partner or family of origin, or exploitative friends.'* Or vindictive ghosts perhaps.

Following this initial confrontation, Steve then suddenly remembered something. He became aware of a memory from his past that in the Mormon faith, unwanted entities can be banished by stating firmly *'In the name of Jesus Christ, go.'* On the second visit of the night from John, Steve tried saying this to him and the apparition turned to leave.

Steve says of this event: **'I think I was in that transition of actually having those priests come in and do what they did, well that church, it's powerless and I remember I was thinking about religion. The reason why "Go in the name of Jesus Christ" popped into my head was because I was thinking at the time – where does religion sit with this, with what's happening and I remembered that I was in the Mormon church. What would they do? I remembered that the commandment "Depart in the name of Jesus Christ" was actually a very strong, powerful thing to say, so I thought well, I was angry and afraid enough to tell him to "Fuck off," so it's not just going to go on my command, so I tried this and it seemed to just suddenly stop and just go. So I thought, well, yeah, it's got to go on that form of command.'**

So after this, things became calm for the first time in five months. During all of these events, Steve was given an appointment arranged by Kate, the Human Resources manager, to see a clinical psychologist. This was carried out in August 2006. Below is a copy of the report:

The Psychologist's Report

History
Mr ** works the night shift. He was working on the top floor on his own when a person ran down the opposite side of the carousel shouting 'help.' He went to find them, but there was no one there. He had a 'funny feeling.' He went to find his team leader, but again, they could find no one although they believed they heard the fire door at the top open and shut.

The second occurrence took place when Mr ** was working on the top floor again. He saw a man 15 feet away with a BR badge on his coat saying 'Help me Dan, help me.' (Mr **'s father who died when he was 16 was called Dan and he worked for BR.) Mr ** says 'I ran, I was shaking, really upset.'

On the third occurrence Mr ** spoke to the apparition. He was told that his name was John, and he was distressed because he had kicked his daughter out because she was pregnant. The apparition 'turned and went.' Mr ** says that 'I seemed to take on his despair, I felt really upset.'

Following this, there was a period until the night before the present interview when Mr ** did not see the apparition again, but strange occurrences continued.

Mr ** reports that his employer has been extremely helpful and someone worked closely with him. The next strange occurrence was when he was working with a colleague, Lizzie, she being on one side of a carousel, he on the other, when the carousel started moving. Both he and Lizzie were 'really shaken up.' He reported being hit on the face by the clothes, and what he refers to as a 'branding' appeared on his face. This comprised a red wheal extending across his forehead and down the right side of his face. (This was apparent on interview, with evidence of scratching.) A similar incident occurred when he was working on the ground floor and several carousels collapsed, the mark on his face again appearing.

On a later occasion he was working in A chamber when he heard a voice say 'You're not helping, help me.'

A colleague who was with him said 'I heard somebody say something, although I don't know what he said.' There was a further occurrence of this, the colleague on this occasion saying, 'Was that your stomach?'

This has naturally caused both interest and alarm in the workplace. 'Everyone's got a ghost story,' Mr ** remarked. Also, however, 'I've had people not wanting to work with me.'

On the night before the current interview, Mr ** was picking and felt someone behind him. The apparition on this occasion began shouting, although Mr** says he does not know what was being said, only that the apparition was 'so angry.' He felt himself being 'hit continuously' to his face. This was the first occasion of any incident for a week and a half since a priest visited the depot, blessing it. Mr ** says that 'I'd been coming in not thinking about it.'

Previous Personal History

As noted above Mr **'s father died when he was 16. His mother died seven years ago and his sister between one or two years ago. All were natural deaths. Mr ** says 'I've had lots of death in my family.'

Mr** was married for 35 years having one child. Some months ago he began a relationship with a new partner with whom he is currently living, happily. He did, however, refer to an unresolved problem in his relationship at the end of his marriage*.

Discussion and Conclusions

Mr ** says' I don't believe in God, and don't believe in ghosts.' He also says 'I really thought it could be me making this.'

There are a number of potential explanations for what is happening:

- Mr ** is experiencing supernatural phenomena. However, he views

---

* This refers to the issue of Steve disclosing to his wife the existence of his new partner. Once this was achieved, however, the manifestations of the apparition continued unabated.

himself as an unlikely candidate for this as he has no previous sensitivity, or even belief in the possibility of such phenomena.
- Mr ** has some physical condition causing hallucination. However, he reports no other changes in cognition etc.
- Mr ** has developed some sort of psychotic phenomenon causing hallucination. Again, he reports no other phenomena typical of psychosis, and no one has told him of any changes in his behaviour.
- Mr ** is experiencing some sort of dissociative phenomenon, As a result of undealt with stress, Mr ** is temporarily entering some sort of state split off from his normal consciousness in which he believes he is experiencing these phenomena and is causing things to happen. It is notable that whilst others have seen the aftermath of these occurrences, no one has been with, or been looking at Mr ** when they have occurred.

The current writer has no grounds for ruling the first explanation in or out. The second two explanations seem least likely as there is no other supporting symtomatology. Mr ** is happiest with the last explanation. Indeed, he was able to identify a source of major stress in his personal life which he has been avoiding resolving. Resolving it will cause some distress to those closest to him, but it is easily tackled once Mr ** has the will to do so. Mr ** is a person for whom control is important, and by tackling this issue he will be resuming control of his life**.

After having the appointment Steve observed: **'It was fascinating in a way that I didn't think it was going to be. Actually talking to somebody who had got nothing to do with me so it was not somebody taking sides or thinking of the warehouse or me thinking if I say something to Lou it might hurt her or make her panic or something. It was completely neutral and I felt quite exhilarated that I could actually talk to somebody who will probably find something wrong with me or who will find out where it's coming from. So I was quite open, I was really well up for it, completely open to it. I wasn't hiding anything or holding anything back. I was truly honest because I really wanted an answer.'**

The psychologist, however, did not provide that concrete answer, find anything conclusively wrong with Steve or offer an explanation of where John was coming from. After reading the report Steve was clearly disappointed and his hopes for some insight were dashed: He reflected some months later: **'What a waste of time! There was no way he could tell if it was a ghost or if it was me. So it was like, back to square one. But I did what the firm wanted me to do. It wasn't me saying no, I'm not going**

** Once more we see the supposition that stress and avoidance are having an impact on Steve's psychological state. As we see, however, the elimination of the stress at this point in Steve's life has no impact on any lessening of the haunting experience.

to do it. The firm can say to me well, we've tried this, we've tried that Steve, but you've refused it. It was a case of yes, if whatever you say I should do we'll do it because I'm saying then that there's no way I'm trying to hide anything. Got to be open and above aboard so it was why I got a report from it - though, nothing there.'

As we see from the report the psychologist concluded that Steve may have been hallucinating, shutting off part of his consciousness, using power of projection etc. As we know, owing to my work as a therapist, this was also my initial theory – but I was unable to offer any explanation for the scratches, the 'poltergeist' activity and the fact that other members of the team appeared to also be affected. Some of them were beginning to have an awareness of disembodied voices and others were directly witnessing the movement of objects. Additionally and highly significantly, Steve was only being affected in the work environment, not in our home or anywhere else. Surely if all of this was going on in Steve's psyche, or if there was a malfunction in his brain, he would be carrying the experiences beyond the warehouse? Or, as my own therapist suggested, perhaps this environment was a neutral space which somehow held the triggers to the appearance of the apparition. Steve's banishment of John felt positive though – if John was a ghost, then it was banished effectively, or if John was part of Steve's psyche, then he was also able to stand up to this fearful/angry split off part of himself. Therapists talk of the Jungian concept that we each hold a 'shadow side' which can be accessible via dreams or fantasies. We are thereby able to get in touch with our more unpleasant personality traits or negative qualities which may be *'incompatible with social standard,'* (Fordham 1964). In Steve's case, feelings of toxic rage, fear and powerlessness Jung suggests may be parts which are linked with an *'inferior'* or *'primitive'* part of the psyche.

Important here is the fact that despite occasionally picking up on uneasy atmospheres, Steve does not believe in ghosts – nor do I. Now, however, we were not feeling quite so sure. At this point then, we were left with our reflections and the task of trying to make logical sense out of the whole experience. We obviously wondered if an event at the railway – a fire or accident, probably in the 1950s, took the life of John, who could have been a friend or colleague of Dan, Steve's father. John may have had unfinished business with his pregnant daughter. I searched the web but failed to find any record of any such event or incident on the former railway site. Research did not show any fatalities or particularly bad accidents, with one exception. On a foggy night in the mid 19th century two trains collided resulting in the deaths of seven people, two of whom were children. All of the dead are listed in the records. John's name is not among them. We continued to wonder about John, who he was, what had happened to him and apart from an occasional reference or joke, we eventually pushed him to the back of our minds. Thankfully, despite frustration at not having any convincing answers either psychologically or spiritually, owing to Steve's banishment of John in the name of Jesus, it was all over.

Death on the Railways

'Then it comes to be that the soothing light at the end of your tunnel
Was just a freight train coming your way.' From 'No Leaf Clover' by James Hetfield & Lars Ulrich.

Death by train. Brutal, violent, accidental or calculated act, but always sudden and certain. We may easily project a certain symbolism onto railways. Stations are atmospheric and can provide an emotive backdrop for life transitions. We may hold in our minds photographic images of children with tickets around their necks, packed off like parcels to avoid the bombing during the evacuation in the war. Young men left on trains to fight and return as heroes; mutilated, traumatised individuals, or to not return at all. Numerous Jews were piled onto trains to die in the concentration camps during the holocaust. We hold a collective awareness of these events, even though we were not present ourselves.

Andrew Martin, author of railway fiction, presented a recent BBC documentary *'Between the Lines: Railways in Fiction and Film,'* (2009) in which he confirms that *'there is an entire world of literature, poetry and film dedicated to the railways,'* and that the 'mystique' of the railway, perceived over the centuries as demonic, romanticised or merely convenient and sanitised, has always inspired the creative mind.

Trains and railways indeed abound in our culture, influencing lives that change or end. JK Rowling's famous literary creation, Harry Potter, leaves from platform nine and three quarters at Kings Cross station to return as a fully fledged wizard. Relationships are made or broken as trains pull in or away from stations. *'Oh! My daddy, my daddy!'* cries Bobbie as she is reunited with her father, now free from prison and who emerges through the mist from a train in E Nesbit's 1906 children's book, *'The Railway Children'*. The Milford Station refreshment room in the classic (1945) film *'Brief Encounter'* provides a meeting place for distressed, lovelorn adults to explore their angst. *'Nothing lasts really, neither happiness or despair,'* mourns Celia Johnson's character Laura, as she battles with the consequences of falling in love with Alec, played by Trevor Howard, who, like herself is married to someone else. Laura is eventually tempted to throw herself beneath a train and experiences an accompanying degree of dissociative feeling. *'I meant to do it…I really meant to do it I stood right there trembling on the edge but I couldn't, I wasn't brave enough…I had no thoughts at all only an overwhelming desire not to feel anything ever again – not to be unhappy anymore…'*

Unlike Laura, Tolstoy's tragic heroine, Anna Karenina, does go through with committing suicide on a railway line. Throughout the novel Anna is personally and psychologically haunted by an incident at the start of the book in which she witnesses a man being killed by a train. When she comes to the time and manner of choosing her own death, the incident returns to her. *'In a flash she remembered the man who had been run down by the train the day she first met Vronsky, and knew what she had to do....And exactly at the moment when the space between the wheels drew level with her she threw aside the red bag and drawing her head down between her shoulders dropped on her hands under the truck and on to her knees. At the same instant she became horror struck at what she was doing. 'Where am I? What am I doing? Why?'* With this, her final thought and action, Anna's life and light, *'flickered, grew dim and went out forever.'*

Classic author Charles Dickens provides a neat bridge between the railway - now established following the industrial revolution as an efficient and comfortable way to travel – and the Victorian's escalating fascination with the supernatural. Dickens himself loved a good ghost story especially at Christmas and many of us are familiar with the classic tale *'A Christmas Carol,'* in which Scrooge is haunted in turn by spirits of Christmas past, present and future, in addition to communicating with the spectre of his former business partner, Marley. Dickens was also involved in a serious railway crash which resulted in numerous casualties, ten people dead and forty nine seriously injured. Travelling in a first class carriage on the 2.38 train from Folkestone to London and approaching Staplehurst, human error resulted in this particular engine not being expected for another two hours. Fatally, work on the track was being carried out at the time. Despite the driver applying the brakes it was too late to prevent a tragedy and several carriages plunged to the river below the viaduct they were destined to cross. Surviving passengers have later detailed Dickens's courage and commitment to assisting the dead and dying for a period of three hours, filling his top hat with water to attend to the wounded and comforting the shocked and bereaved.

In his biography of Charles Dickens, Peter Ackroyd (1991) raises that Dickens never fully recovered from the impact of this rail crash and notes that the author's health and spirits suffered as a result. It is clear that Dickens was experiencing a degree of post traumatic stress, finding it hard to travel by rail again and Ackroyd also notes that Dickens in fact died on the fifth anniversary of the accident. Physically Dickens lost his voice for a fortnight following the trauma and suffered from the 'shakes.' He wrote: *'I have sudden vague rushes of terror, even when riding in a hansom cab, which are perfectly unreasonable but quite insurmountable.'* And his daughter added in her journal: *'My father's nerves never really were the same again...we have often seen him, when travelling home from London, suddenly fall into a paroxysm of fear, tremble all over, clutch the arms of the railway carriage, large beads of perspiration standing on his face and suffer agonies of terror.'*

Prior to his death and following the railway accident, Dickens was among the first author to describe in detail travel by rail and also graphic death by train in his novel published in 1848, *'Dombey and Son,'* when the character Carker violently meets his demise. Ackroyd says: *'In much of his fiction the railway is seen as a terrifying and destructive force, no more so than when it tears up the landscape of London and runs down the guilt ridden Carker....'* With the train bearing down upon him, Dickens uses a vivid description as Carker *'...was beaten down, caught up and whirled away upon a jagged mill, that spun him round and round and struck him limb from limb and licked his stream of life up with its fiery heat, and cast his mutilated fragments in the air.'* Reference is also made to a railway accident in the postscript of his 1864 novel *'Our Mutual Friend,'* where Dickens merges his imagination with fact as he describes aiding his characters Mr and Mrs Boffin in a *'terribly destructive accident'* whilst travelling on the *'South Eastern Railway with me.'* He writes: *'When I had done what I could to help others, I climbed back into my carriage – nearly turned over a viaduct, and caught aslant upon the turn – to extricate the worthy couple. They were much soiled, but otherwise unhurt.'*

Clearly impacted, Dickens later went on to write his short story *'The Signal Man,'* further linking the traumatic incident with his love of creating ghost stories illustrative of the literary taste of the time. Haunted by the memory of two previous accidents and the premonition of a third, the signal man is isolated by the nature of his work and emotionally disturbed. Dickens did, however, remain sceptical throughout his life about the actual existence of ghosts and this may be picked up in the Signal Man story when the narrator questions the mental health of the railway man. *'I have speculated since, whether there had been infection in his mind,'* and to accompany him to *'the wisest medical practitioner we could hear of in those parts,'* and he also tries to offer plausible explanations for the phenomena that the railway man is describing, namely the wind and *'the wild harp it makes of the telegraph wires.'*

Railways always have been and still are a popular and effective site for suicide and sudden death in particular. As I have learned, ghosts are, in fact, frequently experienced around railways. If one is hit by a train, it seems that death can come so suddenly that the unfortunate recipient can be jerked so suddenly and violently from one world into another that the soul can understandably be doomed to linger. When he was sixteen years old, my father, who had a railway line running at the bottom of the back garden, witnessed a man being killed by a train. He describes how the man seemed to step out 'from nowhere' was hit and was 'flung like a rag doll.' When he speaks of this the sense of speed and unreality of the incident, it strikes me particularly how the man seems to lose his humanness at the moment of impact – he becomes an object, an inanimate 'doll.' Is this about the man, or about my father's coping strategy when recounting what presumably must be a traumatic memory for him – a need to turn a living man into a 'doll?'

During the course of my research I have discovered a variety of web pages devoted solely to the subject of railway ghosts. I was aware of both the usefulness of such sites but also feelings of being overwhelmed by the intensity and sheer number of reported hauntings. The web site Paranormaldatabase.com provides examples of railway ghosts haunting throughout the United Kingdom. These include figures sighted on the tracks, many of whom inevitably appear to be going about their daily work as in life – signalmen, point's men, lantern bearers, firemen, porters, old soldiers and various waiting room visitations. A few victims of murders, suicides and accidents also make their continued and unhappy presence felt in various ways. Somewhat more obscurely we also read of reports of dogs and cats, monks and nuns and even a wailing Egyptian Princess who was apparently disturbed in the British Museum Station in Greater London. On an auditory level, footsteps, train whistles, screams and various other sounds of the aftermath of accidents provide further rich reporting of railway manifestations. Breathing sounds and sensations of being brushed continue as a popular theme. Slamming of doors and self operational lights bring in the possibility of coincidence, trickery or electro magnetic disturbance. Also included are sightings of disembodied body parts and 'floaters' – people who consist only of hands, heads, legs or suffer from the lack of these. Paranoramldatabase.com go as far as to divide the complex data into categories:

'Haunting manifestations' - *apparently 'normal' ghosts*

'Crisis manifestations' – *those which appear in times of intensity, for example in the echoing or anniversary of railway accidents*

'Unknown ghost type' – *where shapes are too vague to be otherwise identified and*

'Post mortem manifestations' – *where ghost appears immediately prior to or after death.*

Legends also have their place – George Stevenson, inventor of the 'Rocket' is reported to have appeared in solid form and asked for a glass of water years after his death. Winston Churchill's funeral train has allegedly been sighted on a number of occasions and let us not forget that Boadicea's grave lies under platform ten of NW1 Kings Cross Station and she has allegedly also been spotted over the centuries.

How understandable was it for Steve and myself to assume that John had been killed on the railway lines? His ghost appeared in the appropriate uniform and in a location that used to be train sidings. It seemed logical enough for us to make this connection. This has, however, made me wonder how many other inappropriate assumptions I have made during the course of my life and in particular, with the potentially catastrophic implications this may have for my counselling work. I became particularly aware of a need to reinforce Rogers's model of need for the therapy to be client led and for the counsellor to bracket their own perceptions, history, opinion and any premature interjection or interpretation.

Coincidentally, Steve's son was working on the railways at the time. Steve is fully aware of the risks that can be faced by the dangerous and difficult job undertaken by track maintenance staff. As we know, Steve's father also worked on the lines for a while. I have considered the possibility that if we examine Steve's unconscious, he could be carrying some anxiety about his son's welfare and safety in the present, in addition to any memories of tales his father may have shared in the past of tragedies; accident or suicide. Could these factors have been an influence on the nature and appearance of the apparition Steve had encountered, if indeed this had been something that was presenting only in his mind?

Re-encounters 2007

'Been here before couldn't say I liked it
Do I start writing all this down?
Just let me plug you into my world
Can't you help me be uncrazy?' From 'The Unnamed Feeling' by James Hetfield, Lars Ulrich, Kirk Hammett & Bob Rock.

This brings me up to March 2007, a year after the 'ghost of John' first made its presence felt to Steve. Steve and I were having a feeling that John may return as the anniversary of his first appearance approached. Townsend does cite anniversary as significant, raising that original anniversaries have obviously greatly altered and varied owing to changes in calendars over the centuries. Additionally, the introduction of leap years and changes in clocks between Greenwich and British summertime are going to influence time and render precise days and hours impossible. Spiritual healer David Ashworth concurs, adding that time has no meaning in the spirit world – for a trapped spirit, time as a human concept is meaningless. Psychic Sally Morgan, whose work I explore later agrees, posing that: *'The way I've always thought of the spirit plane is as a place that co-exists with our own but is not bound by our constraints of time or place. The notion of time, after all, is something we've developed on the earth plane. It's a unit of measurement. But spirits don't have that. They simply are. I imagine them viewing our plane with bemusement, wondering how they ever managed to cope with being so restrained by space, physicality, ageing.'* Nevertheless ghosts apparently do seem to have a habit of appearing on the anniversary of their deaths or of other events significant to their lives. Townsend suggests that *'nature itself does not operate on a weeks, months, years, system – this is a purely human invention for the convenience of keeping appointments....'* and he suggests that ghosts are either triggered or generally are 'fond' of keeping such anniversaries in co-operation with the desires of the living! Time itself then, is essentially a human invention and is not logical, unless living people seek to impose logic upon it. I am reminded of a quote in an episode of cult television series *'Doctor Who'*: *'People,'* says the Time Lord, *'assume that time is a strict progression of cause to effect, but actually, from a non linear, non subjective viewpoint, it's more like a big ball of wibbly-wobbley timey wimey stuff,'* (*'Blink,'* 2007). Quite. So whether or not the spirit world transcends, co-operates with or finds irrelevant the human constraints of time and are going to appear on their personally significant anniversaries anyway, it seems that John's traditional haunting time takes place roughly between the spring and summer months, given our evidence from the past year.

The early part of March followed a lengthy period over the winter when no sightings took place. Possibly this was influenced by the fact that the agency workers employed over the winter months had swelled the workforce and altered the dynamics of the environment. Despite this, one of Steve's colleagues did claim to have seen John's face through the glass window in a fire door. Simultaneously another colleague, a committed Christian, had a disturbing sensation of John's presence. Steve was away on leave at the time and neither of these accounts could be verified.

Once Steve returned from his absence a few nights later, however, he felt a sensation of something hitting his face and the old familiar mark reappeared. He did not see or hear anything, although the group of workers present all went icily cold. The mark on Steve's face was livid and faded over night, although it was still clearly visible to me the following morning.

Another colleague, very recently employed, mentioned that he used to work in the lace trade, within a building on the same road as a warehouse and he told some colleagues that this building was 'haunted by a railwayman.' He allegedly had not at that point heard the story of Steve's 'ghost.' So we then wondered whether John had a general presence in the area, rather than being solely connected to the warehouse. The railway would have covered a far greater distance than this one site and encompassed several industrial buildings constructed since its demolition.

The random attacks once more became increasingly frequent occurrences. It was at this point that I decided to keep a regular diary. This decision was partly in order to support myself in the situation and keep an eye on my own stress levels, as I was again re-experiencing an escalating degree of emotion including fear, anxiety, puzzlement, frustration and rage. I was feeling the need to be self supporting, particularly as I had left therapy the previous January following a period of counselling for six and a half years. My therapist had followed my progress with the ghost story with interest but as I felt that the focus of therapy had been well achieved, it felt appropriate for us to end. My therapist was, therefore, obviously not available to support me with the ongoing visitations and my feelings around what was happening to Steve. We did, however, meet up much later, on 16 July 2008 when I had decided to write this book and was carrying out research. I taped an interview with her to find out more about her reactions to my telling of the ghost story at the time. A transcript and commentary of the whole discussion can be found at the end of part two. In the meantime, as an advocate of therapeutic writing and art work, I chose to keep a journal to try to alleviate my anxiety and support myself for, as all counsellors are aware, if I'm not supporting myself then I am unable to work effectively with my client group.

I wrote:

22 March 2007: Last night Steve rang me up whilst I was at work and told me that he had received what felt like an 'electric type shock' and was thrown through some carousels and almost into the person working next to him. Steve was marked on the face but didn't see or hear anything. His watch went back in time by two hours. He was shocked, upset and is in bed feeling ill today. Maybe it's an idea to see his GP? I keep thinking about that film, Phenomenon – could Steve have a brain tumour like the character played by John Travolta? He does get headaches. But then surely he would not just be having symptoms in the middle of the night at work? The colleague who is a Christian says 'It's an evil spirit.' A report has had to go in to HR. I feel highly anxious and feel like crying.

'Phenomenon' (1996) tells the story of George Malley, played by John Travolta, who, on his thirty seventh birthday, is apparently struck down by a light that emerges from the sky in '...an explosion, a flash...it knocked me off my feet.' We witness George's resulting insomnia, which affords him with the time to read numerous books, demonstrate a newly acquired talent for learning languages and discover a profound intelligence. In addition he is able to predict an oncoming earthquake and acquire skills in psychokinesis which baffles his doctor, who proclaims, 'I'm a man of science but I feel like a child – I feel scared.' George is now different. He begins to lose the easy camaraderie of his friends in the small town who, initially intrigued, then become suspicious, mistrustful and finally fearful of his change. Aliens are said to be a likely cause. But no, we discover that George tragically has an inoperable brain tumour which is enhancing rather than debilitating his cognitive functioning. As we see below Steve is becoming worried about how his colleagues may be viewing the situation and like George, holds concerns about a gradual rejection by his peers. I continue:

31 May 2007: *Steve has been marked twice and had negative, emotionally low and anxious feelings over the past few weeks, but has not seen anything. Kate has taken some photos of the damage inflicted upon his face. The scars are now quite deep and apparent and taking much longer to fade. Steve is beginning to experience some shame about this 'stigmata' and talks of not being able to go out in certain situations (like visiting relatives) when the marks are livid. Whilst the necessity is to continue working, emotionally, his instinct is to become reclusive.*

He hasn't been working nights much owing to being required as the union representative in daytime meetings. Last night he saw something and got scratched but I haven't seen him nor heard the details yet. We watched a programme on a DVD someone lent us called 'When Ghosts Attack' – very American. We think – or rather we carry the hope - that it was all acting.

I later noticed that the American 2007 documentary 'When Ghosts Attack,' triggered much discussion on websites and message boards. The programme illustrated the story of the ghost of a child, 'Sally,' who was, it seemed, carrying out physical attacks on the adult male living in the house, leaving him with long and bloody scratches under his shirt. Obviously some comments centred on the need for him to have removed his clothing when the alleged attacks occurred, in order to dispel any assumptions of fakery.

It is interesting to note, however, when visiting any site on the subject of the paranormal, (www.yourghoststories.com and www.ghostvillage.com provide excellent examples), the sheer amount of authority with which people speak on the subject whether with agreement, demonstrating empathy, or posing challenge or disagreement with the phenomena presented. Other websites are dedicated to scepticism and disbelief (Arizona Atheist Blog *'Dedicated to Truth and All Its Forms'* for example). Whilst some discussion on the pro ghost websites acknowledge the possibility of rational explanation, using examples of sleep paralysis, lucid dreaming, and 'astral projection' amongst other suggestions, 'Science doesn't answer everything' seems to be a common recurring theme among people engaging in internet 'chat.' Solid commitments to belief, anecdotal 'evidence' and 'proof' abound, citing examples of the presence of ghosts and demons along with firm opinion as to their purpose. Some ghosts, namely the more 'demonic' in nature, are indeed cited as malicious entities that have been known to pinion and assault their victims quite violently. So I have learned that some phantoms do have the power to physically hurt the living, it seems.

Such shared examples understandably serve to fuel individual belief and influence any resulting change or development of personal insight with regard to religious or spiritual faith. I would feel confident in making the assumption that people who contribute to such message boards and chat rooms would hold a strong interest or belief in the paranormal in the first instance, which stimulates an interest to contribute and provide feedback, whilst others who have less motivation would naturally focus their interests elsewhere. Sceptics contribute remarks around drug taking and insanity whilst others urge the need to embrace religion or to actively encourage communing with the supernatural. Altogether I observed a tendency for people to be forthcoming with somewhat insensitive or delusional remarks, exhorting those who seek support or information in this way to either 'Grow up,' 'Find Jesus or go to Hell,' or stop smoking so much weed. To me, such sites illuminate a worrying amount of fantasy, derision and even cruelty in addition to a worryingly high level of illiteracy! I resolved to avoid reading them in the future.

Electric Entities

'I've got electric light
And I've got second sight
I've got amazing powers of observation' From 'Nobody Home' by Roger Waters.

I continue:
I have been doing a bit of research about electromagnetic activity linked with paranormal experiences. My friend saw a programme in which someone was having electrodes put on his head which caused him to hallucinate and experience intense feelings of despair and a sense that the world was ending etc. I wish I'd seen it – could this be the way forward? Steve says that the electrics in the warehouse have all been rewired over the past couple of years and when I was there for the exorcisms, I was very aware of the buzz – the 'hum' and the bright lights and

metal of the place. I've been reading about people who can become amplifiers and can cause electrics (particularly street lights) to flicker and turn off in times of stress. And Steve has never been able to wear a watch without it stopping until recently. You can buy meters that measure electromagnetic activity – apparently the reading goes up near a TV set and near people who are conductors for this sort of thing. I must find out more. But I'm feeling deeply irritated by the rubbish on the net about the paranormal to be honest – how does anyone know what they are talking about – none of it can ever be more than theory.

I found out later that the experiment probably related to the 'God helmet' experiment carried out originally by Dr Michael Persinger. This is explored further in part three. For now, we are going to focus on electrical activity generally. Steve tells me that he has never been able to wear a watch for a sustained period of time with much success, until his son bought him his present timepiece a few years ago. Prior to this Steve tells me that his watches have inexplicably ceased working in a very short period of time. On the occasions that Steve encountered John, his present watch – apparently a highly robust one - would alter in time, usually going back two or three hours. Why is this? Could it be that Steve was having some sort of flashback or episode of dissociation and was struggling to perceive reality, which can result in a sense of loss of time? I was strongly reminded of a question posed by the dissociative woman in *'The Troops for Truddi Chase,'* whose presence also caused electrics to malfunction and her watches to stop. *'How many watches had there been? Many. But no time at all.'* Or could the physical shock of encountering John somehow increase Steve's pulse rate which is influencing the mechanism in the watch to such proportions? Interestingly, this particular watch has a rubber strap, which may prevent the conduction of any electrical activity and whilst altering the time showing on the hands, may be preventing total stoppage. Steve said: **'Obviously I carry a lot of electricity in my body or whatever it is that stops watches because I've never been able to wear a watch. I had a really good fob watch once and that stopped as well. Watches and things around me aren't very good and so they've stopped, but in the case of when I've been close to whatever energy it is, call it a ghost – it's got energy, it sends my watch backwards for two hours. Now that's impossible. My wrist has never done that before. My body's never sent clocks backwards. It's stopped but it's never altered the time. So it's a different scenario.'**

Roland, in his extensive studies of supernatural activity, cites an example of a woman whose mother in law Mary promised to return in some form after death. She tells us that not only do clocks behave erratically but other electrical items malfunction when the spirit of Mary is attempting to communicate with her: *'...two months after her passing all the clocks in the house started behaving strangely. They all showed a different time and a travelling alarm clock rolled off the shelf and crashed at my feet just as I was telling my daughter how oddly they were all behaving. Another day the phone jumped off its holder on the wall and started swinging from side to side. Then the electric blanket and toaster switched themselves on. Each time I felt a chill in the air. It was Mary trying to tell me she was with me.'* Here of course, the author has decided beyond doubt that these incidents prove that Mary is still around and in her desire, she places an interpretation on the events accordingly. Certainly the theme of erratic electrical activity does present itself quite frequently in accounts of haunting. One of the Chaplains assigned to the university where I work cites a sound example when he described a visit to the home of a parishioner who was complaining of poltergeist activity. He had informed her that although he didn't undertake exorcisms, he would gladly pay a visit to bless her flat. Once there he said that she told him that *'The video would switch itself on and play even though it was unplugged, the oven would spontaneously turn itself on as would the kettle. There were a number of other events that had contributed to her sense of being haunted by a poltergeist. I went into each room in the flat and said a prayer of blessing, including an invitation to any restless spirit to leave the house.'* It may be of course, however, that there are alternative reasons for disturbances of electrical gadgets.

Among the rational explanations, a possibility is that some people may be causing such phenomena unconsciously themselves. A web site dedicated to Street Lamp Interference (SLI) describes the phenomena of certain individuals being able to disrupt electrical and electronic equipment, causing a form of psychokinesis. This is also referred to as telekinesis, the ability to move an object with the mind. As the name suggests, street lamps turn off as the person passes who may either unconsciously, semiconsciously and possibly as a result of stressed feelings or at times of heightened emotion cause the lighting to malfunction. A person becomes a small electromagnetic field which can leak and subsequently interfere with the lights and other equipment with which they come into contact. This is deemed to be an unnerving, but apparently harmless phenomenon. Again such themes are popular and often adopted and dramatised by fictional horror writers, such as Stephen King's classic novel *'Carrie,'* (1973). The persecuted adolescent girl of the title proves that such talents are far from harmless as she destroys her hometown and vast majority of its inhabitants through her telekinetic power. The indication is that Carrie and individuals like her can make full use of their ability to use the power of thought and emotion, which in turn can have an impact on the physical environment and the people within it.

The main contributor and author of the SLI website, the 'Eel' provides us with an explanation that *'It's Darwin's theory of evolution at work...we've just adapted to the constant bombardment of radio waves, microwaves and all other forms of electromagnetic radiation,'* (2007).

Unlike Steve, however, the Eel tells us that *'On the other hand, I can wear a watch without frying it.'* It became interesting to me how often I noticed the timepiece issue emerging during my research. Fascinating to explore, the Eel indicates in his web pages that he and his fellow SLIDERS exist as a minority group, as *'electric people.'* Having found each other, they can go on to develop a mutually supportive network. Reading this I was reminded of the experiences of psychologist Carl Jung, who as a child appeared to have been aware of spiritual presences but who did not benefit from internet contact with like minded people sharing similar experiences. He was consequently very isolated and alone with his perceptions. Perhaps similar to survivors of childhood abuse and incest who have no frame of reference to compare their experiences and consequently perceive them to form a normal part of family life, Jung felt shocked and isolated once he grew up and left home to discover that the occurrences and psychic phenomena he had taken for granted as a child were not the common experience. He reflects that *'There were dreams which foresaw the death of certain persons, clocks which stopped at the moment of death, and glasses which shattered at the critical moment. And now I was apparently the only person who had ever heard of them,'* (1989).

Following brief investigations into more complex electromagnetic theory, for example the excellent examples provided in the studies by Dr Jason Braithwaite who developed MADS (Magnetic Anomaly Detection System), which is used to record magnetic fields in allegedly haunted areas and by Maurice Townsend whose work I referred to earlier, it seems that there is a consensus amongst some paranormal researchers that supernatural activity can increase owing to the presence of magnetic fields. Additionally, certain weather conditions can create a higher vibration, affecting both living and 'not so living' beings. How often do thunderstorms create an effective backdrop to horror films and novels – not only providing a suitably menacing atmosphere but possibly also existing as a natural device that encourages apparitions to make their presence felt?

It has been noted that batteries, electrical and computerised equipment used in ghost hunter activity has been drained of energy at the crucial moments when ghosts are allegedly present or their appearance is pending. Lee cites examples of smoke alarms being triggered, electrical surges and faulty equipment all influencing perceptions around being haunted. He cites one example of a man experiencing a 'feeling of dread,' which was traced to a faulty desk fan. Solar flares, a build up of static electricity, the full moon (the increased closeness of which may also affect the earth's electromagnetic field), along with fault and ley lines lying beneath the earth's surface, are all traditionally cited as aiding the ghost hunter's endeavours owing to their potential influence on the earth's gravitational forces and magnetic fields. Lee questions, *'Is it simply due to the natural effect of the electricity and magnetism on the brain, or some unknown force?'*

Steve became particularly aware of the possibility of electrical activity having an impact on his encounters with John: **'People have mentioned that electrics can play a big part so at that point I started looking round to see if there was any big deal. It was right next to this electrical apparatus that runs the whole place that sometimes stuff happened to me.'**

What came first – the magnetic fields, which cause ghosts to appear, or the ghost that influences the existence and surges in energy of the magnetic field? The society ASSAP questions this cause or effect and claims that hallucinations can be induced by particular low frequency magnetic fields and that these perceptions can increase if the person experiencing them is prone to migraines or epilepsy. More will be touched on this subject in part three.

As a (now tentative) non believer in the supernatural and also a non scientist, through my reading, I did finally feel like I may be obtaining some sort of plausible answer. I'd moved on from pure therapeutic thinking – that Steve was splitting off part of his psyche possibly owing to a traumatic life transition - to what seemed like a feasible answer based in science. The electrics in the warehouse had been altered over the previous year or two, about the time John started to appear. I wondered if Steve had been particularly sensitive to this and had some sort of extreme hallucinogenic reaction in conjunction with repetitive psychosomatic reactions or injuries perhaps self inflicted during periods of dissociation.

I watched the (2000) film *'What Lies Beneath,'* which seems to pull in some of the themes I have mentioned. The actress Michelle Pfeiffer plays Claire Spencer, who has recently moved into a large house. In the first scene of the film, a hairdryer electrically malfunctions. Later on a computer screen starts behaving erratically, flickering up initials and names during a thunder storm. As the film progresses, objects move, framed photographs fall, odd noises are heard and doors open before they are touched. Claire experiences insomnia and anxiety. This manifests itself in aggressive sexual activity with her husband and she sees a ghost of a girl during such an event. We of course, by now realise she may have been triggered emotionally, experiencing a degree of post traumatic stress following a car accident the year before. In addition she is coping emotionally with the transition of her only daughter leaving home to go to college. Claire also relates having a dissociative episode at a party which she doesn't remember and is told, *'It was as if you had seen a ghost.'* *'There's a ghost in my house,'* Claire tells her psychiatrist. *'I saw her beside me in the bathtub.'* *'What did she look like?'* he replies. *'She looked like me. Only she had green eyes.'* Typically, her psychiatrist advises Claire to attempt contact with the spirit – *'try to find out what she wants'* – and this urging to communicate is a recurring theme which I continue to explore later in Steve's own story.

From all this, the viewer is led to begin speculation on whether Claire's problems originate from supernatural sources, her own disturbed perceptions owing to traumatic experiences, from malicious human behaviour perpetrated by other characters in the film, or from a combination of all three. Whether Claire is saved by the ghost at the end of the film, has experienced memories or a firm diagnosis of mental disturbance as a result of trauma is left open.

All this thinking, reading, film watching and my tentative conclusions, were, however, suddenly and traumatically challenged by what happened next…

I continue with my diary:

May 2007: *We have another priest, maybe a 'ghost buster expert?' coming in to the warehouse next week to carry out a 'stronger' ritual. This will be at 10pm so I* *probably won't be there. I don't think it will make any difference, I think it's about the firm needing to be seen to be doing something proactive to protect the staff. One or two of the younger ones are quite scared now apparently. One approached Steve after having a nightmare about a man standing at the foot of her bed and Steve had to provide reassurance that the worst that could happen is that she may see things moving in the warehouse. Many of the workers feel 'cold spots' and are certain these are 'real,' so the probability of mass hallucination or 'hysteria' remains open for debate.*

So last night, Steve told me about the latest incident. He was working alone when he turned and saw John standing about eight feet behind him. John didn't move or speak. Steve felt OK and told his colleague Andrew that he was going to phone the team leader to say what had happened. Whilst at the phone he felt a hard blow in the face and the mark appeared. I found it interesting that this occurred near the phone and apparently this is where the PCs are also located. This may fuel the electromagnetic/paranormal theory? Steve then went into feelings of despair and he returned home from work early, getting in about 2.00am. Another colleague noted that this occurred on a Wednesday at 11.45pm, the same as before. Steve was near tears last night, finding it extremely difficult to shake the negative feelings off. When I asked if the feeling 'belonged' to him he replied – 'No, it's nothing to do with me.' He didn't feel able to go to work and had the night off sick, in addition to the following night. Interestingly, Andrew was also complaining of being plagued by being suddenly hit by the most miserable feelings descending suddenly on him at work. 'I'm perfectly happy,' he told Steve, 'but then for no reason I go cold and my mood just plummets.'

Steve described his own emotional experiences and subsequent thinking: **'If there is this entity trying to get in touch with me and I'm ignoring it, I think it's trying a different approach – trying to make me despair or take on his feelings – remember he'd died and he can't do what he wants to do, so he's desperate. I remember how it first happened. Within ten minutes of it first happening to me I felt like crying and I thought well, where's this come from? It's because it's happening to me but it wasn't – the despair was deep – it was like a desperate despair, like the end of the world despair. I'd never felt this before, unless I'd felt it but thought it was me, but this just felt so different....I went to Michael and said, "Look Mike, I feel really, really down," and I started to cry in front of him. I said "Look I'm going to have to sit down in a corner," and he said, "Alright Steve," and I sat and I really cried which is something I've hardly ever done. I mean, I've cried in my life obviously but that was instant, you know, that's not right...it was something...I went to work quite OK, I was quite happy but after this it was "bang" way down down to the bottom of a pit like how you feel when you are high and then hit a real low and it was so deep, it was traumatic. And to do it in front of somebody is something I never do. I'd never blubber** *in front of somebody – if there was something wrong with me I'd go away somewhere. But it came instantly. I couldn't even talk about it. It came on me even worse when I was speaking about it to Michael. I started to cry – now that was terrible.'*

Clearly Steve becomes very vulnerable at this point. The swing from high mood to low made me question whether he could be bipolar. The total despair which feels somewhat displaced and disowned made me wonder whether he was having a nervous breakdown.

A Pivotal Night

This brings us up to **7 June 2007.** The situation reached a climax and resulted in some decisions being made and finally some proactive action being taken. I wrote:

Last Sunday Steve and I had a very restless night. I was having nightmares all night in my room, felt extremely uneasy and at 1.30am woke up suddenly in the throws of a mild panic attack. It took me some time to get back to sleep – I decided to go to the loo but felt the need to put the light on – which I don't normally do. The darkness felt menacing in a way I had not yet experienced living in my home. Overall I was aware of an extremely strong feeling that I didn't want to go to the third exorcism, due on Tuesday night. I got into a bit of state in my head about this. I'd go if Steve wanted me to offer support, but I felt with his work friends present he'd be OK.

It took me a while to get back to sleep. Meanwhile, upstairs, Steve also had an extremely disturbed night. He felt like John was 'all around' - the first time he had experienced him outside of work. He didn't feel that John was actually present, but he said John was 'in my head.' Steve felt disturbed, frustrated, like he was needed to take some action, to find some closure. He then had a dream. He dreamt that a cross, made from clay, was being taken out of a kiln. The cross had a message on it, which Steve couldn't see.

It was as a result of having this dream that Steve was spurred into taking some direct action in tackling his problems.

Prophets, Pareidolia and More Projection

'Tell me one last thing,' said Harry. 'Is this real? Or has this been happening inside my head?' Dumbledore beamed at him, and his voice sounded loud and strong in Harry's ears even though the bright mist was descending again, obscuring his figure. 'Of course it is happening inside your head, Harry, but why on earth should that mean that it is not real?' From 'Harry Potter & the Deathly Hallows' by J K Rowling.

The significance which can be placed on dreams has a long and extensive history. Dreams are mentioned in most cultural histories and anecdotes and many have been taken serious note of in religious texts. Today, individuals still devour popular dream interpretation literature, others work with dream diaries in therapy; many are related in everyday conversations. Jung describes numerous dream experiences throughout his autobiographical work, asking *'Whence comes such a dream?'* and initially, owing to his religious upbringing, he takes it for granted that dreams are messages sent directly by God. Alongside development of his exploration of unconscious processes, Jung then begins to question why such activity breaks through into his consciousness and queries *'Something must therefore have been working behind the scenes, some intelligence, at any rate something more intelligent than myself.'*

Prophetic dreams can capture the imagination of many people and are again embedded in our culture. Examples of such dreams can be quite extreme. In the Christian Bible, through interpreting the dreams of the Pharaoh of the time, Joseph helps to prevent Egypt from falling into a fatal long term famine. Such dreams can change the course of history and prevent catastrophe. Whereas, of less importance, in the popular 1980s American soap, *'Dallas,'* the entire series seven aired in 1985/86, which included the death of central character Bobby, turns out to be a dream! Either way, wherever they are found in ancient history or modern culture, dreams continue to hold a universal appeal and fascination for many people.

Dreams may be fleeting, trivial and subsequently unremembered or they may be symbolic, significant to the dreamer and therefore acted upon. In the latter case in particular, they cannot always be ignored. Or, to be more accurate, we may choose not to ignore them. We can of course, choose to be selective around anything that seems to be of significance and filter out the rest. This selective projection of personal significance is evident when considering supernatural issues and widens when we consider how much we may project generally when seeking to fulfil our own desires.

For example I had a client whose brother had suddenly passed away some six months earlier. Prior to meeting her for the first time, I noticed a small white feather lying on the carpet in the corridor outside my therapy room. I wondered whether or not to pick it up but chose to leave it lying there. Once in the session with the client we spent some time reflecting on any spiritual faith, perception of the afterlife or religious belief she may hold. The client mentioned that she had sometimes felt that her brother was watching her and that she had also read somewhere that feathers were significant in indicating a symbolic presence of a deceased person. It was coincidental that a feather had been present at the time of this session and that I had even noticed it. I did later pick it up and bring it into my room.

This would seem like a simple case of pareidolia – the tendency to observe significance in random objects or seeking to make clear sense of vague phenomena. Hence we come across stories of seeing Mother Teresa's face in a cinnamon bun in Nashville, Tennessee in 1996, numerous reports of Jesus Christ's image on objects from tortillas to table tops and reported sightings of the long dead Elvis in various locations across the world, to name but a few examples. British heavy metal band Judas Priest were taken to court in Reno, Nevada in 1990 to defend themselves against accusations of including subliminal demonic messages in their song lyrics which incited teenagers to suicide, as was Ozzy Osbourne for the same reason a year or so later. The contemporary archetypes of Big Foot, the Loch Ness monster and UFOs all attract a desire to track down specific myths and legends which continue to be carried through the centuries. Many human minds seem to possess a natural fascination towards the spiritual, mystical or the unexplained and fuel a desire to place spiritual interpretations on such occurrences, whether universally or personally meaningful, mundane or downright bizarre. Taking a light-hearted look at Monty Python's film *'The Life of Brian'* (1979), we can see this working effectively when the unsuspecting Brian, at this point mistaken for the Messiah, flees from the crowd, giving away his gourd and losing a shoe in the process. We see the pursuing masses disagree and debate their projections on the 'signs:'

- *'Look!*
- *He has given us a sign! He has given us his shoe...The shoe is the sign. Let us follow his example...*
- *What?*
- *Let us, like him hold up one shoe and let the other be upon our foot, for this is his sign that all who follow him shall do likewise...*
- *No, no the shoe is a sign that we must gather shoes together in abundance...*
- *Cast off the shoes. Follow the gourd!*
- *No, let us gather shoes together...'*

And so on.

It is indeed interesting what we project onto other people and onto objects. We can consider also what we can learn about ourselves if we allow ourselves to follow our personal messages, our gifts from the unconscious.

From a scientific viewpoint, Terrence Hines in his book *'Pseudoscience and the Paranormal'* (2003), raises realistically that since there are five REM phases of sleep occurring each night with each stage lasting from fifteen to twenty minutes, then an individual will experience upwards of fifty dream 'themes' per night. When Hines multiples this by the population of the USA, he concludes that certain dreams will contain prophetic qualities *'by chance alone.'*

Chance or not, Steve's dream had clearly had a personal impact and possibly my uneasy sleep and responses had been unconsciously empathic. Whilst I have always experienced extremely vivid dreams throughout my life and remembered them in detail, Steve tells me that he never remembered his dreams until he had left his marriage and moved in with me. Since then his dream life has been rich and he has frequently remembered and narrated the content of some of his dreams, especially having images of and conversations with his deceased parents. Clearly, something for Steve had been freed up or released in his unconscious as dreams do indicate a shift in what may be occurring within our psyche. We compared notes about our disturbed night in the morning; me telling Steve about my night first. Thinking about the cross made from clay, Steve made what seemed to be an important connection. His sister Lily, who had been psychic and who had passed away some years previously, had lived in a small town called Clay Cross, in Derbyshire. Having dreamed about a cross emerging from a kiln, Steve decided to contact his nephew, Lily's son, and he obtained the contact details for a woman who had been an old psychic friend of Lily's. The two women had attended the same spiritualist church together. Steve wondered if this contact could shed some light on the situation and give him advice. Following a phone call, Steve and the woman, 'Claudia' arranged to meet.

Continuing my diary, I wrote on **11 June:**
He is going there at 3.30pm today and feels much apprehension. Still, he is going into it with an open mind and also he felt the need to explore every avenue....to move the situation on and maybe take some control. Her name is Claudia and all he told her on the telephone was that he was Lily's brother and that he was in 'a peculiar situation.'

This is what Steve said about his dream and about how his decision to see Claudia came about: **'The whole night was like waking up, going back to sleep, waking up and I just felt kind of like something or somebody or whatever was around me and after thinking about it, I'm not sure that it was John after all. I think it was possibly Lily, my sister, with the dream and thinking well, if she was a medium on earth, then possibly she's got some power where she is now. I don't believe in mediums, it's not something I believe in. I scoffed at Lily when she told me, but having such a vivid dream about pottery and a cross – there's no connection in my life which would make me dream about anything like that. So when I woke up it was like a process of, why did I dream that? What's all that about? And through processing it and coming up with the idea was, did that mean something?' and I just thought well, the way I felt and I think it, when Lou said she felt uneasy that night as well, I thought there must be something in that. So I just thought I'd go down that path. I think we were thinking of going down that path anyway, everyone at work was saying, go and see a medium who will get in touch with this ghost and try and get rid of it through medium contact. So when it came about like that and my brain may have picked up on that "go and see a medium" thing and me thinking, well my sister was a medium and she lived in Clay Cross, so the process was there for me anyway, so it was like a choice, do I follow it or don't I? So I decided to just follow it, to try it.'**

The 'ghost buster' expert attended the exorcism with the priest and again some rituals took place. Steve by now had lost his faith in the process and told me that he doesn't feel that *'sloshing holy water around clothes will help.'* He told her he didn't believe in God or ghosts and she informed him that it is unusual that someone in this position would be haunted. I did not attend and Steve was fine with this decision. I did, however, feel very excluded from everything that was going on, which was becoming a familiar feeling for me, but one I had to accept. What was happening was beyond my comprehension. War, abuse and torture I could endeavour to understand, but this was pushing my capacity to believe to the limit.

I was also plagued by a strong sense of powerlessness as I mentioned before. It was hard to see someone I care about suffering and there was nothing much I could do except, at Steve's request *'be myself.'*

The other thing worth mentioning here is that Andrew, mentioned before as the colleague who had been plagued by a sudden feelings of misery in the warehouse for no apparent reason and who is apparently trustworthy, told a colleague that he saw John amongst the carousels on Friday night, when Steve was off. He described John's physical features accurately. Andrew approached Steve himself a few nights later and told him also that he was positive he had sighted John. This is significant as it seems to be the first fully trustworthy and 'solid' sighting of John experienced by someone other than Steve.

I continue in my journal:

I'll write about what happens at Clay Cross next. Steve hasn't been able to shake the depressed feeling off yet. I wonder if this experience will make any sense or whether it's fruitless, but at least we'll know one way or the other soon.....

A Spiritualist's Perception

'So why are you trying to find out the future by consulting witches and mediums? Don't listen to their whisperings and mutterings. Can the living find out the future from the dead? Why not ask your God?' Isaiah 8 vs 19

Spiritualism was born of events that were experienced by an American family named Fox, in 1848. Three sisters were plagued by a series of knockings that appeared to reply to various questions put to them. Following various investigations, experiments and understandably vast amounts of cynicism, it was deduced that a man who had been murdered was communicating with those now living in the house. What remained of his body was later disinterred from the cellar.

Owing to these incidents and the fact that the rapping continued unabated, the family - the two teenage girls in particular - developed something of a celebrity status, albeit the girls were subjected to some distressing experiments in order to attain this dubious honour. It has been frequently suggested that children, particularly females who hit puberty, provide particularly vulnerable channels for psychic energy. Children exist in a state of unknowing and have not yet been impacted by the left brained expectations of an adult society. Children are the ones who have imaginary friends and it may be worth enquiring – exactly how imaginary are these friends? Dr Edith Fiore (1987) whose work on spirit possession I discuss in depth later, writes: *'Young children are much more able to see spirits than adults are, probably because they do not have beliefs that get in the way. Often these become their imaginary or invisible playmates, whom they have brought back from hospital or picked up elsewhere. Sometimes they have died in the home and have remained there for years.'* This argument raises that children are naturally in touch with psychic energy. Owing to physiological changes in adolescence they may then become exposed to resulting poltergeist or psychokinetic activity described by Roland as *'physical phenomena caused by involuntary discharges of psychic energy.'* Hines, however, raises that adolescence also encompasses the age for practical jokes and that *'the case for their reality as anything other than teenage pranks is exceedingly poor.'* He goes on to state that the Fox sisters' activities did indeed turn out to be fraudulent, with their knocks being perpetrated by bouncing an apple on a string to unnerve their mother.

My guess is that Freud would have labelled these 'spiritual' experiences as 'hysteria,' which I explored in part one, and that supernatural activity was increasingly being viewed as a by-product of this state. People claiming to have gained possession by spirits of the dead would also be viewed by the psychiatric and mental health world as displaying dissociative symptoms; clearly defined sub personalities as detailed in part one.

The time of the Fox family's activities was, however, an age when science and religion were both being questioned by the more sceptical and forward thinking members of society at the time. The spiritualist movement developed once it was felt that any possible discourse with the dead that was more satisfactory than the crude knocking techniques lay with the spirits themselves being able to use the bodies of those living, in order to communicate their needs. Thus the defined role of the spiritualist or 'medium' came to the fore and triggered a huge interest in all things supernatural for the Victorians in the latter half of the nineteenth century. Use of tools to aid communication with the spirit world such as Ouija boards, groups conducting séances and experiments with ectoplasm became popular pastimes of choice. This was obviously deeply uncomfortable for the Church which condemned such activities, in addition to emphasising a hefty split with organised science.

This was also the age of the club. Most notably the Society for Psychical Research was co-formed in 1882 by a group of scholars including Frederick Myers mentioned earlier, and its members included noted intellectuals such as Mark Twain, Lewis Carroll, Alfred Lord Tennyson, John Ruskin and Sir Arthur Conan Doyle in addition to Prime Ministers William Gladstone and Arthur Balfour. Consistent meetings, ponderings and investigations by the group resulted in the publication in 1886 of the definitive work *'Phantasms of the Living,'* whose main author was Edmund Gurney, along with Myers and Frank Podmore. This comprised details of a series of about seven hundred 'supernatural' cases which were investigated, carefully scrutinised and often exposed as fakes. The team became expert in examining the possibility of trickery and illusion whilst maintaining a healthy awareness of desire for belief in the supernatural and mindful of the wishful thinking humans may hold when pondering on the possibility of life after death. Some paranormal activity, however, was cited as being unexplainable and apparently the collection makes interesting albeit somewhat dry academic reading.

Roland raises that at the time the scientific community remained 'unimpressed.' This seemed to be owing to the fact that witness statements and evidence of apparitions did not add to the scientists' understanding of the universe, nature, or cast any further enlightenment on the purpose or functioning of the human being. Roland goes on to state that: *'...this attitude has been the bane of believers ever since. Phenomena in themselves tell us nothing about the nature of the universe or human potential. No amount of table-turning, inexplicable rapping sounds or phantom materializations add to our understanding, only to the catalogue of anomalies. In the end a person either believes in ghosts or they do not.'*

There are of course many people who do believe in 'ghosts' – or at least, that their loved ones endure in some form or another following death and that these residual spirits are somehow able to communicate with the living. Some of these psychically attuned people continue to share their experiences within the spiritualist community and today, there are over four hundred spiritualist churches in the United Kingdom.

I continue with my diary:

8 June 2007: *Last night we learned a lot of things. Steve went to the woman's house. I will call her Claudia. Before Steve said a word, Claudia told him: 'Lily is OK, she is in a place of peace. But this isn't about Lily is it? It's about John.' This, Steve said, was the scariest part of the dialogue between them – she was straight in there, using John's name, without any word at all from Steve.*

Apparently she could see (or sense) that Steve is *'covered in the essence of John.'* Claudia kept using this word 'essence.' Claudia was able to give Steve John's surname and place of birth. Her information seemed very specific. Fifty years ago John had a heart attack and died in the railway signal box where the warehouse is now located. He had found out that his daughter was pregnant and he had thrown her out immediately prior to his own sudden death. He subsequently found out she had been made pregnant by his own brother, her uncle. This man's name was Dan. So Dan was John's brother and not referring to the Dan who was Steve's father – hence us travelling down the wrong lines of thinking and making faulty interpretations.

Apparently John has been looking for Dan for fifty years and it may have been that there was some sort of confrontation between them just prior to John's sudden death, which has left John's rage unresolved. Claudia then explained that John probably thinks that Steve is Dan, possibly as they may have similar physical features. Perhaps Steve's beard has an influence. Steve reflected to me later that over the seven or so years he has worked at the warehouse his appearance has changed continually, as his wife disliked him wearing a beard. He would, therefore, periodically shave it off, change the shape of it or then grow it back again. It is only within the past two years that Steve's physical appearance has remained consistent. Claudia says that John is present and can travel in a three to four mile radius, hence him not being around at home as we live further out from the warehouse than this. Also this would explain his periods of absence and possible sightings by other people in other locations as he journeys to search for his brother.

So John is dead - physically and cognitively. The thinking, logical part that would fully recognise Dan and be aware that the location in which he haunts has changed completely has gone, but his 'essence' – the part of him that feels angry, is still around. This may explain the violent attacks, although Steve chose not to disclose to Claudia about the facial scratches as he only wanted to impart the most basic information. As we know, there are many charlatan clairvoyants who will manipulate clever guesswork and pick up on the slightest verbal and non verbal clues that are offered to them by the more naïve of the public.

This is Steve's verdict on his visit to clairvoyant Claudia: **'It was like - What!? It was painful in a way. It was her saying well yes, you are being haunted by a presence that has got problems. It was like - Oh my God! – it hit home. Very solidly. And the fact that she said it before I even said anything to her made it more, it was like, this person must know – it's something that I've not said. She said about my sister being in "A safe place," well, that's what everyone says – and I remember thinking as she said that, Here we go, it's not going to be helpful at all,' but when she came out with that stuff about John, I was dumbfounded. It was like something out of a film – you go on set and it's all staged – it was - What's all that about? And it hit home, it was like, it was really happening to me, although before it was fifty fifty – is it me, is it a ghost? But when somebody said all that, you have to accept that that person says that's what it is and you go, God, no it's happening to me, and I'm going to a place where there's spiritual things happening. All these things happening to me – it's scary, it's reality, or it's not reality – it's something that's come out of thin air, really weird, it's I don't know, I don't know what it was. I remember feeling entirely different from going in and coming out.'**

We can see how Steve's natural stubbornness and refusal to be bullied kicks in here as he adds: **'At that point I thought I'd got something to communicate in that if he came to me I can say, well I'm not your brother, you know I'm not. Do I have a shave, do I have a haircut, do I look different and it's a case of well, no, you are who you are, regardless of this thing happening to me. It's a** *case of does it make that big a difference in my life and I was like saying no, it doesn't. It's nobody I know so why should it make a difference, why should I look different, be entirely somebody that I'm not so it's a bit of like, a war between us. It was like 'I'm not going to do what you want, I'm not going to hide from you, I'm not going to change just so you don't start hitting me. Having said that I'm aware later on that I did start to feel like swapping my identity – but at that time I was thinking no – no, and I should be able to confront this thing now and say, I am not your brother, I don't know what to do for you, I can't help you, I don't know your daughter, whatever, whatever it takes but when you are face to face with this thing, it becomes an entirely different process. You can't stand in front of somebody and know they're not actually there and they are a ghost come from a different dimension or wherever they come from. I can't stand and have a dialogue with him, its flight or fight. You can't help yourself. It's like "bang," oooh, so it's helpful to know but how do you approach it now in a different way? It's not me that's doing it; it's something pretty powerful there.'*

The Nature of an Essence

'Essence n. the basic nature of something; an indispensable quality or element; a concentrated extract' From' The Oxford English Dictionary.'

Medium Jill Nash, cited in Roland raises that *'I know nothing really dies. Energy can't die. It can only be transformed.'* I am reminded of the belief held by a young client of mine who was having bereavement counselling. She said quite simply, *'I know a human person means too much to be entirely destroyed.'* Of course, hope for an eventual reuniting with the departed loved relative and her own defence mechanisms play a part here. But let us for a moment remain with the essence theme and imagine that some sort of transformed energy which lingers after death is a possibility. Roland posits the significant point that *'ghosts appear to be an emotional residue rather than a conscious presence,'* and Dr Edith Fiore explains that for an essence *'Memories, personality, perceptions, emotions, thinking continue without a break.'*

This seems extremely important given what Claudia was telling Steve. Essences do not hold conscious or cognitive awareness but do have some sort of presence and continuity with regard to emotion. This also links in with Oliver Lodge's Stone Tape theory of emotional residue recorded in matter. I am also reminded of a client I saw who told me that her boyfriend had seen an apparition of his dead mother on the anniversary of her passing seven years before. She had been an alcoholic and her ghost was indeed, dead drunk, if you forgive the pun. Ashworth explains this concept further: *'the spirit maintains the same essential self, the spirit maintains the integrity of the same personality after the physical body passes away.'* He continues: *'the personality remains the same...the spirit will continue to live out its emotional self as determined by its consciousness.'* So we can see how John is in a state of rage about Dan making his daughter pregnant. Ashworth says: *'Spirits are just like people, differ greatly, one from another. If a person was very disturbed and angry in life, then the spirit of that person will be the same...'* 'Essence' or not, physical appearance does seem to play a part as well. I guess an angry ghost who dies wearing a 20th century British Rail uniform will reappear wearing a 20th century British Rail uniform whilst continuing to express his frustration.

I then wrote:

So with regard to what action Steve can take now. Claudia advised that he needs to confront John, which will be difficult – and tell him he is dead. John is dead; he needs to accept this and find peace. He may need to be told several times before this takes effect. John needs to realise that he has died.

How Do We Know We Are Dead?

'Don't mull over it. It does no good. You're dead and you have to accept it.' From 'The Lovely Bones' by Alice Sebold.

At this point, therefore, we now need to be thinking in terms of 'essences' rather than 'ghosts.' John's 'essence' lingers and forms an angry, rageful part that doesn't know he has died. Jung cites a dream in which he encounters the ghost of a customs official who had died many years previously and who is described to him as *'one of those who couldn't die properly.'* Indeed, returning spook Jamie in the film *'Truly Madly Deeply'* queries: *'Maybe I didn't die properly, maybe that's why I can come back.'*

So how do we know whether or not our own death has actually occurred and if so, whether we have died *'properly?'* Our lack of knowledge and clarity surrounding our own demise seems to be a popular theme in twentieth century entertainment. In the 1990 film *'Ghost,'* Patrick Swayze's character, Sam, dies after being shot during a mugging. We see Sam running after the mugger only for the camera to pan back to see Molly, played by Demi Moore, cradling Sam's dying body. This event occurs quickly – too quickly for Sam to realise he has been killed. During attempts to resuscitate him, we then witness bright lights enticing Sam upwards. He does not take the chance to leave; however, and his spirit lingers until the conclusion of the film. In a confused and bewildered state, Sam struggles with going through doors and other physical objects as live people walk through him and other discarnate entities communicate with him in a new world. We see the translucent souls of other newly dead persons ascend to heaven whilst demonic creatures carry off the perpetrators of evil elsewhere.

Sam visits fraudulent spiritualist Oda Mae Brown (Whoopi Goldberg), who does, much to her own surprise, turn out to have some auditory psychic ability. She later explains to Molly that Sam is stuck between worlds - *'He's yanked out so quickly – the essence still feels it has work to do here.'* She later exhorts Sam to *'give up the ghost,'* and that *'you're holding onto a life that doesn't want you any more.'* We see in this film the powerful themes of a fast and shocking death, the slow realisation of the event and the 'essence' not feeling ready to move on. This particular film also encompasses a neat definite, good versus evil theme and the comfort of loved ones 'waiting for you.' There is a strong sense of future in the afterlife.

Similar but considerably darker themes are illustrated in the film *'The Sixth Sense,'* (1999). Highly disturbed nine year old Cole (Haley Joel Osment) describes to his psychologist, Dr Malcolm Crow (Bruce Willis) his continual horrifying experiences of seeing ghostly manifestations in the following exchange:

'Cole - I see dead people
Dr Crow - In your dreams? While you're awake?
Cole - Walking around like regular people. They don't see each other. They only see what they want to see. They don't know they're dead.'

Upon exploration of this movie, we can see many familiar issues emerging. Dr Crow takes into consideration the child's trauma owing to the recent divorce of his parents. He also observes cuts and scratches on Cole's body suggestive of abuse either by another or through the little boy's own self infliction. He eventually dismisses either of these possibilities. We witness Cole's psychological disturbance at school as he is labelled a 'freak' and his suffering at the hands of bullies who sense his difference. Cole shocks his teacher by drawing a picture of a corpse with a screwdriver in its neck. He writes *'upset words.'* He steals religious artefacts from church in a bid for protection from the horrors of the ghosts he can see. He also creates his own 'safe space' in the construction of a red tent in which to sleep. This is a child who is clearly suffering, feels alone in his trauma and is unable to communicate, chiefly through his fear of being disbelieved.

The focus of the film then switches to visible signs of psychic activity and we are invited into the reality of Cole's world. The colour red is used throughout the film effectively as an indicator of any meeting between the spiritual and physical worlds. Cold spots and drops in temperature predominate as indicators that Cole is about to encounter an apparition. He sees these at home and at school. The school is a former legal courthouse where people were hanged and also the scene of a tragic fire, so entities are plentiful. Cole also describes to Dr Crow his feelings, *'sometimes you feel it inside, like you're falling down really fast, but you're standing still.'* Also this simple emotional desire he confides to his therapist, *'I don't want to be scared anymore.'* During the course of the film we witness Dr Crow coming towards the gradual realisation that his own death has shockingly already taken place. Cole can see him as an entity, not as a living man working as a psychologist. Crow becomes aware of the selective seeing he has employed in order to defend himself from the fact of his own death, until, following a period of shock and disbelief, he knows it's time to go – to where or to what we do not know.

The film *'The Others'* goes one step further – virtually the entire cast either already knows it is dead or spends the film travelling towards this realisation. Against a backdrop of a large house kept in darkness and shrouded by permanent fog, it is once more the children who are initially in touch with ghostly entities. Themes around breathing, suffocation, footsteps, piano playing, doors and curtains opening and closing occur throughout, hinting that all is not as it seems. Ghosts persecute other ghosts, vying for control and tangling with the living across the years as realities collide. *'The world of the dead gets mixed up with the world of the living,'* the ghost of the elderly housekeeper, Bertha, informs us. Bertha's mission is to endeavour to convince the central character, Grace, that she has murdered her two children and then killed herself and that the three of them are all dead. Bertha says, *'The children will be easier to convince. It's the mother who's going to cause us problems.'* As we know, trauma can shock and trigger denial as in Grace's case. The shock of 'going mad' and smothering her children, then shooting herself in the forehead clearly has not enabled her to believe the fact of her death. She assumes in relief that her children have survived when she hears them laughing from the next room and thinks that the gun failed to fire when she put it to her head. This belief causes her and her children to linger on in the house in spirit. Even after the realisation of death, it seems that these particular ghosts will continue to inhabit the location to which they are emotionally and spiritually attached. Eventually once realisation dawns for Grace and her family, Bertha goes on to tell her, *'We must learn to live together – the living and the dead.'* The living who subsequently take up residence in the house are perceived as the 'intruders.' Families move in and out over the years, and sometimes they are sensed by the ghosts and sometimes not. We also witness the medium in the film possessing the daughter - not the other way around as we are led to expect. Essentially therefore, roles around who is living and who is dead are reversed.

Convincing a phantom that it is dead and encouraging it to move into the spirit world accompanied either by loved ones who have also passed on or with other spirit guides, forms a major task according to spiritualists and psychics who habitually communicate with deceased folk. In *'The Sixth Sense,'* Dr Crow asks Cole, *'What do you think the ghosts want when they talk to you? Help, even the scary ones. Listen to them.'* Cole replies, *'What if they're angry and just want to hurt someone?'* Good point. We have seen already how ghosts (or essences) can hurt the living if they linger long enough.

Part of Fiore's work with clients in her book *'The Unquiet Dead'* (1987), comprises persuading spooks that they are dead and that the resulting appropriate behaviour is to depart from the physical world with the assistance of their fellow dead. She cites a case study in which the spirit, George, is frightened and initially refuses to leave:

'Dr Fiore: All right. Here's somebody to help you leave.
George: I don't know him (Frantic & crying)
Dr Fiore: Yes you do.
George: Uncle Jim.
Dr Fiore: What does he say to you?
George: He asked me to go. But I don't wanna go! (Crying) They're all dead! But how can I go with dead people? (Crying hard.)'

It clearly isn't easy being dead. We can see how powerfully fear has a hold. Not only do the living often fear the dead and take time to accept their presence, as with the small boy Cole's experience in *'The Sixth Sense,'* but the dead themselves also have the potential to fear other dead people - the latter need to deal with the implications of being dead themselves.

If I can again quote another source of fiction, contemporary this time, Marian Keyes, in her novel, *'Anybody Out There'* (2006), writes beautifully of a tragic car accident which heroine Anna survives but which kills her husband. Physically injured and emotionally traumatised, Anna progresses painfully to the gradual realisation that her husband will not be returning to her. She searches for clues to his whereabouts as she projects Aiden's image onto strangers, put significance into smells and other signs which all ultimately present rational explanations. The reader shares Anna's journey as she emerges from denial. She writes of a dream in which her husband, Aiden, for whom she has been yearning, finally 'shows up:'
'Happy to see me?' he asked.
'Jesus Christ, Aiden, I'm so happy! I can't believe this. I was afraid I'd never see you again.' He was wearing the same clothes he'd been wearing the first day we'd met. 'But how did you manage it?'
'What do you mean? I just walked in here.'
'But Aiden, - because I'd just remembered -' you're dead.'
I woke with a jump...I closed my eyes and went straight back into the same dream. Aiden wasn't smiling any longer, he was upset and confused and I asked him, 'No-one told you, you were dead?'
'No'
'That's what I've been afraid of. And where have you been?'
'Hanging around....'

Poor Anna acknowledges that Aiden is going to *'hate being dead.'* I wonder how John feels about it or will feel about it, when he gets to know. That is if Steve or anyone else can get close enough to see him and to tell him without becoming intimidated, frightened or attacked. We can only speculate on the cause of John's death, but it seems it may have been a swift process. He is clearly left trying to communicate with Steve and has formed some sort of an attachment to him in a forlorn hope – a hope that the living will somehow resolve the outstanding issues that linger from the lives of the dead.

Fiore says of the spirits she has cleansed from her clients: *'many were unaware of their deaths, since they felt alive, and were totally confused and frightened, especially when they could not make any impact on their survivors. These individuals remained earthbound – tied to the physical plain – despite the fact that they had died.'* She says that this is particularly true of suicides or sudden deaths as discussed before. Spiritual healer Ashworth agrees: *'the trauma of an accident victim who dies soon after the event often leaves the spirit in turmoil, not realising it is dead and failing to make the right connections for transition, desperately trying to retain access into its physical body, but of course, failing as the body's life support mechanisms are now defunct. They all need to find somewhere to go or somebody to be with.'* Such incidences can leave the discarnate *'roaming the physical realm as a lost soul.'* I am strongly reminded of the long term emotional impact of childhood sexual abuse and other traumatic events in Ashworth's statement that: *'Certainly the event will have created an instant and enormous mental and emotional pattern, which may well not have had time to balance out in the panic and terror of those last moments.'*

Ghostly Motivation

'For the living at least know that they will die! But the dead know nothing; they don't even have their memories. Whatever they did in their lifetimes – loving, hating, envying – is long gone, and they have no part in anything here on earth any more.' Ecclesiastes chapter 9 vs 5-6

As in life, it seems that attachment issues have a significant impact on behaviour for those who have passed on. Apparently attachment can be a strong motivation for the essence of dead folk to remain on earth and for the living to yearn for signs of their presence in an afterlife. A sound example in literature is displayed by the dead Cathy in the novel *'Wuthering Heights.'* We learn how hard it is for Cathy to part from Heathcliff in death and how he exhorts her to haunt him indefinitely rather than leave him alone in his suffering and grief for her loss. Film is no less emotive on the subject. *'I longed for you,'* Nina tells the ghost Jamie in *'Truly Madly Deeply,'* as he obligingly returns from the grave as he *'couldn't bear'* Nina's pain. *'The capacity to love that people have, what happens to it?'* Jamie asks later. In this case, love is clearly stronger than death and Jamie is able to reunite with the still living Nina.

Another perception of the ghost's purpose, however, is that ghosts linger or return in an attempt to resolve their 'unfinished business.' In John's case the need to communicate with his daughter and tackle feelings of unresolved anger with his brother for impregnating her, whether through seduction, serial abuse or one off rape, seems to tie in with this theory. In literature especially, ghosts are often a device used to communicate important messages to the living in order for significant actions to be followed up or for revenge to be carried out. Shakespeare's spectres provide a good example of this. Macbeth leads his life in accordance with the prophecies of the three witches (or mediums perhaps) which incites him to commit murder. Plagued by prophetic apparitions, he alone experiences the silent ghost of his victim Banquo sitting in his place at the table. Lady Macbeth's symptoms of guilt, however, take a more psychosomatic form during her sleep walking activates and ultimate suicide. Her actions cause her doctor to comment on a need for psychic or religious intervention rather than medical treatment. *'Doctor: Unnatural deeds /Do breed unnatural troubles. Infected minds/To their deaf pillows will discharge their secrets/ More needs she the divine than the physician' (Act V sc i).*

Another Shakespearian spectre, that of Hamlet's murdered father, however, chooses to appear to more than one person initially, albeit silently. By eventually informing Hamlet of the facts of his demise, this ghost becomes far more talkative and eloquent and he seems sure of who he is and where his final destiny lies. *'Ghost: I am thy father's spirit/Doomed for a certain terms to walk the night/And for the day confined to fast in fires/ Till the foul crimes done in my days of nature/ Are burnt and purged away' (Act 1 sc v).*

He goes on to declaim the necessity for his son to take some positive action and *'Revenge his foul and most unnatural murder.'* Likewise our John has been able to specifically request help verbally from Steve – to find his daughter and tell her that she can come back home. Claudia told Steve that the fact John often stands in silent purpose watching Steve is also his way of trying to communicate. It does feel remarkable that Steve and John reached a point when they were actually eventually able to engage in a dialogue.

Whether the ghost's function in making contact with the living is mundane, life changing or downright confusing, what seems to come across strongly is that ghosts will, more often than not, be found frequenting the location where they lived. There is a notable exception cited in Roland's book concerning the war poet Wilfred Owen, however. Owen appeared to his brother on the day of his death, which occurred one week before the war ended. Harold Owen was a navel officer aboard his ship at the time and a physical visit by his brother would have been impossible. Harold Owen helpfully recorded what happened and how it made him feel: *'...to my amazement I saw Wilfred sitting in my chair. I felt shock run through me with appalling force and with it I could feel the blood draining away from my face. I did not rush towards him but walked jerkily into the cabin – all my limbs stiff and slow to respond. I did not sit down but looking at him I spoke quietly: 'Wilfred how did you get here?' He did not rise and I saw that he was involuntarily immobile, but his eyes which had never left mine were alive with the familiar look of trying to make me understand; when I spoke his whole face broke into his sweetest and endearing dark smile. I felt no fear, only exquisite mental pleasure at thus beholding him. All I was conscious of was a sensation of enormous shock and profound astonishment that he should be here in my cabin... This not speaking...was not only in some inexplicable way perfectly natural but radiated a quality which made his presence with me undeniably right and in no way out of the ordinary. I loved having him there: I could not and did not want to try to understand how he got there. I was content to accept him, that he was here with me was sufficient. I could not question anything; the meeting in itself was complete and strangely perfect,'* (2007).

After sleeping for a while following this encounter, Harold goes on to explain that he wakes, somehow knowing with absolute certainty that his brother has been killed. This provides us with a sound example of a *post mortem ghost* – those who make an appearance after death pretty much straight away, sometimes before news of their demise has filtered through to the living. The incidence of our loved ones popping in immediately after death to say farewell reminds me of my grandmother, in the 'dream' which I described earlier. The associated feelings of calm, peace and comfort seem to enable the living to achieve closure.

Although it seems impossible that the deceased Wilfred Owen could appear in the middle of the sea, there is a suggestion that ghosts do tend to be on the move. Railways and the underground tube trains provide a sound example of this. In the film *'Ghost'* the spirit of Sam is able to travel across town and whilst taking the tube he encounters an angry and emotionally disturbed solid essence that haunts the subway after being pushed in front of a train. This ghost's ownership of his 'patch' comes across very strongly as he violently protects his space demanding: *'Like trains? Get out! This is mine!'* Having then formed an uneasy relationship, this ghost teaches Sam how to move and throw objects in the physical world, telling him – *'You still think you're real – you got to move with the mind – the finger is dead – take emotions and let it explode like a reactor.'* With practice Sam is enabled to learn how to make his presence felt, torment his murderers and eventually gain justice and closure with Molly. This motivates his reluctance to leave immediately, although when he does, he is accompanied by inviting white lights.

Roland raises the interesting point that most ghosts may not have such significant missions and merely go about their daily lives commuting from home to office and back again, which may explain why spirits often communicate what may seem to be fairly mundane messages via mediums. In *'Truly Madly Deeply,'* when she feels the presence of the deceased Jamie, Nina explains to her bereavement counsellor that he *'Never says anything profound or earth shattering. You know he doesn't say 'Well God thinks this' or about the planet or world events or 'There is no God.' It's all 'Go to bed, brush your teeth.'* Ghosts then may simply be motivated by their own normality. Given this argument, maybe many of the travellers on the tube are in fact, ghosts as three dimensional and as solid as our railwayman, John. This has certainly challenged my perspective on my daily bus journey as I now stare intently at my fellow passengers and wonder if they are, in fact apparitions!

When excavations were commenced in Victorian London many sites of burial, including pauper's graves and plague pits were uncovered in order to complete the task. This resulted in disturbance, re-burying and potential disrespect of numerous long dead people in order to satisfy the need for scientific progress. On the whole, however, Roland cites that ghosts don't tend to linger around graveyards, maybe as they don't know they are dead, or simply because they don't wish to be reminded of the manner of their demise. He tells us that: *'Ghosts tend to linger in locations where they lived or where they died and rarely where their body is buried. They do not associate themselves with their physical shell and many believe they are still alive.'*

My assumption would be that the places populated by the living are generally more exciting and less morbid than hanging around in a graveyard, which must be one of the most static and least energised places possible. By this argument I guess potential ghost hunters need to be aware of the comparative waste of time if they choose to examine relatively lonely or unpopulated locations. I have found during my research that is the problem with ghosts – so many examples, stories and evidence illustrates such a great variety in behaviour, temperament, location, culture, appearance and the physical and emotional impact upon the living, that it becomes hard to make sense of them other than as 'discarnate' entities we have yet to understand. Any study of the supernatural, I am learning, seems flawed. All ghosts seem to be as individual in manner, demeanour and behaviour as they were in life. There are no common links and all I can describe and speculate upon is Steve's own personal experience with his particular ghostly essence.

Returning to the **8 June 2007**, I continued in my diary:

'Steve felt very relieved last night, and somewhat lighter. We went for a long walk around the park talking it all through and trying to take it all in. We do wonder how Claudia could possibly have known all of this detail without any apparent prompting, but as Steve was in the situation and feeling somewhat shocked, I guess such logical questions and ponderings come up later. His main worry is that he may be psychic like his sister, an ability he doesn't want. The thought of having to start dealing with uncontrollable visitations from any other entities seems intolerable but hopefully this is a one off situation. He talked to another sister and learned that Lily was only affected once or twice in her life, however, which is reassuring. If he is indeed a psychic, then Steve is a reluctant one.

He also isn't sure whether to say anything to the priest at his next visit as this priest discouraged Steve from visiting a spiritualist. Likewise Claudia specifically didn't want her name giving to the priest in case of possible persecution from the Christian church. Talking last night Steve and I don't feel that our views have changed with regard to the existence of God, afterlife, heaven or hell. But we feel strangely at peace with all this information we obtained and personally I remain open minded about the dead leaving behind certain legacies – which Steve feels may even have some connection with DNA. I do find credible any thoughts on DNA, genetic heritage or predisposition to psychic ability providing some sort of explanation in the future. We also wonder if ghosts are time travellers who cannot quite 'get through' or are failed reincarnates. I am now fully open to any suggestions...

11 June 2007: *Of course at this point it may be logical to try and track down records of John's life and death. We feel, however, that at the present time it's not* *that necessary to gain further detail. No sighting of John yet – maybe he's gone wandering again....*

14 June 2007: *Night before last both Steve and his colleague were really cold –Steve felt the hackles rise on the back of his neck. His colleague showed him a definitive 'cold spot.' Everyone on the shift avoids the fire doors now, the main area which triggers feelings of unease. Then last night Steve was 'hit' again and marked – again he feels the despair. It's too quick and too shocking for him to put any idea of talking again to John into any sort of action. I suggested he just try saying John's name (or surname) straight after being hit as a way in.*

20 June 2007: *All is quiet at the moment. Three priests came in and did their bit the other night – I don't think they intend to return again though. Their take is that spirits are all around us but only certain people can be susceptible to seeing them.*

26 June 2007: *Horrific night last Friday. Steve had been given a cross by the priests, which they had blessed. It was made of wood and a very tactile shape, designed to fit neatly into a hand and if held used to aid a sense of comfort and protection. Steve was working alone in an area directly below the section he fears, owing to having had the worst supernatural experiences there. He was feeling somewhat apprehensive and was holding the cross in his hand whilst picking the clothes. I think he was bearing in mind the possibility that John could appear and that he may be able to communicate.*

Then, as carousels started being thrown violently at him, he saw John standing next to him in a state of total rage and malevolence. Steve got marked on his face and this time was burned quite badly on his hand also. He later showed me the cross – it was all completely charred and blackened in the top corner. Steve left the area and had medical treatment for the burns. He says that he now has no doubt that this is something external to himself and is present in the warehouse. He carried on working as he wanted to combat the feelings of depression that hit him later – this seemed to work. The sight of the burned cross is very unnerving. Needless to say, his watch went back (or forward) from about 12.30am to 9 o'clock. The colleagues who remain sceptical – a very few of them at work now, still maintain that Steve must be doing this himself – for attention? – but since the workers are searched pre and post work there just does not seem to be a way that anyone can take in a lighter or any other means of self harm. Steve is going for promotion as a trainer and he really wouldn't jeopardise this by acting in strange ways. Myself I have witnessed his reactions too often now to be sceptical.

I would mention here that Steve does have noticeably warm hands. I have often thought he would make an excellent masseuse or reflexologist. I do not believe that it would be possible for Steve's body heat to ignite wood however! Ashworth talks of the extreme physicality of his own psychic experiences: *'My physical body was going in and out of some kind of torment, building up so much real, physical pressure that I was convinced that at any moment I might explode. Spontaneous human combustion seemed a real possibility.'* The blistering on Steve's hands was clearly painful and the desecration of the beautiful cross was puzzling.

Steve described the incident: **'I was badly burned on the palm of my hand where I was holding it. My hand was blistered and there's no way, no physical way, that could have happened. And it just says that this thing is more powerful than we can imagine and everybody was so astounded. I was physically shaken, I had to go and sit down. I must have been sitting down for two hours. Michael was there with me and he was just saying, "I don't believe it; I just can't believe that this is happening," We just sat there talking about it and everybody in the warehouse was aware that it had burned me and everybody was scared – well, not everybody, there were still people believing I had done it myself – but then it became stronger, it was a different force, it felt malevolent, it felt as if I was going to die with it. It wasn't a case of this thing wanting to know something now, it was a case of, I'm having you. And that's scary. And it's angry because I'm carrying a cross – it's angry that I'm carrying a cross or whatever, that's what I put it down to at the time. This cross was an act of aggression towards him and he answered in an aggressive way. That's how it felt. It was a different kind of thing I was being faced with.'**

29 June 2007: It's been quiet the past couple of nights. However, Steve did a half night earlier in the week. After he had left, three guys were working in the 'scary' part of the warehouse and all three simultaneously had a feeling of anxiety, fear, dread and as if they were being watched. They all went to find each other at the same time and compared emotional experiences. Whilst they were talking, footsteps went past them – but no-one was there.

It was now the end of July and things had been quiet. Steve and I took a week's holiday together. Several of the night workers who had witnessed cold spots, seen ghostly legs pass beneath the carousels and experienced anxiety, individually or collectively, had not reported anything further of this sort. People on the afternoon shift had also reported items shifting and witnessing disembodied parts of John's body, mostly his legs, occasionally being seen. He had by this time become a generally acknowledged phenomenon within the warehouse and approximately one third of the night shift claimed to have been directly affected by him. John was becoming a much discussed topic of conversation. One or two people, however, refused to speak of what they had witnessed; openly acknowledging that to speak of their frightening experiences would make them 'real.' They declined to be interviewed for my research, a view which I respect. Perhaps avoidance was their way of staying psychologically safe.

It did seem, however, that it had once more reached a point when we thought that John had absented himself, perhaps embarking on an extended search for Dan and acting on the need to disgorge his rage further afield. We must remember that the cognitive, logical, thinking part of him had been eliminated and it seems the essence was caught up in some sort of loop. If the situation follows the same pattern as last year we may expect his presence to become very strong, before he then left altogether. The whole situation was subsequently near forgotten about. Thoughts of him lingered, however, along with a sense of apprehension as to a possible reappearance. Whilst we had no answers as to what may happen next, it did seem, if we followed Claudia's line of belief, that we had acquired more information this year. All remained quiet throughout the autumn and the early part of winter until Christmas, when an unexpected attack incited me to re-commence my writing.

Further Encounters 2008

'I don't feel sane, I don't even know what the word 'sane' means any more – so why assume this little girl is unbalanced, or abnormal or mad? What are ghosts? What does it mean to be haunted?'
From 'Landscape of Love' by Sally Beauman.

13 December 2007: Steve arrived home last night at 12.30am. He had been 'attacked' and scarred on the face and his clothing was covered in blood. He had not seen or heard anything, however. A colleague cleaned up the wound and said it was 'healing up before her eyes.' Steve was distressed, needed to cry and to be alone. He had been sent home from work. I cannot believe this is happening again – and at this time of the year. So unexpected. I am very upset.
14 December 2007: Quiet last night, Steve worked with others around him. The HR manager, Kate, was again sympathetic.
9 January 2008: Steve was 'hit' again last night – only a very slight mark this time but he had a severe nose bleed – the first one he had had since he was a child. He read his book for a while to distract from feelings of despair. Again there was no actual visible sign of John. It has been suggested that he consider changing shifts as all this paranormal activity is disrupting the night shift. Steve is considering this option but wants to stay put at the moment. I suggested he see a GP and request a brain scan. I am deeply worried.
14 February 2008: 'It's the first time I've seen him for ages' Steve told me following this night. Steve turned around and John was standing behind him. Half an hour later Steve was 'hit' and marked in the face, which was very sore and bleeding. He coped by talking for half an hour to a manager about mundane work issues. Steve and I had a discussion about 'freezing' and the impossibility of rational speech or action once shock takes higher thinking temporarily out of action. This is why the questions of why doesn't Steve communicate or throw an object at John are rendered problematic. Shame is also another issue – Steve feels self conscious about the scarring – 'People may think I'm a rapist or something.' The woman who manages the local shop asked him about the marking which brought this point home to him. It was hard to evade the questioning.
Steve's watch went back by an hour and fifteen minutes.
27 February 2008: Steve felt a 'brush' past and was marked very slightly. An hour later there was an earthquake which measured 5.2 on the Richter scale. This

occurred at about 1.00am, caused many people to wake up in the night and many, including myself, were talking about it the following day. This again makes me wonder further about energy distribution within the environment.

29 February 2008: Steve was working with three others when he felt 'hit.' He asked his colleague about his face and the scarring appeared before his colleague's eyes. One of these had been a sceptic. These were the worst marks so far in terms of breadth and severity. I took a photo but this was three days later. Steve came home early, very despairing, withdrawn and tearful. I think we need to go down the electrical route – Steve was holding his hand held device and standing near the computer at the time of the 'attack' – I think getting a report on the electrics in the warehouse and the work which was done there two years ago may be worthwhile.

7 March 2008: Very, very active events occurred last night. Steve was preparing deliveries to the lorries, working in an area with about eight other people close by. About four other colleagues were working in hanging, a separate area. Someone emerged from hanging and said to Steve – 'I bet you are pleased you aren't in there, it's all hell let loose.' Now white faced, colleague Tom had been working alone but was highly disturbed by noise, shouting, footfalls and a presence in the area next to him – yet no one was there. Someone else had to leave a work station (T86 the little girls clothing section) owing to the intensely cold drop in temperature. Others felt watched. Nerves were high. John was clearly present and going berserk – it was speculated that he was actively searching for Steve. Whilst standing within this larger group of people later, Steve was hit and marked – hurrah! Witnesses! Steve felt very pleased about the significance of this. Having this experience with many others present meant he could now feel more confident in his awareness that he clearly isn't self harming whilst in some sort of dissociative mental state. Even the sceptics present couldn't avoid this occurrence. One colleague described what happened after Steve reported being 'hit.' He said: 'I don't believe any of this and I'm not interested. But once Steve said he had been hit in the face I turned to him and saw a slight mark on his forehead. Then, before my eyes, the scars went all around his face and began to bleed. There was no way that Steve could have done this to himself. I don't know what to make of it and I can't explain it.'

Steve then went into a different area and saw John at the end of the gangway – quite a long distance away. John remained still and silent – Steve maintained eye contact, hoping that someone would come behind him and also be able to share what Steve was looking at. Steve knew if he turned around John would, however, vanish. Eventually Steve himself left as no-one joined him – this felt like a shame, a missed opportunity.

Steve did feel an element of the usual despair after being attacked; however, he also described feeling 'buoyant' as he hadn't been alone on this occasion. I felt his energy when he came home this morning and told me about the events of the night. It really does seem that, similarly to this time last year, John's activity is escalating in ferocity. This time, however, Steve, whilst continuing to be the target *for psychic attack (if that is what it is,) is no longer so isolated in his continuing distressing experiences. Others saw him be 'hit' by something invisible and the resulting bloody marks appearing on his face with no apparent cause. Fear of being disbelieved is a universal issue, particularly when significant highly unlikely events happen in our lives.*

Steve said: **'It's still something that galls me that people think that I'm actually doing it myself still and when it happens in front of somebody, whether it be one time or ten, it's something that's saying it's actually happening to me and I'm not blanking out, I'm not marking myself and those people who say that I am, it kind of like worries me that I still actually believe possibly I am, because it's still an unbelievable story I'm telling. Then the fact that it happens in front of people says that there is no way I can make a scratch. Not only that, but part of the time people actually see me being struck and physically going backwards with my head, things like that, so it's like saying, yeah, that's what's happening. And other people saying well, I don't believe you and he's doing it himself – let them come forward and say how I'm doing it myself because it's a fact that people have said no, he's not, I've seen it happen. So it's like the other side's got to say how they think I can be doing it for myself in front of people without them actually seeing me do it myself. So it's like saying see! I've got my tongue out – see I can prove it and I am not doing it myself. Now you prove to me that that's what you think is happening. So it's like a positive thought.'**

Steve continues, describing how the debate on belief and the dynamics in the warehouse were being challenged: **'The whole warehouse at night time had changed. We'd got different camps. We got a camp saying I was doing it to myself and a camp saying,"Don't be ridiculous, we know, we've seen things happening as well." They believed me, they were on my side. I'd got some true friends on the night shift. These friends saying I believe you Steve.'**

I continued in my diary and wrote: *Isn't it strange how people come into our lives when we need them? My newly arrived and temporary sessional colleague (another therapist) who I will call Rose, has been telling me that she has had many psychically challenging events occur and she holds warranties on all electrical goods as she destroys so many merely by touch and ordinary use of them. She feels watched, objects move and odd events happen in her home. Her mother's watch inexplicably restarted two years following her death. At a psychic event someone drew an accurate picture of her mother. She does not feel threatened as none of these experiences feel connected to evil or malevolent entities.*

My mind changes continually as I explore possible explanations - from health reasons – the possibility of brain tumours – to electromagnetic activity. Rose, who seems to be something of an expert, tells me that entities can gain energy from places where electrical energy will be present. So I journey full circle to the possibility of essences existing following death and fuelled by such energies. Ghosts.

11 March 2008: On the radio this morning a woman rang in who said she is 'full of static electricity,' gets through lots of appliances, lights blow when she switches them on etc. She is no longer permitted to fill up her car at petrol stations – the first time she tried, she unscrewed the cap and a spark hit the fuel tank. The man in the car behind her had to douse the flames with a fire extinguisher – fortunate as she most likely would have been killed. The fire brigade were called and the petrol station was closed. It seems that many people are indeed 'human batteries,' full of chargeable energy.

13 March 2008: Steve was speaking to his colleague Nathanial who said he had been discussing the situation with some of his church members. Apparently some members were able to describe John accurately. It seems he is already known in the area as a 'railwayman' ghost who has always haunted locally. Steve remembers places where he used to play as a child with his friends. The locals always used to joke that the public toilet nearby was haunted...so it seems that John has been lingering around the three to four mile vicinity for many, many years. It seems that this is a ghost with longevity – something of a legend known to the local community, even before Steve was born, after the war.

14 March 2008: Wednesday night Steve saw John staring at him and, with his heart in his mouth, Steve felt able to speak to him. He noticed that the longer he lingered the more pronounced the pain and scarring to his face was becoming – and indeed scratches spread across his cheek to his nose on this occasion. Bearing in mind the instruction from Claudia regarding letting discarnate entities know that they are in fact, not living and entirely deceased, Steve told John 'You do know that you are dead don't you?' Much to Steve's horror the ghost continued to regard Steve and calmly replied 'Yes, I know I am.' Steve left rapidly, feeling very shocked. How can an 'essence' know that it is dead if the living, cognitive part had died? If John knows he is dead, then could he be a demonic presence with the sole intention to persecute Steve and cause him the utmost harm? Or does Steve's greatest fear remain that John is a dissociated part of his psyche – a shadow side? Steve felt very shaken. And I feel helpless. Completely.

Steve said afterwards: **'It was like being powerless. It was like, total, well, I can't help you then. It was thinking afterwards, well, I've got this for the rest of my life while I'm here then because he knows, there's no way he's going to retreat from what he's doing. It's a positive "I know I'm dead." We weren't expecting that. I just couldn't believe it and just to go back to square one, right from the beginning what do I do? What can I do to stop this happening? After that, there's no answer to it.'**

Steve was then asked by the team leader to take a look at unusual activity on the CCTV. As Steve had passed through to leave for home, all of the signage suddenly and violently fell down. Probably coincidence or another healthy case of Pareidolia, but unnerving nevertheless. I told Steve that I was beginning to perceive John as a bully. Steve hates bullies and did make the connection that having something of a powerful personality, he is unused to being a victim. This is a new experience for him and an extreme one.

22 March 2008: After a quiet few nights Steve got marked last night. We've been discussing electricity again. There are open fields behind the warehouse which may well have pylons in them. Steve also feels a 'hum' in his head when he sees John. Ironically he remembered last night that his sister Lily became psychic in her late fifties...the age Steve is now...

26 March 2008: 'We are all in it now' Steve told me. It was a chaotic night last night (25th) and the first night back after four nights of Easter break for Steve. Many people felt disturbed, particularly his colleague Lizzie, who was emotionally and physically shaken for the first time, feeling an unseen John stamping near her and finally jumping on the gangway right next to her. Lizzie had been reassuring herself that he was looking for Steve and unthreatening to her but this time she was finding it hard to detach herself and be stoical. In fact Lizzie had been saying that she is more than happy to tell it to just 'piss off.' Others experienced intense cold spots and the smell of sulphur. Colleague Tom in particular got very stressed by his disturbed sensations and a sudden sense of depression which he had not brought into work. The prevailing sense seemed to be that John was in need of attention. John was very present but left Steve alone until Steve was marked in the face far later on in the night. Steve felt a 'roar' as John passed him by and once more he went into terrible feelings of despair. Meanwhile, at home I was having a nightmare of being possessed by an elderly man, seeing my face in the mirror and likewise him screaming at me in impotent, absolute rage.

The colleagues are now feeling involved. To the point that they want something done as work is becoming an unsafe environment for everyone.

Colleague Tom made these comments: 'Occasionally while working in the hanging section of the warehouse I have sensed or smelt the odour of sulphur but unfortunately I did not time or date these experiences. Where this has occurred I have had no direct witness but have mentioned it later to colleagues. Sometimes it has been so intense that I could taste sulphur on my lips. Also when I arrived home on occasions I could smell odour on my work clothing. I thought I was being over sensitive but it kept happening. I don't understand the experiences because they come and go, they are never in the same place or area and if I sense the smell it's gone if I call someone to witness it. Also I wondered if it was only coincidence if it happens with any of Steve's terrible experiences. I feel very sorry for Steve is going through and it is the first time I have been in contact or worked with someone who has been subjected to supernatural happenings. My experiences are trivial compared to Steve's though. I have an open mind on the subject of the supernatural but I have no personal experiences. My experiences of sulphur odours only concern me when I hear gossip that it can be connected to the myth of demons. Believe or not, mankind's limited sense can only show us

so much. There is more to life and the universe than our human perception of it.'
Colleague Bernie adds: *'The last time Steve was attacked I had smelt sulphur earlier in the evening. Later Steve approached me and told me he had been 'done' by the ghost. I told him I could not see any mark on his face. Then, before my eyes the mark appeared. I had often seen the mark after the fact but never actually witnessed it. It was amazing. I can not see any way he could have faked this.'*
27 March 2008: *Quiet night last night. I, however, had nightmares and sleeplessness. I feel I am holding the trauma. I'm not sure how much longer I can go on like this.*
Steve booked an appointment to see his GP for 18 April with my encouragement. I think that a family GP with knowledge of Steve's history may prove trustworthy, hopefully reassuring and helpful. I would suggest that Steve requests a session with a neurologist or even a psychiatric referral if it helps. Steve made the appointment as he thinks that the issues are all lying within him – 'I still think it's me' he said. When I asked what makes him think this was the case, he replied that it was on the basis that 'I don't fucking believe in ghosts.'

Scents and Sensations

'The lunatic is on the grass
The lunatic is on the grass
Remembering games and daisy chains and laughs
Got to keep the loonies on the path.' From 'Brain Damage' by Roger Waters.

Agnostic philosopher David Hume (1711 – 76) posited that *'Only that which can be perceived through the senses should be accepted as real,'* (Roland.) Anecdotal evidence which utilises the senses suggests that apparitions tend to be seen, rather than heard – often from the 'corner of the eye.' Sceptics will cite tiredness, brain misinterpretation and the general sensitivity and likelihood of peripheral vision on this experience. Ghosts can, however, be heard and not seen – footsteps providing a popular example along with the occasional voice. Various odours also crop up – this is the case especially with colleague Tom, who relates his experiences via his senses, smelling and tasting sulphur and owning that he is very sensitive in this area – albeit that he is aware that he could merely be being 'over sensitive.' I am also aware of Steve's first brush with what may have been a supernatural experience, the presence of his dead father - or perhaps another helpful psychic guide - who communicated via the familiar smell of petrol, all those years ago in the park. Let us examine further the issue of our senses and how this may inform our reality.

Spiritual healer Dr Edith Fiore poses the question: *'Have you ever felt something like cobwebs across your face? Or a cold caress? Sometimes these are strong enough to be considered a push or a light hit.'* The cobweb issue is a fascinating one, mostly because this is phenomena in the warehouse that virtually all of the colleagues have experienced, even the ones who have sensed nothing else untoward. It may be possible to argue that light touch of this nature is the first point of contact with those people who are less 'psychic' than others. Steve describes the cobweb sensation as follows: **'It's like being touched and it feels like cobwebs but there's no possible way there's cobwebs there. I mean there's no possible way you can have a cobweb because hundreds of people have walked by or its been worked day in day out taking clothes, moving clothes, whatever. There's no way a spider can form a cobweb and especially in the middle of the aisle although loads of people say they have been swept by cobwebs. You stop and think because it feels like, Oooooh, I've got a spider web on me, but it isn't, so therefore something's getting our attention, be it whatever. My attention's deflected onto a cobweb because I've been hit. Everybody says that it does feel like somebody's trying to get your attention and I believe that's what people put it down to. And I think somewhere, I don't know where it was, it is a big thing in ghosts or haunting – somebody's said to me that the feel of cobwebs is a normal way that the other side is communicating. I mean, I never knew that.'**

In her interesting novel *'The Lovely Bones'* (2002), contemporary author Alice Sebold writes from the viewpoint of a fourteen year old murder victim, Susie, who watches her still living family's activities from a personal heaven. Occasionally, she chooses to mingle with the living in the company of the friend she has made after her death. Susie describes the light touching by souls: *'Holly and I could be scanning Earth, alighting on one scene or another for a second or two, looking for the unexpected in the mundane moment. A soul would run by a living being, touch them softly on the shoulder or cheek, and continue on its way to heaven. The dead are never exactly seen by the living, but many people seem acutely aware of something changed around them. They speak of a chill in the air. The mates of the deceased wake from dreams and see a figure standing at the end of their bed, or in a doorway, or boarding, phantom like, a city bus.'*

A sensation of feeling touch, or passing through cobwebs is something that has been experienced by many members of Steve's team. Steve's colleague Bernie describes such an experience: *'I was picking stock down an aisle on the top floor of B chamber when I felt what I thought was a cobweb brushing against my face. I went to brush it away but there was nothing there. I felt another on the back of my head. Again I tried to brush it away and again nothing was there. Suddenly I felt as if my head was covered in cobwebs and ended up frantically trying to brush them off. I felt as it something was deliberately trying to intimidate me.'* Bernie believes in the existence of supernatural phenomena and he goes on to describe his emotional response to the event: *'At first I thought I was imagining it but then realised it was really happening. I was also angry that something was annoying me in this way. My annoyance quickly faded though as I wondered if it was just something trying to make contact in the only way it could.'*

Senses have also been assaulted in other ways; the smell of sulphur has again been a particular example. Interestingly, Steve noted that the sulphurous scent emerged periodically and in full force following the incident with the burned cross. Whilst the closest I have got to a smell of burning has been smoke from the neighbouring shop's bonfires permeating through my windows and the walls of my house, in the warehouse the sulphur seems to have been a theme for many of the workers, even more so than with Steve himself. A friend of mine once turned her flat upside down in an attempt to find the source of electrical burning she could smell. This, however, turned out to be an olfactory hallucination caused by a migraine. Indeed, the mind plays strange tricks upon us, but it does seem odd that the sulphur smell seems to be a collective experience in this case, although it is fascinating to note that Steve himself has not been overly affected by this particular phenomenon.

Cold spots also abound in the warehouse. These seemed to move location but again many workers were affected and had to remove themselves from certain areas. Scientist Terrance Hines and other sceptics put cold spots down to undetected draughts; however, personally I am not convinced by what appears to be such an over simplified explanation. Cold areas in the warehouse have apparently never been a problem prior to the manifestation of John, nor are they likely to occur in major frequency or intensity in a vast open plan area which is windowless, virtually door-less, air conditioned and has its temperature controlled. In my opinion most people are intelligent enough to be able to detect draughts, which tend to be directional, easily located and remedied. Other explanations include phantoms extracting energy from the air or merely a biological effect similar to a shock state once one feels 'spooked.' Of course, the power of suggestion, that some of the workers were wanting to share some part of the 'ghost' is another likely possibility.

Steve tells me that the experience, however, feels deeper than 'cold spots,' which simply provides a satisfactory explanation for the sensation of feeling cold. He tells me that a description of the experience even goes further than being 'chilled to the bone.' This sensation is instantaneous – a cold shiver, a 'thrill' - a sensation of goose bumps and anticipation of another presence. So the cold is not only physical in nature but also holds an emotional content. I am reminded of author J K Rowling's creation Harry Potter, who, when in the presence of his persecutory dementors, illustrates a depth of cold which delves further than a mild image conjured up by 'cold spots.' *'An intense cold swept over them all. Harry felt his own breath catch in his chest. The cold went deeper than his skin. It was inside his chest, it was inside his very heart...He was drowning in cold.'*

On one occasion Steve and his colleague Tom both shared an intense feeling of cold and this is what Steve said on the subject: **'I'll give an example of the time I was with a colleague and we met in a place where it was freezing. There's no way it was freezing, there's no way it was a little cold draught and it thrilled us to death. It was like** *having the biggest thrill you could actually have – a thrill in a positive way – it was really weird. It was like from top to bottom – frozen. We just stood there with goose bumps – every part of our body was saying, what the hell is that? We started to laugh because it was like something out of this world. So cold and yet the whole warehouse is warm. Oooh, I've never felt anything like it in my life. It was a thrill, a deliberate thrill, it wasn't like anything else. I have been through cold spots before but this one was entirely different. Some cold spots I went through were like a dread, because you know something was happening, but this one was solid, it was like, oooh, this one had an entirely different quality to it, because you don't stand there laughing like buffoons, I mean we couldn't help ourselves. It was like having an emotion with somebody, having a terrific laugh because of a joke or being down because someone had died; it was an emotion like you never feel again. It was a heightened emotion and it was two people sharing it. If it happened to me I couldn't explain it to anybody but the two of us explained it quite well, what it felt like. Because people had said "I've had a cold spot," and we'd say "Well, you've not had one like us." In fact we'd never felt like that before, like goose bumps on top of goose bumps on top of goose bumps. No directional breeze involved because it came from the inside, it didn't come from the outside. It came from the inside and that's the difference, it was the inside getting really frozen and coming out.'*

11 April 2008: *It's been quiet for some time. We had indeed been speculating on the possibility that John had disappeared for this year. Quiet that is, until last night. Steve had been feeling relaxed and happy prior to going to work. He was then working alone when he began to hear voices which were 'enticing' him. He wasn't sure if the voices were external or internal but he chose to ignore them. The 'enticements' were of the nature of 'You aren't cooperating so we will have to show you.' His memory of any further detail is blurred. This attempt at communication went on for a fifteen minute period. When I later asked why Steve didn't go to others for support he replied that he wanted someone to come to him, to check out their experience and to see if anyone else could witness any sounds or visions of apparitions – for shared involvement – for 'proof.'*

Finally John appeared visibly and solidly in front of Steve. This was, as usual, shocking enough, however, this time Steve could clearly see a child peering around from behind John. This child Steve interpreted as being his deceased sister, Lily, in the form of a young girl. This deeply upset him – he was then marked, albeit this time extremely faintly, in the usual places down the right side of his face.

Steve was very depressed and close to tears following that night. I came home early from work to be with him. He cancelled the appointment with the GP as he didn't feel in any state to see him – fears for his mental health were growing. 'They'll put me away today with what I've got to tell him,' Steve said. Unfortunately we had watched 'Poppy Shakespeare' on the television a few nights before – a drama depicting a catch 22 situation in which a woman becomes unable to extricate herself from a disturbing closed mental health system (televised on Channel 4 on 31 March 2008). *This had unnerved Steve, understandably under the circumstances. Steve was discussing what had happened with colleague Nathaniel. Nathaniel, who has been supportive to Steve from a religious viewpoint has been feeling presences and spending time in prayer at the warehouse itself. He told Steve that he had a dream a month before about a man, a woman and a child appearing to haunt the warehouse and the activity escalating severely before the situation terminates. Both Steve and Nathanial were feeling shaken by this newly perceived presence of the child. From the Christian viewpoint, these apparitions are demons. If John is in fact a demon, it seems this child (about 10-12 years old) may be a second demon. So was she Lily? In the cold light of day we speculated that Lily had passed away as an adult and she would not hurt Steve in any way. We also wondered if this child may be the ghost of the child that Dan had molested, but she obviously would, I assume at this point be too young to have become pregnant. Steve had thought of this too and had felt 'pained' when I raised this - 'It's as if I'm responsible,' he told me. He was feeling enmeshed in the ghostly family drama.*

Steve reflected on this incident later and said: **'Thinking about it, when I did see it, my brain was confirming that it actually was my sister at that particular time because I remember my sister when we were young, when I was growing up. I was younger than her but I remember her. She always used to have blond hair and she'd wear a blue dress, to make her blond hair look blonder you know. My mother used to dress her like that. I remember thinking, that's my sister. I can't remember if this apparition had the hair and dress but it's the aura she gave off similar to the one I remember when Lily was a little girl. She was probably twelve or something and I was thinking, that's my sister. It's like seeing her again, it's like confirmation that is my sister but – it wasn't my sister. When I went away and thought about it, I was thinking well, she hasn't said anything and if it wasn't my sister then, who was it? But at the time, it was definitely my sister, but then I began to doubt it. But there and then it was definitely my sister. Now, I don't know. I'm fifty fifty. I think it was because there is no reason why – why would she come as a small girl? It could even have been the child that was born.'**

I wrote: *Steve's relieved that I don't feel frightened. He still intends to go the GP much to my relief. Of course, all this activity, particularly with the hearing of voices and the 'enticement' points to the fact that Steve is psychotic, possibly schizophrenic. Or at least, having psychotic episodes, triggered by the environment. But how likely is it, that if he has a mental illness, that symptoms are not in existence in any other location or under any other circumstances? As we know from the copy of the psychologist's report, the psychologist presumably did not pick up any mental condition nor recommend any further course of action.*

What is going on here? Love of course, is blind – so am I missing anything here? Or am I simply refusing to see anything obviously wrong with my partner? I feel unnerved and low in mood. I also feel highly angry. This, as I said before, is bullying. This ghost is such a fuckwit he needs to go off and find a mate, albeit a little girl 'demon' hiding behind him, to intimidate his victims further.

18 April 2008: *Stressful two days. Steve went to see his GP yesterday afternoon – a long standing doctor who is aware of Steve's history. He was intrigued, talked to Steve, gave him a sound physical examination and concluded reassuringly 'You aren't mad Steve.' He shone a bright light into Steve's eyes – and he couldn't see any brain swelling or diagnose an indication of mental ill health; schizophrenia, psychosis, epilepsy, migraine, tumour or any confirmation of my other medical theories and fears. He finally told Steve that the problem seems to be 'Supernatural in origin' and suggested that Steve should 'be on TV.' That, however, is the last thing we would want – who needs freak show reality TV and publicity. Why on earth do so many people seem to suggest such methods as a first point of help? And Steve just wants to disappear.*

Steve said of the visit: **'I was saying can I have a brain scan please? And I explained what was happening to him and yes, he said, it could be part of the brain that's doing it, let's check you over. And he checked my reflexes and everything and he did look straight into my eyes and he said "Steve, I'm not going to spend that amount of money – nothing's wrong with you. You've obviously got a ghost on nights."** This brought a smile to my face when he said it, I think he just looked at me and smiled as well and he said "Go on days." And I said "What, go on days?" and he said "Yeah, because ghosts only walk at night." And I thought well, that's an odd thing to be getting from a doctor** (he laughs), **talk about placebos. Yeah, that was funny…Not being mentally unwell was a big thing. After seeing that programme "Poppy Shakespeare" I thought they might just put me away for having the thoughts.'**

Ultimately the GP said that Steve should consider going on the day shift for a six to eight week period – if no ghost appears then it's a nocturnal type. If the ghost is still around then maybe Steve can go ahead and have an MRI brain scan, but this will cost the surgery £400 and the GP can't see any physical reason via his medical examinations why this would be necessary. It's interesting to note how many people seem to be under the impression that ghosts only come out at night! Much to my surprise, he didn't suggest counselling!

After this Steve felt considerably lighter. Congratulations, you have a ghost. They don't exist but you have one anyway. I was certainly much relieved that it doesn't seem to be a mental health issue. We were feeling really quite euphoric and went out to celebrate. Then, it all went horribly wrong last night….

21 April 2008: *Steve came home early and distressed at 2.30am – I was in bed and waking up, becoming aware of someone walking around the house. Once I* realised he was home I knew he had had another 'visitation.' Not only that but he had arranged with top management permission to take a tape recorder into the warehouse. Armed with the small machine I've on occasion used to tape my clients and supervisees, Steve once again had begun to hear indistinct 'enticing' voices for some time, so then he switched it on. What can be heard on the tape recording seems to be beyond anything human I have ever encountered. Pop music from the warehouse radio (which is continual in the background) can be heard and then the roar of a man's voice cuts in twice over a period of a couple of minutes. To me it sounds like a strangled, enraged, primal, 'pushing' of rage, distress, fury, inhuman. It sends cold shivers throughout the bodies of those who hear it. Steve said he sensed that the entity knew what he was doing, watching and reacting to Steve's actions…It seems there are a few words which cannot be made out – the managers will be trying to figure this out, once Steve gets the tape to them. Until then, it stays in the car – Steve doesn't want 'any part of him' in the house. I must admit, I handed over the tape recorder not expecting any of this – I thought either nothing would be picked up or there would be static/white noise only - certainly nothing this loud, definite, other worldly, a tortured soul. Steve hadn't seen anything, but again got marks on his face, faint lines once more.

1 May 2008: Steve is considering visiting the Mormon Church on Sunday. Despite his loss of religious belief, he trusts the people there and thinks they may be able to bless and shift the ghost for good. Julian, Steve's Mormon friend, should be doing a ritual soon. Steve hasn't said much about this conversation beyond his belief in that it should help, even temporarily. He may go on the day shift and is thinking about this. But he worries that the apparition may shift its attention onto others – colleague Lizzie in particular has continued to be affected by stamping near her and having the cranes she been working in shaken violently. My thought, however, is 'Fuck them, let some of the other night shift workers bear the brunt for a while.'

At this point, not surprisingly having felt stressed and angry over a period of months, coupled with doing a stressful job, my health began to break down. I really felt the possibility that I was beginning to experience some symptoms of vicarious traumatisation. I wasn't sleeping well, I felt edgy and I was catching colds and flu viruses. I think it was only being out at work and having the welcome distraction of this that was helping me - that and talking to Steve and one or two of my friends about the ongoing events.

Steve had a welcome break by going out of town to a conference for a few days. Whilst he was away and I spent nights alone, I did start to feel a sense of shock about the tape and I did choose to take some time away from work. My colleagues assumed that I was in 'burn out' from my heavy therapeutic work – but I had in fact been finding that my counselling work was providing a containing, structured routine, which was helping to 'hold' me in all of this. With Steve back in the house, I returned to work after a week off and I was feeling better. The cycle of ill health coupled with my feelings of stress had eventually manifested itself causing an enforced period of inactivity I had found beneficial.

Vicarious traumatisation or traumatic counter transference which I mention here, is likely to revive any personal issues for that therapist who may then notice that imagery linked with the client's trauma is occurring within her own dreams, fantasies or feelings. Of course, the risk of such secondary traumatisation is a consideration for any therapist who is working extensively with trauma clients, to be aware of and to protect ones self against. In her book *'Trauma and Recovery'* Herman says: *'Repeated exposure to stories of human rapacity and cruelty inevitably challenges the therapist's basic faith. It also heightens her sense of personal vulnerability…The therapist also empathically shares the patient's experience of helplessness.'*

Here of course, the cause of the trauma does not appear to be of human origin although it is of course being repeated. I am left with the continual uncertainty as to what may be occurring to my partner during the time when I am trying to sleep.

2 May 2008: *A student today told me about seeing a spiritualist who gave her much accurate information about her deceased grandfather and also her cousin, who had been murdered and was the reason she had entered therapy. I've had many clients who've seen clairvoyants and one or two who have been psychic. I am striving to work effectively with them and use supervision to support me in this. I do find that I can bracket my own situation and focus on them, but of course their issues are going to catch at my own stuff.*

During this period of feeling ill and closed off, however, I've become aware that I'm feeling especially 'atheistic,' conforming to my historical non believing 'blue print' as a clear defence. Maybe I need to open up again and see how this feels.

6 May 2008: *The Mormon quorum of priests are preparing a service on Wednesday evening to undertake a clearing and protection. They are not going to be present at the warehouse; it seems that this can be carried out remotely. Steve will be present at this service. If that doesn't work, then we have a card with a spiritualist contact – this was given to us by one of the night cleaners, who attends a spiritualist church regularly. The last time she went, apparently a member raised an issue about 'the railwayman' having a problematic presence at her place of work. Interesting if this true how this somehow got picked up. Personally I'm hopeful that the spiritualists are the answer. From my research and from what has been reported by other people, I have a sense that they know how to deal with discarnate entities. It does seem to have been confirmed that Steve is a 'conduit' for psychic forces that he cannot control. Spiritualists and psychics learn how to harness their energy and channel an ability to communicate and work with such forces. As an immediate measure, however, Steve has faith in the Mormons. We will see…as long as something works.*

Steve said of his return to the Mormons: **'I think it was like going back to old friends saying "I'm in trouble." and they accepted it almost instantly. It was reassuring. To be honest I'd got more faith in**

them than in any other church so obviously its more grounding for me, perhaps more likely to work if I think it might and most importantly, it's acceptable to them.' We can contrast here his attitude between this pending ritual and the exorcism carried out by the Anglican Church earlier, which had triggered scepticism from both Steve and the priests involved.

15 May 2008: Well, it seems to have 'worked' as far as Steve is concerned. As a non Mormon I'm not entitled to discover the details of the exchange between Steve and the priests nor how they actually carried out their 'banishing of unwanted discarnate entities' ritual. I am aware that whilst no rituals or prayers or 'cleansing' of the actual area is involved, the focus of this work very much lies around protection of the individual and a need for positivity. Steve has been given coping strategies on how to protect himself, guidance in how to think positively and, most significantly, techniques on learning how to close himself down to psychic awareness. Although it has only been a relatively short space of time since the last time John felt present, all has been peaceful for Steve since practising his 'closing down' methods. He has been feeling physically, mentally and emotionally fine at work and even going into areas in which he had previously felt apprehensive and avoidant. T86, mentioned before, is one such area, where the majority of the most distressing haunting has taken place and where myself I felt watched when walking there with the priest during the first exorcism way back in 2006.

Not the same sense of security and confidence exists for everyone else however! Several colleagues experienced being haunted last night and I must admit to feeling a wry and possibly even cruel amusement over this circumstance. Steve and I went so far as to having a bit of a laugh over the way it seems things are turning out – but I sense our motivation stems from relief over the continuing and increasingly likely fact that others are actually genuinely being affected and it seems, not as any sort of collective hysteria or trickery. Colleagues affected can, therefore, present themselves as viable witnesses, further proving that this doesn't appear to be any form of internalised disturbed mental perception on Steve's part, triggered within his psyche for whatever reason. Not only can others become more fully involved through being directly targeted by John, but they can take some responsibility and action which has up to this point been Steve's sole burden. Won't it be interesting to see if anyone starts to get marked on the face or on any other area of the body as the ghost transfers its attention to another conduit?

So it seems that owing to the latest intervention, Steve is now protected but others are not. So the ghost is still very much present in the environment despite the fact that the individual himself has been 'exorcised' or perhaps to be more accurate, 'closed down' to the possibility of communication or attack by discarnate entities. Steve described this as a 'strange night' and by the end of the shift incidents he had been told about included colleagues seeing the shadow of a figure, smelling sulphur, experiencing the sense of cobwebs on faces and heads and hearing directive, angry voices 'giving orders.'

Below, quoted in its entirety, although names have been removed, is a report Steve's colleague Russell put in to management as a result of the disturbing experiences he was having on this particular night. Again, it is interesting to note how this colleague was affected physiologically. We also gain a valuable flavour, particularly for those of us who have little awareness of how working a night shift in a warehouse operates; of the culture of binning and hanging areas along with the general nature of the work.

A Colleague's Report

'I would like to place on record some occurrences that happened on Thursday night, 15 May 2008, and Friday morning, 16 May 2008.

I came into hanging, binning after first break. At 1.30am the team leader Michael told me to bin T19. As there was not much in there I binned them and went down to T86. I was binning T86 near fire door one, when I thought I saw a shadow. Immediately after this I began to feel nauseous and dizzy. On finishing the carousel I walked back to the top of the aisle whereupon I felt better. Picking another carousel, this time of dressing gowns, at the fire door end I felt totally unwell again. Having binned the dressing gowns near to the top of the H I felt better. This I repeated numerous times having the same results. I confided my observations to my colleague Tom who told me that he has smelt sulphur within the top floor of hanging. (The sulphur smell is the smell we got when Steve was getting his scratches on his face.)

Then just before second break around 3.55am my colleague Hassan was doing a bin map, and was in T54. Coming out and on the H, he cried out that he had walked into a cobweb. He was trying to pull it off his face and from his hair but from me and Tom's observations nothing was there.

This has now happened on three separate occasions over a period of time to three different people. We then proceeded to break at 04.00am whereupon my colleague Paula was at the door to go out of the warehouse when she informed me that as she opened the door a voice was heard to say 'Come on, come on.' When she turned to see who it was, no-one was there. She tested the door to see if it was that that had made a noise but it was not.

Another occurrence possibly around 01.30-01.45 happened when my colleague Lizzie was binning top floor when she heard her name called. She looked all round her but could see no-one.

I'm sure I do not want to scaremonger but would like these matters to be recorded.'

This is the end of Russell's very useful report. As we observe here, a total of five people, including Russell himself, are affected.

I continued to write in my diary: *I'm interested to find out more about the incident with Lizzie. She's is the one who previously reported stamping near her, feeling*

John's presence generally and seems to have more recently been a focus for the spirit trying to gain her attention, which she has been doing her best to ignore. Did Lizzie have her name called? Does this mean that the ghost knows her name? Again this is suggestive of a cognitive ability. I'm also aware that Steve has never been mentioned by his own name - he has always been called 'Dan'.

21 May 2008: I learned today that yes, apparently Lizzie's name was called, and it seems that this has also been the case with several other people. Surely this means that the ghost can cognitively identify and recognise individuals by name – an interesting and unnerving thought. For others, however, it may be that it is the 'essence' (for example of brother Dan) that is enough to enable an entity to latch onto an individual conduit.

Steve said of these recent events: **'It's very hard to stay closed down when people are coming up to me talking about it in the warehouse. It's like yes, OK, that's fine, I'm sorry it's happening to you, but then I have to go away and close myself down again because it's opening me up again. So it was a case of going away and coming back, going away and coming back. I have very mixed up feelings – should I be doing this? Other people are starting to be affected whereby it's just me usually being affected – is it fair on everybody? But nobody's getting marked so I decided it was fair.'**

28 May 2008: Something strange and unnerving happened at home yesterday. I was in the bathroom; Steve was lying on my bed. Both doors to each room were shut. I came out of the bathroom into the hall just as Steve was emerging from the bedroom – he thought he'd heard me shout his name, with a sense of urgency or distress. I hadn't. What I did think I may have heard myself was a sudden wall of distorted sound – for just a split second – I remember thinking Steve may have turned on my radio on the bedside cabinet and got some white noise. Steve was then frightened – he said he was sure it was a female voice saying his name. It was the first time he'd experienced this in years, although he has a history of hearing his name called or spoken since he was a young child. I am frightened – I keep thinking about Steve's colleague Nathaniel's dream – that involved a man, a woman and child. We've seen the man and the child – what if the woman is now in our home?

Didn't get much sleep last night – I was listening out for voices in my head...

Voices

'I heard a voice somewhere cry – Jane! Jane Jane!' nothing more. 'Oh God what is it?' I gasped. I might have said, 'Where is it?' For it did not seem in the room – nor in the house – nor in the garden: it did not come out of the air- nor from under the earth-not from overhead. I had heard it-where, or whence, for ever impossible to know!' From 'Jane Eyre' by Charlotte Bronte.

Steve has on rare occasions, heard voices since being a small child and he takes this for granted. Voice hearing, however, is often regarded as symptomatic of psychosis. Dissociation and trauma may also have their place. In their book *'Accepting Voices'* (1993) Romme and Escher make links with voice hearing as a dissociative coping mechanism which *'is brought into play to cope with threatening situations, particularly in early childhood.'* Deciding to research the subject further I discovered a website called *'Intervoice; The International Community for Hearing Voices'* which I found fascinating. *Intervoice* cites that between four and ten percent of people world wide experience voice hearing with 74% occurring after the age of twenty. Such voices can be either male, female, or an undetermined gender, adult, child, human or non human. They may be single voices or multiple, although one tends to dominate. Some people report being able to tune in and out of their voice hearing, similar to use of a radio, whilst for others the experience is far more random and uncontrolled.

Voices may be experienced in the head, ears and other body parts or outside of the body within the environment. Intervoice acknowledge that between twenty and ninety percent of people who have the experience will do so as a result of a traumatic event and they explain that *'voices often reflect important aspects of the hearer's emotional state – emotions that are often unexpressed in the hearer.'* This concurs with the issues illustrated in Steve's psychology report and in the discussions on projection and splitting explored earlier. Traumas or events which may trigger voice hearing include divorce or a relationship breakdown which would be significant in Steve's case, illness, bereavement and interestingly for me, living alone for the first time. This last factor links in with memories I have now had of moving into my first house and periodically hearing the shouts of crowds just before falling asleep.

Other interpretations and reasons for voice hearing cited include schizophrenia – perhaps incorporating an urge or instruction to hurt the self or others. Drug addiction, a link with diabetes, demonic impersonations posing as God, or voices sent directly from God to test our strength are also illustrated. Statistics cited in this website inform us that eighty percent of people who have endured torture hallucinate and Bennett (1972) has observed that the phenomena was also common amongst long distance yachtsmen and others who spend much time alone.

Much depends upon the reaction of the voice hearer and how they and others interpret their experiences and this has changed over the course of time. The Greeks habitually accepted voices of the Gods and Julian Jaynes, cited in this website, makes the claim that *'the people who hear voices today are carriers of an evolutionary residue from this ancient time.'* Biblical and historical figures, for example the pious young girl who became Joan of Arc, may have been undisturbed by voices. Joan was, however, then labelled as a liar, witch and impostor by others before finally being revered as a saint. In modern times voice hearing is perhaps less likely to be interpreted from a religious model and more pathologised. Whether theories vary from spirit guides, insanity or symptomatic of genius or creativity, we see once more how individuals may be steered towards the mental health services. Intervoice state that more often than not, voice hearing is deemed to be pathological today and that psychiatrists tend not to *'buy into patient's delusions.'* Romme and Escher 2001 state that: *'Psychiatry in our western culture unjustly identifies hearing voices with schizophrenia. Going to a psychiatrist with hearing voices gives you an 80% chance of getting a diagnosis of schizophrenia.'* Subsequently, engagement with the voices is discouraged. The emphasis, as in most forms of therapeutic contact, should, however, ideally focus on the reactions of the hearer, rather than on the fact of the voices themselves. The community suggest a need for mental health workers to *'accept, understand, consider helping communication with the voices and to meet others with similar experiences to break down isolation.'*

Voices can either provide benefit for the hearer, perhaps giving trusted advice, providing wisdom, wit, companionship or they can be detrimental and persecutory – negatively affecting the hearer's actions, confidence and self esteem. We witness voices working positively for the hearer in the uplifting (1989) film *'Field of Dreams,'* in which, Ray Kinsella, played by Kevin Costner, periodically hears a mystery voice instructing him to build a baseball field on his farm land. Whilst a team of 'solid' deceased baseball players avail themselves of practice on the newly constructed pitch, the ultimate message of the film is around faith, redemption and healing the relationship between Ray and his dead father.

Accompanying visions, smells, taste and touch sensations can be experienced alongside the voice. Fits or physical pain may also accompany the episode. Voices may shout or whisper and often, as sometimes in Steve's case, say the hearer's name only. Interesting points around falling asleep, hearing voices triggered through the use of water (for example when washing in the shower) or when electrical equipment is activated, are all speculated upon in discussions. *Intervoice* summarises that: *'Some people perceive the voices as helpful and they evoke a feeling of recognition. These people feel the purpose of the voices is strengthening them and raising their self esteem. The voices are experienced as positive and as an understandable aspect of their internal selves. Others experience the voices as aggressive and negative from the very beginning. For these people the voices are hostile and are not accepted as part of themselves. They suffer from negative voices that can cause chaos in their minds, demanding so much attention that communication with the outside world is extremely difficult.'* Fortunately, Steve does not have to cope with such extremes, despite having to do battle with the 'ghost' phenomena. Whilst not fully understanding the reasons behind voice hearing it is feasible once more to see how many of such experiences could be interpreted as supernatural in origin.

Specific individual examples of voice hearing on the *Intervoice* and similar websites are included and these organisations do much to normalise the experience, providing lots of useful information, dialogues and research on the subject. This includes providing groups, events and training, issuing self diagnostic questionnaires, commentaries on television programmes and strategies for coping. The last includes a need for acceptance and *'to set limits and structure the contact'* and as in the work with DID sufferers Sybil and Eve discussed in part one, to work towards integration. We see how Ray's response to the voice in the film *'Field of Dreams'* and how he chooses to act on it is significant: *'Until I heard the voice, I'd never done a crazy thing in my life,'* he informs us. Fortunately his wife and young daughter are empathic to his voices and subsequent actions, which may perhaps be a less likely response beyond the cinematic world.

Ignoring voices, distraction techniques and denial, we are informed, rarely works effectively. Certainly we witnessed this in Steve's case as he was being attacked verbally, emotionally and physically. His is a ghost that requires attention and will do its utmost to gain it. Panic and feelings of powerlessness are also generally replaced by anger – which we also saw in Steve's case when he ordered John to 'fuck off.' Significantly, it is recommended that affected persons do not allow the voices to rule their lives and whilst Steve may continue to ignore the occasional voice calling his name, he has now of course, finally been able to close down, emotionally and/or spiritually, to anything more problematic.

We can see how some of these themes, particularly around trauma and creativity are pulled together when we consider this list of famous voice hearers, which includes: Poet and visionary William Blake; Winston Churchill who was plagued by voices during his 'black dog' depressive episodes; Charles Dickens, who was able to hear his fictional creation Mrs Gamp making jokes in church and Sigmund Freud, who said, *'I was living alone in the foreign city…I quite often heard my name suddenly called by an unmistakable and beloved voice.'* Others include Mahatma Ghandi, Saint Ignatious Loyola, whose history combines loss of his mother at the early age of seven, enduring a battle wound, experiencing religious visions and a nervous breakdown as part of his contributory factors; Noble Prize winner John Forbes Nash, a diagnosed schizophrenic who was periodically institutionalised and on whom the 2001 film *'A Beautiful Mind'* is based and composer Robert Shuman, who was tortured by angels, demons and sleep disturbances, which inspired his finest works. The 'divine madness' of Socrates which, like epilepsy, has been described as a 'gift from the gods' has inspired art, poetry, philosophy and mysticism.

Traumas and life transitions are clear triggers to voice hearing. In 2006 Romme and Escher raised that: *'In research concerning people who hear voices it was found that 77% of the people diagnosed with schizophrenia and the hearing of voices were related to traumatic experiences. These traumatic experiences varied from being sexually abused, physically abused, being extremely belittled over long periods from young age, being neglected during long periods as a youngster, being very aggressively treated in marriage, not being able to accept ones sexual identity etc.'* A common trigger for voice hearing is cited as a negative social environment or severe early childhood distresses. Voice hearer and actor Anthony Hopkins says: *'My school days were not always happy and I wanted to get away from Wales and be someone else. I was stupid at school; I just didn't know what was going on. I thought I was on Mars, I didn't know what they were talking about.'* This reminds me of Steve's citing his experience of the pointlessness of school, his frustrated potential and his desire to integrate into the adult world with all possible speed. Here I am also reminded of Sybil's psychiatrist, Stanley, in part one, reflecting on the fact that there may be a case for particularly gifted and intelligent children but who are perhaps thwarted and restricted by their environments and some of the people in them, that may trigger psychic ability and other phenomena. Medium Doris Stokes, whose story is told later, writes specifically of *'Voices In My Ear'* and actress Zoë Wannamaker is also affected, the latter acknowledging a hefty level of *'chatter.'* And so the list of famous voice hearers goes on.

Steve's experience of voice hearing is mild by comparison. He explains: **'All through my life I've heard my name being shouted or said or whatever. Sometimes, if I remember rightly, it's possible I do have some sort of reach to people, because every now and then I'd hear my name being said. There's nobody ever around. I've felt, like tugs in my hair, so I don't know, I mean, can that confirm I'm a medium or what, I don't know.'**

30 May 2008: I'm still feeling uneasy and not sleeping well. I'm also raging again about the female voice Steve heard in our house – I'm not prepared to share my home with another woman. Particularly the whinging, needy undead. This feels like a violation of my safe place.

For my living as a counsellor I endeavour to enable people to feel better about their lives and this, as all competent therapists know, involves the implementation and maintenance of firm boundaries. Knowledge of contracted appointment times, private space and confidentiality offer as much safety within the therapeutic environment as can be predicted through the provision of such boundaries. The therapeutic contact – at least, in longer term work - also involves striving for the utmost patience and the monitoring and celebration of any progressive movement within the client, however slight and however lengthy the process. The randomness and unpredictability of spiritual attack clearly does not offer such boundaries. I have learned that the stuckness of spirits who appear to operate, in Transactional Analytic terms from the victim position, is an irritant to me. It seems that John may have been around since Steve was a child – for over fifty years in fact. He may appear to ask for help but then it seems he may not be enabling himself to gain what he needs. This is because he is not being explicit and he is being violent - bullied himself by a demon perhaps. John himself, intentionally or not, is a persecutor towards the living. From feeling bullied by our ghost/s, the bully is being brought out in me and I am feeling angry and persecutory myself. I'm aware of how bullies may bully from fear, however, and I'm very in touch with my fear. So our wheels of trying to maintain a sense of control and power in whichever way we can, continue to turn and patterns of behaviour are set.

Over the years I have become increasingly aware of the challenges that arise for the partners of therapists. I also wonder how the partners of psychics cope, particularly when any ghostly forces visit a psychic who has either not yet learned to fully channel their presence, or has not in some way invited them in by arrangement.

***9 June 2008:** Steve's had a week off with food poisoning but finally went back to work last night. Whilst he was still functioning OK, apparently for much of last week one of the more sceptical colleagues had to leave the chamber in which he was working as he felt watched, sensed a constant presence and was experiencing the 'cobwebs' in the face phenomena. Less sceptical now I suspect.*

As for me, I've relaxed back at home after a few uneasy nights. I don't think there is anything here. It was, however, a useful learning curve in terms of wondering how on earth people cope with unseen but sensed forces in their homes. Accounts I have read from various people indicate that they don't feel threatened by any of their own ghosts and some may even welcome their presence or at least, grow to tolerate them. There is an assumption in such anecdotes that ghosts have as much right to be there as the living and are essentially benign and benevolent. Many seem harmless apart from the odd poltergeist who may cheekily hurl a plate to the floor. Some people, however, do move. And given the nature of our ghost, I think it would be highly unnerving to share a house with John...

I was shocked and disturbed in particular by my sense of violation. Home no longer felt like a safe place and it gave me a sense of what it may be like for those people who are bullied, abused or otherwise have to exist in unsafe and unpredictable environments whilst in a state of constant tension and hyper alertness. It took me a while to relax and to regain a sense of ownership and control in my safe space.

Steve continued to work and was fine, with one exception. In July 2008 his elderly uncle passed away peacefully in hospital and Steve was the only person with him when he died. I wrote:

***July 2008:** Steve's uncle passed away aged 96. He died in hospital during the night and Steve was the only person able to be with him at the end. Steve feels deeply distressed by this bereavement – he acknowledges that it triggers feelings around the sudden loss of his father – this uncle was Dan's elder brother and the last link with Steve's father's family. The following night, unsurprisingly Steve was feeling his grief and presumably his aura was vulnerable – leaving him 'open' to psychic attack. He was working and talking to his colleague Tom, when they simultaneously went extremely cold. Steve tells me it was the weirdest feeling 'as if someone put their icy frozen arms around me.' He was then badly marked on the face. He then went into low mood, intensified by his grief for his uncle. So we know that John still haunts the building – he hasn't disappeared over the summer as in previous years....Just because Steve has been closed down to his presence, doesn't mean he has gone...*

Since this event, Steve experienced cobwebs brushing him, particularly if he was feeling particularly vulnerable or low in mood. In our day to day life, we may be walking – whether in the park or down an urban road in the city - and he may on occasion feel a cobweb-like sensation over his face, although whether this is merely the creation of a spider or the more mystical touch of a spirit, we were not always sure. At work, his psychic 'armouring' and techniques from the Mormons seemed to be effective. Interestingly, however, on one occasion whilst on leave he visited work briefly to fetch something and upon entering the premises he was instantly marked with the familiar scratching down the right side of this face. Knowing that he would only be on the premises for a matter of minutes, Steve had not prepared himself in the way he now would before commencing work on a long shift. Fortunately he was also not present in the environment long enough to feel any of the old alien emotional content but nevertheless he beat a hasty retreat.

For the remainder of the year 2008, whilst not seeing or hearing anything from John, Steve continued to be attacked and scratched in the face on thankfully rare occasions. Most notably, an unpleasant event occurred during a night in September when he received a bad 'electric type shock' whilst pushing a metal carousel. Witnessed by a team leader, Steve felt his face to be violently knocked sideways and with his face bloody, he returned home in the familiar state of deep temporary depression. Steve has concluded that these rare incidents may be triggered owing to two facts. Firstly, that many colleagues still report strange events to Steve and expect him to listen. Their detail and energy seems to be serving to 'open him up' when he needs to be focussed on 'closing down.' Secondly, and significantly, Steve is aware that on occasion, he had become somewhat 'complacent' in his psychic armouring. He has learned that he is safe, but only if he continues with a commitment to the nightly performance of his protective rituals – a level of preparedness and what authors of the *'The Haunted Self,'* Van der Hart, Nijenhuis and Steele term as *'pre-encounter defence.'*

Other colleagues seemed to be having more of a sense of John's presence and were continuing to be plagued. Clothes were flung, carousels have been known to be uncontrollable and somewhat to my amusement, to 'follow people.' John had been spotted and recognised, standing, watching one or two particular individuals, perhaps gathering energy for a more forceful attempt to communicate with others in due course. He was present on some level all year round and was clearly much stronger in energy than he ever was at the start of the situation back in March 2006. The work force continued to live with the situation and it seemed that paranormal activity continued to be rife for some. There was a meeting held with all affected colleagues which resulted in some vague talk of 'Getting the ghostbusters in' in the spring, when activity would probably make itself felt more strongly. No-one really knew what to do and some seemed to be actively enjoying the dramatic events. Maybe some didn't really want to let go as they hadn't yet witnessed any haunting at all or enough to satisfy themselves. I was feeling angry with everyone.

We awaited the coming of spring then, when traditionally John's activity escalates even further, albeit with a sense of anticipation rather than trepidation, as we now knew that Steve could as least psychically defend himself. I continued to feel frustrated with the group, however, with the general 'collusive fog' around the haunting and I was reminded of how society may collude with the silence around abuse of any type. Whilst in this case, some people had become aware of the elephant in the room, there were no attempts from anyone to shift the elephant.

Individuals may respond with fear, avoidance and the maintenance of silence. Others respond with fascination, over questioning, a dwelling on detail and a self absorbed interest in the sufferings of others. What was apparent was that no action beyond the arrangement of the failed exorcism was being taken. The abuse remained the problem of the abused; the ghostly abuser was left to manipulate it's power in the environment. This was the position at the conclusion of the year 2008.

Outstanding Questions

After reading of the account of events so far, I am aware that it may be worthwhile pausing to ponder on two or three questions which may need to be asked:

What happened to the tape? The audio tape of the appalling demonic screaming, of course, is a powerful indicator of 'evidence' when it comes to the existence of the entity, John. It was left with Kate who was intending to send it off to be analysed by some sort of recording expert. The tape was never returned to Steve. It seems it was, perhaps somewhat conveniently, 'lost' en route by management. I can only speculate on what happened here. Perhaps management did not want to acknowledge the existence of the tape which may have led to adverse publicity for the warehouse. Perhaps it was genuinely mislaid. Perhaps it was lost by Steve himself as he used to keep it in the car boot, reluctant to have it within our home.

Why didn't Steve simply leave the job? Colleagues repeatedly asked this and indicated that had they had deeper experiences of the ghost, including being directly attacked during the haunting, they would most certainly have left their employment at the warehouse. Others held the opposite viewpoint. Steve says that, for him, there were several reasons not to quit. Firstly and most significantly there was a question of belief. Steve simply did not and could not believe that all this was actually happening for many months. He did not believe in ghosts. The attacks were so random it was evident that there was a sense of *'this just cannot be happening to me...'* Healthy denial and a sound coping strategy for survival on a day to day - or rather a night to night basis – was an obvious psychologically protective route to take. Also the question of fear was ever present. Something along the lines of: *'I fear I'm going mad. If I leave work, this fear will become visible through my taking action and maybe then this fear will be somehow confirmed. I will have to have implemented a change in my life which confirms that there is something wrong in my life.'* So we can track a clear progression for Steve from *'I don't believe it's happening'* to *'It must be me,'* to *'I'm doing this* to myself, or something within me is doing it and therefore I'm not OK, so I must be 'mad.'

Then, with a gradual change in emotional response, there was for Steve an acceptance of what was happening. *'Whatever it is, it's happening, the feelings about it are survivable and temporary and I have faith in myself to get through. I can be resilient in this experience.'* Also, significantly, another coping method was the knowledge that the feelings were *not his*. Steve could therefore put some psychological distancing between himself and what was going on for him; he was able to maintain some boundary between the 'me' and the 'not me' elements of his interactions with the spiritual presence. Certainly John has a unique physique, a strong individual personality and an emotional presentation that made it easy for Steve to realise that he could define John as a separate entity, beyond himself and with no blurring between them.

Initially at least, it also seemed that the added factor of John's presence being only seasonal would help Steve to survive as he could then prepare for visitations at certain times of the year. Of course, as time wore on, John's presence became more permanent, however, at first the definite timing to John's warehouse visitations enabled Steve to think along the lines of *'Well, I'm safe for the winter so I'll carry on for now.'*

Following on from this, Steve cites 'truculence' as a reason for staying put. This I would re-term as 'stubbornness.' He is simply not the type of character to allow himself to be persecuted into any action he is reluctant to take. The ghost, or to be more accurate demon, was bullying him. There was no way Steve, given his historical and emotional 'blueprint' would budge. In Transactional Analytic terms, I was interested to observe the interplay of Steve moving between victim, survivor and *'I'm not OK, you're OK/not OK'* positions during his journey of events. I was certainly also aware of my own *'I'm not OK either'* experiencing from time to time.

Another reason Steve did not leave was an honest ownership of the excitement incited by these highly unusual circumstances and the different type of attention he was getting. This situation was affording the workforce with an unknown; a heightened stimulation of the senses and a new highly charged working environment, away from the mundane and the nocturnal grind of accepted routine. It provided a challenge that went beyond doing one's job for the night and remaining awake to do it. Whilst many people were becoming affected and involved, it was Steve who remained the focus for the activity and afforded him with a role of story teller, provider of 'evidence,' mediator between opposing opinions and to some extent the 'expert'. People were approaching him with their own stories and experiences and seeking advice. This altered his situation – changed his relationships with others – enabling him to broaden and deepen his contact with his colleagues. Steve did come home and tell me about the viewpoints and spiritual and religious stances his colleagues took – knowledge which he would not have had privy to, had none of these events taken place. He was consistently surprised and moved at the responses and empathy of others; one Christian colleague, Nathaniel, in particular, who would walk the gangways and areas praying for Steve and the one who openly sensed and dreamed about John himself. Other colleagues also took time out to undergo research, one giving him a website specifically dedicated to 'Railway ghosts.' Perhaps Steve was finally feeling stimulated in terms of being challenged and stretched to a limit he had not really encountered in his life before. I have speculated that we need to remember that Steve is an intelligent man who has not fully realised his potential in a working environment before, been at times frustrated and bored and perhaps had accumulated some sort of energy to burn off which has manifested itself into a bizarre form of psychic activity. My thoughts on this re-routing of energy and the implications of this may become clearer when I consider the accounts of psychics and mediums in part three.

It perhaps could be interpreted therefore, that this was an enriching learning experience for Steve and he received support – sometimes from unexpected sources, which sustained him during the distressing circumstances. He also felt the support of management who were of course, also involved in dealing with a highly unusual and bewildering situation which no-one had been trained to work through and resolve. Work and work people were really the only places to go with this. This is why he did not leave.

Finally and realistically, although I feel this may have been my idea rather than Steve's, there were practical issues for not leaving a job he enjoys. His age, the fact he had moved into a new relationship and was personally and financially insecure for a while meant that it simply was not practical to walk out. The haunting had commenced just six months into our relationship and we were working through learning to live together, to make compromises, to manage conflict and to generally get used to being together, in the way of all new couples. The trauma of displacement, of being forced out of a secure employment or any other life situation before one is ready to go, to have one's choices eliminated, should not be underestimated, whatever the circumstances.

Speaking some months later, Steve said: **'Recently, it's a case of do I really want this in my life? And I think recently I really don't want it anymore. I was seriously thinking about leaving my work and finding something else, but when you reach my age it's hard to get a job full time so I'm hanging on there until I either want to do something myself or I'm forced out. There's part of me can't take any more – it feels as if - You've made your point and I'm going to go.'**

Why did Steve not bring in a spiritualist or psychic to do a clearing of the building after the more 'conventional' exorcisms had failed? This, Steve says firmly is owing to his background as a Mormon. Along with Christianity and many other religions, demons are deemed to be nothing to do with deceased souls but are disturbing apparitions sent by evil forces to confuse and tempt the living away from a righteous path. Such religions advise a 'close down' to the supernatural and do not generally advocate an invitation to explore or access it. We have seen how the spiritualist Claudia was aware of this fundamental principle and did not wish her personal input into the situation to be made known to any priests.

As we know, the Mormon faith formed a significant part of Steve's life for a few years and elements of it lingered in his unconscious mind long enough to be called upon at the crisis point when he was able to banish John, albeit for a temporary period of time. Interestingly, article seven of the thirteen articles of faith doctrined by the Mormon faith states that: *'We believe in the gift of tongues, prophecy, revelation, visions, healing interpretation of tongues and so forth'* (2009). My interest was captured by the fact that *'visions...and so forth'* may well include ghosts, apparitions and an openness to their existence, albeit in this interpretation they are perceived to be messages from God, rather than anything to do with returning spirits of deceased people. So Mormons do recognise that entities exist, possibly as God has reasons to reach someone on earth and message them accordingly. Demons, however, are another matter and the Mormons will advocate a need to learn to repel anything malevolent – and this is the difference. Steve tells me he cannot understand why any person interested in spiritual matters would want to invite anything so potentially dangerous into their lives. Sadly, inexperienced people in the name of psychic experimentation will still endeavour to open themselves up to things that cannot subsequently be fully controlled or understood. Personally, it surprises me that I now find myself writing such a sentence with authority and a near sense of belief.

Of course, if Steve went along the route of pursuing his psychic abilities (if that is indeed what this is) he could have made different choices. He may have opened himself up, learned to channel his energies and perhaps in time even become an effective psychic and healer. As it is, he did not want this. Three exorcisms from a church to heal the building and rid the entity had failed and this was enough. Steve was being persecuted, attacked and injured. It was up to Steve to close himself down on a personal level in order to survive. I also considered later, that if the clearing or exorcisms did in fact work, then Steve may well have been left with the daunting task of re-considering his lost faith. If he was 'rescued' by the church and had as a result returned to his faith, then he would have had to deal with a re-evaluation of his beliefs and his life, with all the resulting implications, challenges and losses. He would, in fact, have probably been expected to return to his marriage, and to give up the 'good' things in life, for example the occasional drink or gamble. To return to a commitment to the faith would be unnerving, so additionally, to close down on all levels made sense. Of course, these thoughts were causing some ongoing anxieties for me – would I need to join Steve and develop my own belief with a resulting change in my own way of thinking and behaviour, or would I lose him altogether?

Many people desire or envy psychic ability and some strive to perfect it, but Steve rejected this. The hauntings continue – and it is up to those affected to choose their personal ways to cope. Maybe someone else, management or another colleague will invite a spiritualist in to cleanse the warehouse. Steve does not want the task. This is a powerful and persistent entity or demon with longevity – stories of a railwayman have been in existence in the area since Steve was a child. If this is a ghost, then this is not his personal ghost, even if Steve has the potential to have more access to it than many other people. It seems to us that Steve cannot 'close down' in the way he has learned to survive and simultaneously also risk 'opening up' by inviting any spiritualist – genuine, effective or not - into the workplace to deal with the entity. Ridding it is not his sole responsibility.

This makes me feel sad, for the lonely suffering of the phantom John, however, if we are in fact dealing with a demon, I acknowledge the need to leave well alone. We need to be in touch with our thoughts, feelings, fears – and our limits.

Whatever our conclusions – or lack of them - Steve describes himself as a *'The dog that saw a rainbow.'* Dogs are colour blind and cannot perceive rainbows. But, seen or not, rainbows still exist in our skies. Steve remains adamant in his views on his supernatural experiences over the past couple of years. He says: **'I don't want this to be happening to me. The main thing is I don't want it and people who say to me, "You're doing it..." what am I getting out of it? What am I getting out of it? I don't want it. I don't want it out in the open; I don't want to make a big thing over it. When it happens to me I just want to go away and lick my wounds in a private place. The only people who ask questions are the people who see me, therefore I answer questions. I don't want it. If I could give it up I'd gladly give it up. I'd give it to anybody else yesterday, I don't want it. So anybody who thinks I'm getting something out of it, like being centre of attention, like I've got to be somebody to whom something happens differently, well whatever they're thinking, I know I'm not doing this to myself and that's a big step forward for me. I know I'm not doing it to myself.'**

This was my final diary entry for the year 2008:

July 2008: *Do I believe in ghosts? Almost. I do believe that the sheer volume and weight of anecdotal material and narratives on the subject gathered from the experience of so many individuals must count for something. I have myself witnessed, albeit second hand, a supernatural experience. I do not believe that science will be able to reach any conclusions imminently on these matters but I am sure that this will not stop the need for humans to share their knowledge, beliefs, fears and fascination – ultimately I think we hold a basic primitive need for the supernatural. To me it seems that spirituality and science are two sides of the same coin – forming a whole but each looking outwards away from the other and destined never to meet face to face. Whilst they face away and I research each side I come back to just one conclusion – whilst I cannot speak for the experiences of others – for me personally, I now think John exists and that he is - a ghost.*

Here at the end of the year 2008, we are going to leave Steve's story for the moment and return to him later. Before we leave him entirely, however, I am going to end this section with the transcript of the conversation I had with my therapist, who, you may remember, I visited to reflect upon the situation on 16 July 2008. In this way I continue to focus on myself and my own responses, as a partner and as someone involved in the counselling profession.

Counsellors in Conversation

One issue I was aware of during my experiences was my need to keep working as a counsellor. I mentioned in my diary that I found my work psychologically containing as I was able to fully focus on my clients and bracket my own anxieties. I chose not to share what was happening with colleagues, as I was aware of possible judgment, particularly from one or two who possessed negative religious backgrounds. I did not want to lay myself open to any discussion or potential interpretations on my partner's mental state of mind which may have been difficult to hear. My work at the university was a safe place for me at the time and I wanted to maintain this helpful boundary. I was thereby defended. My supervisor was aware of what was occurring in my personal life and I trusted that we would together be able to hold an awareness of whether my work with clients appeared to be negatively impacted and negotiate any necessary change accordingly. Apart from a couple of friends who were aware of the ongoing situation and with whom I was able to share my feelings, there remained one other relevant place and person where I could take my experience.

I mentioned earlier that I re-visited my former therapist in the summer of 2008, with the intention of taping an interview with her to gain her perspective on the parts of our therapy when I had brought the supernatural experiences. I had had weekly sessions for a period of six and a half years and we had ended our contract eighteen months previously. I was excited and apprehensive about returning for this one off meeting and I was not sure what would emerge. I had prepared some questions beforehand. What follows is a complete transcript of the tape, with a commentary illustrating my thoughts and reactions, which I added in later.

Lou: *I'll read though all the questions first then we'll go through them one by one. OK, so the first question is what you remember about the sessions in which I did describe the events with the ghost. Then I ask what it was like for you to actually hear about at the time, any specific thoughts, feelings that you had or any physiological reactions perhaps during the sessions and any counter-transference during the sessions, and then once the sessions had ended. And then what sort of reflections you had, any thoughts or feelings or any particular changes that you had once you did reflect on these sessions, perhaps any changes in your own beliefs or your own thinking and just generally your rationale after the sessions had ended. And then finally if and how you used supervision if you remember and then just anything else that you would like to contribute.*
Therapist: *OK.*
Lou: *So if we can perhaps start with what you do remember of any of those*

sessions in which I did describe the events with the ghost. I actually remember very little about what was happening and how much had happened and how often I brought it.

Therapist: Yes, I suppose, I mean I could actually spend the whole session, the whole time that we've got talking about things that I remember. I do remember quite clearly what was going on. I have an awful lot of memory around it and the reason why I have an awful lot of memory around it is that it impacted me a lot at the time and it's interesting on lots of different levels for me so I remember first of all the big thing was Steve coming back with the scratch down his face and how that continually kept reappearing. And I suppose I remember, when it first started, there was a feeling of excitement, I felt very excited, like 'Oh God, this is a bit different from every day issues that come into a therapy room,' and I was also aware that you did your dissertation on - can't remember the exact title, but the supernatural, ghosts...

Lou: Yes, yes.

Therapist: So I was aware that I was interested that this is happening to you. And I was aware that you would be quite open to that – it's not something that you would have shut off, basically, so I was sort of holding that but at the same time and - also holding - and I'm sure we actually talked about it in the sessions - that it could be absolute total and utter projection and that projection can take on, you know, people can experience physical things from projection, some people can hear, smell, see things. I was also aware he had just split up with his wife so there was also a question mark around what is being acted out, played out, and it could be, like, suppressed feelings that are actually being acted out in some way.

Lou: So you went down very much a therapeutic route.

Therapist: Yes, projection and suppression and all of that lot. It was not as though I was split, so there was that side of me, looking at it from a purely therapeutic way...so that was that side and this happened in supervision as well as my own thinking. So there was all the therapeutic side of it as well. And in some respects, Lou, I could talk to you for a long time on, maybe it was this and bit of transference and what was he carrying from his past – and dah-de-dah and were his family trying to give him messages, you know so I could very much go down that, and we could make sense of it in that way, but then there was another side of me that at times sitting here, I felt, and I'm sure I said this to you at the time, like shivers down my spine type stuff. And I know for myself that I'm very, as a kid, I wouldn't be scared of someone coming in with guns and violence, I would be scared of the unknown, scared of ghosts, scared of supernatural, and I've had a couple of experiences growing up where I've really thought there was something not OK in my room sort of thing. And I've never been able to make sense of it – it wasn't just my experience, it was also my sister's so I have been sort of open to that...

Lou: Have you tried to make sense of it – you thought about it later on in life but haven't been able to come to any sort of rational explanation?

Therapist: No, it's like keeping it open in my mind. Yes, it's like I could still get spooked – I would definitely, definitely get spooked and I would...So I'm aware of that side of my personality that can be feeling that I'm open and in that feeling that I'm open to it and therefore attracted and I certainly as a kid growing up believed in ghosts, supernatural and the afterlife, so that is my background, that was my blueprint. I question that now. I'm more open to 'Maybe, maybe not, I don't know.' It's more like I just don't know.

It interested me to hear of my therapist's 'blue print' and that she herself had encountered something inexplicable and potentially supernatural. I was aware of the need to not become in any way distracted by any desire on my part to ask for details as this would disrupt the focus of our conversation. I was aware of feeling relief at her 'don't know' and 'staying open' position and I was aware of a similarity with my own process – the therapeutic exploration coupled with the holding of the unknown.

Lou: Yes.

Therapist: And just because it can't be proved doesn't mean it's not happening. I've got no idea.

Lou: Yes.

Therapist: So I suppose when you were talking about it I was open to both, I was open to - I held both in fact – that yes the therapeutic which is so easy to wrap it up in all of that, but the one thing that I remember was thinking, that it's hard to wrap it up when it wasn't just Steve's experience. And other people started to have the experience of the clothes racks and things starting to move.

Lou: Yes.

Therapist: Then that's when I, that's when I probably thought, 'Oooh well, gosh – what the hell is happening here?'

Lou: So if you were to wrap it up therapeutically, let's say, given Steve's background, and life transitions etc - and I know you said you could talk about that for a long time – but in brief...

Therapist: Briefly, OK...

Lou: What would be your rationale if you were coming from the purely psychological viewpoint?

Therapist: OK, that Steve had just split up with his wife that he'd been with, since God knows – I think they'd been teenage sweethearts.

Lou: Yes, that's right, it was over thirty years.

Therapist: Which is a lot. And it had been pretty volatile to say the least, where he was expressing a lot of anger and things within the marriage. Suddenly he is with you, there wasn't that expression of being that angry and also he'd split up with his wife and so it was like, because he was a blokey bloke and not expressing very much of his feelings at that time, I could put it down to OK, it's suppression of feelings being acted out, being projected out, and I'm sure if I had all the you know, had it in sequence, then I'd be able to go yes, well that would be Steve projecting – stuff on his face, the scratch on his face, well I could put that down

to – if I were wrapping it up therapeutically – that he was somehow doing it to himself, as a way of expressing his pain basically.
Lou: Anything else at all or are those basically the two?

I had particularly wanted to check out here that I was not 'missing' anything further that could be deemed to be significantly therapeutic. Projection and the result of trauma or life change were the two basic potential triggers I had considered regarding Steve's situation and I wanted to be sure that I had not overlooked any other psychological aspects to think about.

Therapist: I think those are the two main things really. And it also got him the attention and the support that he needed to go through the difficult time he was going through. Losing his family as well and starting a relationship, so I could do that – and he was getting that without having to be lying on the floor all screaming and shouting and having tantrums sort of thing. I'm also aware - I think he was a Mormon as well.
Lou: That's right.
Therapist: So I was also aware that he was very suggestible in his belief system as well and therefore something supernatural happening – a bit like me growing up with that – it's more suggestible to someone like him than to - say a friend of mine who would throw it out the window immediately – don't be ridiculous – she'd just laugh, so I was aware of that so yeah, those.
Lou: Yes. Is there anything else you were aware of physiologically in the sessions – you mentioned shivers going up and down your spine. Anything else going on sort of bodily?
Therapist: Yes, I think fear – coupled with, yes fear and excitement – actually excitement that – oh gosh this is different – don't often get – I've NEVER had anyone bringing supernatural to therapy.
Lou: So it was new.
Therapist: Yes, that's right and it was interesting to think of it. Yeah, it was new and it was like – how am I going to see this? So but, yes, so excitement, fear and I was left with an after taste. I was left with an after taste on a regular occurrence, basically – so it wasn't something that – if I had another client following you, then it was easier to put down – but it was easy to pick up again and return to that sort of like, looking over my shoulder. And I can remember, late at night brushing my teeth before I went to bed – there was more of like – ooooh, not liking to put my head down and have my back turned, basically. And I know that that's part of me, as I said to you before – so I was aware that's my stuff, definitely the volume was turned up big time if I'd seen you that day and we'd talked about ghosts...
Lou: So you carried it with you quite strongly.
Therapist: Yes, there was that and I was surprised at how I carried that and that was one of the reasons I took it to supervision because it was like oooh gosh, it was poking that part of me sort of thing.
Lou: So having to separate out your stuff from my stuff.
Therapist: Absolutely, yes, exactly. And just one more thing on the physical,

you sent me an e-mail afterwards – after we'd finished in fact – just to update me on things that had happened and I look at my e-mails last thing at night and I happened to read it – like last thing at night and I can remember feeling really like 'Oh my God' – feeling very spooked from what had been written and holding the rational side but also again there was a very strong looking over my shoulder. So there are the two but I am aware that I can go down that route myself. It is, as I said at the beginning – it is something that I... that would be my fear as a child not guns and whatever but something supernatural so it fed in beautifully to my stuff, my fears, my conscious fears, yes.

Lou: *And yet I also remember in our sessions that you rationalised quite a lot by saying you used to work on night shifts and it was very easy for colleagues to get spooked – I remember quite a lot of that coming up in the sessions.*

Therapist: *Yes, that's right, I'm glad you reminded me, yeah, that's true and maybe that's because I've done night duties myself and really aware of at night time, silence, nothing is going on and people's imaginations running away with them and I think that's one of the reasons why I can get spooked, as my imagination is vivid – and actually he seems quite an imaginative guy – he doesn't seem you know, black and white.*

Lou: *He's very creative.*

Therapist: *Exactly. That's right. And then that mass hysteria bit so that was the other bit, you know everybody basically getting on the band wagon and getting spooky and I've seen that happen lots of times within institutions at night time. People spooking each other basically and like a sound or whatever can get amplified beyond belief, so I was aware of that and that's how I sort of rationalised my own spook as well.*

This ties up nicely with my reflections on group hysteria which comes up later when I also explore what may be a natural desire to experience or believe in ghosts or the potential to see a ghost. I am also aware of how the significance of night-time itself may affect people, causing a degree of suggestibility despite the fact that the warehouse itself is brilliantly and artificially lit at night as there are no windows. Pop music also blares out through a sound system and contributes to the sense that this is the last place one would expect to feel spooked, despite the vastness of the place and isolation of the individual night workers.

Lou: *Do you think there was something in that about how you were protecting your inner kid?*

Therapist: *That rationalising?*

Lou: *Yes, that looking wider, certainly we need to look at rational explanations.*

Therapist: *Yes.*

Lou: *I was kind of wondering something about you needing to protect yourself, particularly if you were feeling spooked after the sessions.*

Therapist: *I think because I know I can go much more down the spooked line than to rationalise it, like I have to work hard to rationalise it, so yes, it was good to have some theory on whatever was happening – making it a little more rational,*

logical to myself. Don't think it was me soothing my kid, I think it was more me soothing me at that time.
Lou: Yes.
Therapist: And also looking at it in a way – wanting to be open to it on lots of different levels I suppose. I was also aware of what impact it was having obviously – what impact it was having on you – and so I was aware that this would tantalise and excite you as well and so was I picking up on some of that from you.
Lou: Mmmm, absolutely.
Therapist: It titillated my - something that we can't make sense of.
Lou: Was there anything else that you remember about how I was during that time?
Therapist: Excited.
Lou: Right.
Therapist: It was the time that I saw you most animated in your sessions – you were definitely – this was exciting for you and it was something, whereas you could be really timid – suddenly you became – like the white witch – if that makes sense – and had power. So I saw you becoming empowered at that time.
Lou: Right, that's interesting. Anything else at all or is that basically the main thing that you remember at that point?
Therapist: That was the main thing – because it was such a contrast and the relationship with Steve was very empowering full stop anyway for you. But this was another area where you could shine in some respects, so I was aware of that. (Pause.)
Lou: It sounds like when we were meeting it was quite a new and exciting experience for you to move into. (Indistinct.)
Therapist: No, around the ghosts and things, sometimes you would be pissed off and 'Oh it's happening again' but actually it was OK, it wasn't a big deal and at that time in therapy it was like great, Lou's getting angry about this and you were able to say it to him – so that all felt very empowering in some respects.

This surprised me. I had indeed been aware of communicating excitement until I remembered that the majority of anger, fear and bodily symptoms had occurred for me after the therapy sessions had concluded. No doubt I would have had much more to share had I continued with therapy.
Lou: What was it like when we ended our therapy and you were obviously left with – the ending – which we managed very well – but obviously that situation was ongoing and I'm just wondering how you felt about that? If indeed you had feelings about that, or if it was really part of the ending.
Therapist: Yes because it's interesting because earlier on I was just thinking I also saw it as you separating out from me as well, a time of you separating out from me and very much attaching to Steve and everything that went with him at that time. So no I didn't feel, I didn't feel left with anything actually – like anything was unfinished and left in the room. No I wasn't going to find out what happened but I wasn't attached to it you know, enough to sort of be phoning you up and

going 'Oooh, Lou, what's happened,' and such and such...but when I got your e-mail – with sort of the next bit of the story in it – I could feel myself being pulled back into it and feeling the same sort of fear, excitement, titillation, interest and actually when you said you were going to write a book as well – I thought well – it would be very readable because its exciting and you've got not only your personal interest but also as a therapist as well you know all that side to it – so it felt really rich – 'Oooh I wonder what would come out of that' – but no, so, really I was OK.

Lou: Yes, yes. Is there anything else you want to say about how it was for you after the sessions had ended? Reflections, thoughts, feelings, any changes in your beliefs or thinking and your rationale after the sessions – and I know you've said a lot about that – is there anything else you want to add to that before we look at how you used supervision?

Therapist: I think as I said, very much so that I had therapy on one side and that's what I was wanting to engage and I think I brought both of them a little bit together in here with you anyway – the 'Oooh I just got shivers down my spine' sort of thing but when I went out yes, I was holding the two really, rational and scientific. No my belief system didn't change because I felt open to it and I stayed open and that's how I still feel now really.

Lou: So did you actually take this to supervision – I presume you did – so how did you actually use supervision?

Therapist: Really it was about separating out what was my stuff and my stuff from the past, my belief system there around – very much supernatural and ghosts, being drawn to that side of things but then sort of finding a rationale – a therapeutic rationale of what might be going on – and what I was aware of within the sessions – it was group as well – the other people had all sorts of reactions to it as well which was quite interesting the fact that they were – some people were getting spooked – it depends on what their belief system was – that's one of the things I was very aware of people responded differently to whatever belief system they held. And my supervisor didn't feel any spooky bit at all – it was just purely and utterly rationalised in some sort of therapeutic – and was open to other people – but other people who had more religious beliefs – they were the ones that were really spooked – so it was interesting. And also brought up church every Sunday for me – I was aware of that.

Lou: In that particular context, did you come across anybody else who had any supernatural experiences or had any clients who'd presented with such stuff?

Therapist: No nothing at all, nothing came up at all – that's why it became quite a sort of fascinating – 'Oooh, any more on the ghost, what's happened with the ghost...' People would be interested to know and wouldn't be talking about what is Steve projecting out now but more around 'Oooh, has he had any more marks on his face?' – so I was aware of the excitement and how stimulated people got with this sort of subject really.

Lou: Did you find the attention seemed to go onto the ghost, not onto Steve and not onto me?

Therapist: Yes. Absolutely, yes, yes. Even though I had that and I did talk about the fact that you had done your dissertation on that. Yes, obviously that was an area of interest full stop for you. So my supervisor – that was the group – but my supervisor was 'OK so come back to Lou and what does this mean for Lou in the relationship.'

Lou: I'm quite surprised actually because – usually it feels like everybody has a ghost story somewhere along the line – so to actually know that there people have not come across it either personally or -

Therapist: Ahh, they might have personally. Sorry, I went with the client work there – no they hadn't in client work.

Lou: Ahh, I see, yes.

Therapist: Yes, stories did come up.

Lou: It's a very universal thing – it does attract people.

Therapist: Yes, it does.

Lou: Desire as well – the desire to see or to believe.

Therapist: That's right, that's right. But no-one had had a client that was coming in with supernatural.

Lou: So I was unique!

Therapist: Totally and utterly unique! (We both laugh.)

Lou: And I still am by the sound of this.

Therapist: Yeah, yes!

Lou: OK. So I think that covers everything that I'm interested in – it's been really, really useful. Is there anything else you want to say about anything that you remember or anything you want to add generally? (Pause.)

Therapist: I was just thinking of the split between rationalising therapeutically and also and as you just said and as I was saying earlier on people's belief systems and desire to want there to be something after life basically. Want there to be something else rather than this realm of existence, dimension or whatever and I was just thinking of when the exorcism happened, a couple of times I think...

Lou: There were three, from the Church of England, yes.

Therapist: Three, OK and yes it sort of brought some more – gosh, sinister element to it but at the same time I also felt a split between the two camps – could have been brought together by an exorcism because it was sort of like – if he has belief in priests, God and all of that – which he had grown up with even thought he might not have had it at the time –

Lou: He didn't actually grow up with it though, that came later, in his twenties.

Therapist: Oh, OK.

Lou: And he shopped around a few religions.

Therapist: Right.

Lou: And settled onto the Mormon one for a while.

Therapist: Right – there was a search.

Lou: As a child I think there was a Bible in the house, but they weren't church goers or anything like that.

Therapist: Oh, OK. So when the exorcism actually happened, it was like, whether it was psychological or whether it was supernatural, it's like, it would have, the exorcism would have lent itself to both of them just in terms of what he would believe at that time and everything would be fine because this priest had come and splashed some holy water.
Lou: But it didn't work.
Therapist: Yeah.

Here I was checking out the themes of universal appeal, the apparent rarity of the phenomena coming into the therapeutic context, the 'blue print' or belief systems and desire for rituals to 'work' which individuals may hold. Many of the themes I had reflected upon were coming together.

Lou: Did you ever have any thinking along the lines of mental ill health and perhaps brain damage or anything along those lines?
Therapist: With Steve? I think I actually asked you about had he had any accidents or anything and nothing was coming out so I sort of put that to bed in some respects but yes that did go through my mind and like I know that some of my questioning to you was around Steve and I certainly had questions around his mental health. I wasn't sure how stable he was at that time and I had – I suppose – it was more for me my focus was very much on you actually rather than on him and at times with him I felt very protective around you with him. However, I was also aware that you came out of your shell hugely during that time and although it might not have been particularly healthy, sometimes I was concerned at times for you in it – so yeah, there was a concern in it about mental health. And his lack of sleep because he wasn't sleeping properly and I know that when you don't sleep properly there will be lots of hallucinations.
Lou: Sure.
Therapist: So there was that as well.
Lou: So what's it like for you to be talking about this now?
Therapist: I suppose I'm enjoying meeting you again and it feels quite a long time ago. And I'm sure that when you go I'm going to be going – 'Oh yes, oh God fancy not mentioning this and that!' (We laugh) and whatever, but I can put those thoughts and feelings down and e-mail you...
Lou: Just get in touch or ring or e-mail, or we can meet again – which again may happen if something comes up with my writing but you've said loads - it's really tied in with a lot of what I've been writing – it's been really helpful.
Therapist: Oh good!
Lou: And I'm really struck by how much you remember as well – and I think I feel very valued by that. It feels like – it was six and a half years but Steve was very much – 'Well, will she remember anything?' Of course she will – six and a half years and this is what I'm going to find out, but you've obviously remembered a lot about the situation – a lot about what I told you, so it feels like the relationship was important – what happened to me was important – so it was a very containing experience for me.

Therapist: *Oh good, I'm glad. Yes, I remember very well.*

I felt overall that many of the issues I had so far expressed in my research and writing were tied up well in this encounter and I left feeling reassured and energised. We can also see how the therapeutic relationship works – with transference, supervision and above all, the benefits around feeling valued in a non judgemental relationship, all forming significant themes.

******

Throughout 2008, I undertook some research about spiritual matters and mental health issues on a deeper level in order to try to make some further sense of Steve's experiences. Some of this is detailed in the following section. I am then able to further reflect on Steve's situation later whilst holding a new awareness of the wider possibilities pertaining to the impact of mental health, spiritual healing and the work of mediums and psychics.

Carousels from which clothes are hung. These are often reported to move unaided

T86 – The most powerfully haunted area of the warehouse. The fire door is at the end of the gangway

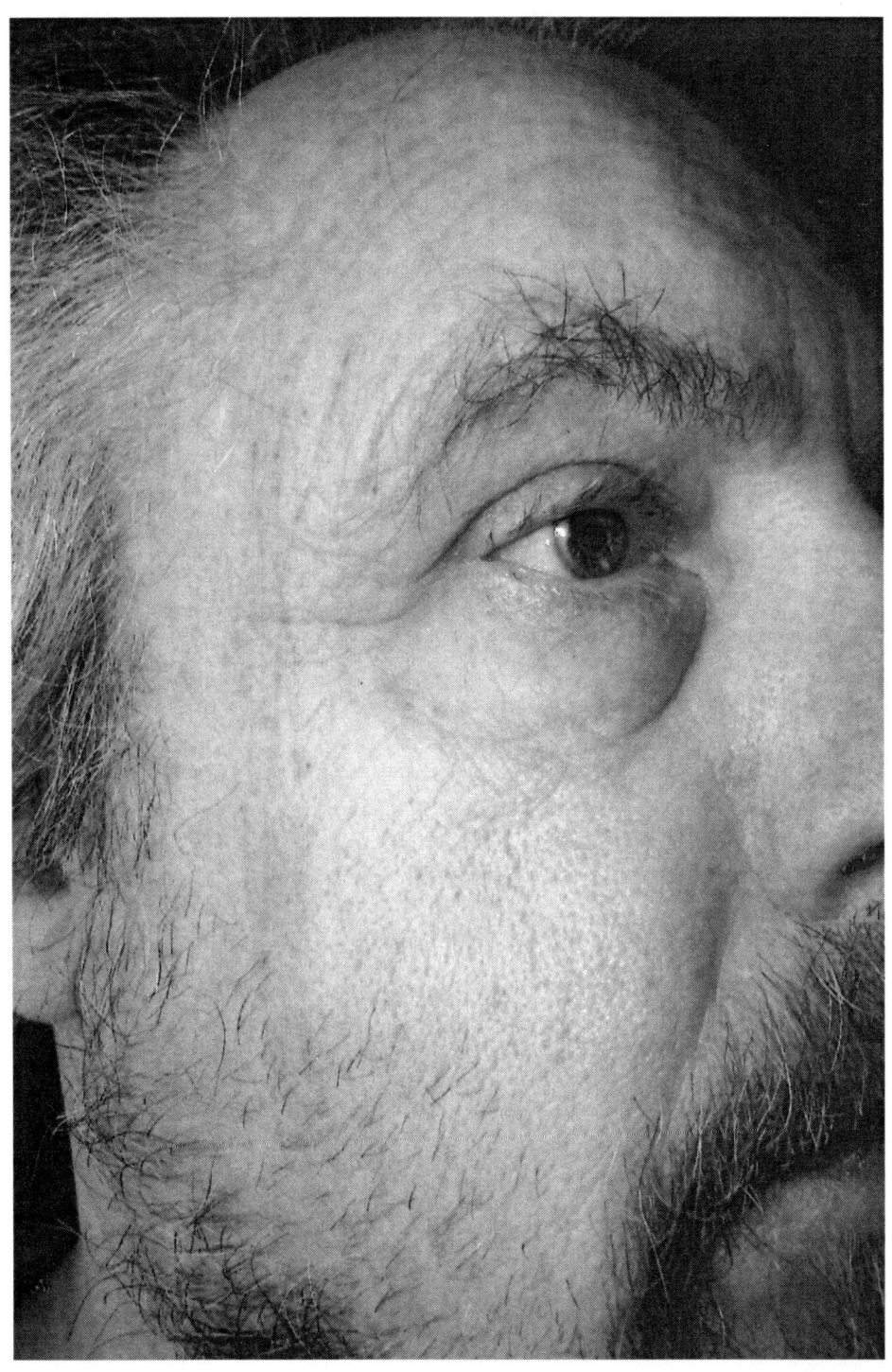

The strange scratch marks on Steve's face after being 'hit.' The position of them never varied

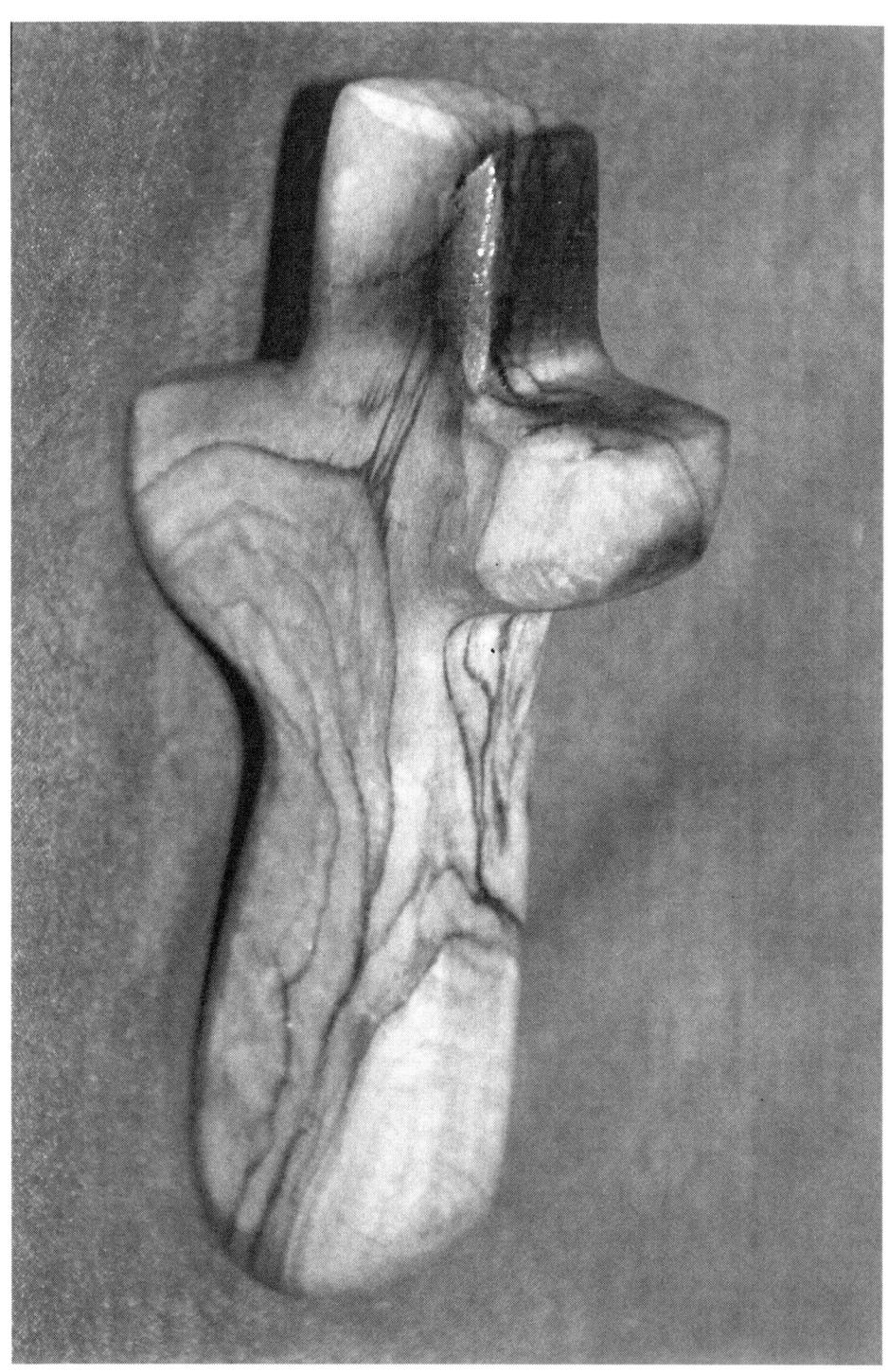

The wooden cross given to Steve by the priest. It is blackened and burned in the top corner

Steve's artistic impression of the ghost, 'John'

PART THREE

PSYCHIC OR PSYCHOTIC?

'There is more to human existence than sheer material existence' From 'Why God Won't Go Away' by A Newberg, E D'Aquili and V Rause.

Belief and Desire

'God is literally a state of mind' From 'Can We Be Good Without God?' by Robert Buckman

Do you believe in ghosts? This is a question that most of us have either asked or been asked of since early childhood. Other questions which may provoke a variety of reactions include whether we believe that adults are really capable of sexually abusing small children, whether trauma can have an extreme long term emotional impact, whether the holocaust actually happened, or whether man really did land on the moon back in 1969. Our personal history, access to information and opinions gathered through dialogue with others forms our beliefs. What we believe influences our answers.

In his book *'Pseudoscience and the Paranormal'* (2003) Terrence Hines raises that *'Truth is independent of belief and that it is belief that determines the structure of reality.'* It is of course, widely acknowledged by the majority of therapists that our personal worlds are constructed through our set of belief systems. Cognitive behavioural therapists may for example cite that what can be learned can be unlearned and that it makes logical sense likewise that what can be believed, can be 'unbelieved.' 'Belief' also perhaps suggests an element of choice and flexibility – after all, a person's beliefs may change over the course of their lifetime. The ability for the brain to alter its cognitive and neurological brain patterns which therapists will be aware of when treating conditions such as obsessive compulsive disorder or phobia is evident.

As we have seen in part one of this book, if the experience of abuse is denied for the child by the others around her then it may be logical to re-route, deny or 'forget' ones own subjective reality. Likewise, what are the implications for those individuals who see spirits or ghosts but those realities are denied by those who cannot share such perceptions? I will be looking in this section at the conflicting realities between science and spirituality, mysticism and mental health and finally how naturally psychic children may struggle in a material world that denies them their experience. Firstly, however, we need to do some ground work on the natural inclinations of human nature when it comes to belief and group responses.

What, then, is the nature and purpose of belief for the human being? I would suggest that belief in the human condition fulfils some of the following historical and contemporary purposes:

Coping with fear of the dead - It can be argued that a basic emotional response to a dead body is necessary for the survival of the human race. For prehistoric people, emotions such as unease and disgust would have triggered them into taking practical action with regard to the disposal of swiftly rotting corpses and therefore preventing the onset of disease amongst the living. It seems to have been a natural process in early cultures to have buried their dead with tools and other possessions, indicating a belief in an afterlife or a resurrection when such items would once more be required by the deceased. Neanderthals were buried in a foetal position to be perhaps 'born again.' In the book *'The Spiritual Brain'* (2001) the authors, Mario Beauregard and Denyse O'Leary, make the important suggestion that an afterlife in these particularly early times may well have been an *'assumption'* and not merely a belief and therefore the fear of death becomes obsolete. Beauregard and O'Leary argue that religion is culturally universal with a belief in a land of the dead being widespread across the world so *'it must be a genetically inherited instinct.'*

Buckman in his book *'Can We Be Good Without God?'* (2002), which I have made reference to extensively here, agrees, raising the possibility that this is a human urge or instinct, a coping strategy, rather than a conscious choice: *'...the action of believing in an external deity performs the function of a coping strategy in the human psyche.'* He argues that religion in particular gives people *'ready made'* and shared cultural ways of doing this.

On the whole, it is a very human instinct to fear death. Religion, belief and ritual take their place as a way of coping with this anxiety. One way to combat this anxiety is the need to place the dead into a neatly boundaried environment, preferably with the assistance of a relevant burial ritual.

The need to stave off evil - Rituals are significant in most cultures not only as a way of marking life transitions – birth, marriage, death, but also act as a way of warding off evil entities. Exorcisms are an obvious example of this. In most cultures, rituals generally fulfil the needs of providing comfort, a sense of order and hope for improvement in the life condition. Additionally there exists an instinct for humans to feel that they have done everything possible to stave off unwanted entities and earn rewards from benevolent deities.

Rescue and responsibility - Linked in with this idea of protection, I would suggest is rescue – a need for the human being to move from the victim position with the aid of a rescuing higher power, deity or spiritual person perceived to be more authoritative. Buckman cites that: *'It is the strong hope that we all have for salvation and a saviour.'* Many therapists at one time or another have been elevated into this position, mostly unrealistically, by their client's hopeful projections. If, however, clients do hold a fundamental healthy belief that therapists will aid them in their healing, then this will potentially be helpful when it comes to therapy 'working.' If they do not hold this faith, or hold the hope that the therapist will 'rescue' them without believing in their own potential for healing, the therapeutic encounter may potentially be more complex. Buckman argues that a desire to believe means absolving ourselves of responsibility. Life's problems and dilemmas can be resolved though application of a set of rules or code of behaviour. People can blame fate, or a higher power, clients can be 'cured' or not 'cured' according to their faith. Dr Edith Fiore, writing about spiritual possession puts forward an idea that her clients in particular may be able to blame their spirit possessors for some, if not all of their behaviours and be tempted to absolve themselves of the responsibility for more negative aspects of their life choices or addictions. We look further at Fiore's interesting work later.

Belief as an inherent need - Everyone dies. The prospect of some sort of life after death is quite simply, universally appealing. A desire for a continuity between life and death fuels belief in many people. Such beliefs cannot be proved or substantiated by factual data. Definite proof spells the death of the belief. It seems from this assumption that hard scientific evidence and religious belief will never sit comfortably together as one threatens to challenge or destroy the other.

Buckman argues that belief is an urge innate within the human psyche, that *'myths are part of the human mindset.'* By our belief in God or the supernatural we are, therefore, doing what comes naturally. A belief in God, therefore, or some sort of afterlife helps mankind face a natural fear of death and the vast unknowns within the universe. Quite simply, Buckman cites that human beings have *'always employed the activity that we call "believing" in order to conceptualize, understand and cope with the world about us.'*

Inspiration - Behaviour and the way humans order and illustrate their world are influenced by belief. Buckman cites art and the creation of cathedrals as positive examples directly influenced by religious belief. A sense of inspiration may be interpreted as evidence that such creativity emanates from an external source. He tells us that the emphasis, however, lies with the response of the person who is creating such works, rather than with any external divine intervention. This is, therefore, an internal process. *'The focus is not on the existence of the presence of an external divinity, but on the change of the individual's psychological state into a more spiritual frame.'* Again we can see a link here with the therapeutic process – the client responds to changes within their inner world, given the right conditions or interventions provided by the therapist. On the flip side of the positives of creativity and healing inspired by a sense of divine intervention, Buckman cites wars, torture and destruction as negative impacts caused by religious faiths.

Buckman concludes that: *'In simple practical terms, belief may be defined as:*

any set of perceptions which are sustained by a person as a consistent attitude or view and which extend beyond any factual information available, or even contrary to relevant factual information. Therefore, by that definition, beliefs are systems of thought that cannot be proved or disproved.' He goes on to state that: *'Building a system of becauses quells the anxieties we feel when we meet a cluster of whys.'*

So to summarise, as humans we need belief, we need hope, and we need the possibility of rescue. If we consider the basic fairy tale innate in our culture, in which the princess is saved from the dragon by the hero, or the films directed by Steven Spielberg or George Lucas who use the theme of wish fulfilment in much of their work, we can see how our needs are satisfied as we want Darth Vador to achieve redemption following evil acts, Indiana Jones to escape ridiculously perilous situations and we certainly want ET to go home! We hold the hope – and the belief - during the stories, during the films, that all this will happen.

Buckman then further goes on to categorise the different types and levels of belief we may hold. These are:

Complete or total belief – This is an absolute state, completely integral to personality and ways of behaving. Day to day living will be impacted by the belief of the individual, for example those following religious orders or who are exceptionally or ritualistically devout.

Partial belief – This affects those who are *'ready and capable of believing in the object, but most of the time the individual does not hold that belief as part of their daily life.'* Such a belief system can be shed without undue disruption to daily life. I would suggest that counsellors arguably need to hold this position in each session entering into each session without *'desire, understanding or memory'* (Bion cited in Casement, 1994). This is essentially an agnostic state, for example one which affects most people who celebrate Christmas or take part in various transitional rituals in churches but think little about faith at other times of the year.

Contextual belief – This encompasses belief to a slight extent, for example in the pursuit of alternative or occult therapies, comprising astrology, the tarot, crystal gazing, palmistry and the various ways of gaining contact with the dead. *'Many people, for example, feel that they do partly belief in the ghosts or in spirits, or that contact can be made with people who have died,'* (Buckman). We have already seen how there may be an element of this when we consider the rumours of ghostly sightings of a railway man in Steve's childhood play areas and how the warehouse is now being cited as a definitive source of supernatural activity – even by some of the non-believers and sceptics.

Beliefs of childhood – Rewards and punishment and belief in figures that can be used to reinforce and teach children acceptable social behaviour for example Santa Claus, the tooth fairy or the monster under the bed. I am reminded of the link with the experience of childhood sexual abuse perpetrated as the trusted adult advises the child that this is 'our secret' and perhaps 'you are bad or something will happen to you/your family/your pets if you tell.' This reinforces the child's belief in the unshakeable power of the adult. A literal belief disperses with age and psychologically a five year old who holds absolute belief in Santa Claus will be treated significantly differently from a forty year old who holds the same belief. Similarly a child who holds the responsibility for being abused may be able to unlearn any belief that she was 'bad' for being abused, given the right healing conditions.

Beliefs of small minorities – for example those who believe they have been abducted and experimented upon by aliens. A select few holding specific beliefs – this would include some small religious groups who live as isolated communities.

Superstitions – *'Behind superstitions there is a belief in some form of indefinable, ineffable force that needs to be placated and propitiated'* (Buckman). We have seen how Steve was given crosses to take to work for protection, for example. One was given to him by his colleague Paula, who is a regular churchgoer and the wooden one was given to Steve by the priest. The origins for superstitious belief probably lie in animism, one of the earliest belief systems, when power was invested in the natural world of sun, moon, stars, rainbows, thunderstorms, significant animals and other natural phenomena. Once humans became more sophisticated, realised their potentialities and dominance over nature, however, the need for animistic belief was mostly replaced by alternative systems. According to Buckman, however, the premise for superstition is similar to organised belief systems – to cater for a need to gain comfort and to stave off evil.

Whilst it is evident that religious belief may endow people with feelings of calm, peace and goodwill, my sense at the moment is that the supernatural in terms of ghosts inciting fear, trauma and causing confusion does the opposite. This is unless individuals or groups are actively seeking out the spirit world for their own purposes or in an attempt to aid others, for example through channelled mediumship. Whilst Buckman argues that *'...the development of myths, legends, belief systems, and religions as humankind's attempt to understand the natural order of the world,...'* I would suggest that supernatural phenomena may be arguably less defined and more representative of chaos. We can therefore understand the belief that entities could be an opposing force to the one for good, for example a Christian God. Are ghosts also more intrusive than God? Although there are examples of people becoming Christians in sudden, drastic ways, on the whole I would suggest that God is sought out and invited into our lives, certainly more easily if the believer has a sound religious blueprint from which to explore. Ghosts on the other hand, apart from the hopeful few who actively seek out their presence through ghost hunting or spiritualism, seem to be more unexpected, more intrusive and it is certainly difficult to make sense of any purpose of those who appear to be malevolent in intent. My feelings at the present time, certainly given Steve's experiences, are that ghosts represent disorder.

The desire to seek them out, however, has continued over the centuries. Ghost hunting groups and TV programmes prevail and even for people who are not interested by such activities an attraction to 'alternative' therapies and methods that are not regulated by hard scientific evidence have increased in popularity.

Even today studies in astrology, dowsing, past life regression and various holistic and spiritual healings continue to fuel the public imagination and influence the lives of those who choose to explore such paths.

Myself, I connect with the rationale of sceptics such as Hines and Buckman who argue strongly from the Humanist stance. Their arguments are undeniably logical and carry a lot of rational weight. They are clear in their opinions that 'supernatural' experiences occur owing to environmental or biological causes and how this may be happening given the combination of brain activity and electromagnetic stimulus which we go onto explore soon. Yet I cannot help but conclude that neither of them has ever seen a ghost nor had their own belief systems violently disrupted, which is turn leaves the hauntee with the dilemma of whether or not to carry forward any sort of cognitive belief in ghosts, whether the entity is benign or destructive. The perception from sceptics also often concurs with the view that many psychic people prostitute their talents when it comes to demonstrating their skills; that money is to be made and the public are to be exploited. I am left pondering on the 'ordinary' people, those who have no interest or desire to ring radio shows, be on television or make a living from professed psychic ability. When there is no financial gain or fame involved. Those people who have been haunted but keep their experiences and perceptions to themselves. Those who still have to live alongside their ghosts.

Group Belief

'The destructive potential of groups is equal to their therapeutic promise' From 'Trauma and Recovery' by Judith Herman.

Attitudes to hauntings are indeed interesting. Lee (2007) describes people who have seen ghosts as 'lucky.' It was also noticeable to me that a firm believer in ghosts, Steve's colleague Bernie, speaks in August 2007 of his positive sense of excitement and joy about his own brush with the entity at the warehouse during his sudden battle with the freezing sensations and the cobwebs. He says: *'I felt slightly scared but also very excited and overjoyed that I had had what I believe to be a supernatural experience. I only wish I had stayed in the aisle instead of running out. I have always believed that if I was ever in that situation I would keep calm and try and communicate but unfortunately my bottle went and I made a hasty retreat. But I have no doubts that I had a supernatural experience.'* Desire for either the individual or more widely the group to take part, share and be excited by supernatural experiences seems often to be strong. A need for witnesses to collude with such events seems similarly powerful. As we have seen, there exists a need perhaps for something more than what we already possess physically, materialistically, emotionally and above all temporarily, whilst we are alive.

For the group, this desire can turn up the volume and incite a need for the witnessing of hard 'evidence' of supernatural activity, once a general awareness has been ignited in a particular environment or context. Hines refers to collective belief incidents occurring within the group as *'collective delusion, also known as mass hysteria',* and that such delusion or hysteria accounts for *'a situation in which a significant part of the population of an area, which can be as small as a single building or as large as a nation, becomes convinced that some strange event is taking place for which there is no immediately obvious explanation.'*

Mass hysteria at its most powerful can be illustrated in Arthur Miller's play *'The Crucible,'* (1953) which details the Salam witch trials in the late seventeenth century. As a group of young women denounce members of their own community, condemning them as witches and thereby to death, we see how the situation escalates beyond control in this increasingly volatile exchange:

'Betty: (calling out hysterically and with great relief) I saw Martha Bellows with the Devil!
Abigail: I saw Goody Sibber with the Devil! (it is rising to a great glee)
Putnam: The marshal, I'll call the marshal!
Betty: I saw Alice Barrows with the Devil!...
Abigail: I saw Goody Hawkins with the Devil!
Betty: I saw Goody Bibber with the Devil!
Abigail: I saw Goody Booth with the Devil!
On their ecstatic cries. The Curtain falls.'

How far, therefore, will people concur with the theory that there is a ghost on the night shift in the warehouse and how much of this is delusional? We have seen how some of Steve's colleagues have been directly or partially affected by the supernatural activity in the warehouse, mostly through the experiencing of their own senses. It seems from the evidence presented that one or two may have genuinely shared Steve's experiences of John, although not so clearly or directly as Steve himself. I would also suggest, however - and Steve strongly agrees - that others are caught up in very real states of suggestibility, fuelled by anxiety, over active imaginations and a need or desire to contribute to the group experience. No doubt some of Steve's colleagues are more suggestible than others through the blueprint of their own belief systems, whether religious, or having had previous experience of events perceived to be of supernatural origin. We can understand how factual evidence may become obsolete in the face of a desire to believe. Indeed, Buckman agrees that *'Suggestibility is no respecter of scientific status.'*

He also observes that *'crowds are more readily motivated by emotions than they are by reason.'* What, however, is the definition of a crowd? Le Bon, cited in Buckman, wrote on the subject, suggesting that a group of people does not form a crowd but is composed of a number of people who maintain their own individuality. Once a stimulus or event occurs which cause the individuals in the group to *'subjugate their own differing individual decisions and behavioural patterns into a common frame…they become a crowd.'* Buckman points out that this is an unconscious process – people do not suddenly decide to become a crowd. The crowd holds power; thereby individuals or smaller groups may be elevated, manipulated or annihilated. Crowds may unite to cause others to be stoned to death; torn apart by the mob or less fatally but still dramatically, the tribal angst or celebration of the football crowd may cause havoc. Political uprisings occur, the Bastille is stormed and the Light Brigade charges towards certain destruction, all driven by the force of the tribal or crowd influence.

Steve holds a fear of being rejected and destroyed by the group of his colleagues who have the potential to become a persecutory crowd. What may partly be saving him from this, however, is what Le Bon has explored as *'prestige.'* This comprises the perceived qualities that leaders have to hold in order to survive in their role as leader. Steve, whilst he may not be personally liked by everyone on the shift, is undoubtedly a leader, not only owing to the longevity of his employment with the firm, but also as his role as the sole Union representative on the night shift and as a trainer. Significantly, however, it could also be through a 'taking no prisoners' personality which lends others to hold him in a degree of what Le Bon terms as *'social value.'* On a practical level, his story is being heard by the majority, corroborated with by some and the scars he carries on his face are clearly visible. This 'evidence' will of course also be helpful to his claims.

Let us consider other factors which may be influencing the other workers to share, or partly share, Steve's more dominant experience of the ghost in the workplace. Buckman posits that *'Ideas, beliefs, and emotions can be transmitted to large numbers of people very quickly, but there is a necessary precondition and that can be termed 'suggestibility' or 'impressionability' or even 'persuadability.'* Stage tricks or conjuring are an obvious example and once more we may consider the influence of spiritualist illusion popular in the Victorian age when 'ghosts' were mysteriously conjured out of cupboards, mediums were somewhat violently possessed by the dead and ectoplasm was produced in abundance. Whether it is a decision made to discover an image of Mother Teresa's face in a cinnamon bun, spot Elvis in a supermarket or to see a vision of Princess Diana whilst in the queue to sign a book of condolence following her death, the desire to believe, whether conscious or unconscious is illustrated. It is becoming evident that desire and attraction to the supernatural are significant.

Not only is it possible to be swept up in the mass desire of the crowd, but also the desire to conform to the group or to the sub group within the larger group, is a powerful one. A need for acceptance born out of social organisation is a basic instinct. If a group of people are reporting sensing a ghost in the warehouse, then for some there will develop an active wish to follow this belief, for others to avoid it and for yet more in another sub group to deride it. The power of persuasion, coupled with the nature of individual personality and how susceptible this may be to the influence of more powerful others are to be held in mind.

It is necessary to consider all of these factors when exploring group illusion or 'mass hysteria.' It is noticeable, however, that Hines, in his collective delusion theorising, focuses chiefly on the 'Sick Building Syndrome' phenomena and other purely physical symptoms, whilst little mention is made of psychological examples. In our case, however, there remains strong evidence of other workers sharing a genuine personal awareness of a ghostly presence in the warehouse themselves with accompanying physical sensations. Whilst Steve may be the focal stone which hits the water, it seems that some of his peers are caught up in the ripples within the pool.

Given such circumstances and reflecting therapeutically, let us consider what Steve would need from the group and from his environment, in order to heal. Trauma specialist Judith Herman tells us that *'if the environment encourages and supports the person, you can avoid the worst of it'*, and when illustrating cases of traumatised individuals, she informs us that the first task is to ensure the safety of the survivor, both physically and within the environment. This of course, provides a problem in the case of Steve as it appears to be the environment itself that is triggering the trauma. Herman goes on to advise: *'In the aftermath of trauma, the survivor must assess the degree of continued threat and decide what sort of precautions are necessary. She must also decide what actions she wishes to take against her attacker...she may feel confused and ambivalent herself and may find her ambivalence reflected in the contradictory opinions of friends, lovers or family.'* In Steve's case, contradictory opinions clearly emanate from all of these sources, in addition to the diverging perspectives from his colleagues. Attitudes and varying degrees in belief in what is occurring is no doubt a subject of debate and disagreement amongst those possessing knowledge of the situation. Further ambivalence may even be present in the question of who is the real victim here - that the needs of the 'poor ghost' or lost wandering entity may even overtake the necessity in supporting Steve and result in the shunning of him as helpless and hopeless 'victim.' Whilst this often occurs for example in the cases of rape, when for some people it becomes more psychologically comfortable to employ a defensive stance and place blame on the victim, it is perhaps less likely to occur in this case. But it could happen. We have indeed observed how Steve increased his empathy with John as time passed – feeling the pain and desolation of over fifty years worth of despair and unresolved issues. I have certainly been aware of my own flashes of pity observable in my diary.

Tasks of healing according to Herman further involve the rebuilding of trust (again, not possible in the case of Steve until the haunting is finally eliminated and his environment is made absolutely safe) and assurances of *'safety and protection'* from the *'presence of a sympathetic person.'* Crisis intervention is a necessary component of any working organisation and needs to focus on *'mobilising the supportive people into the survivor's environment, for she usually prefers to be with familiar people than strangers.'*

We saw during the recordings in my diary, of course that sympathy and support from management, particularly Kate, appeared to be solid. In due course, in part five of this book when we return to Steve's story; we will start to see how such assurances became inconsistent, less reliable and increasingly untrustworthy as managers began to play out their own agendas.

Herman goes on to say, *'Trauma isolates; the group re-creates a sense of belonging. Trauma shames and stigmatises; the group bears witness and affirms.'* Yalom terms the discovery that one is not alone as *'universality'* which helps breaks down a sense of isolation and alienation. This is why survivor groups may work well. The group can provide *'collective empowerment'* holding an increased capacity to bear and integrate trauma than that of the individual. The group, in Steve's case is uneven. Nor is it, of course, a therapeutic group with boundaries and commonality of experience or themes. All Steve may hope for is a witness or two who can share the experience of John and for some attempts at empathy from those who do not. Steve holds on to the need to remain on the night shift with the support that he has obtained so far. We can start to see how a sense of being cast among strangers on another shift may have problematic repercussions for him. Herman cites that for the soldier, research found that mutual support and lessening of traumatic impact can be achieved by not separating out the individual from his fighting unit. To do so *'greatly compounded the trauma of combat exposure.'* Steve's emotional needs comprise a desire to continue with his familiar 'fighting unit.' Whilst he may not be able to trust his 'environment,' at least he can trust some of his colleagues. Trust itself has been compromised for him. He can no longer trust his own sensory perception and cognitive interpretations of the events that occur to him randomly. He can no longer fully trust continuing to attain the unconditional support and acceptance of colleagues who are faced with a fear provoking situation that is unusual, unique and unexplained.

Shame indeed, as mentioned above by Herman, has been another continually present issue for Steve. Rothschild points out that shame itself has survival value and observes that *'shame, at least through evolution, has served to keep an individual in line with cultural norms that further 'survival of the tribe.' It socialises.'* Being a victim can be shaming. Being alone in a crowd can be potentially dangerous.

Once Steve does move shifts, which occurs in 2009 and is detailed later, he becomes adamant that he wants no further incidents to occur. He is reluctant to seek support from other team leaders less known to him, particularly as the shame and stigma associated with the recurrent injuries to his face would be visible for all to see. He may become safer in one way by this move, but not in terms of experiencing difficulty in an unfamiliar group.

To summarise, Herman concludes: *'The response of the community has a powerful influence on the ultimate resolution of the trauma. Restoration of the breach between the traumatised person and the community depends, first upon public acknowledgement of the traumatic event and second, upon some form of community action. Once it is publicly recognised that a person has been harmed, the community must take action to assign responsibility for the harm and to repair the injury. These two responses – recognition and restitution – are necessary to rebuild the survivor's sense of order and justice.'*

Clearly, in the case of the haunting of Steve, such desirable reparative action was always going to be a challenge on an individual, group and institutional level.

So we have explored belief from several angles, for the group, for the community, as a part of human nature. Opinions on science, spirituality, religion and mysticism vary, however, and often incite strong feelings and opinions. We now go on to explore more specifically the relationship between science and spirituality and issues that arise directly out of belief and the desire for proof.

Science and Spirituality

'...have you ever wondered how real your world actually is? As you sit there, you perceive things in a certain way and assume all of it is real. That's only natural; it's your frame of reference. But how can you be sure that somewhere another world doesn't truly exist wherein your reality, as you perceive it, is just as ridiculous, or at least as strange, as you perceive ours to be?' From 'When Rabbit Howls' by the Troops for Truddi Chase.

What is reality? I still hold in my memory a powerful picture of my tutor, standing before his eager eyed group in the first session of a counselling skills course. Virtually the first thing he told us was that *'There is no such thing as reality.'* All we have are *'differing perceptions of a situation.'* My immediate response to this statement was a sense of absolute relief. I was aware of a sense of being somehow freed up from the restraints of opinions, beliefs and theories held by family, my peers, society and the wider world in general. I was going to enjoy my journey learning to be a counsellor and viewing life in a different way. Reality I felt, can perhaps be somewhat restrictive. From a spiritual viewpoint psychic Darrin Owens agrees: *'It all hinges on perception – how you see yourself, your situations, and the world you are living in...Your perception shapes your thinking, your thinking shapes the way you act, the way you act affects the people around you – and it all gets reflected back at you'* (2006). The 1998 film *'The Truman Show'* pursues this theme effectively, but in a considerably more sinister manner as we observe the central character's journey through the movie and gradual realisation that the world he has always known is not as it seems. He is in fact, the central protagonist for a continual television show with all of his actions and interactions with others having been controlled and stage managed. *'People believe the reality of the world with which they are presented'* explains the director. It is only when the cracks in Truman's reality begin to show that he starts to suspect that his life has in fact been contrived to satisfy the demands of an audience obsessed with reality based television.

All we have, therefore, are a collection of the subjective perceptions and opinions of the individual. Most of us remain rooted in the reality of what we perceive through our senses. This is what Newberg, D'Aquili and Rause term a 'baseline' reality. This acquired information is collated and needs translating into something meaningful for the individual. A sense of cognitive meaning is then achieved by the channelling of information along the appropriate neural pathway in the brain. As we have seen, we are then in a position to form our beliefs which in turn influences our perception of reality. Newberg, D'Aquili and Rause point out that *'our experience of reality – all our experiences for that matter – are only "second-hand" depictions of what may or may not be objectively real'* and this *'raises some profound questions about the most basic truths of human existence and the neurological nature of spiritual experience'* (2001).

For those 'ordinary' people (by which I mean apparently non-psychic) who suddenly see ghosts, however, it may not be as clear cut. Steve was aware of a state of confusion induced immediately when he perceived the presence of John, either by sensing him through an intense feeling of cold, seeing objects move, feeling the infliction of the marks to his face or actually seeing him in solid form and hearing him speak. The area of Steve's brain that sensed John came repeatedly into sharp conflict with the part that logically and consciously informed him that John could not possibly be there. Similarly to a state of shock, the higher cognitive function became temporarily disabled owing to the conflict caused by the information Steve was receiving through his senses. Conversion of the image of the ghost into a logical explanation, into an articulate expression of language becomes extremely tricky. Even now, Steve says he does not 'believe.'

So what then, do people generally believe? On the surface, it seems that there are two clearly opposing arguments in the 'scientific' versus 'spirituality' debate. People may follow either a purely scientific viewpoint based on indisputable proof or they may hold strong fundamentalist religious beliefs based on firm faith systems. I would suggest that most people in the West would probably describe themselves as falling somewhere between the two, perhaps describing themselves as 'open minded' to the existence of phenomena that has yet to be proved. For some, however, the die hard atheist scientists versus the hard core immovable creationists, the split between scientific proof and spiritual belief is definite, absolute and there is little room for manoeuvre.

Spiritualists and scientists are doomed to disagree it seems. During the course of the film *'The Entity'* in particular we witness scientists and psychics in direct opposition following their lengthy debates on Carla's mental health state versus the potentiality of a haunting. An experiment is subsequently performed to wire up a replica of Carla's home and to try to freeze the entity with liquid helium and prove that her appalling supernatural experiences are not *'just a psychic projection.'* We are somewhat disappointed in the scientists' lack of conclusion. Emerging from the chaos that this procedure produces as the make shift home is destroyed, a witness concludes, *'It could have been anything,'* and the film ends, telling us that the supernatural sexual attacks on Carla Moran continue, although *'decreased in intensity and frequency,'* (October 1976).

Exploring scientific viewpoints we find some strong arguments against the existence of the paranormal. In the fascinating book published in 2001, *'Why God Won't Go Away: Brain Science and the Biology of Belief,'* which I have quoted from extensively, authors Newberg, D'Aquili and Rause observe that: *'Science and common sense...tells us that such a thing is not possible. Nothing can be more real than the material universe within which all real things are contained.'* They add: *'Science has no choice, of course, but to find such natural causes for 'supernatural' events. From rational points of view, it's hard to imagine that the claims of mystics could be based on anything other than delusion.'* The authors' observation on science concludes that: *'Science concerns itself with that which can be weighed, counted, calculated and measured – anything that can't be verified by objective observation simply can't be called scientific.'*

In his book *'Pseudoscience and the Paranormal'* which strongly opposes the existence of the supernatural and raising that believers in the paranormal will always argue against scientific proof, scientist Terrence Hines posits that studies of paranormal and supernatural phenomena provides unfalsifiable hypotheses and a lack of hard evidence. He informs us that: *'The use of non falsifiable hypothesis is permitted in parapsychology to a degree unheard of in any scientific discipline...No matter how many experiments fail to provide evidence for psi and no matter how good those experiences are, the nonfalsifiable hypothesis will always protect the belief.'* The burden of proof, he says, will always lie with the sceptic to disprove every single paranormal claim. He also raises that for believers in the supernatural, commitment to belief is *'stronger than the data on which that commitment is based.'* Professor Richard Dawkins, evolutionist and author of *'The God Delusion'* (2006) concurs, citing in a channel four television documentary series *'The Enemies of Reason'* (2007) that *'Personal feelings are validated over scientific evidence'* and despite the failure of experiments to ascertain the existence of any proof by psychics carried out for the purpose of the documentary, that *'People prefer to remain in a state of denial in the face of hard evidence.'*

For sceptics, my guess is that a cognitive behavioural stance (which takes into consideration the impact of thoughts which in turn define belief which then influences behaviour) is a logical one and therefore that indeed *'belief determines the structure of reality'* (Hines). Hines also suggests that it is scientists who are more open minded and willing to flex their attitudes once presented with hard evidence whilst it is the mystics who remain close minded.

For the firm believers in spiritual reality, however, answers are not provided through such logical means. Paul Roland argues that *'We are naturally inclined to disbelieve anything outside our personal experience unless a case can be made for its existence on rational grounds.'* Stanley, the woman's psychiatrist in the book about dissociation, *'When Rabbit Howls'* is well aware of what the potential 'mysticism' and non rational dictates of the brain and personality hold when he raises that not everything concerned with the workings of the mind can be neatly labelled into *'Boxes, compartments, niches, neatness, chronological order.'*

Turning to mystical matters, it is argued that spiritual, or 'non rational' experiences occur on a continuum and are not necessarily obvious. Most people may not have a conversation with a spirit, but can experience a sensation of oneness with nature, an uplift during prayer or whilst singing for example. A level up from these experiences can comprise stronger mystical experiences, perhaps sensing the presence of an absolute higher power. For the religious this may indicate a feeling of divine presence, a felt sense of God's love. For others this perception may be more threatening, perhaps punishment from spirits or demons. For psychic children and adults, it seems that such a 'higher' reality is just as concrete as that 'reality' we perceive through taste, touch, auditory and visual perception. Newberg, D'Aquili and Rause endorse this view, although: *'The reality of the mystics cannot be considered real because it cannot be verified scientifically.'* They go on to inform us, however, that: *'Mystics, however, have different ideas about what is fundamentally real. They believe they have experienced a primary reality that runs deeper than material existence...Science rejects this claim, not only because it holds that nothing in existence is more real than the reality of matter, but also because it cannot accept that something other than science, especially something as subjective and immeasurable as mystical experience, can yield useful truth about what is fundamentally real.'*

Mystic psychoanalyst Jung himself concurs, arguing for the spiritual viewpoint: *'Everything in the unconscious seeks outward manifestation...I cannot employ the language of science to trace this process of growth in myself, for I cannot experience myself as a scientific problem.'* He adds: *'Myth is more individual and expresses life more precisely than does science. Science works with concepts of averages which are far too general to do justice to the subjective variety of an individual life.'*

For the many people who have been affected by a sense of spiritual presence and who are in receipt of meaningful messages from their deceased loved ones, perhaps through having a sitting with a medium, enough proof and enough scientific evidence has been provided. The saying *'For those who believe, no proof is necessary; for those who doubt, no proof is enough'* fits in with this view (Roland). For children who are psychic and for anyone who has powerful mystical experiences and senses, the presence of an absolute higher power - this 'higher reality' - is just as concrete as that we perceive through our reality of taste, touch, auditory, olfactory and visual reality. Certainly the marks on Steve's face are real even if his other perceptions are playing tricks. Medium Doris Stokes endorses this view in her comment: *'Time and again I've heard them say that the spirit world is a real world on another dimension – as real to them as ours is to us,'* (1980).

Mystic experiences may not be invited or strived for, however, and they may arrive unexpectedly, afflicting people who do not desire them nor want to make sense of them: the reluctant psychics. Roland argues that we all have an innate sixth sense which cannot be regarded as abnormal or supernatural in origin, but exists as a sensitivity to natural forces around us. He claims: *'Some people are born with an acute psychic sensitivity or 'sixth sense' which enables them to see and communicate with discarnate spirits while others seem to develop this ability as the result of a traumatic event.'*

We have seen how I have born in mind the possibility of Steve's change in life circumstances as potentially significant in triggering a defined 'psychic' ability. Whether or not people are actually born psychic, it seems that most people choose not to learn to utilise this fully owing to the need to defend ourselves from unsettling disturbances in our sense of reality. I have certainly been aware of such defences myself in some of my diary entries.

Mystic and spiritual healer David Ashworth, whose work I explore later on, argues that *'We need to learn to accept. We do not need to understand everything in a clear cut scientific way, labelled, packaged and put into a compartment, that we can take off the shelf now and then and say this is it and these are the limits, we know because we have measured them.'*

Ashworth also argues that fear is the major reason for the rejection and persecution of those particular people who may have psychic ability. He informs us that *'Fear breeds limitation'* and that *'scientists are the most limited of all.'* He raises the need for those working with scientific research to *'Dissolve their fear of the unknown and embrace it. Dissolve their fear of holding on to their own perceptions as being the absolute truth.'* Thus Ashworth and mystics like him perceive the limits of being brought up (particularly in the West) in a predominantly left brained society, a society that refuses for the most part to acknowledge or to work with a spiritual quality in people's lives. Intuition is rejected on the grounds of being improvable, immeasurable and he suggests that evidence of right brained activity, with the exception of artistic, poetic or musical pursuits, is generally much maligned.

To conclude this section then, Roland summarises the possibility that the problems in the warehouse may indeed be owing to ghostly activity by arguing strongly for the existence of the supernatural and paranormal generally: *'...paranormal phenomena do not violate or contradict nature; the supernatural is an extension of the natural world and conforms to universal laws.'* He adds: *'Most people have never seen a ghost, but that does not mean that ghosts do not exist. There is considerable experiential evidence that discarnate spirits do exist, but in an alternate reality to our own. This is a non physical dimension of which we are not conscious because our perception of this greater reality is limited by our five senses.'*

Just what some of those laws may be remains debatable and are yet to be explored. Hines, however, views all of these claims with suspicion, arguing that in contemporary times, the obsession with the parapsychological and supernatural has taken the form of *'a quest to dethrone materialistic science and re-establish the dominance of a spiritual approach to the world.'* Psychics, spiritualists and mystics are basically deluded and wasting their time in their beliefs and paranormal pursuits.

And so the argument between science and spirituality continues and probably always will endure, certainly beyond my lifetime. Below, we begin to look further at the argument for how mysticism may in fact be linked with brain function, and how mental health issues may have influenced our beliefs and viewpoints when it comes to examining the possibility of the existence of ghosts.

Mysticism and Mental Health

'It's been said that if you speak to God it's prayer but if God speaks back you're a schizophrenic.'
From 'Am I Normal?' Spirituality BBC 2

A question posed in the book by Newberg, D'Aquili and Rause *'Why God Won't Go Away'* quite clearly examines whether spiritual or mystical experiences are induced by *'emotional or psychological imbalance'* or *'a delusional state brought on by brain dysfunction or any number of psychological factors...fatigue, or emotional distress, to obsessive thinking or even mental illness.'*

When there is no explanation for a behaviour in a person - particularly in Western culture - and someone who acts in a way we cannot easily understand; unpredictably or bizarrely, the temptation may be to describe them as 'just crazy.' Those who look deeper than this may pinpoint a diagnosable mental health issue or illness. Stigmas around mental illness predominate in society even today, despite the best efforts of various individuals and organisations who seek to challenge stereotyping. Many people still fear, misinterpret and misunderstand mental health issues. In the past of course, those people who may have had psychic ability may have feared speaking out of their abilities, which may have resulted in ostracism, ridicule, incarceration and in some cases, potential execution as a witch.

Mystics, however, have also played an important part in many religions, including Christianity, Islam, Judaism, Hinduism and others (Owens). It is clearly observable how society has changed over the centuries, previously often designating religious or spiritual reasons for acute mental ill health, for example demonic or spiritual possession and holding an attitude towards spiritually inclined people which often revered them as above the ordinary. A religious model was, therefore, often used to account for mental ill health. Emotional or mental disturbance was quite clearly explained by the presence of demons, which possessed the individual and would then need to be exorcised. The individual would then enjoy a healthier state once the demonic forces had been evacuated. In the 1800s the brain was examined more carefully as a potential source for mental processes and experiments were carried out. Whereas some of the barbaric practices may seem inhuman to us now – for example misdiagnosis, subsequent incarceration, freezing baths and electric shock treatment, these methods contributed to a critical turning point in research into mental health and the development of modern psychiatric services. Such studies are less than two hundred years old, yet the leaps in mental health treatment and care are now far removed from the harsh practices of the past two centuries. It is interesting to ponder that the study of the psychic individual even today is yet to develop fully in an 'acceptable' and public way, beyond certain individuals displaying their talents in theatres or on television. It is evident, however, that colleges catering for supernatural studies, workshops and groups for serious psychics who want to develop their skills beyond the need for public entertainment are on the increase.

During the nineteenth century then, scientific experimentation accelerated and gradually medical and psychological reasoning grew in strength and evidence when seeking answers for the disturbed 'hysterics' who were claiming paranormal sensations. Beauregard and O'Leary raise that: *'The study of mysticism was largely neglected during the twentieth century, the heyday of Freudianism, behaviourisms and evolutionary psychology. The question was no longer "What do mystics experience?" but "What's wrong with them anyway? Can it be fixed?"* Given this trend, the argument that primitive religions could be annihilated in time by the continuing development of science is, perhaps, a powerful one.

Newberg et al summarise the growing conflict between scientific and spiritual belief and research: *'In ancient and mediaeval cultures, mystics were often held in high esteem as the wisest and most spiritually attuned members of a society. The rationalistic and empirical demands of Western science, however, seem to leave professional observers no choice but to regard these modern mystics as the victims of damaged or deluded minds. Certainly, there is evidence to support that point of view. We know, for example, that certain pathological conditions such as schizophrenia and temporal lobe epilepsy can trigger voices, visions, and other hallucinatory effects that often possess religious connotations and that occasionally these hallucinations can lead to an abnormal fascination with spiritual affairs.'*

Science it seems has no shortage of rational explanations for the strange accounts of the mystics, and whilst these explanations may vary in approach, they all agree on one important point: *'The mind of a mystic is a mind that has somehow become fundamentally confused. Mysticism, in other words, is the result of mental pathology, and mystics, whether they suffer from neurosis, psychosis, or functional problems of the brain, are people who have clearly lost track of what is real,'* (Newberg et al). The authors, however, argue that mystics and psychotics tend to respond in different ways – mystics tend to describe their experiences as *'ecstatic and joyful'* whereas psychotics tend to be rendered fearful and confused by their experiences that often incorporate a vision of a God who is angry and vengeful. Other research agrees that people who access genuine mystical experiences regularly enjoy a higher level of psychological well being and self esteem with lower anxiety levels and a more positive outlook. When I consider the potential differences between psychic ability and schizophrenia for example, it is noticeable that psychics often perceive voices as helpful or protective (which is especially clear when we consider the stories of psychics Sally Morgan and Michele Knight later in this section). Schizophrenics, however, tend to risk danger, for example through voices instructing them to harm themselves or to perceive themselves as indestructible. This may lead them to take unnecessary risks, for example attempting to fly.

From film examples, both the demonically possessed little girl Regan, in *'The Exorcist'* and Carla, persecuted rape survivor in *'The Entity'*, follow a mental health route prior to seeking spiritual aid for their traumas.   Logically for Carla, her terrible childhood is taken into account by the medics as a potential explanation for her paranormal experiences. Afraid of the dark, she was terrified of her strict minister father who indulged himself in 'inappropriate holding' of the child Carla. The medical team agree that she is suffering a 'mass illusion' triggered by the links with the incestuous father. Running away from home at an early age, Carla's first boyfriend is killed whilst she is pregnant at the age of sixteen. Following this, her second relationship collapses, leaving her as a single parent of two more children. Her psychiatrist logically tells Carla that *'early psychological phases can come back with the vengeance causing delusions, anxieties, hallucinations.'* When Carla's car is taken out of her control whilst she is driving, this is interpreted as a suicide attempt. Furthermore, an underlying Freudian interpretation of Carla's possible sexual desire of her own teenage son also runs through the film as the psychiatric services seek to explain and contain Carla's escalating haunting attacks.

Likewise Regan, in *'The Exorcist'* is subject to medical and psychiatric tests once she starts to behave erratically. When studying this horror film, Hines makes some links for Regan with Tourettes syndrome. Alternative potential diagnoses actually appearing within the film include *'disorder of the nerves'* linked with early adolescence, *'overreaction'* to depression, as a result of her parents' split until the final interpretation indicates that a *'lesion in the temporal lobe'* is the logical answer. This is a curable condition.

There are indeed strong indications that the right temporal lobe may influence paranormal sensations and hallucinations.   DSM 4 informs me that: *'Hallucinations can occur in any sensory modality (i.e. visual, olfactory, gustatory, tactile or auditory) but certain etiological factors are more likely to evoke specific hallucinatory phenomena. Olfactory hallucinations, especially those involving the smell of burning rubber or other unpleasant smells, are highly suggestive of temporal lobe epilepsy.'* I am reminded of the smell of sulphur that has so often been reported by Steve's colleagues here, although this is something that Steve himself has not been unduly bothered by.

Robert Buckman (2002) in the book I have already quoted from quite extensively *'Can We Be Good Without God: Biology, Behaviour and the need to Believe,'* has listed specific additional hallucinatory effects associated with right temporal lobe activity. This appears to provide valuable and pertinent information and I have, therefore, quoted the list in its entirety:

- *"Auditory experiences:* sounds or hearing voices (auditory hallucinations), often talking directly to the person, sometimes voices of people from one's past.
- *Visual experiences:* seeing lights, patterns of light and dark, sometimes including the white-light-at-the-end-of-the-tunnel, sometimes entire images from one's past including images of deceased relatives and friends.
- *Vestibular experiences:* the sense of whirling through space, going into a tunnel and other changes in orientation and position.
- *Taste and smell experiences:* sometimes smells that are familiar from the past, sometimes new ones.
- *Memory changes:* déjà vu (the sense of having seen something before – when one hasn't), jamais vu (the sense of never having seen something before when one has).
- *Extracorpreal experiences:* the sense of being outside one's own body.
- *Morning highs:* people who get a 'high' in the morning have higher scores than average in temporal lobe signs.
- *Drama, poetry and other creative acts:* activities that require the person to 'get into' another world or another mode are associated with high temporal lobe scores.
- *Sense of presence:* the feeling that one is in the presence of another intelligence (sometimes religious – i.e. God – sometimes an alien, sometimes a spirit or ghost).
- *Other religious and spiritual experiences:* many different kinds of deep and spiritual experiences including a sense of peacefulness, being at one with nature, understanding in some intangible way the working of the cosmos.
- *Signs of special significance:* the feeling that various things that happen in the world are specific signals directed at the person.
- *Pseudocyesis* (false pregnancy): women who have experiences of cessation of menstrual periods, enlarging abdomen, and breast changes (when they are not in fact pregnant) have high scores on temporal lobe signs.
- *Near death experiences:* the white light and the sense of peace often associated with near death experiences (e.g. drowning or hypothermia).
- *'I would kill in God's name.'"*

This final issue Buckman describes as *'an important feature of the right temporal lobe'* and he discusses it in detail later on in his book. So we can see from this argument that the brain indeed may have evolved naturally to experience anything that could be translated as mystical or supernatural. What, however, happens if the temporal lobe is either artificially stimulated, perhaps by electrical impulses, or simply goes wrong?

Temporal Lobe Epilepsy

I go on to briefly examine Temporal Lobe Epilepsy (or 'Complex Partial Seizure Disorder'), a condition which clearly can trigger sensory hallucinations causing a powerful impact on an individual. TLE itself is often misdiagnosed as a mental health disorder and sufferers are often referred on to psychiatric services. Feelings of déjà vu or jamais vu, altered states of consciousness and auditory, visual and olfactory hallucinations are common symptoms. In TLE a sense of unreality can be experienced, however, reality can still be clearly cognitively defined by the sufferer and this therefore offers a distinction from psychotic episodes. TLE symptoms can also be confused with those of migraine.

Mystical and spiritual experiences can arguably be held within the mind, which, Newberg et al strongly argue, is actually hardwired for the purpose and can be artificially stimulated to produce effects symptomatic of TLE. Having previously researched issues surrounding the healing power of prayer, near death experiences, epilepsy and schizophrenia, the authors go to describe an experiment in which a volunteer has his brainwaves monitored whilst in a deep meditative trance. It is noted that whilst in a state of deep calm, God, or mystical experiences generally can be 'let in.' They continue to observe that the experiencing of such events are: *'not outside the range of normal brain function. In other words, mystical experiencing is biologically, observably and scientifically real'* and that *'spiritual experience, at its very root, is intimately interwoven with human biology. That biology, in some way, compels the spiritual urge.'*

The philosophical question of whether God created the brain, or whether the brain creates God through neurological functioning has been around for a long time. Beauregard and O'Leary (2007) enquire whether the brain function is inclusive of holding a 'God Gene' and if *'brain disorders trigger a sort of God module or God circuit?'* Many scientists pose the theory that humans may be hardwired through evolution, genetic or DNA inheritance to perceive God, supernatural activity, or both. Along with trigger hallucinations of voice hearing, senses of taste, smell, retrieval of forgotten memories or other intense feelings that continue to be widely discussed in various research, TLE can also trigger experiences of depression and anxiety along with more positive feelings owing to visions and senses of religious or spiritual ecstasy.

Specific experiments on temporal lobe stimulation have been carried out most notably by neurologists Hughlings Jackson and Wilder Penfield during the earlier part of the twentieth century and much knowledge was gleaned from these tests. Further extensive research on magnetic activity and its impact on the temporal lobe and monitoring of associated sensations were developed by Michael Persinger during the 1980s. Persinger is also noted for developing the God helmet experiment. The God helmet was demonstrated on television by atheist Richard Dawkins in 2003 exciting great interest and speculation. This experience is examined in interesting detail in Beauregard and O'Leary's book

'The Spiritual Brain'. Briefly, these experiments found that temporal lobes could be stimulated by weak electrical activity which could trigger 'religious or mystical experiences' along with a felt 'sensed presence.' Persinger had hypothesised that: *'Magnetic fields may cause a burst of electrical activity in the temporal lobes. The sensed presence might in turn account for both traditional mystical experiences and modern accounts of alien abductions.'* He raises a link with *'increased global geomagnetic activity all over the earth'* and concludes that about a third of the subjects *'attributed the presence to a deceased member of the family or to some cultural equivalent of a 'spirit guide'* (Beauregard and O'Leary). Of course, this view would concur with my reflections in part two, when Steve and I are considering the possibility that visions of our ghost, John, are being triggered by the amount of electrical activity which is evident in the warehouse.

It appears that such stimulation of the temporal lobes can trigger feelings of *'terror of nothing in particular.'* There is, however, a question of psychological suggestion when such experiments are performed and the circumstances under which the subject is experiencing this stimulation to the brain. We will experience an effect if our surroundings encourage us to anticipate it. A subject protected under laboratory conditions is more than likely to have a different experience and level of exposure to an anxiety experienced by someone who is in a 'haunted' house in the dead of night. Buckman agrees: *'A belief in ghosts or spooks is unlikely to be a prominent feature of a person's outlook on a sunny day in a crowd, but more likely to be prominent in a creaky house at night.'* This concept is particularly evident in the film *'The Entity'* when Carla undergoes the controlled experiment to attract the entity into her re-created home environment. She is considerably safer here, with scientists around monitoring and supporting her, rather than on her own when she was in a state of abject fear from the constant threat of being terrorised by the malevolent being persecuting her. Buckman is convinced of the accuracy of the temporal lobe experiments and the findings and observes that: *'This proves conclusively that temporal lobe mediates experiences of ghosts and haunting, but it does not explain – yet – what precipitates those experiences in nature and outside the laboratory.'*

I have discovered that the magnetic or electrical influence on the temporal lobe argument is indeed a compelling one. Lee posits that *'stimulation of the brain by an external magnetic field can rekindle old, dormant memories and "create" new hallucinations ('Temporal Lobe Epilepsy') this may explain the many cases of Alien Abduction prevalent throughout the world.'* He also raises the possibility that certain environmental conditions may also be required in order for individuals with TLE to experience such sensations and apparitions and with this he includes religious experiences. Newberg, D'Aquili and Rause raise that *'patients with TLE have a heightened response to religious language, specifically religious terms and icons. The suggestion from these findings is that the temporal lobe is very important to these experiences.'*

In 2007, News-Medical Net firmly concurred and raised that experiments conducted by stimulation of the temporal lobe through exposure to weak magnetic fields, have resulted not only in feelings of terror and anxiety with indeterminate cause but also with subjects experiencing the *'presence of a sentient being'* which has been open to interpretation as either religious or supernatural. They are, however, less likely to accept such experimentation as conclusive and absolute and they do once more take into account the environmental conditions and the personality traits of the subjects undergoing the tests. Such investigations are therefore worthy of questioning and the News-Medical net conclude that *'highly suggestible individuals had paranormal experiences to a larger extent, but this had nothing to do with the magnetic fields. Paranormal experiences were particularly pronounced among participants with personality traits indicating openness to shifts in consciousness and a new age lifestyle orientation.'*

It seems as I read about them further that similar experiments on this subject appear to have been carried out quite regularly but are flawed, unsuccessful in some way or have had their authenticity challenged. It is clear, however, that generally, altered states of perception can be triggered not only by the stimulation of the flight/fight response under stress, but also through more pleasurable activities such as dancing, running, meditation or the performance of rituals. This *'points to a clear link between the autonomic nervous system and the brain's potential for spiritual experience'* (Newberg, D'Aquili and Rause).

These are complex and persuasive arguments in favour of the view that all supernatural experiences are linked to neurological activity within the brain. This, however, does not prove or disprove the existence of God or ghosts, it merely informs us that the brain is designed in a way that can be more receptive to those experiences through artificial stimulation. Buckman logically raises that just because an area of the brain can be stimulated to create a bright light, it does not, of course, mean that there is no such thing as a bright light in any other circumstances. For some people, such activity is stronger than in others, perhaps owing to health, or to the stimulation by specific environmental conditions which may have an impact on the temporal lobes. Similar to the possibility that Steve's scars could be psychosomatic in origin, in the way a nervous rash and skin conditions such as eczema or psoriasis can appear in times of stress, the warehouse and the workers in it could be being affected by artificial stimulation of brain patterns. The warehouse could be shaken by trains; the proximity of electrical pylons, or any other prevailing atmospheric conditions which could be resulting in TLE symptoms in many of the staff.

Newberg et al dismiss these possible causes, however, when considering how genuinely 'real' experiences of mysticism seem to the individual who has them. The authors argue that: *'We do not believe that genuine mystical experiences can be explained away as the results of epileptic hallucinations or, for that matter, as the product of other spontaneous hallucinatory states triggered by drugs, illness, physical exhaustion, emotional stress, or sensory deprivation. Hallucinations, no matter what their source, are simply not capable for providing the mind with an experience as convincing as that of mystical spirituality.'*

The healthy functioning of people who have religious, spiritual or mystical experiences is repeatedly normalised along these lines by researchers who have made studies, for example that of Carmelite nuns which Beauregard and O'Leary describe in detail in their book *'The Spiritual Brain'* which ascertains definite changes in brain activity during a course of prayer. It seems that people can indeed induce such states by taking specific actions and the authors conclude, quite comfortingly I think, with the suggestion that *'there is no need to choose between science and spirituality…Science cannot prove or disprove the existence of God.'* They go to relate that such mystical experiences are a natural part of human nature and a *'sign of mental health…A transcendence of the personal identity and an enhanced sense of connection to and unity with others and world.'* A state that is difficult to attain when immersed in the mental health system. Beauregard and O'Leary go on to claim that whilst some religious patients may be regarded as delusional, many clients do in fact indicate a preference for therapy from a positive spiritual perspective. Additionally, some potential TLE sufferers have indeed had a significant impact on the world, for example Newberg et al go on to cite St Paul Mohammed, Joan of Arc, St Theresa, Mormon founder Joseph Smith and Vincent Van Gogh as examples. After presenting interesting arguments which are beyond the remit of this book to reproduce, they do conclude, however, that religious experiences are not linked with TLE and do not provide a 'God spot' and that relatively few epileptics in fact report having religious or mystical experiences during their seizures.

Discussion, argument and lively debate about the links between mysticism and disturbed mental health rage on in fact and fiction, but any firm scientific progress apparently remains unsatisfactory, although the examination of brain activity is fascinating and I am sure, there is much more to learn. Despite this we are perhaps left for the moment with evidence which is quite compelling, that Steve may be suffering from TLE, which is triggered by working alongside low magnetic frequencies in the warehouse. Or, if not TLE, he may have a sensitive right lobe which would naturally lend itself to imagination. Steve is a bright, artistic man working anti social hours within a creatively restrictive environment and it may be that he is frustrated by this. My view is that he is someone who has not reached his potential academically or creatively owing to the environmental and situational factors of his life. Be that as it may and whether or not Steve is creating his ghost for himself, I am aware of fellow colleague's Lizzie's less subtle viewpoint when she comments: *'How does that explain what's going on for the rest of us – are we all suffering with fucking epilepsy then?'* Possibly, Lizzie. It may indeed be that a number of Steve's colleagues are having TLE sensations triggered by the same magnetic activity present in the warehouse, which explains why no-one has confessed to having symptoms elsewhere. Some colleagues remain unaffected. We are, however, still left with the mystery of Steve's repeated physical scars and the violent invisible assaults which physically knock him flying.

Schizophrenia

In the light of Steve's experiences I considered the possibility of him being traumatised, dissociative or that he was having some sort of mental or emotional breakdown. I did also consider the possibility of him being schizophrenic. This was a potential explanation that we both found frightening. Despite my history of working closely with clients displaying all of the above in addition to some quite extreme mental health disorders, it felt like a totally different ball park when such issues were arising within my own personal life. I needed to undertake yet more research in order to confront my fears and examine every avenue. There are of course, many mental health conditions and episodes of psychosis which involve the experiencing of hallucinations but schizophrenia is certainly one that I felt was worthy of closer examination.

My starting point was once more to find a definition in DSM 4. Through reading this I was informed that auditory hallucinations tend to be more common when diagnosing schizophrenia, often manifesting as voices which are distinct from an internal frame of reference. A running commentary or voices in conflict may occur. Hearing one's name called, as in Steve's case, or hallucinations that are a normal part of religious experiencing in some cultures, hypnagogic or hypnopompic hallucinations are all considered to be within the range of normal human experience and therefore are not considered to be characteristic of schizophrenia. Delusions may often be persecutory and it is evident that Steve is feeling persecuted. There are several types of schizophrenia and the Paranoid type in particular may fit comprising as it does: *'the presence of prominent delusions or auditory hallucinations in the context of a relative preservation of cognitive functioning and an affect.'* The delusions *'organise themselves around a coherent theme.'* Presumably a persistent sight and sense of a railwayman is consistent and coherent and the delusional themes themselves may be indicative of anger, anxiety, aloneness, aloofness and argumentativeness. There may be a sense of thoughts being inserted into one's head or that sources from outside of the self, for example the TV or radio, are speaking directly to the schizophrenic individual. Onset may be later in life than in other types of schizophrenia. All this fits in with Steve's experiencing, but only during the night and in the warehouse.

Reading more widely, in the work *'Schizophrenia, Symptoms, Causes and Treatments'* by Bernheim and Lewine (1979), the authors inform us that schizophrenics suffer a *'split from reality'* which may range from one psychotic incident, to occasional episodes. It is certainly not a permanent state of mind: *'the word psychotic refers to a temporary state in which various aspects of the environment are falsely perceived or interpreted.'* They do go on to explain specifically that: *'There are various symptoms of disordered thinking, the presence of any one of disturbances include hearing one's thought spoken aloud, hearing others' voices talking or commenting about one, believing that another's thoughts have been put into one's head, having and believing that one's feeling, thoughts and actions are not one's own, but rather dictated by outside forces.'*

The significance of hallucinations is therefore taken into account when diagnosing schizophrenia. Assuming that John is a hallucination, then hallucinations are obviously the most common manifestation of Steve's experiences in the warehouse. Bernheim and Lewine inform us that: '*...there are a number of ways in which thought disorders may be manifested. By far the most common is hallucinations. Hallucinations are sensory experiences in the absence of the appropriate external stimuli. The schizophrenic may hear voices talking to or about him when no-one is speaking. He may see a vision of a dead relative. He may feel insects crawling over his body or an electric current running up and down his spine. Patients may or may not be aware that their experiences do not match reality.'*

As we have witnessed, Steve is clear that his experiences with John do not of course, match his reality. Despite his sense of shock and confusion on encountering John and seeing John in real and solid form albeit as if through a mirror, it was obvious that Steve was never going to interpret these events as part of his ordinary life experience. For Steve, the intertwining of fantasy and reality could easily be untangled. For him, he is not experiencing disorganised speech patterns or any other symptoms which presumably could have been picked up by his GP or the psychologist.

Experts on schizophrenia develop a case for genetic inheritance and additionally how the condition may be fuelled by the responses of the family and wider society to the schizophrenic individual. The significant point is also raised that schizophrenia may be triggered by positive events and not traumatic ones. Cases of diagnosed schizophrenia rise, however, in particular when someone has undergone a negative life experience six months previously. Of course, Steve underwent a life transition when his marriage ended and the beginning of his relationship with me is perceived by him as positive. Something certainly has been disrupted for him, whether the causes are mental ill health or supernatural in origin.

On an optimistic note therefore, schizophrenia is controllable. Symptoms include sensitivity to a bombardment of sensory perceptions which the schizophrenic can learn to deal with effectively, perhaps through medication. Patients can work, function and learn to ignore their voice hearing, hallucinations and sense of phenomena which seems to have no bearing on material reality. It may also mean, rightly or wrongly, perhaps learning to cope with societal prejudice by not broadcasting the effects of their symptoms, for example voice hearing, too publicly.

We have so far examined the possibility that people experience themselves to be haunted for a variety of reasons including a natural result of early neglect, severing of attachment, dysfunction or abuse in childhood, post traumatic stress, dissociative identity disorder and underlying physical and mental health issues, from sleep deprivation and temporal lobe epilepsy to schizophrenia. There are of course, many other reasons people may experience disturbances in perception and the triggering of hallucinations, including the use of illegal drugs and prescribed medication.

So perhaps we return to the argument that supernatural experiences are created within the mind and are perceived to be as real as 'ordinary' material reality. That the people who have such experiences are not mentally disturbed but are merely acting in accordance with natural brain function, or at times, dysfunction. But what of experiences that seem a little more complex than this – not only that 'ghosts' are created in the mind, but are actually present physically within the body? This is an issue we have not yet explored and which is detailed below. This is the challenging and unsettling possibility of actual spirit possession.

Now is the time to further examine the evidence provided by those therapists and spiritual healers for whom ghosts are a sound reality – facts in their own right and present within our existence. It was time for me to take on some serious reading around spiritual possession, demons and the nature of the work that some people employ with clients who are presenting with supernatural issues. This was reading that I had never considered picking up before, either through any personal curiosity or interest, or as part of any research to aid me with my training in counselling. I found the book *'The Unquiet Dead'* (1987) by Dr Edith Fiore which I have already referred to in earlier chapters particularly helpful. I am also indebted to David Ashworth whose book *'Dancing with the Devil'* (2001) proved an extremely useful and interesting read at this point in my investigations into Steve's experiences. I have referred to and quoted from these texts extensively here and I hope that I have summarised and interpreted work on energy, vibration and psychic healing accurately.

Spirit Possession

'Spirit possession has been reported since ancient times. Is it real?' From 'The Unquiet Dead' by Edith Fiore.

Many spiritual healers cite the disturbing fact that people are caught up in the mental health system who need not be in that situation, had they been given the 'correct' diagnosis - that of spiritual possession. David Ashworth, a practising psychic healer, states that *'Often psychological problems are present simply because there is damage to the aura of the person who is under psychic attack and any energies which penetrate the person's aura can then create panic attacks, delusions and many other symptoms of imbalance.'* In other words if our energy is off balance, perhaps caused by a life transition or trauma – and I'm thinking of Steve's major change when he ended his long marriage and moved out - it may have a detrimental effect on the aura, which will then need attunement by a healer.

Some people may then literally find themselves under *'psychic attack.'* A spirit may step into that person's psyche and physical body. Ashworth argues that such a psychic attack may leave the possessed with mild symptoms, such as insomnia, through increasingly severe symptoms from nightmares, mood swings, anxiety, hallucinations, severe depression and even personality disorder. With regard to multiple personality, Ashworth argues against theories formed by the psychologists who study dissociative identity disorder and the splitting off of parts of the personality. Ashworth is emphatic that whilst people can switch in and out of differing personality states without full awareness, it would be impossible for these personalities to display certain skills and abilities unless these skills were accessible to them via the life experience of the entities who possess them. Edith Fiore cites an example of an initially brilliant student who goes on to inexplicably and suddenly lose his ability and almost quit college. We can also see the example in *'Sybil'* illustrated in part one, of Sybil's interchangeable skills in maths, music and art, which fluctuate according to which personality is dominant at the time of her performance. The phenomenon of speaking in tongues also provides a sound example of this. From the spiritual possession viewpoint, such skills cannot and do not emerge from somewhere within the individual's divided personality but belong to the spirits who take up residence within that person. Fiore answers the question of multiple personality thus: *'My view is that these cases are probably uncontrolled mediums who are multiply possessed. The 'personalities' are actually other people – spirits. The reasons these patients are generally unresponsive to therapy – at least with lasting cures – is that the main cause, possession, is not treated. When it is, the personalities disappear.'* Using hypnotherapy with her clients, Fiore cites that some spirits are temporary visitors rather than permanent lodgers and are just *'flitting through.'* A little girl who has possessed a patient Fiore is treating for example, suddenly emerges by asking Fiore to play with her and is then never heard from again. Such entities are either just passing by and are not spirits who take up full residence, or they may be echoes from past lives rather than full possessors. Ashworth adds that *'Our psychiatric wards are full of spirits and entities attached to people and manipulating their personalities.'* Demonic possession which I explore later, it is argued, is particularly linked with sectioning under the mental health act and treatment in psychiatric units. Whether this is fully believable or not, it is certainly a fascinating thought.

Edith Fiore is clearly experienced in such situations and has written widely on the subject. Her work, along with that of David Ashworth, is worthy of extensive consideration here, as some of it does in fact seem to make some sense of our situation. She cites cases of clients who experience alterations in consciousness which don't fit neatly into categorised mental health conditions but seem to correspond with the idea of 'possession' which can be found in mediaeval and other ancient literature. In these cases spiritual and demonic possession remained unquestioned for centuries as the absolute causes for physical and mental ill health. Such examples include those carried out by the ultimate psychic healer, Jesus, in the Bible. Coupled with these experiences comes a variety of experimentation with regard to exorcism and ridding of unwanted entities. Dr Fiore goes on to describe her own methods of depossession as *'a new perspective for understanding human behaviour'* and she goes on to tell us, quite sensibly that she is still learning. *'The inner mind, I now believe is our greatest challenge and just as worthy of research as outer space.'* Fiore uses her hypnotherapy techniques as *'working hypothesis'* – she is not herself fully convinced about spirit possession but significantly, has noticed that it 'works.' But how does it work and how would one measure the success of such methods, in common with any type of psychotherapeutic intervention? I would perhaps assume that part of the healing process as patients begin to integrate and function in a more satisfactory manner may link with placing either conscious or unconscious faith in the therapist. Significantly, clients may hold hopes, beliefs and desires in a method of healing which may help them – particularly when all else offered in the mental health system has failed.

So let us turn to what spiritual possession actually involves. Put very simply, Dr Fiore argues that spirits are those who have died and who have not achieved the *'proper transition between the earth plane and the "other side" at death.'* They have, therefore, become *"displaced persons"* These then inhabit the bodies of the living on earth and thereby procrastinate over joining the spirit world. They may either be trapped or remain willingly. One motivation may be that in life they have themselves, like living people, refused to believe in life after death and simply don't see the spirits who come to aid them in their transition to the spiritual realms. These are the *'discarnates'* – the dispossessed who seek an aura of a living person on which to attach.

Fiore then observes that the personality of the living person is altered and vacillates between two (or more) character states – at times the possessor having only a slight influence, at others a dominant one – often struggling for control and even issuing 'insults and commands.' This we have seen in Steve's case as he and his colleagues experienced voices bullying, ordering and enticing them. Voices may also be critical, demanding or undermining. Fiore cites the possibility that entities speak through 'unwilling mediums' and the patient – and also noticeable in Steve's case of severe despair – recognises that what they know of their own personality seems to be at odds with how they are behaving. A frequent claim at such times is *'That's just not me!'* I must admit, I have noticed that this is a phrase that clients use quite often and having had my awareness raised from reading and researching the subject of spiritual possession, I have caught myself wondering at times just how many of us there actually are in the therapy room!

Ashworth likewise states that hosts can notice themselves participating in odd behaviour which can be deemed to be 'out of character.' He says, *'They will confront themselves bemused, and say 'why did I do that? It's not like me at all.'* Fiore cites an example of a man who, despite being from an upper middle class background, felt attracted to heavy drinking bouts in the company of working class men. He also became increasingly badly behaved towards his wife, sensing on occasion that someone was *'speaking through him.'* Upon depossession, he learns that he is possessed by a couple of entities who come from different backgrounds and employ quite opposite ways of behaving to the client's natural way of being. When considering Steve's case, however, it is noticeable that he was always able to separate out his own emotional world and the ownership of his feelings from the alien content of the ghost's projections of despair quite easily.

Why do spirits stay with their hosts? Fiore cites reasons around fear, ignorance, and obsessive attachment to the host – perhaps an overprotective parent who cannot let a bereaved child grow up or a deeply attached spouse who is reluctant for their partner to move on into another relationship. Unattached or solitary ghosts, those who actually have no relatives or friends to lead them into the astral realms, will attach to any stranger whose energy matches their own and make them feel able to function on some level. One entity in a case study tells her: *'I joined many, many people. I found I could join them when I wanted to and leave when I wanted to. It was interesting. When I got bored or depressed, I could just leave and find some other person to join.'*

It may be that the living hosts are chosen specifically as they remind the possessors of others. Fiore cites an example of an entity feeling reluctant to leave a teenage girl who reminds her of her own lost daughter. It is also possible for several entities to possess the same host but for the entities to have complex and aggressive relationships with each other. This may be the case when I go on to look at the possibility that Steve has more than one entity, or possibly an entity and a demon attached to him, later on. We also saw such cases when considering the interaction of the personalities of the troops inhabiting the woman in *'When Rabbit Howls,'* although of course this was attributed to entirely different reasons from those of spiritual possession.

Sinister reasons around unfinished business, for example entities motivated by hostility or bullying tactics are possible. Perhaps spirits latch onto hated persons for such reasons. More sinister still, a motivation for entities to attach to the living may be the desire for revenge. We know that John thinks Steve is his brother Dan and we know that John is angry and presumably revengeful against Dan, whilst also having the motivation of needing Steve to contact his daughter and ask her to return home following the disclosure of her pregnancy. In other words – such entities have their own agenda. This makes sense of the experiences of Steve and his colleagues being aware of the 'enticing' nature of John's communication with them. Ashworth says '*...the spirit can act out its own desires using the energy of the person.*' This can obviously result in serious consequences. The entity quoted above who roams around attaching indiscriminately to any available aura and then leaving them, continues: *'I made most of those people miserable. I gave them some power, some got very interested in the occult, but they all became depressed, and I didn't like to be around them for long.'* We can therefore see how unhealthy and how debilitating it is for spirits to hang around for long, especially if the cost of the process is their hosts losing happiness, risking relationships, careers and ultimately having to use psychiatric services in their despair.

In particular, however, Fiore cites addictions such as drugs, alcohol, smoking, food or sex as strong reasons for entities to possess living persons. It may be that alcohol and drug use weakens the aura itself and makes it easier for spirits to attach. Additionally, however, it may be that there is a need for spirits to fulfil their own compulsions and thereby they disregard passing onto the spiritual world in order to continue to fulfil them. One of the possessed clients with whom Fiore works has suddenly developed a binge eating disorder and tells her *'Someone is forcing me to eat! It's like somebody is taking my hand and making me do it. I don't want to! There's a person saying "Feed me!" I feel like I'm almost out of control of my own consciousness.'* Ashworth adds that people who *'live on challenging housing estates'* are also particularly vulnerable. He says: *'The people who have to live in these situations are often unaware of the psychic forces governing their very existence. All they see is the fabric of society breaking down around them and their own tolerance and moral fibre being eroded in the cess pit of psychic misfortune.'*

So it becomes easy to ask, does the spirit cause the addiction or does the addiction cause the spirit? One particularly strong issue that came up for me when I was carrying out the research on these themes was that of personal responsibility. Whilst Fiore questions: *'How many murders, suicides, incidents of child abuse and other crimes are committed by possessing spirits?'* she does acknowledge that if we are to absolve ourselves through the defensive stance of 'something just came over me,' then issues around taking responsibility for our actions and implementing positive change becomes 'muddied.'

In addition to an attraction to a person's energy, spirits may also have an attachment to a place or land. We saw in part two that theories such as the one put forward by Oliver Stone, spirits may become embedded within the fabric of a specific location and that this may be picked up by living people who are prone to be psychically skilled. An interesting example of this took place in a church in when Steve and I were on holiday in Greece and I mention this incident when we pick up my diary again in part five. As soon as Steve entered that particular environment; he felt cobwebs and cold spots. Take him out of the environment and the experiences cease. As mentioned earlier, Steve has been informed of a railwayman being seen in the town prior to his childhood. The public toilets, near to where Steve and his friends used to play, were widely reported to be haunted and were universally avoided. We may conclude that John haunts the vicinity simply because he wears a uniform and worked on the railway, so may have died there and has a strong attachment to the place. We witness this theme in the film *'The Others'* when in the final scenes the entities have driven out the living 'intruders' from their domain, declaring *'This house is ours!...No-one can make us leave this house...'.*

Ashworth says, *'No matter what need they are desperately seeking to fulfil, earthbound spirits are immensely frustrated, confused and unhappy; they can find no peace or lasting satisfaction while inhabiting other people's bodies. They are truly lost souls who do not know they are hurting themselves.'* This seems evident in John's demeanour and illustrative in the feelings Steve is picking up.

All of this leaves us with the question, is Steve possessed? This is his main fear. Personally I think not, as despite having very strong feelings that seemed out of character, Steve's personality did not change and also the phenomena was clearly rooted in the warehouse. Unless, that is, this is an entity that steps in and out of Steve's aura every now and then as he begins and ends his shift. Additionally, the fact remains that Steve's ghost is rooted in external sources. Steve can see and hear him as a separate individual, rather than experiencing the less visible 'acting out' aspects of possession.

One theory offered is that the scratching on Steve's face may be a somatic re-experiencing of the injuries John may have received when falling, following his fatal heart attack. I also wonder if the scratch may have been the result of a confrontation with Dan, following discovery of the abuse of John's daughter, which is being transmitted to Steve's face in the present. Maybe this is something to consider when we ponder on the possibility that John is using Steve's body whilst he delays his departure to the afterlife.

Energies, Auras and Vibrations

In its most simplistic form, Ashworth argues that the *'physical universe is composed of matter...sub atomic particles which make up atoms, which in turn make up molecules. Each and every atom is in a state of vibration and movement and consists of electrical charges and magnetic forces; therefore every atom is electro magnetic. As everything in the universe is made up of atoms, therefore everything in the universe is electro magnetic.'* The earth can be described as a living thing – consisting of ley lines, power points and electrical storms etc, all vibrating at different frequencies and in infinite numbers. As we have seen, radios and tape recordings also present as significant issues in Steve's case and several observations have been made about the increased use of electrical equipment not only within the warehouse itself but in society generally as we now all use computers and mobile phones regularly and in escalating numbers. Ashworth goes on to state that people are made up of atoms also and it therefore follows that humans also hold magnetic forces, electrical charges and that electricity is created in the brain. This ceases at the point we know as death.

According to my research on this subject, and I have been extremely brief in reproducing much of it, we all have a physical body and several 'light' bodies. Together they form the 'Aura.' Vibrations exist at differing frequencies depending upon each 'body.' The ***'physical body'*** is exactly that – the matter that makes up our bodies – tissues, muscles, bone, blood vessels etc. This body can obviously be seen. Ashworth informs us that: *'The physical body is no barrier to the vibrational frequencies of other dimensions for the beings who dwell therein... this is why we see a spirit pass through a solid wall, because the vibration is so high that physical matter cannot prevent its passage. It will pass through the solid wall without disturbing a single molecule.'*

The other bodies, having higher and faster vibrations than physical matter, are not visible to most people. Descriptions of these seem to vary according to what I read. Basically, however, these seem to comprise of the **'etheric body'** which radiates anything from a couple of inches to about twenty inches outwards from the physical body and is, according to Fiore, a duplicate of it. Not only does it look after our health but this body acts as a transmitter and link from the higher frequency bodies to the physical body. It can frequently be perceived by clairvoyants. The **'emotional (or astral) body'** implies exactly that. This is involved with processing our emotions, leaving an impression on the physical body which can be experienced as our feelings. This extends outwards from anything from a few inches to between six to eight feet again, depending on which account I read. This body changes in resonance, according to which emotions are being experienced. Significantly, I am aware that owing to the traditional positioning of the seating in a therapy room, this is the area in which a counsellor would be typically exposed and it is the 'emotional body' with which most therapists would be focussed when working with clients. This leaves another component, the **'lower mental body.'** This is the most mundane perhaps, dealing with day to day thinking and functioning – regular processes such as eating, sleeping, working and so forth. This is generated about twelve feet from the edge of the emotional body. Again I am aware that a counsellor would be impacted by the day to day thoughts and functioning of our clients. It follows, potentially, that a cognitive behavioural therapist would be focussed on and working with a client's thoughts, feelings, belief system and the consequences of their behaviour. Symbolically speaking, sitting on the outskirts of the client's aura. A humanistic therapist, on the other hand, may well be focusing on the emotional content of a client's life – literally getting closer, not only on an interpersonal level but also on a psychic level, to the client's inner world.

Psychic energy, according to Ashworth, has a *'magnetic attraction.'* We all know that we can potentially pick up 'vibes' from others. When working in close proximity with another person's aura, people in professions such as counsellors, police officers, medics, those working with addictions or violence and those who have any 'hands on job' such as hairdressing, massage, or tattooists may all experience a negative energy transference. How often have we felt the need to wash after shaking hands with some individuals, felt a shiver when walking past a stranger in the street, have avoided seating ourselves near a certain person on the bus and all for no discernable reason other than a sense of unease or repulsion? Consider how many times as therapists we may have described certain clients as 'vampires' – those who we have probably all worked with at some point in our careers, who leave us feeling totally physically and mentally drained after a session in their company. Sometimes it can feel that these vibes appear to go beyond non verbal communication, the difficult content of material presented and travels deeper than our usual level of countertransferencial responses.

Our energy changes all the time. Clients will become aware of the rise and fall of emotional energy during the course of their sessions. Counsellors may take particular note of how our energy rises and drops when seeing different client after client. We can all be aware when our attraction to others is ignited or when we feel repelled. Ashworth informs us that: *'New frequencies of energy bring forth new perceptions and desires as our lives begin to change in a positive way.'* Perhaps this may match in with what Carl Rogers may be referring to as the *'Actualising Tendency'* but a spiritual version of the potato endeavouring to grow towards the light despite adverse circumstances of environment! We can clearly see the impact here of Steve's change in history. Leaving a negative situation and becoming happier, more in tune with himself and perhaps initiating an alteration in his psychic energy through his life transition may have caused a shift in his psychic energy, meaning that John was then allowed in.

Our light bodies surround us but cannot generally be perceived through our senses of touch, taste, smell, visual or auditory senses. These bodies of light, however, can be accessed through clairvoyance – literally meaning 'clear seeing' - once one begins to develop such ability. Ashworth says we all can become aware of the higher vibrations of the light bodies, especially in our peripheral vision and particularly when relaxed. This is when we see 'ghosts' or 'spirits' from the corner of our eye, something that Steve's colleague Bernie has previously mentioned. Ashworth states that most people are rooted inflexibly in the physical realm and are not open minded enough to learn of or develop their higher functioning. He goes on to claim, however, that it is possible for us all to achieve this skill with varying degrees of success. He informs us that most of us do not access other light bodies or dimensions quite so naturally though, similar to birds or fish being unable to access both air and sea.

Under Psychic Attack

Ashworth tells us that *'Psychic energies are all around us. Psychic Vampires or Entities are everywhere and you would be amazed and most probably horrified to learn how many. People in the street are carrying them around with them and these energies are interested in one thing: food. The food they crave is our energy; our electromagnetic life force energy; the energy within our chakras and our aura, which is the very essence of our light body or spirit body'* (1999).

Whilst our physical body by its very nature obeys physical laws, it can be penetrated, either harmlessly or maliciously by our other light bodies or by the beings that dwell within other dimensions. The aura provides a 'protective shield' and is part of each living human being, but only so far. If the aura is weakened, torn or damaged in any way, it can make us vulnerable to psychic attack. Fiore likens an aura to the immune system – possession can be physically and emotionally debilitating, rather like having the flu. Being unconscious either through accident or through anaesthesia can make us particularly vulnerable to possession. Hospitals are cited as places full of entities seeking hosts. Those spiritual possessors who have been cared for and may not have realised that they have died may willingly seek a medic, visitor or fellow patient as a safe place on which to attach.

Ashworth argues that since spirits 'feed' from the energy in the aura this can leave the host with a physical body that feels *'drained and debilitated.'* We can see this happening repeatedly with Steve. Not only is he finding the strain of being haunted highly emotionally problematic, but also he is sensing the despair and heavy depressed feelings linked with the entity that is literally eating him, whilst he remains working in the warehouse. His physical health has also suffered somewhat. This reminds me of the dementors described in J K Rowling's Harry Potter books, fictional figures emerging from the author's imagination and personal experiences of depression. Dementors are the sinister cloaked guardians of Azkaban prison who feed on the energy of others leaving them drained and feeling like *'I'd never be cheerful again.'* Associated with death, despair and decay, dementors feed on the fears of the living… *'And then the thing beneath the hood, whatever it was, drew a long, slow, rattling breath, as though it were trying to suck something more than air from its surroundings.'* Dementors can literally suck out one's soul with a kiss.

Ashworth tells us that psychic attacks can be 'passive' (or undirected) or 'active.' These attacks can be sub divided into 'accidental or deliberate' and of the deliberate attacks, these can be 'malicious or non malicious.' Whichever form such events take, they can be categorised as 'attacks' since the ultimate result is the disruption in the energy state of the host's aura and chakra system. Most attacks, therefore, result from the transference of energy from an entity attaching to an aura and increasing its own energy as your own depletes.

So we are aware of why Steve may be under attack but why a warehouse as a location? Ashworth informs us as we are now aware, that *'spirits arrive in one's life for two main reasons. They are either attracted to the energy of a person or attracted to the energy of a place.'* It follows that our John has some sort of attraction to the location of the warehouse, particularly if he is bound by his history as a railwayman, on a site that used to be the sidings of the railway where he may have worked. Ashworth says: *'Every place has its own distinctive energy. Every building or piece of land has its own personality signature by the nature of its energy imprint or by way of the energies which move through it.'* He elaborates that *'the energy absorbed by the fabric of a building can affect people.'* Most people, whether believers in the supernatural or not, will have picked up on atmospheres in certain places. The local Women's Centre, where I used to work as a counsellor for example, does not hold a cheerful history within its walls. In the present it is used as support for women experiencing sexual abuse, domestic violence and other life traumas and before that, as a private children's clinic (for dental treatment and tonsillectomies), we can safely assume the building has been associated with fear, disempowerment, physical and emotional pain. Prior to this, indications are that the centre was used as a refuge for 'fallen' women and may also have been used temporarily as overspill for the nearby workhouse. It seems that the basement, now used for small workshops, was where children were kept separately from their parents and it is suspected, provided the scene for the deaths of at least a handful of these suffering little ones. Whilst myself I always felt comfortable working in this location, it was notable that a significant number of women would not use the building after dark and many in particular refused to go down to the basement area. In such cases of unease, or of any experience of direct 'haunting,' the right hemisphere of the brain would briefly dominate the left and disallow us to cognitively process such feelings or argue them away, perhaps until we have left the location. Ashworth goes on to cite the importance of psychically clearing homes of objects that hold the energy of deceased people, describing this as an *'energy spring clean.'* I guess that in its most simple form, most counsellors would agree that it is particularly important to consider our rooms carefully in terms of decor, positioning of the chairs, temperature, lighting and the need to present a neutrally comfortable environment – in other words, radiating the 'right' vibration!

To summarise, spirits may try to find someone whose energy is the same as someone to whom they were positively or negatively attached to when they were alive – or a place with a similar energy and affiliation. This would make some sense of why Steve has attracted John. We may assume that Steve may have a similar essence – or energy – as John's brother, Dan. We are also holding our awareness from the suggestion posed by Claudia that Steve may also bear a resemblance to Dan physically, particularly when he has his hair and beard styled in a certain way. The fact that Steve's father was named Dan and also worked on the railways for a time, I suspect remains a coincidence, although at this point, we do not really know. There may be other reasons for this, as yet undiscovered. Ashworth, agreeing with Claudia, also argues that spirits travel – in John's case, a radius of three or four miles, which is perhaps why he has not attached to Steve's aura and made himself felt within our home, much to my relief.

How Healing Works

The essential need and goal for psychic healers is to persuade possessing spirits to depart in peace, to leave; the destination being the appropriate realm we settle in once we have died. To merely cleanse the host of their presence would escalate problems - causing spirits to once more become wandering discarnates, hungry to latch onto yet another unsuspecting person's aura. It is noticeable that whilst owning humility on the subject generally, on this particular issue many psychic healers write with authority on the subject as alleged experts. Promises of a happy afterlife in which addictions and disabilities will no longer be experienced seem to be strong enough to persuade entities to depart with deceased loved ones or spirit guides and are strong themes in the examples I have studied. How do the healers achieve this aim?

Again put very simply, psychic healers are able to channel the energies from the universe through their own bodies and into that of the client or patient they wish to heal. Ashworth claims that we all have the ability to do this – either through being born with this power, or becoming aware of it, some in a more drastic way than others, and perhaps in a manner which can cause excessive disruption to life, relationships and future plans. As we have seen, a trigger for Steve may have been the movement in his own life in terms of loss of a long relationship and change in living accommodation. The only thing that remained a constant was his work location, the site of the haunting. I guess that relationships can become strained and even dissolve as a result of newly discovered spiritual abilities and my own anxieties around living with a psychic for a partner and what impact this may have on our future are evident in my diary. The psychic ability to channel energy is at first uncontrollable but can then be opened up and shut down at will with practice and the increase in knowledge. Energies can be re-attuned, for example through practices such as Reiki, or specialist working with the chakras or auras. Ashworth also goes on to advocate the value of palmistry and tarot as *'accurate divination tools'* but only when used in practiced hands.

He tells us how he goes about healing, using his own aura to soak up the energy of the aura of the affected person and thereby he is able to *'transmute the vibrations through my etheric aura into the mind/brain, which then translates the energies into words, pictures and perceptions which I can relate to.'* We can clearly see here that this is what has been happening in Steve's case. Steve is clearly able to see, hear and perceive John in terms of visual images, auditory messages and internalised thoughts and feelings. For him, however, as an unpractised healer, the experience is uncontrolled, the contact is highly random and this causes pain and distress.

Ashworth confidently tells us that: *'...the universe never sends you a job you cannot do. You carry enough light to tackle successfully anything which is thrown at you.'* Fiore likewise confidently calls upon greater powers: spirit guides, various saints, angels and Jesus Christ if she requires aid in her work.

Psychic healers, like the supervisors required by counsellors and other therapists, need regular healing sessions from others, who are their 'energy equal' in order to undertake the work well. As I said before, when I chose to record all of the events in an attempt to support myself, if we are not doing this for ourselves, we cannot effectively support others, either in our personal lives or in our work as therapists, whichever methods and theories we employ with our clients.

Facing Demons

Ashworth also believes that *'all forms of energy work involves opening doorways into the other dimensions....where dwell other beings such as spirits, entities, psychic vampires and others.'* Therefore an active psychic attack is from an energy source that embodies some sort of life force from an alternative dimension or the other light dimensions previously explored and of which most of us remain unaware. These beings may inhabit different dimensions simultaneously. Ashworth also describes malicious attacks which may be instigated by one person upon another – black magic, voodoo and witchcraft for example. We return to this issue briefly when looking at client examples in part four. I am, however, not going to argue a case against the possibility of curses, voodoo and witchcraft, particularly when it forms part of a basic belief in a client's culture.

I am also reminded of my sense of Steve's ghost's seemingly malicious bullying tactics on Steve and Steve's sense that the apparition is out to 'get me.' Fear itself is of great attraction to a spirit, entity or demon that can absorb and feed from the energy released by this emotion. Perhaps this is why we are naturally afraid of ghosts. Ghosts cannot exist without our fear. Perhaps we do indeed function like batteries in such circumstances, charging up the power of these visitors from other dimensions.

Finally entities, spirits and others may be manipulating people within other dimensions and this seems the most likely scenario in Steve's case, if Ashworth's work is to be noted seriously.

At this point, let us take a look at demons and explore the question – what are the differences between them and discarnate entities, if indeed either of them actually exists? In short, it seems that demons are nasty types. Ashworth describes them as *'A step up the energy ladder from spirits'* and as much more *'Solid and evil than that of a spirit or entity.'* He says of them: *'In a case of demonic possession, we are dealing with beings who will lie, cheat, hide whenever they can to avoid being seen, and even do their best to attack you and damage your energy system.'*

Fiore cites that the demon phenomena have never actually been human. She goes on to claim that there are numerous well documented cases of Catholic priests performing the Roman Ritual to exorcise demons which can cause physical and mental trauma and even many deaths – I am unsure as to where she gets her evidence for this claim. Fiore says she has never worked with cases of demonic possession in her clients. Ashworth, however, has. Demons, in fact, can not only attach to the living but may also attach themselves to entities – Ashworth cites one example of a demon who is feeding from the anger and fear experienced by an entity who was a murderer. The murderer/entity remains in possession of a client as he fears punishment in the afterlife. The demon is, in fact, holding the entity hostage.

Demons also seem to be highly physical. Whilst tackling the demon/entity/murderer, Ashworth experiences an attack himself as: *'what can only be described* as a kick in the abdomen. It came with such force as to lift me off the chakra a little way as I let out a startled groan.' He feels the emotions of anger and fear as he *'was kicked again a number of times.'* Ashworth also cites an example of a demon attached to a female client who is *'hiding in the solar plexus chakra.'* As Ashworth works to cleanse the woman of the demon, it pushes upwards into the unfortunate woman's heart chakra – which she could, apparently, feel moving upwards – this is accompanied by thoughts that seem not to belong to the possessed woman and, most interestingly, by *'a foul odour of cooking.'*

How simple, logical and much to my increasing sense of discomfort upon reading this, does this research seem to fit in with Steve's experiences – particularly the later ones – his face being repeatedly scarred, the violent forces with which objects move or are thrown causing disruption to the warehouse and the internalised negative emotions causing his alien feelings of despair, depression and debilitation. These, Ashworth describes as a demon preying on the victims fears and ultimately becoming *'A powerful force of negativity.'* We also have evidence of smells, unnervingly of sulphur, traditionally associated with the devil. Worse than that, Steve has had sight of a small girl standing behind John – and both are 'solid' figures - seemingly posing as Steve's deceased sister, although Lily was an elderly lady when she passed away. And, if that isn't frightening enough, we have, on tape, what we would all describe as *demonic* sounds of screaming. It seems that John, pleading for help is an entity who has at least one demon, one that harms, one that entices, screams, attacks and frightens, attached to John, attached to Steve...

At this point I suspect that I may be challenging the belief systems of some of my readers. It may be that our disbelief needs to remain suspended, however, for those of us who struggle with discussion of the spiritual dimensions, psychic healing and perhaps in particular the subject of demonic possession. For some people, however, such issues are not so unusual and form an acceptable and fairly ordinary part of life experience. They are the natural psychics.

Three Psychics

'Psychic adj. of the soul or mind; of or having apparently supernatural powers n. a person with such powers' From 'The Oxford English Dictionary.'

It may now, therefore, be useful to continue to pull together some of the themes that have recurred throughout this book. It seems it is becoming increasingly possible to observe the similarities, some differences and a few links with Steve's experiences when considering his story from differing angles and seeking an answer for his situation. Mental health, trauma, spiritual or demonic possession have been discussed in brief. That leaves the possibility of natural psychic ability. Could Steve possibly be psychic? And what exactly is a psychic? Owens defines a psychic as one who can tap into the mental energy or 'divine essence' of another person which is why, allegedly, a destiny of that person can be ascertained in some cases. A mystic, on the other hand taps directly into the energy of God, or a divine being. Owens himself who describes himself as a *'Reluctant Psychic'* cites that it was once he entered puberty that his psychic skills began to 'skyrocket.' Becoming very depressed and withdrawn he considers the possibility that the cause may be owing to a brain tumour and he is also sent to a psychiatrist who diagnoses him as socially unskilled. The possibility of mental ill health diagnosed for psychic people is never very far away it seems. For me, however, it is starting to feel highly unreasonable to assume that all psychic people have mental health issues or are fraudulent, any more than it is reasonable to expect mentally disturbed patients to possess psychic ability.

In order to illustrate the potentiality of natural psychic ability further I have included the more detailed autobiographies of three mediums that have each enjoyed a high profile displaying their talents at communicating with the spirit world. Individuals who are not, it seems, to be viewed as supernatural survivors, but as psychic thrivers.

Beginning with the classic medium, Doris Stokes, who gained public attention in the 1970s and who wrote several books detailing varied *'Voices In My Ear,'* Doris is among the first of the twentieth century published psychics to gain world wide and media attention. I also explore the work of contemporary 'Psychic to the Stars' Sally Morgan and 'Soul Coach' Michele Knight.

Doris Stokes

'There's something strange about our Doris.' From 'Voices In My Ear.'

Doris Stokes, a 'cold' reader, admits in her first autobiographical book to occasionally having to 'perform' for her shows and incorporating *'a bit of cheating.'* Following her death in 1987, claims of fraudulence prevailed for a while. Whether or not it can be argued that to make a living out of delivering psychic readings for the entertainment of people and filling concert halls for the purpose of profit is morally wrong, Doris was undoubtedly one of the 'greats.' Perhaps indeed she was either a great psychic or a great fraud. Let us examine her experiences in her own words, in her first autobiographical book *'Voices In My Ear.'*

Doris, born in 1920, tells us that she was an ordinary working class girl from Grantham in Lincolnshire, who discovered herself to be psychic at an early age. Doris is supported in this learning by her father who seems similarly inclined. She is, however, maligned by her mother and labelled as likely to *'end up in a mental home one of these days.'* Indeed, it is likely that this could have been her destination under other circumstances when we consider the links between psychic ability and mental ill health as previously discussed. Doris's first childhood psychic experience involves her catching sight of the charred remains of a neighbour who has been burned to death in an accident. Doris witnesses a vision of the man, intact and seemingly alive, standing beside his own body as it is removed by the stretcher bearers.

Doris realises that this is a *'strange gift I was born with'* and she initially tries to suppress it – quite understandably wanting to be like every other youngster.

Like Steve, as a child Doris is very ill, in her case, suffering with impetigo and rheumatic fever. Unlike Steve, however, she reports having contact and communication with imaginary friends whilst recovering: *'I realise now my friends were spirit children, yet at the time I didn't even wonder about them. They were as real and solid to me as the members of my family.'*

As she grows, falls in love and marries, Doris becomes interested in the spiritualist church. On one occasion, her husband having gone to war, she is told by a spiritualist member that he has passed away, although this turns out to be false information. Doris is in fact informed of the truth by her father, dead some years previously who visits her in 'real and solid' form. Later, Doris has a prophetic dream about the death of her baby and then again sees her father who explains that he will come to take the child into the spirit world at *'a quarter to three next Friday.'* This is indeed the time Doris loses her child and literally passes the baby's body over into her father's arms when he arrives to take him away. There remains a continuing link with madness as Doris questions her sanity over these distressing experiences.

Her husband returns, injured and shell shocked from the war: *'Depressed and restless.'* The couple settle as regular members of the church as Doris learns more about her psychic abilities. Some of the experiences she describes are quite graphic in nature, for example witnessing a stream of ectoplasm emerging from a medium and holding the resulting fully formed *'warm, living'* hand allegedly from the spirit world. Doris concludes that *'Either I'd been conned, or anything, absolutely anything, was possible.'* The family move to a cottage where Doris feels watched and it becomes apparent that the place is haunted by an unhappy elderly woman who is attracted by Doris's energy and psychic abilities. Aided by her spirit guide, Ramonov, Doris develops the ability to often hear voices clearly, sometimes singularly or in multitudes. She learns to tune into particular messages from the deceased for those clients who attend consultations with her: *'...the more practise I had, the more experienced I became at distinguishing the voices. At first, it seemed to me like one voice speaking inside my head, but after a while I realised it was outside me, and then that it wasn't one voice but different voices. Soon I was able to tell if they were male or female, old or young.'*

Amongst her many anecdotes on spiritual experiences, Doris describes one where she at first does not realise that the elderly man who has rudely interrupted her demonstration during a church service is, in fact, an apparition. As with so many ghosts, it seems that this one also does not realise he has passed on: *'What a ruddy cheek coming in at this time, I thought in my young, arrogant way. Fancy interrupting the great Doris Stokes…I was so inexperienced and tactless I leant straight over the rostrum and said, "Do you know you're dead?" Little gasps sounded all over the hall and I realised for the first time that nobody else could see him. "Don't be so bloody silly," he said.'*

This is not the first time Doris mistakes a dead person for one living. I am reminded of the first time Steve saw John, running across the warehouse floor. *'Are you OK mate?'* Steve had asked, completely convinced that this man was either a security guard or a new member of staff in distress, present on the night shift for whatever logical reason but having a few problems.

In time and with practice, Doris normalised her psychic abilities: *'I'd lost all trace of fear, and by now it seemed quite natural for me to talk to spirits – particularly as there was nothing "spooky" about the conversations. They were like earthly telephone conversations. With the fear, I'd also lost the sense of being a bit odd, a bit different from other people. I realised now that I was an ordinary wife and mother like millions of other women, but just as some of them were also brilliant cooks, gifted artists or wonderful athletes, I too had a talent. I'd been born with ears that could hear sounds other people couldn't hear and eyes that sometimes saw things other people couldn't see.'*

Doris has a near death experience with an ectopic pregnancy. During her sink into unconsciousness, she reports seeing her deceased father and the baby son who also died at the foot of the bed. A tunnel of bright light, an image which is so often reported by people who have had such near death experiences and a feeling of relief are apparent before she is rushed for emergency surgery. Doris eventually recovers and fully rejoins the physical world, alive. Other major life incidents include her decision to train as a nurse in a mental health ward, directly maintaining perhaps a link between mediums and 'madness.' Doris is attacked by a patient and this incident results in her receiving a severe physical injury. Having her thyroid gland removed necessitates a need for medication for the rest of her life. She suffers from severe post traumatic stress disorder following this event, which possibly includes a dissociative incident when she forgets to give patients their medication. She also suffers a serious debilitating physical paralysis whilst trying to get out of a car, resulting in hospital treatment and a diagnosis of 'tension paralysis' coupled with the statement that *'There was nothing organically wrong, it was all in my mind.'* Doris is clearly severely clinically depressed at this point in her life. Eight weeks in hospital and suffering a relapse after returning home, she is heavily medicated, angry and bitter and reacts by 'closing down' to the spirit world: *'I fell out with the spirit world and closed my ears when they tried to talk to me. It felt they'd used me badly to allow my life to be ruined like this…I wanted nothing to do with any of them.'* Some time later, however, Doris forgets to set up her psychic block and the spirits re-engage. We can see a parallel with Steve and the way it seems it can be possible for those people who are subjected to communication by entities to reject, close up and to tune spiritual contact out from their lives. It seems necessary that there does exist a degree of chosen control for the practised psychic to cease contact, perhaps born out of changing life circumstances, an increase or decrease in traumatic events or from emotions such as rage, fear or stubbornness.

Doris concludes that: *'The spirit world is more concerned with proving to us its existence, than interfering with our lives down here.'* She details being able to track down what happened to murder victims in order to assist the police in addition to giving out seemingly accurate messages to ordinary folk.

In addition to her delivery of individual and group psychic readings for the public, Doris undertakes a variety of exorcisms of haunted environments. She details cases of particularly disruptive entities that damage property, telling us that: *'Over the year another interesting development of my work began to build up – the job of tracking down "troublesome" ghosts! People either laugh about "haunted" houses if they don't live in them, or are terrified of them if they do, but in my experience "hauntings" aren't usually sinister.'* She describes on one occasion how she is able to help some occupants who, like Steve with his requests for help from the church and the occasion he carried a cross during his shift, have sought traditionally religious methods in an attempt to protect themselves. *'There were containers of holy water everywhere, crucifixes nailed to the walls, garlic strewn about, everything the girl could think of to protect herself from this 'evil.'* Whilst Doris is convinced that such haunting spirits are far from malevolent, we can see how this viewpoint again conflicts with Steve's experiences, which are not only sinister but cause him physical and psychological pain. This is especially disturbing when we recall from his experiences that there could be an indication of some sort of 'demonic' presence.

Similarly to Steve's responses in his early encounters with John and the telling him to 'fuck off' episode, Doris's initial reaction to such disruptive situations is one of rage: *'I was too angry to be frightened. "Bloody well cut that out!" I shouted and, to my surprise, everything simply dropped to the floor and a watchful silence settled over the flat.'*

It must be nice to have developed such power. If only such rageful responses had been as effective for Steve!

In her book, Doris also informs us of the significance of a recurring theme, that of cold spots. She says: *'You walk through the room backwards and forwards and if there is anything there, you stand in this spot, and an icy sensation creeps up from your feet over your whole body. I never say anything to the others. I just ask them to walk behind me, putting their feet exactly where I put mine and they feel it too.'*

Other familiar themes are present when we consider the life of Doris Stokes. Like Claudia, the spiritualist Steve went to visit, Doris is aware that the Catholic Church in particular is strongly disapproving of spiritualism and she does come up against some strong opposition and organised protests during her world wide travels. Another theme in common with Steve's experiences occurs when Doris describes giving shows in Australia. On one particular occasion she mentions that the many clocks backstage all go 'berserk.' *'The hands were whizzing round an hour every minute.'* She orders them to stop, and of course, they do. It seems that Doris had an effective way of dealing with mischievous entities by taking a dominant attitude and refusing to be bullied. But as we have seen this did Steve little good – and presumably is likely to be ineffective with any aggressor, living or dead, who chooses to continue on a persecutory path.

There is also a highly physical aspect to Doris's psychic work. She informs us that spirits draw their energy from her solar plexus area, which causes physical debilitation and a feeling of exhaustion in the aftermath of the contact. Doris provides an example of one particularly strong bodily sensation during a sitting when communicating with a female murder victim. This seems somewhat reminiscent of injuries inflicted on Steve: *'As she talked I began to experience some weird and unpleasant sensations. I saw blood spattered all over a bed, felt blows in my face and teeth being knocked right back in my mouth.'* Clearly she is experiencing the parallel injuries from a particularly violent beating and murder. Giving another example, Doris tells us following communication from a murdered spirit that: *'by the end of his communication I felt limp and drained. The violence and pent up emotion came over so strongly, I felt this man wouldn't rest until his killers were brought to justice.'* It seems that unfinished business indeed provides a strong theme which links the dead and the living. It may be up to those living psychics to attempt to bring some cessation to such issues and the suffering caused to deceased people.

Let us consider aspects of Doris's life, assuming for the moment that she is genuinely psychic and not fraudulent as has been strongly suggested since her death. Growing up, she was not physically or sexually abused, although interestingly there is a suggestion that on the way from school she narrowly avoids molestation by a lurking man who continually attempts to grab her. Witnessing the sight of a burned body at such a tender age would have been a traumatic shock to her. She feels different from her young peers owing to her psychic ability and her contact with the spirit children. She experiences some disapproval and possible rejection from her mother. She will have been further traumatised by the early death of her much loved father and later on by the belief that her husband has perished in the war. Doris then endures the sudden illness and death of her baby son and subsequent miscarriages and infertility. She clearly suffers with post traumatic stress following the attack by the patient in hospital which in effect, ended her medical career. Exhaustion is a constant theme in her book. Doris works hard, travels much, suffers periodic serious illnesses and is physically frail. In older age, she describes an out of body experience and witnesses the viewing of herself sitting in a chair, a sensation she finds highly unnerving. We can only speculate on how many of these incidents would have triggered or fuelled her psychic ability. It is without doubt that Doris Stokes certainly led a colourful life, at times rich in traumatic incident. Whether she was severely mentally impacted which triggered hallucinations and other supernatural and paranormal experiences, whether she was a genuine medium, or a combination of both, she was certainly convincing and popular enough with the public during her lifetime to fill large venues around the world; making successful appearances on television, allegedly demonstrating genuine psychic talents.

In further consideration of Doris's autobiography, the role of the media seems significant, as does marketing and money. It was interesting for Steve and I to note the reactions of so many people who were becoming aware of Steve's alleged psychic ability. The universal response, including that of his GP, seemed to suggest that appearing on TV or radio was a logical next step in order for Steve to progress and demonstrate his newly found talents. There seemed to be an expectation that sharing his story would be beneficial, that a joint exploitation (of both Steve and the public) was acceptable and that a fortune could be made. Or, if not to actually contemplate making either a high profile or quieter living from all this, then at least there was present some pressure from folk that Steve should develop his awareness of spiritual presences and to learn to channel them. Undoubtedly, individuals can and do make a thriving living from psychic readings either privately or to groups and have undertaken this historically over the centuries, becoming particularly popular during the Victorian age, as we have seen in previous pages. It is evident, however, that there are also many psychic people who do not take such routes and who do give readings without a financial charge, presumably out of a desire to genuinely assist and give hope to distressed or curious clients. One thing Doris was clear about, whether paid or not, was the actual function of a medium. She described this as not holding any ability to 'tell fortunes' but to pass on literal messages through clairaudience or clairvoyance. There exists in the profession much preoccupation with expectation from sitters, the conscious or unconscious hope of the clients perhaps in a way similar to clients of counselling and the constant seeking for 'proof' of the spirit world.

Reputation becomes significant in order to attract the work. Doris had to perform on stage and was under pressure to produce satisfactory results for her expectant audiences who had bought their tickets. She does admit to some 'filling in' when the voices go silent, some spying on conversations in the public toilets and a few other tricks in order to give her public what they required. She does also admit to getting it wrong on occasion, *'Mediums do make mistakes sometimes just like everyone else.'*

It is perhaps partly owing to such honesty in her books that Doris Stokes' reputation became sullied following her death but during her life she did attract a devoted following and clearly provided a role model for those practising mediums who followed her into the limelight. She was undoubtedly aware of the ongoing work and research to be done in the spiritual world and ends her book quoting these words from her father: *'then, through it all, came my father's voice. 'Remember Doll, never look back, progress, always progress.'*

Following the death of Doris Stokes in the 1980s and acknowledging the impact she had, there was room for other mediums to fill her shoes and continue to develop psychic work. Let us therefore focus on another famous medium who again holds a high profile in the public eye, but who, this time, is more contemporary. Sally Morgan, advertised and revered widely as *'The Psychic to The Stars.'*

Sally Morgan

'One minute I'm a dental nurse, the next I'm Princess Diana's psychic. You couldn't make it up, could you?' From 'My Psychic Life.'

Author of *'My Psychic Life'*, published in 2008, Sally Morgan was born and grew up in Fulham in the 1950s. Her Grandmother Gladys, known locally as 'The Witch of Fulham' sold newspapers for a living and through this activity she made frequent physical contact with the hands of strangers and regular buyers alike when taking their money and passing over the papers. Nanny Gladys would subsequently tell people personal things about themselves, making predictions and then dissociating - not remembering what had been said. Whilst Sally tells us that she was too young to remember her, again there seems to be an indication that psychic ability could be genetically handed down the generations.

Sally herself sees her first ghost at the age of four whilst at nursery. This is the deceased grandfather of another little girl and who Sally can clearly see standing behind his granddaughter's chair. Sally, who cannot understand why she is not allowed to have her own granddad with her as well, is punished for making up stories – a typical reaction from adults who perceive children to be somehow stepping out of line, whether through an over active imagination, or displaying behaviour or distress that is labelled as problematic. Her intimidating father displays reactions to Sally's ongoing perceptions of spirit people of *'puzzlement, curiosity, suspicion.'* Sally says, *'I didn't know it then, but would have to get used to that look as I got older.'* Sally learns to stay quiet about the fact she can see ghosts – *'ghosts only I could see'* and she begins to experience psychic sensations on average once every couple of weeks and details several examples of the spirits she encounters.

She tells us that her home in a dark basement on Waldemar Avenue had a significant emotional impact on her. Sally makes particular mention of the bathroom inhabited by a spirit who *'would make her do things.'* She goes on to keep the details confidential other than to describe these activities as *'naughty... too dark and too frightening.'* Hints of abuse perhaps? Or simply some personal psychic activity Sally chooses to keep to herself as she claims.

One particular night, Sally describes her intense fear when she suffers the trauma of waking in the night and knowing that her parents have gone – undergoing the terrifying fears incited in the abandoned child. This occurs repeatedly as her parents, a young couple, leave the children to go out socialising on a Saturday night. Abandonment, attachment issues and the later severing of her relationship with her mother altogether – she informs us that she has not spoken to her mother for twelve years - are all interesting themes for psychic Sally.

Sally details some of the spirits she encounters and tells us that *'They appear for as long as they're needed and no more.'* For example she is aided by entities when she is a small child and unable to reach a light switch. The switch is turned on and off for her by an unseen spiritual helper, much to the bemusement of her father. Once she was tall enough to reach the switch, the convenient switching on and off to light her way ceases. Electricity and cold chills are once more recurring themes in this home although Sally tells us that she continues to blow light bulbs on the stage as she gets older and becomes famous.

Among the spirits she sees in childhood, Sally spots the lifeless body of a woman who broke her neck on the stairs before Sally's family moved in. As we know from the experiences of Doris Stokes who saw the burned remains of her neighbour or of Eve White being forced to view her grandparent's corpse lying in the coffin, for a child to see a dead body is undoubtedly highly traumatic.

Like Steve, who is about the same age as Sally and among his childhood illnesses suffered a form of mild polio, and like Doris Stokes before her, Sally is seriously ill as a child. She suffers with whooping cough on an annual basis and on one occasion, again like Steve, what seems to be a mild form of the polio virus. A resulting high temperature can of course induce delusions and Steve did tell me that on one occasion his fingers swelled up and he could also see 'little people' at the foot of his bed. Likewise Sally explains of her own experience: *'What used to happen was that I'd get delirious and have minor hallucinations. I'd look at my hand and think I could see my fingers swelling, then I'd start crying, telling mum and dad that I had fingers like sausages.'*

During one particularly severe illness, Sally clearly perceives the image of a man on the ceiling and it is only later that she identifies Jesus from a religious painting. There is evidence of a religious blueprint in Sally's childhood as her mother attends the spiritualist church to try to contact her mother, Nanny Gladys. At fifteen, Sally is invited into the medium's circle to find that what others strive so hard for comes easily to her. She can see spirits. Over the years she learns to control and to tune in and out of her contact with the ever present spirits that she picks up naturally: *'I see everything. It's as though it appears around and behind the sitter. What I get is images, fragments of images, random stray thoughts, snatches of speech. It's like I've switched on a television, turned on the radio, opened a book and started a telephone conversation – all at the same time. It's a bombardment. It's all I can do to control it.'*

Do near death experiences as children have an impact on psychic ability? Is this ability triggered or developed through trauma or illness? Why do some children have protective spirit guides? Could it be a way of gaining some healthier parenting and nurturing that is lacking from primary attachment sources? Clearly we see how Sally somewhat neglected and, with a father who intimidates her at home, survives through her perception of being supported by a benign, protecting spirit or two. *'To me these spirits were part of the house. I felt almost as though I belonged to them, and that they would protect me: from getting burnt on the iron, from catching a chill and from seeing fingers like sausages. I had nothing to fear from them. Not from the dead people. It was the living who scared me.'* What pre-disposes some people to be psychic when others are not? Why are Sally and Doris psychic when their sisters are not? Why, among Steve's many sisters was it only Lily who professed to be a medium? Does the premature experiencing of issues such as change, sex, death, of views of corpses, of lack of control, of powerlessness, have an impact on the child's ability to respond and develop coping strategies that are maybe less generally understood than those diagnoses offered by mental health models?

Sally actually visits Doris Stokes for a reading describing Doris by then as becoming a 'household name.' Not hugely impressed by this experience, however, Sally gets on with being a teenager in the swinging 1960s. She marries young, quickly separates from her husband and becomes a mother. After a second marriage, Sally sees the spirit of a man sitting on her feet at the foot of her bed one night. Men at the end of the bed are a common vision for abuse survivors, as we have learned and I do continue to hold the question in my mind that there may have been deeper issues during Sally's childhood and youth at Waldemar which continue to haunt her. She says: *'There was a darkness in that house, I always knew that. Waldemar was the source of so much that had happened to me; it had shaped my life. Our family belonged to that house. It wasn't happy that we were leaving.'* Perhaps like Sylvia Fraser, author of *'My Father's House'* the home as the scene of early abuse means that Sally also projects a great deal onto the house. The house itself subsequently burns down after the family have left, leaving an unidentifiable dead body in its upper rooms. Sally observes that the fire itself starts in Sally's old childhood room. *'It's that spirit, I thought as we drove. It's the spirit in the bathroom. What happens to them, I wondered, when their home burns down? Where do they go?'* And we, the reader, never do find out what occurred in that family bathroom.

Sally cuts off her relationship with her mother, choosing this severance of what has been an insecure attachment to a primary care figure. Her mother has remained in denial about Sally's talents, and plays up her illnesses as a possible cause for Sally's delusions and odd behaviours. Sally acknowledges that illnesses do indeed play a factor. Increased vulnerability enables her to 'see stuff' and to be more open. I am reminded of how often counsellors comment that we can actually be capable of doing some of our most effective work when we are tired and our natural defences are more limited.

In Sally's view, spirits have a right to exist and she will not get rid of them. She tells us that: *'If your house has a spirit and you can see it the last thing you should be thinking about is getting rid of it. Congratulations, it's proof that you've got a touch of psychic ability. You should be pleased.'*

Sally also believes that the intention of any spirit is to help those on earth and that is why her messages are never malicious or harmful. I am sure that in light of his own experiences of being haunted by a highly unwanted entity, Steve would disagree. Sally does let us know, however, that there is a place for exorcism in certain cases, for example that of a certain Mrs Walters, a particularly unhappy entity who haunts Sally's own home and family for a while. When the exorcists arrive, Sally observes the normality of the ritual: *'I suppose we both half expected them to arrive at midnight, smack bang in the middle of a thunderstorm, and start chanting or something, like a scene from The Exorcist. Instead, it was so...normal. More like afternoon tea with the Waltons than a Hammer Horror.'* Holy water is sprinkled and a few prayers said and following a *'post exorcism cup of tea,'* this particular ghost has been banished, clearly wanting and choosing to leave.

Sally learns to 'open' and 'close' down her ability to hear the voices and likens herself to a 'radio.' Somewhat bombarded with images, sensory input and disturbing material, it takes her longer to learn to control its randomness and to acknowledge that yes, she is in fact, a medium. Sally realises with time that: *'One thing I knew; I should have been scared, but I wasn't. I wasn't seeing a ghost, not in the horror movie sense of the word. He was someone on another plane who had as much right to be there as I did. I never used to try and communicate with the spirits I saw. Sometimes a spirit will try and make contact...but most of the time they were simply part of the fabric of the house; doing whatever it is they did...they were there. They were often around. But we didn't really share the same reality.'*

She acknowledges that she is ready to use this gift after decades of not understanding, trouble and shame about its use or misuse, particularly during her childhood and learning from adult reactions to try to re-route or ignore it. She learns to describe to her increasing client load what she sees, without attempts at interpretation or analysis. Sally also believes that she can help others but not to gain anything for herself and that she can only view so much – and what she views is never 'crystal clear' – else she would solve the world's problems. Possibly in achieving this, mediums would become God-like all knowing figures. The lack of clarity can be frustrating and on occasion thwart client expectation. Sally observes: *'...it's as though the messages passed on from the spirit world are deliberately oblique. Why? Who can say? I mean, why bother giving out fully? If the spirit world wanted people like me to be taken more seriously on the earth plane then why not give us specifics? Details?'*

This is illustrated when Sally's daughter Fern becomes dangerously ill and Sally berates herself for not seeing it coming. It seems she holds the ability to access much trivia in the dead and the living alike – who is in love with who and what they had for dinner, but not things of great personal, political or worldly importance. She advises to *'Never interpret, always give the message literally.'*

Interestingly, as Sally contemplates the nature of her gift and develops it into adulthood, becoming a sound and successful psychic reader, she recognises that she is exposed to a great deal of trauma. She witnesses murders taking place, women being raped and on one occasion, the multiple drownings as a result of the Zeebruge ferry disaster in 1987. She sees a man being horrifically buried alive by the notorious criminals the Kray twins. She predicts the fall of the twin towers and is involved in readings and healing in the aftermath of those 9/11 terrorist attacks. She also sees the death of the Princess of Wales before it happens, despite believing that the death she is witnessing is that of the Queen. A continual display of blood, terror, body parts, abuse. But she did not see such sights during her early childhood. She feels that logically she was not ready nor would the spirit world expose her to such events before she was old enough, with the exception of the women with the broken neck on the stairs. Sally herself asks: *'These days, I wonder what was the start of it all, that gift? Was it Waldemar, the darkness of my childhood, the trauma of events with Fern, the problems with my mum and dad? I don't know.'* It is interesting to contemplate this chicken and egg situation. What comes first - a psychic ability triggered by trauma in childhood which is then maintained through repeated exposure to further traumas such as those perceived by Sally, or does the post traumatic stress caused by such exposure keep the psychic in a state of stress which maintains the perception of psychic ability?

Whether or not there is any real link between trauma and medium activity, this is Sally's summary of what the spirit world is all about: *'I believe that when we're talking about spirits, we're talking about a person's soul, and that it continues to exist long, long after the physical body has died, but on a different plane: the spirit plane, or spirit world. I see this soul as a ball of energy lodged in the middle of your chest, the place where you feel sorrow and anguish and joy and love. When we die (I call it passing over) the soul moves from the earth plane to the spirit world, where it's drawn towards the living with whom they shared a connection. It's always a benign connection – I don't think I've ever met anyone with a person in spirit wishing them ill. Mainly spirits operate out of love, because if you ask me, love is the guiding form to the spirit world.'*

I think that there are two interesting points here. Firstly, when we think of Steve's entity, John, we may recognise that indeed he may be essentially a benign spirit, as Steve increasingly feels pity and empathy for the decades of misery that John has endured. Also that it seems more likely that the part which is causing destruction, distress and harm could be a demonic presence that has attached itself to John and that this part is actually nothing whatsoever to do with the vast majority of spirit cases that Sally, Doris and mediums like them illustrate. The essence of John, therefore, could be fundamentally harmless, but unfortunate. Secondly, the issue of a great all encompassing, unconditional love as a major positive force is significant and also emerges as a strong issue as we see for our third and final medium, Michele Knight.

Client attitude is an interesting issue for Sally. She says: *'I know that as a psychic you are always being tested. Every reading is a test; everything you say is scrutinised, and that's fine. Whether someone believes in a psychic or not affects how they feel about some pretty major issues; life and death and destiny, maybe even God and religion.'* All clients are also testers, that also seems to be the case with those hearing ghost stories – a client may be asking how mad is the story teller? Or how much of a liar? Or how much am I being taken for a fool here by the story teller?   On the question of belief Sally says: '*I do have a theory: even for those who believe in my work, their belief is never absolute. By which I mean there's a safety mechanism in there somehow, something in their mind that stops them truly believing. Otherwise how could they leave?...I think that even those who think they believe must have something deep inside that allows them to walk away. Doubt? Fear? And if we truly believe – then what are the implications for living, for bothering to live?'*

Sally works her way through a variety of celebrities to become psychic to Diana, the late Princess of Wales.   Like Doris Stokes she is undoubtedly commercially successful. She says in her autobiography: ' *...since Star Psychic was on TV it's gone mad. We worked out the other day that I've got an 18 year waiting list. That's 72,000 people on a database that my youngest, Fern, keeps. Fern gets through 100 calls a day, so if you're on the list and you're in when she calls and you make the slot, then you can see me.'*

I did actually attend an audience with Sally Morgan in the summer of 2009 when she was touring the country and happened to be appearing in my hometown. Ordinarily I would never have considered attending such an event but it seemed like too good an opportunity to miss. I went into the hall feeling open minded, somewhat apprehensive and suitably cynical. I admit to leaving feeling pretty much the same, although I did find the experience interesting. It was noticeable that the audience consisted predominantly of women, some of whom were clearly vulnerable in bereavement. Myself I was one hundred percent certain that there would not be a message from the beyond for me. Partly because I don't feel aware that any of my very few deceased friends or relatives would particularly want to speak to me, or I to them. Not that I don't care, I just don't have much to say beyond 'Hi, how're you doing over there?' As far as I'm aware they have all departed seemingly in peace and it is not my belief that we have any unfinished business to confide in each other. I also knew I would remain uninvolved in such an active manner partly because I still consider myself to be a highly grounded woman who will never actually see a ghost, spirit, demon or whatever. That, it seems, is my partner's remit! The brave friend who accompanied me to the audience does have a spiritual belief and nature, however, and she did close herself down psychologically before we went – she wanted to avoid any potential contact. Needless to say, there were no messages throughout the evening for either of us.

Sally herself was very polished as a show woman, enthusiastic, empathic and professional. She was warm, humorous and entertaining as she felt her way through her messages, searching for information, embroidering on the snippets she was fed by the individuals she worked with over the evening. Statistically of course, amongst the hundreds of people present, she was likely to find someone who had lost a relative called 'Bob' and I had to make an effort to curb some of my scepticism. As time passed, it was clear that she had many 'misses' with names but her 'hits' were indeed quite impressive. As a therapist it was of course interesting for me to read the reactions of the respondents, see what I could pick up myself from the more expressive ones and to monitor my own feelings during the process. At one point I was powerfully aware of wanting to cry – however, when witnessing the tears of women who have lost their children to illness, suicide or stories of relatives who have gone missing – who could fail to feel moved?

I left with a bad headache, but having found the evening worthwhile, and there was plenty to think about. I did notice that my anxiety and insomnia levels rose significantly for a couple of days following my attendance at the audience with Sally. I felt like something had exposed me to situations and events and had opened me up emotionally in a way that I was finding hard to close down. I was aware that I had experienced a level of emotional intensity that I rarely achieve during my interactions with clients and perhaps I should have allowed myself to shed the tears instead of holding them back, to be masked over by this anxious state. I was left feeling unprocessed to an extent.

Sally did make one or two interesting points, which, when I consider Steve's story, I would have to challenge. Firstly she told us, *'Spirits are in heaven – they are happy - always happy – we are the unhappy ones.'* Clearly, from the examples I have included in parts one and two, not all 'ghosts' demonstrate this perpetually blissful state and John himself is obviously deeply depressed and trapped as he wanders and searches for a way to resolve his unfinished business. Secondly Sally informed us that *'Everything we get from the spirit world is about love and them wanting to help us.'* Again, I'm somewhat cynical of this view in light of what Steve has experienced over the past few years and the fact that it is John who appears to have been seeking help from Steve.

Like Doris Stokes, Sally Morgan agrees that there is much to learn in the spirit world and takes a stance that would, of course, infuriate the scientists. *'What I do defies explanation...Some things just cannot be explained.'* She also fully acknowledges that there is an evolutionary aspect to the development of the work carried out by mediums. She concludes: *'I don't understand everything and I don't believe that we are meant to at this moment in time.'*

Let us move on to my final psychic example, Michele Knight.

Michele Knight

'I never knew if I'd be woken by screaming and yelling from humans or scratching and whispering from spirits.' From 'Touched by Evil.'

Michele Knight's experiences are particularly interesting as she experienced long term childhood sexual and physical abuse which she details in her autobiography

'Touched by Evil: The True Story of the Psychic Powers that Saved Me from Abuse' (2008). Her story therefore provides a useful study when considering how deeply entwined the influences of her early traumatic life experiences may be with her developing skills as a medium and psychic. Michele began to develop psychic abilities from the age of two. Additionally, at an early age and beginning to hear the *'telepathic communication'* from her spirit guides, Michele becomes aware of the presence of one particular constant guide, companion and spiritual protector. It is not until Michele reaches the age of thirteen (an age of course traditionally associated with the 'hysterical' prepubescent female), that she discovers the identity of this spirit guide. It is her own twin sister, Lucy, who died at their birth.

Michele's Italian mother is volatile and unbalanced. She is verbally and physically violent and highly inconsistent in her parenting skills. She is also a psychic and her own grandmother was said to be a witch. Michele's mother comfortably incorporates ardent Roman Catholicism with superstition and Michele tells us that she would have no problem working with the combination of holy water, tarot cards, communicating with Jesus and tangling with demons. She splits her work between the healing of others and placing curses on them. She gives readings, séances and speaks in tongues, inviting both playful and malevolent entities into the family home. The young Michele is fully aware of these supernatural visitors as she senses, hears and sees presences throughout the course of her mother's activities.

Michele's mother has a history of abuse experiences herself, having been raped by her own father at the age of seven. She also witnessed traumatic events during the war when the men of the village were all slaughtered and the local priest refused help to the remaining women and children. Michele also learns later that her mother was raped by a group of American soldiers shortly after her marriage to Michele's father. As her mother and probably her maternal grandmother were also highly experienced mediums, Michele holds no doubt that psychic ability is genetic and inherited: *'So I was branded from birth, as a psychic. I was going to follow in my mother's footsteps as someone who can look into different realities, who isn't held in my time or place. I can look at you and just 'know' what is going on in your life, what has happened in your past, and what may well happen in the future...As I learned from my mother, prophecy and magic are in my blood. Sadly, I also inherited a pattern of abuse that stretches far down the generations. Back down through time the children in my family were abused by their protectors, by the adults around them. All families are complex, but mine doubly so. First it was overshadowed by the sadness and loss of power that abuse brings. But, second, it was a family in which power came from other worlds – the dead walked with the living, uneasy spirits scratched on the walls, and tormented souls shrieked for attention and retribution. I grew up both powerless and full of power – it was a strange and perplexing combination.'*

So here we are witnessing a direct combination of psychic gifts, a history of personal abuse, the longevity of trauma filtering down the generations and a mother with a lack of boundaries or the ability to protect or comfort. Bullied by her brother, beaten or ignored by her mother, Michele is repeatedly sexually molested by her neighbour, a series of male lodgers and random strangers. She also seems aware of having been a part of satanic ritual abuse accompanied by sado maschochistic group sexual activity, probably incited by a mentally unbalanced female family friend. Michele has never recovered the memories of these latter experiences and acknowledges a need to build up a defence around these particular traumatising events. When illustrating her own abuse memories, we can see clearly how spirit sister 'Lucy' may be a manifestation of another part, a dissociated alter that copes with the abuse whilst it is happening. She explains: *'I think that, when I was very young, Lucy used to take my place sometimes, so I could blank out the worst of times. She would gently push me aside and I would simply go into the blissful darkness whilst she faced the horrors instead of me. It's similar to what happens when a personality splits off (like Sybil, the other famous multiple personality case) in order to protect the fragile self.'* So whilst Michele is open to the possibility of dissociation during abuse, fully acknowledging that she learned the skills of 'blanking' large segments of her life, I am left to ponder on the possibility of psychic awareness being one more, further extreme division. Can it be possible that some suffering children cope through a displacement into psychic awareness – a sense of 'there must be more to the horrors of life than this?'

Like so many other abuse survivors, it takes Michele years to remember in entirety her distressing experiences and also like so many others, she leads a life employing chaotic behaviours that make her vulnerable to further abuse, taking drugs, becoming addicted to sniffing solvents, self harming, rebelling as a punk, narrowly avoiding being forced into prostitution and being unable to perform conventionally at school or in a workplace. This is not helped by the fact that her unbalanced mother has no boundaries and remains unaware of her daughter's suffering and the reasons for it, despite holding supernatural powers and therefore the alleged ability to 'see' beyond what exists under her nose. In agreement with both Doris Stokes and Sally Morgan, Michele does, however, point out that physics have 'blind spots' particularly when it comes to personal issues. This does indeed appear to be a strong recurring theme when considering the lives of these psychic individuals.

Michele does, however, have a sound early attachment figure in her father. Once more, similar to the cases of Eve and Sylvia being expected to kiss a corpse, at the age of six Michele is pressured into kissing her much loved but now unrecognisable father as he dies from a debilitating illness. She thereby loses the last remnants of any safety, being left with her mother. Her mother's acting out behaviour, the failure to protect, the way in which she invites strangers into the house to live – always males – and her own need to enter a series of violent unstable relationships - is clearly the legacy of Michele's mother's own childhood sexual abuse. Michele remembers: *'It was totally unpredictable, totally arbitrary. There were no rules or reasons; she simply expected me to tune in and know when she was home. Of course the park and canal left me horribly vulnerable to yet more sexual predators.'* One such incident occurs and Michele describes being able to extricate herself from a dangerous man through Lucy warning her, possibly putting a definable voice and in some way externalising what may be a natural instinct for self preservation. On several more occasions, Michele employs an inherent protective instinct, again personified as the warning voice of her stillborn twin sister Lucy. That she is protected forms Michele's fundamental belief system and presumably, enables her to go on living, despite some suicidal inclinations.

Michele, like so many other children in similar situations, has limited awareness that such treatment within her family is not 'normal' and acknowledges that looking back she was severely depressed. She remembers that she did in fact contemplate suicide for the first time at a children's party when she perched on a window ledge, wanting to jump but then was prevented by a combination of the facilitator of the party and by Lucy, her spiritual inner voice. In addition to the abuse, the deterioration of the family relationships and the resulting problematic emotional and behavioural legacy that Michele carries, it is ironic that the continual psychic and supernatural activity she regards as *'normal as eggs and bacon.'*

As she grows up, Michele details various events of haunting. One particular incident, whilst staying in Italy, occurs during a violent electrical storm, a natural occurrence as we have seen which may have an influence on the arrival and strength of power of an entity. An inhuman violent presence invades the lodgings in which the family are living. Clearly, a demon has attached itself to one of the relatives and it is only with ardent prayer that the spirit finally departs after causing fear, distress and near death for all of the family. Their home remains the one structure untouched by the destructive storm - so much for spirits never intending any harm. At least Michele is on side with Steve about the potential for destruction by the more malevolent entities, as she acknowledges that not all visiting entities embody peace, love and goodwill to the living.

From the age of seven or eight, Michele tells us that she gets in touch with previous incarnations, has prophetic dreams, for example of a serious bus crash, and she predicts world disasters, including the destruction through terrorism of the twin towers in New York on 11 September 2001, fourteen years before the event. The age of seven (although some argue that it is the age of five that is significant) is an interesting age in that it is perceived by many mystics to be the time that children may fully join the physical world and leave behind the natural psychic awareness that they were born with. It can be then that for children generally, imaginary friends tend to fade away in the face of exposure to and contact with 'real life' peers. Alternatively, at this age or thereabouts, psychic children may be able to develop their powers further, given the right conditions. At seven, Michele informs the reader that she was given 'choice' about whether she wanted to become fully clairvoyant – to achieve the ability to 'see' spirits themselves. This occurs when she hears a conversation from unseen entities exploring the possibility and requesting that Michele invites them in to talk it through. A reluctant medium, Michele declines and she then outlines details of a 'visitation' to her room. She hears the voices of several entities discussing her and realises that: *'I was at a spiritual gateway and I almost feel as if my destiny was decided upon there and then. I was given the choice and I made it. I did not want to be a traditional medium – I didn't want to see dead people.'* We can see an uncanny resemblance here to Steve's experiences from the warehouse. Whilst Steve chose to close down altogether, Michele re-routes her psychic ability into healing using spirit guides – 'higher forms' or 'angels' for her work rather than encouraging the communication from past un-living entities who she feels, may try to 'take over' in the unhealthiest way. In this she acknowledges a lack of separation between this world and the next.

Michele also likens the voices she hears to a muffled tone on a radio and again we can observe here a marked similarity with the claims from Doris Stokes and Sally Morgan in addition to Steve's own involvement with radio activity in the warehouse haunting and the voices evident on his tape recording.

Michele's abuse continues unabated when she narrowly survives being murdered as her drunken stepfather tries to slaughter her and her other family members with an axe. *'It was as if he were possessed,'* says Michele. It is noticeable here that there is a sense of the man being 'taken over,' temporarily spiritually possessed by entities, reminiscent of the examples provided by spiritual healer Dr Edith Fiore earlier. Themes of possession abound in Michele's account of her life. She describes going to see the movie *'The Exorcist'* and her reaction to it: *'The film absolutely terrified me. Unlike the others in our group, I had had direct experience of the supernatural and the demonic. I knew, from my own bitter experience, how easily spirits can get out of control. I also felt incredibly lucky no worse had happened to me, although I remembered with a shudder all the scratching and scrabbling and the occasions when I had even felt my bed shaking.'*

What saves Michele from her murderous stepfather is a sudden awareness of an all encompassing surge of total 'unconditional love.' She projects this forwards and the man backs off. Like Sally, Michele holds great faith in a wide all conquering power of unconditional love. *'I truly believe that, if you have unconditional love for others even in your darkest hour, the universe will mirror it back to you.'*

Meanwhile, however, Michele's mother also attempts to kill her through drowning her in a bath. During this Michele understandably dissociates: *'I remember watching it as if it were a film – all of a sudden I was no longer in my body but floating above it. I could see myself from above and being held under.'* Michele's response to this is typical of her coping mechanisms: *'I think Lucy must have taken me out of myself to stop me being scared – it was like a form of astral projection.'*

Somewhat reminiscent of abuse survivor Marilyn Van Derbur's comment in part one of the neural thermostat becoming stuck on high, long term effects of trauma are evident when Michele is finally taken into care. She says: *'Primal and feral, I reacted to the slightest thing with adrenaline. I was stuck in survival mode with my foot rammed on the accelerator.'* Interestingly whilst gaining the benefit of safer boundaries in care, Michele observes that the place appears to be haunted by a poltergeist, attracted by the 'disrupted' energy of the chaotic adolescents who inhabit the children's home.

Finally, in adulthood Michele discloses her history of abuse to her mother who had 'assumed' that Michele would be safe. This results in a suicide attempt by her mother. Michele eventually works towards achieving some empathy, however, acknowledging the abuse that has been a toxic presence coming down the generations and that her mother has been acting out her own traumatised responses. Following her mother's death Michele experiences a strong sense of protection and love, eliminating malevolence and anger when she hears her mother's voice from beyond. This affirms Michele's belief in an afterlife, which she had previously somewhat intellectualised despite her psychic experiences, and brings for her a sense of closeness to her mother unachieved in life. *'We are not our past: we are our future. The past moulds us, but should never shape our reality.'*

What is interesting from all three accounts is how the psychic child's family organises itself around the child's psychic tendencies. Whereas for Michele psychic ability is perceived as normal and even expected, for Doris and Sally, the sense of them being strange or different is apparent, as they are regarded with mistrust and disapproval by at least one parent. The expectations on a child, to be weaned, to learn to crawl, walk and talk in logical stages does not generally take into account the possibility that the child may have access to a reality that is not shared by others. That by, say, the age of seven or eight, a child could well be communing quite naturally with the world of the paranormal.

There is of course, great potential here for the child to find herself in a double bind situation. The child who displays psychic ability may be scapegoated or rejected and may run the risk of being diagnosed as mentally disturbed. As a consequence he or she may seek to hide, limit or subdue her ability altogether and this makes me wonder how many potentially psychic children have not developed what may have been important and amazing gifts which could have been nurtured under other familial or environmental conditions. Perhaps Steve may have been one of them. The adult psychic, who is 'coming out' is likewise open to social stigma, religious persecution and above all continual testing and judgement. He or she may tussle with the risks, gains and losses with any such coming out process. Like Steve, however, who was told by his GP to appear on television, such cases may be expected once they have 'proved' themselves adequately, to be built up by the media and worshipped as a celebrity.

Unlike Steve, all three of these women began their psychic lives from early childhood. Apart from the occasional voice, which he normalised or ignored, Steve shares no such similarity. What of the mediums, whether reluctant or actively seeking such activity, who develop psychic ability much later on in life?

Would they be more or less likely to be diagnosed with a mental health condition, or to simply 'close down' more easily than a child, perhaps dismissing such experiences, as 'imagination' 'nonsense' or simply 'I must be getting old?'

I have in fact, quite by chance, been able to track down one psychic who did develop her abilities well after infancy. Confirming my theory that major life changes may have an impact on 'psychic' responses, Spiritualist Minister and medium Simone Key told me that: *'I do believe that life transitions have an impact on psychic ability that arises later on in life. In my own case, I was very much like your partner, not at all interested in anything to do with a spirit world, life after death, psychic phenomena etc. I certainly believed that when we are dead, we are dead (a staunch atheist, as a matter of fact). However, around the age of thirty four I became very ill, suffering from extreme anxiety attacks, passing out and hypersensitive to anything and everything. I was suffering from nervous exhaustion caused through over work. This lasted around three years but towards the end of the illness (which may have ended because I was doing something about it) I became aware of people's energy and moods, as well as seeing things and spirit people out of the corner of my eye. I also had many premonitions at this time too.*

I do believe that in order to see/sense feel/hear the spirit world, one has to have a very sensitive nature and perhaps one that suffers from anxiety helps, i.e. not a calm, serene or composed personality. I know it is that anxiety and sensitivity that gives us that extra 'edge' or energy we need to communicate with the spirit world. Hence, those people who are calm and tranquil may find mediumship too difficult to achieve. Also, times of extreme stress can trigger the psychic faculty, perhaps because of changes to our energy and our conscious state. When we are anxious, the chances are we don't sleep well and this usually becomes a very difficult time, when we are in a highly sensitive state.'

Simone then goes on to explain how visiting a healer was helpful and led her into exploring spiritual matters more directly, despite her extreme cynicism at the time. She certainly was not easy to convince during her investigations and felt highly reluctant during her gradual involvement before finally becoming convinced of the existence of a spirit world. She also informed me that she is not aware of any other mediums who would admit to not possessing their psychic skills as children, although I expect that there are examples of other mediums having similar experiences in adulthood.

Simone makes several interesting points in her comments. We see how she concurs with the view that major life transitions can shift our energy significantly and possibly have an impact on psychic ability developing and I regarded with some amusement the view that an 'edginess' can have an influence. Steve certainly could not by any stretch of the imagination be described as 'calm and serene!' After leaving his wife, he came into our relationship with a raw and angry edginess; a degree of pent up emotional material. As we have seen, he encountered John a neat six months later.

Simone also raises that during her illness and subsequent explorations she became increasingly sensitised to peoples *'energy and moods.'* This strikes me as being part and parcel of the role therapists and those who work in the caring professions take. Humanistic counsellors in particular work with tuning into a client both verbally and non verbally, perhaps via counter transference and projective identification as we saw earlier, and the need for extra self care in the event of vicarious traumatisation is paramount.

What is also evident here is the potential for a misunderstood psychic child to become isolated and a therapist working with such issues would need to take this alienation into account similarly to any other child who was perceived to be different and vulnerable to being ostracised and rejected. The adult psychic may be bombarded with images and hear the screams of violated and dying individuals, sense the powerlessness of witness inaction and suffer from secondary traumatisation.

The experiencing of ghosts and haunting are a reality for many people, whether based in neuro-function, mental disorder, electromagnetic reactions, trauma responses or emanate from genuine supernatural sources. The believers in ghosts may search for incidents that corroborate with or validate their beliefs, or that may aid them with the formulation or sustaining of such beliefs. Some haunted people present with their issues in therapy. The next part of this book takes a more direct look at how counsellors may want to take supernatural issues into consideration when we are working with this client group.

PART FOUR

TILTING THE MIRROR

Implications: Why this Person? Why this Problem? Why Now?

'Knowledge is an attribute of the mind, and wisdom is an attribute of the soul.' From 'Reader of Hearts' by Darrin Owens.

So having researched scientific and spiritual viewpoints, thought about the links between trauma, childhood, life transition and psychic ability, I am left with further personal thoughts about my work and my relationship. What I now need to begin to address towards the end of this book are the implications of this haunting for me, as a person who has witnessed this, lived alongside someone close to me who may have encountered a ghost, or who may have suffered with a temporary psychosis. I need to consider what the implications may be for me as a person who will one day die, as a partner to Steve and as someone who also happens to work as a counsellor. I will begin by thinking about therapeutic work generally and the questions that have been raised for me as a result of my personal experiences with Steve's 'haunting.'

When I underwent training as an external clinical supervisor some years ago, I became aware of the following question. Exactly how many people are there present in a therapy room during a session? From the physically 'real' point of view there are of course exactly two, the counsellor and the client and this is as 'exact' as it gets. On another level, however, the client will be 'bringing in' - although not physically - her partner, her children, her parents, her family with issues coming down the generations, her friends, acquaintances, neighbours, strangers – on some level virtually everyone she has had contact with, past and present. Add into that the counsellor's own people. Take into consideration if I am in the role of supervisor, listening to a supervisee's people, to their clients and to their client's people. And what of group therapy – the number of people 'present' in the therapy room quickly has the potential to expand into a multitude. These are the people, the 'entities' that counsellors and supervisors carry in our heads, in our notes and hold in our awareness during the course of our work, either consciously or unconsciously. For people of faith, God is also ever present, forming a definite triad alongside the counsellor and client.

Consider the possibility that in addition to this awareness of the 'I, thou' and (on another level) 'others' dynamic, that actual unseen entities (ghosts) may also be present, albeit for most of us they remain undetected on any conscious level. For some people, however, those who are psychic, these entities make themselves known via the psychic's own direct sensory perceptions and are seemingly as real as any solid person that a non psychic person perceives. So maybe on occasion there are ghosts in the room and outside of it. Maybe there are clients presenting for counselling who claim to see them.

A Ghost in the Therapy Room

'If you can keep your head when all about you
Are losing theirs and blaming it on you,
If you can trust yourself when all men doubt you,
But make allowance for their doubting too...' From 'If' by Rudyard Kipling.

Imagine then, this client. The client tells you that he is being frequently visited at work by a ghost, dressed in a British Rail uniform and who is claiming that his name is John. Believing that the client is his brother who made John's daughter pregnant, the ghost wants resolution to this situation. The client tells you that the ghost gets very angry and frequently causes some scratching type injury to the client's face. Following these incidents the client is left with feelings of depression and despair that don't seem to belong to him.

What do you do? How do you assess the risk to the client? Is he psychotic or delusional? How, or if, do you proceed with therapy? How do you use supervision to learn about yourself in relation to this client? If you are humanistic, do you tell yourself – this client is no different from any other and I must therefore offer unconditional positive regard – in which case – how unconditional and empathic can I be given the implausibility of this story? Many clients present in therapy with issues that do to an extent, during or following the therapeutic process, provide them with some sort of answer, resolution or increased ability to function despite certain givens in their past history or present circumstances. The growth in awareness towards this and the way forward ultimately, as humanistic therapists advocate, is that the client knows best. Our clients may be combating anxiety, depression, relationship or sex issues, working through abuse, spiritual or self identity - seeking a way forward in a variety of life situations. Ultimately, the client is asking, consciously or unconsciously – how can I be happier? And do I really want to change? The client described above, however, may actually be a little different from others – why? Because 'answers,' whether the client's or your own as therapist, are not readily accessible. In this case, the counsellor needs to hold a significant capacity to tolerate the unknown and to hold the client in their own unknowingness - whether this encompasses containing the anxiety around inevitable death, the fear of the thereafter, the randomness of psychic attack or, simply the *'what next?'*

In the film *'Sixth Sense,'* Cole asked Dr Crow *'How can you help me if you don't believe me?'* Therein lie the pivotal questions – Do I believe in ghosts and do I believe the client? Do I have to believe in one to believe the other?

A client may be asking himself 'Do you, as my therapist, believe in ghosts? If I take the risk to tell you my story – will I be believed?' Once Cole has built up a relationship of trust with Dr Crow – they even go on to solve a murder mystery together – Cole is able to function better in his unique world – that of seeing and communicating with dead people. Following on from a horrific history of being attacked by them, he is gradually able to combat his fear, form more positive contact with the apparitions he comes into contact with and significantly, move into a state of self acceptance. His mother, perhaps somewhat conveniently in my view, provides a solid attachment and also offers unconditional positive regard once he finally discloses his circumstances to her, which presumably will contribute a tremendous amount to her son's emotional healing. This, however, is just a film.

Issues of belief are significant and we return to it soon. In the reality of the therapeutic alliance, what are the further implications for the therapist who encounters a client who is claiming to have had or is having supernatural experiences? I also pose the question – how does this sort of experience compare with any other type of traumatic experience? I want to make it abundantly clear here that I am not advocating a theory that claims that to have an experience that appears to be supernatural in origin can fully compare to or encapsulate the degree of long term trauma suffered by survivors of rape, childhood trauma or neglect, violent physical or mental abuse, war, terrorism, torture, bereavement or any other extremely distressing life issues presented by our clients and who continue to combat the legacy of such stresses on a daily basis.

Let us, however, consider what may be an interesting and pertinent statement from Finkelhor and Browne (1986) on the subject of childhood sexual abuse: *'We theorise that a basic kind of powerlessness occurs in sexual abuse when a child's territory and body space are repeatedly invaded against the child's will. This is exacerbated by whatever coercion and manipulation the offender may impose as part of the abuse process. Powerlessness is then reinforced when a child sees his or her attempts to halt the abuse frustrated. It is increased when the child feels fear, when he or she is unable to make adults understand or believe what is happening, or when he or she realises how conditions of dependency have him or her trapped in the situation.'*

Now let us repeat the statement but replacing some significant words, to fit more closely with Steve's situation: *'We theorise that a basic kind of powerlessness occurs in <u>being haunted</u> when a <u>person's</u> territory and body space are repeatedly invaded against the <u>person's</u> will. This is exacerbated by whatever coercion* and manipulation the <u>apparition</u> may impose as part of the <u>haunting</u> process. Powerlessness is then reinforced when a <u>person</u> sees his or her attempts to halt the <u>haunting</u> frustrated. It is increased when the <u>person</u> feels fear, when he or she is unable to make <u>colleagues</u> understand or believe what is happening, or when he or she realises how conditions of <u>employment</u> have him or her trapped in the situation.'

Adults of course, do have considerably more power than children generally and, unless prevented by a more powerful adult, can usually change their life situations to suit their needs and improve their situations at will. Finkelhor and Browne go on to state that *'The dynamic of powerlessness distorts children's sense of their ability to control their lives.'* Whilst Steve, of course does have choices about his work location and how much discomfort he is prepared to tolerate, most adults generally cannot control contact with supernatural phenomena. Let us now explore how a therapeutic alliance may aid Steve and others in a similar situation when it comes to supporting haunted people, given that a degree of uncertainty, anxiety and stress can be undeniably present.

Challenges for the Counsellor

'In every consulting room there ought to be two rather frightened people; the patient and the psychoanalyst. If they are not, one wonders why they are bothering to find out what everyone knows.' From 'Brazilian Lectures' by Wilfred Bion.

As in any therapeutic encounter the offering of belief can be pivotal in healing. I have over my years of counselling abuse survivors observed how the disbelieved child in particular may generally experience a more complex reactive degree of long term distress, hurt, betrayal, rage and powerlessness. Whilst Rogers advocates the basic core considerations of unconditional positive regard, empathy and congruence in providing the best possible healing conditions for a client, how easy is this for a counsellor to achieve given the circumstances of the unknown and horrific nature of being haunted? What effect does this potential turmoil have on the therapist? Does it actually matter whether or not the counsellor believes in ghosts or not as long as she is aware of the impact on the client and the importance of providing a therapeutic alliance that can hold the client safely whilst the client's issues are explored? What of the counsellor who has himself had supernatural encounters and may be biased towards a belief in such perceptions, only to be confronted by clients who are struggling to integrate their own experiences? In such circumstances how much does the counsellor allow the therapeutic work to be influenced by his own history and experience and how much does he need to hold back on any opinions or self disclosure?

As a therapist I would also need to bear in mind the cultural contexts and norms in which I am counselling. For example in parts of China it can be believed that the deceased co-exist with the living and for a Chinese client it may be taken for granted that on certain occasions a place at table is set for those family members who have passed away and who will join the occasion in spirit. An entry in DSM 4 raises that: *'Ideas that may appear to be delusional in one culture (e.g. sorcery and witchcraft) may be commonly held in another. In some cultures, visual or auditory hallucinations with a religious content may be a normal part of religious experience (e.g. seeing the Virgin Mary or hearing God's voice.)'* In some African cultures, the existence and significance of evil spirits can be fairly mainstream experiencing. I have certainly come across cases when my clients have been cursed. As I write this I am thinking of one young man in particular who was cursed by his father's lover, which appeared to have caused his mother to have several miscarriages before giving birth to my client, who was then also targeted by witchcraft. At the age of five the brakes on his bicycle inexplicably failed and he was almost killed by oncoming traffic. He placed the responsibility for this near fatal mishap firmly on the jinx. For such cases, the possibility of voodoo, witchcraft and cursing others can form part of a traditional belief culture and are to be noted seriously. It would be equally inadvisable to assume that people of the same faith would interpret doctrines in the same way. Many pastoral counsellors emphasise that *'Each individual has their own unique personal religious and/ or spiritual experience'* (Foskett 2003). Williams (2003) agrees and shares her opinion that *'Assumptions are often more powerful than beliefs because they happen out of awareness.'*

When Steve had his consultation with his GP which was perhaps long overdue, I became aware of his fear of being disbelieved, ridiculed, or diagnosed as mentally ill. He had perhaps 'assumed' that he would be disbelieved and that the GP would 'assume' that a diagnosis of 'madness' would automatically follow. It could be that this is a significant consideration when exploring haunting and I would suggest that in many cases, it takes much courage to make disclosures of this nature. The right environment and the building of a relationship of trust with the therapist are clearly of paramount importance. Perhaps the starting point is the tussle with belief. I would believe the client – offer belief to the client – or at least, I hope that I would endeavour to believe as much as I can. When working with his haunted clients healer David Ashworth advises us to *'Remain neutral but open minded.'* He further advises: *'Don't believe anything. Don't disbelieve anything. Be open to everything, no matter how far out, ridiculous or bizarre it may seem...Follow your intuition and develop knowledge and truth from your own experiences. Then you will truly know; then you will truly evolve.'*

Some people, thankfully now in the minority given the amount of awareness raising over the past few decades about childhood sexual abuse, still refuse to believe that such a horror exists. They do not believe that the most dangerous place for a child to be can be its own home, or that anyone is capable of doing such damage to a child, or even that such experiences can have a significant long term impact as we briefly explored in part one. Marilyn Van Derbur raises that some people cannot conceive that the effects of child abuse or rape can be anything more than *'A bad twenty minutes.'* She goes on to describe her responses to callers on a radio show who were expressing levels of disbelief at her story of incest and she expresses her shock: *'I was astounded. It was something I had never even considered! There were people who didn't believe me? How so could that be? Who would lie about such a shaming thing? I said: 'If people don't believe a 53 year old me, then, dear God, who is going to believe a child?'*

I include this point because I have indeed encountered a few individuals who refuse to believe that adults are capable of sexually molesting their own or someone else's child. I was certainly exposed to many myths and wildly outrageous comments about rape and sexual assault during my years as a counsellor in the local Rape Crisis Centre. Another minority of people will persist in disbelieving that the holocaust ever occurred, which is a crime in some parts of the world. Most people are shocked by the possibility that some people will persist in their denials of such events which, to most of us is an abhorrent reality in our history. War, ethnic cleansing, persecution, rape and child abuse continue unabated in contemporary society. How we defend ourselves from such horrors and behave in ways that reinforce our defences remains a pertinent factor. It can become easier and considerably more comfortable to disbelieve than face the horror and identify with a victim.

Issues around the supernatural, however, perhaps differ. In Western culture it is perfectly reasonable and acceptable for people not to believe in ghosts and to own such a belief openly without fear or ridicule. In fact, this particular disbelief can often be cited as a sign of robust mental health. I doubt that many people would feel unduly disturbed in viewing haunted folk with disbelief or judgement, shaming them or labelling their mental health states as questionable. Foskett in his article *'Is Religion Counselling Last Taboo?'* (CPJ Vol 14, no 8 October 2003) describes reactions in a psychiatric ward when he quotes a patient pleading for spiritual support: *'For God's sake somebody get me a Bible!' and they looked at me with horror in their eyes and no-one would get me a Bible.'* Foskett goes on to raise issues around dominant secular thinking in psychiatric professions, with a threat of patients who have strong faith being pathologised. He also raises that for a religious counsellor, many feel pressure to remain 'in the closet' about their own faiths. Whether or not this is true, it is evident that tension between mental health and religious or spiritual viewpoints remains an issue in contemporary society as we have speculated upon earlier.

Moving on, if presented with a 'haunted' client, I would reflect on how the client is being impacted, which of the client's senses are being affected and whether any physical injury, perhaps a head trauma or underlying ill health issue is present. How is the supernatural event being perceived? Is the client being affected in ways that are visual, auditory or affecting other senses? Is the event positive or negative for the client? It seems that for the most part, people affected by supernatural phenomena report a sense of comfort, happiness and hope from departed loved ones. Others may be afflicted by poltergeist like activity;

disruption, harm, mischief and confusion with regard to moved or thrown objects. How is the client responding emotionally?

I may need to explore whether there is indeed a possibility of actual or perceived terminal illness, or any recent changes in such conditions? How does the client feel about death and dying? What is their past and recent history of bereavement? I would be reflecting upon any magical thinking of the client; their perception of any afterlife; their hope for an afterlife; their defences against death. Is the client seeking out something in the spiritual world that they are lacking in the material one? In turn what are they seeking from the therapist?

I would certainly consider any life transitions, whether loss, disruptions to attachment or change in working life, their age, relationships, any geographical relocation, cultural shock and any other alteration in life circumstances that may be having a conscious or possibly unconscious impact on the client. I may be reflecting 'Why you, why here? And why now?' What are the conditions for this client pre and post the haunting events?

I would need to respect and explore the beliefs, culture and any previous 'mystical' history of the client. Perhaps I would explore whether they have had any experiences in the past, maybe as a child, which could be interpreted as supernatural or if any other family member has, but avoid interpretations and guesswork. I would need to make myself aware of any faith or religious 'blue print.' I would also, of course, need to evaluate any neurobiological disturbance or mental ill health. I would need to take on board a personality disorder and consider if they are presenting in ways that are anxious, grandiose, dramatic, eccentric or bizarre. Is there any evidence of a need for the client to be viewed as different – do they need to stand out from the norm? I would of course, need to consider whether referral would be appropriate.

Spiders, Spooks and Spaceships

'Our mortal minds want to rationalise everything and figure it out, but the divine is meant to be experienced, not figured out.' From 'Reader of Hearts' by Darrin Owens.

Let us consider some clients who have presented with a variety of issues that could be interpreted as 'beyond the normal.' Two are clients I have worked with myself and other examples are from therapists who were happy to share their experiences of 'haunted' clients.

Firstly a student I counselled at the university some years ago presented with disturbances of perception comprising visions of being threatened with weapons, eaten by lions, or bitten by large snakes, rats or spiders, which would accumulate on her bed during the night. The client also told me that when she looked in the mirror she 'did not recognise herself.' That sometimes she perceived the face of an old woman, sometimes that of a child, or even a dog. Her handwriting would change and she was noticing spells of 'spacing out.' This client was clearly in a state of deep long term anxiety and was having dissociative spells. To my mind, she had been abused in some way in childhood and was on the brink of attaining some memories. The client fled from therapy once it felt like we were getting close to any disclosure, however, but was then well supported practically by the mental health team. It is possible to see that certainly in the past, some may have interpreted her issues as spiritual or demonic possession. This client is reminiscent of those we explored in part one and her 'supernatural' issues seemed to have some source within her psyche owing to external factors. This had disturbed her psychologically and she had then internalised mentally, emotionally and symbolically. Interestingly, mirrors do seem to present a theme with regard to self perception, distortions of image and implications for mental health.

Another counsellor, based in a GP surgery, had had a client referred to her who had become phobic about looking into mirrors. The counsellor reported that: *'She looked in the mirror and her grandmother looked back. She couldn't look in mirrors any more. She was being haunted.'* Client and counsellor worked successfully together as the grandmother's positive and negative attributes were explored and amalgamated, along with the impact she had had on the client's life, both dead and alive. The client was gradually enabled to gain a healthier and more autonomous sense of self separate from her relative's influence and unwanted 'presence'.

My next example illustrates a client whose presentation is clearly less routed in symptoms of mental distress and who presents issues which may hold more of a sense of 'supernatural' and in terms of 'I may have actually seen a ghost.' This was another student client of mine, who was grieving the loss of her father. He had very suddenly passed away whilst working abroad. The client was six years old at the time. Her long term grief reactions were complex as she had not understood his death then, being told he had 'gone away' and 'not to be silly' when she spoke of him. She had also witnessed her mother crashing into depression and this further withdrawal of security clearly added another layer to the loss of her father. The client was now aged twenty. Grief was re-triggered and intensified with each life change coupled with feelings of being out of control. She was comforted, however, by vivid dreams of her father throughout her teens, although he was now beginning to feel 'further away.' She recalls being told by her mother that as a small child she had often claimed to see the ghost of her father. He would visit her frequently, then 'turn into an angel and fly out of the window.' The client did not remember these experiences from her childhood and a sense of her faith or belief in such spiritual contact remained illusive. In this case, we may also hold an awareness around the desires and potential projections of the mother.

Another client and this time not one of my own, was perhaps more clearly defined in terms of inviting in experiences of the paranormal as part of her presentation. This woman believed in ghosts and the spirit world and could talk to the dead. The latter were people who had passed away, some to whom she had been emotionally close. She believed them to be essentially benevolent. The counsellor in this case described the client as very 'matter of fact' in her descriptions, having had the experiences since being a teenager and not feeling unduly bothered by them. She did, however, feel concerned by visions of large insects when triggered by distressed feelings and was on anti psychotic medication for anxiety. She had been diagnosed as schizophrenic when younger but this diagnosis had been overturned by both the counsellor and her present psychiatrist. We can see how the labelling and 'threat' of mental ill health shadows this client. She was indeed worried that the counsellor would perceive her as 'mad' owing to these perceptions and hallucinations of insects, rather more so than the alleged psychic ability. The counsellor raised that this client had been through some difficult times in her life and her beliefs in visitations from her loved ones in the afterlife greatly sustained her.

Moving on to another more extreme example, the same counsellor, who works from a psychodynamic model, had worked with a client who was considerably more disoriented by his 'supernatural' experiences. The client believed that God was sending ghosts to haunt him because he had sinned. Often in such cases, a 'sin' has been carried out in childhood and the adult continues to be plagued, often triggered by every perceived misdeed thereafter. For this client, God was a punitive, Old Testament type, persecutory and vengeful. The client felt that he had drawn God's negative attention because of his sinfulness, although he never disclosed what these misdemeanours were. He believed that if he died and was buried then the Devil would find his grave and carry him off to hell. This was triggering insomnia and intense fear in case he died in his sleep. The counsellor describes him as being understandably in a state of terror. She used supervision frequently to discuss the risk of this client tipping into psychosis. He was indeed under the care of psychiatric and mental health services. The counsellor believed that in this case the client was experiencing powerful projections out of his rage and hatred of those around him.

Another client, this time working with a person centred counsellor, described a similar experience with severe examples of hearing voices inciting her to rise above a wretched and worthless humanity. Somewhat worryingly, this young woman was being persuaded to *'evolve into something superior, to trample mankind and use humanity as a foot stool and rise above them.'* From a strong faith background, this client regarded the voices as repeated spiritual attacks and as a result of their influence she felt bad, guilty and of minimum value. She also experienced some quite extreme physical reactions of temporary bodily paralysis, a sense of burning up and being 'forced out' of her body. She was prayed for at her church and the voices and physical sensations ceased immediately. She also began to take anti depressant medication. The counsellor focussed on her low self esteem amidst other issues and again one or a combination of these interventions may have influenced the cessation of the attacks.

In none of these latter few cases was there a sense of a clear and tangible ghost to get hold of, more a level of disturbance being sustained by the client's ongoing beliefs. Whether 'ghosts' exist or not, the perception of such phenomena; benign or malevolent, positive or negative, loving or punitive, clearly plays a huge part in the client's responses, although in none of these examples were issues around supernatural phenomena the main presenting concern.

Finally, consider this interesting case provided by an NLP therapist. He describes a client who told him that he saw a spaceship parked in a field when he was driving his car in the early hours of the morning. The counsellor goes on to say: *'He was able to describe the ship in detail and see and hear the occupants inside. No one else drove down the road at the time and he was able to stand and observe the craft for several minutes. He was even able to hear the sound of the ship, which suddenly flew away at high speed, following a non linear route until it was no longer visible. He told me it was real.'* Strange as this event was, this was also not the main theme or reason that this particular client had sought therapy. He had broken up with his wife suddenly when she had left him for someone else. The counsellor observed that the client became more articulate and 'came alive' when talking about the space ship experience. He reflected that the client may have internalised several messages from his wife, her lover and some of his friends that he was 'boring.' The counsellor reflected that this client may therefore have constructed this story to make himself interesting to the therapist, to others or as a way of deflecting the hurt caused to him by his partner. The therapist did observe that to encounter a space ship would indeed provide *'A great distracter.'* This client was on no medication and was not diagnosed with any underlying physical or mental health condition.

Anything Else Out There?

'What have I learned? That humans are funny old lot....!' A psychodynamic therapist

I have provided examples of clients who have been disturbed in some way by supernatural perceptions which are all based on true client experience. Additionally I have worked with a handful of clients who describe themselves as actually 'psychic' although this has also to date not formed the main focus of the session.

When I was thinking about this part of the book it became obvious that I was not going to find vast numbers of counsellors who have worked with clients presenting with supernatural or psychic experiences in therapy. Aside from the strong examples cited above, further client work I could illustrate is somewhat limited. Working with bereavement issues, however, does seem to be an obvious trigger for examples of clients encountering 'ghosts.' Pastoral and church members in particular are presumably going to be targeted for the sharing of experiences of this nature. This priest argues that: *'In funeral visits, it is common for the* bereaved to talk of seeing their loved one, hearing their voices and so on. This could be put down to the trauma of grief, but why can't it be a genuine form of experience, a residual presence or memory? People talk of entering a church and "feeling" a sense of peace, the presence of those who have prayed there. There can be a palpable sense of calm.'* Messages of comfort, hope and companionship also seem to present frequently in the therapy room. When counselling for bereavement issues, it follows that therapists are particularly aware on some level of the nature and 'presence' of the deceased during sessions and will be tuned into what this means for our clients. It is observable that many grieving clients fully accept presences themselves in their daily lives which are then related to the counsellor. Many bereaved people report sensing a presence of departed loved ones, objects are moved and once more scents, lights and glimpses of people in apparently physical form are often cited as pertinent examples. One bereavement counsellor observes: *'All of the clients were obviously emotional, but whenever they talked of their experiences, they either smiled or remembered it fondly and would almost always ask my opinion, which I couldn't give them obviously. Every one found the experience wonderful and a message from their loved ones that all was well and nothing to fear.'* Rose, my psychic colleague and friend observes that of her bereaved clients, many see apparitions that appear 'real and solid' and often at the foot of the bed. They are able to interact, providing reassurance and comfort but she also cites an example of a client who was given a clear instruction by the spirit to go to the cupboard and locate an important document that would assist with the finalisation of the details of the deceased's will; clearly an example of an entity with some urgent unfinished business. Rose concurs that entities want the living to know that they are present and many clients respond in one of two ways. They seem either reasonably comforted and unfazed by such appearances or they will question whether or not they are going mad, particularly if there is no loss as a triggering factor to the perception of a ghostly visitation.

For counsellors who find themselves enmeshed with a client who is actually psychic rather than 'haunted,' sessions can be truly unnerving, particularly if the therapist finds themselves on the receiving end of clients sharing their spiritual perceptions during sessions. One example of this comprises a counsellor who had worked with a client privately for some time before the client disclosed her psychic skills and abilities. Like so many others, as a psychic child who could 'see people who weren't really there,' this client had been alienated from members of her family as a child and accused of being 'not right in the head.' She was also a survivor of childhood sexual abuse. During the session with this psychic woman who was now an adult, the counsellor told me: *'The client saw people in the room we were working in. They seemed to appear unbidden.'* She goes on to detail feeling surprised and upset when it becomes apparent that the client is able to perceive the counsellor's recently deceased mother, describing her personal attributes accurately.

Another counsellor describes some seemingly quite straightforward therapy with an openly psychic client who performed professionally on stage in an array of *'exotic clothes, turbans, beads and makeup...using her empathy, insight and psychic powers she would tell people that their loved ones were in contact and sending them encouraging messages.'* Behind the scenes, however, it was a different story. The counsellor said: *'When she came off the stage and was divest of her finery, she could not so much as look in a mirror, let alone the full length one in front of which she would have admired her costume as the psychic star who dazzled and sparkled. She would return to her house and young son, wearing dreary colourless clothes and feeling thoroughly bad about herself.'* Clearly this client was separating out the 'despicable' side that had survived a 'rocky' childhood, the *'side of herself that needed to be split away and left in the dressing room',* from the 'acceptable' part that could astound, amaze and bring comfort when performing. The counsellor's task was to enable this client to *'make sense of the bad she felt and the good she was.'* Once this was achieved, the client did in fact walk away from the stage. The 'psychic star' was no longer needed.

Casting my net a bit wider I encountered therapists who are psychic themselves, and again the vast majority appear to have held such abilities since being very small children. I have again been reliably informed that on occasion there may be more than counsellor and client present in the room. Rose tells me that she has an ability to sometimes gain an impression of entities whilst counselling. The image may be a face, an item of clothing or a general impression of how the person looks. She may hear some words which can add to the sensing of something present beyond her client. She also raises that these deceased significant others in the room always seem to present to the right hand side of the client in front of her. She has even witnessed entities tapping her clients on the shoulder during sessions. Sometimes her own spirit guide may intervene and provide observations. When I asked Rose if she was ever afraid during such encounters she said not, but related one incident when a deceased relative hung around long after the client's session had ended and had left Rose's home, where counselling was taking place. This entity followed Rose into the kitchen and had to be ordered to leave. Rose was aware of frustration and invasiveness, however, rather than any sense of fear or disquiet.

In both cases, that of psychic counsellor and psychic client, one of the major tasks for the counsellor is quite clear, that of maintaining professional boundaries. For the counsellor disturbed by the client's speaking of the presence of her mother; it felt like a role reversal which needed holding, containing and supporting. For psychic counsellors, the role of therapist rather than medium needs to be clearly defined and most did not disclose their psychic abilities to their clients. This would of course, muddy the waters of the role. Rose cites how frustrating this can be. *'I can't pass on messages,'* she says. *'And this can be hard when the spirit clearly wants to communicate so badly and also if the clients themselves don't believe.'*

The role of supervision is clearly paramount when it comes to discussing the need to demonstrate an empathic, congruent response to the client's issues. This may include a client's psychic ability which can be present in a session, often in a way that can be highly personally shocking to the counsellor. Additionally the need for the sessions to remain focussed on the client and not be overtaken by the counsellor's responses was often cited in the research I gathered. Many counsellors expressed either a triggering of or a re-emergence of interest in spiritual and supernatural matters as a result of counselling psychic clients. For psychic counsellors, their beliefs were reaffirmed rather than changed. Atheists and non believers appeared to remain firm and immovable in their viewpoints.

It did not offer any great surprise to me that virtually all counsellors who have worked with clients presenting supernatural experiences have cited a client centred approach as being a model of choice when it comes to encountering such issues, or at least the offering of a model of non judgement and a quality of being fully present. The core conditions were cited by humanistic counsellors as providing a healing environment, particularly for clients who had been on the receiving end of negative reactions to their alleged psychic ability as a child. A warm, empathic relationship offering belief and unconditional positive regard were enabling clients to be self accepting. Significantly, however, as we have seen, none of the cases I was provided with cited supernatural experiences as being the main presenting issue and any psychic abilities seemed to emerge either much later or as part of working through issues, particularly around loss, change or bereavement. Several counsellors did raise the issue that there was a fine line, however, between colluding with a client's hope, one telling me that: *'I am person centred, so I listen and sometimes gently challenge if I feel it is appropriate. I am aware that people can want something so badly, they can almost 'make' it happen – convincing themselves it has, when in fact, it hasn't. I can see this and will challenge what a client is saying to find the truth.'* How to manage such haunting events is a major issue and counsellors often cited that they were mindful of not leading clients down a particular route. If they are open to the supernatural then so is the counsellor. Permission giving and normalising are key ways of working with such issues whilst perhaps bearing in mind issues around adaptation to change, loss, and the intricacies of grief reaction and neurological functioning. One therapist offers the opinion that: *'It all confirms what I think myself tempered with the awareness that it could all be wrong...it might all be some weird phenomenon that isn't what we think it is or hope that it might be.'* A hefty challenge also seems to be when clients ask the counsellor directly what they believe and counsellors may need to manage the tension around truth, congruency and tact according to their own belief system. The attitude of acceptance of clients presenting with supernatural phenomena is obviously going to be more of a challenge for some support workers than others. From a firm Christian viewpoint, the tussle with faith and belief may be viewed as less personally problematic although values around acceptance remain fundamentally the same. This priest observes: *'As a priest the pastoral relationship is distinctively different to the clinical or therapeutic interventions made by counsellors and other professionals. I am not looking for diagnoses; instead it is a relationship of empathy and getting alongside, a therapy of love and acceptance. The notion of hearing voices, prophetic insights, or paranormal activity has to be treated with legitimacy, since faith demands the possibility of these things.'* For anyone presenting with supernatural issues, it does seem that a sound therapeutic relationship can provide an important source of healing, alongside a need for an awareness of any underlying psychological disturbance which may perhaps require medication or liaison with professionals beyond the therapy room. The majority of the clients provided here as examples were free from medication, apart from a few who had been prescribed anti depressants or anti psychotics and it seems that most did not drink alcohol or take drugs excessively.

Finally, this research enabled me to consider generally any taboos that therapists may hold in terms of talking of either their own psychic abilities which could, of course, impact what is occurring in the room, along with the psychic or supernatural issues emerging from the client and any resulting transference and counter transference issues. I am aware that shame always holds the potential to be present despite the fact that on the whole, we are becoming used to openly discussing painful life events such as childhood sexual, physical or ritual abuse, illness, death and sexual issues including orientation or practices. Mental illness is increasingly becoming 'out there' and it is noticeable that the number of students coming into higher education with visible psychiatric histories has significantly increased over the many years I have been present as a university counsellor. For people from all walks of life accessing higher education, such issues may no longer be the barriers that they once were. Behaviours such as self harm, whilst still mostly a private activity, are also being increasingly openly discussed and I have observed that scars, once hidden by most individuals under long sleeves, may now perhaps for a few, be more visible. We observed how Steve felt shamed by his own 'stigmata' which unlike self harm was not self inflicted and was not employed as a coping strategy.

I wonder, however, if counsellors or clients becoming the subject of a serious haunting may remain something of a misnomer to share for practitioners in situations such as case discussion. I notice that I did not take Steve's situation into my own work environment, although it is customary for team members to 'check in' our personal feelings as a group at our weekly meetings. Whilst I needed a boundary here and wanted to keep the situation away from my work with clients, I was also aware of a degree of shame about what was happening in my life. It was bizarre, it was unusual and I feared that my partner could be immediately labelled as psychotic. Are the ghosts and apparitions brought by clients into the therapy room likely to be perceived by practitioners as products of delusional thinking? I sincerely hope not. My supervisor has been aware of my ongoing struggles with the haunting and appeared to demonstrate an open mind. There is of course, also a place for personal therapy in such situations, with the right therapist.

Thoughts and Reflections

'Those who stubbornly refuse even to consider the possibility of life after death are fast becoming the modern equivalent of those who once asserted that the earth is flat' From 'The Complete Book of Ghosts' by Paul Roland.

To conclude, therefore, if I were to continue to make something of a reflective 'checklist' for myself for such cases, it may read something like this:

- All clients are worthy of belief, however challenging their situation is to believe.
- I need to endeavour to suspend and bracket anything of my own disbelief in the here and now to be reflected on later. Beliefs are reconstructive and subject not only to growth and change but also reversal. The NLP counsellor who had the encounter with the client who saw the spaceship emphasises a need: *'To utilise every aspect of the client's experience, the client's model. If a belief is painful for a client and the client wants to change it, then the best way to do it is to enter into the client's model and change it from within. If the client's belief is not damaging and the client is happy with it then don't change it.'* Enabling a client to gain an understanding of their world may be an aim of the therapeutic support, an understanding that makes sense to the client and taking into account any faith background which may be influencing their reactions to their experiences. In his research paper on mental health, beliefs and voice hearing (2008), Dr Michael Marriot urges mental health workers to approach the client's spiritual or religious blueprint: *'without inhibition: in some circumstances they can represent a valuable resource from which therapeutic options might be drawn; in other circumstances, they may be presenting focal points of distress that could be invaluable for sensitive exploration.'* He continues that the findings of his study *'support the suggestion that spiritual/religious beliefs can heavily inform individuals' understandings of the experiences that might be causing them distress, and it could be suggested that a therapeutic intervention that does not seek to understand these aspects of a person's values and beliefs might struggle to engage with important issues.'* Whichever way they tilt the mirror, a client needs to be enabled to find their own truth.
- Most importantly, use supervisory support for education, exploration, containment, reflection and personal learning with regard to the client and their presenting material. Reflect on my own reactions generally, consider how they influence the therapeutic encounter and examine my responses and counter transference with my supervisor. In this, I need to monitor and own my defences. The NLP counsellor described above clearly used supervision in challenging his reactions to his client. He said: *'I had a feeling of amazement and disbelief. My initial thoughts*

were *"He is making this up."* I noticed he made different eye movements to when he was talking about the spaceship experiences. I wondered if he had created this story in order to say to me *"I am interesting."* The counsellor goes on to state that: *'In supervision we explored the concept that this was his model of the world and that it should be accepted as such. We explored that it was not my model. We also explored how this communication to me could be utilised to help him achieve his goals without discrediting what he had said.'* It sounds important to retain a healthy observing presence and balanced view, bearing in mind that the client may be projecting much of their current distress onto the past, the behaviour of others, or even 'spirit possession,' all or some of which may be enabling the client to absolve themselves of taking responsibility for their own emotions and actions.

- Remain open minded, non-shaming and respectful. Consider whether the client is looking for a need that cannot be met by the physical world, for example this may be rescue, or having needs met through an experience of perceived persecution or punishment. Equally a supernatural experience may provide a way of self soothing, or a need to feel chosen, special, nurtured or any other number of factors that meet a client's conscious or unconscious requirements, perhaps for validation or increased visibility. This was particularly clear in the cases of two of the clients cited above; the one persecuted by a vengeful God and the one comforted by the presence of her deceased loved ones. The client who saw a spaceship may possibly have been searching for that 'specialness.' Or he may have actually seen a spaceship.
- Reflect on the possibility that the client is being haunted by an entity, whether perceived by the client as amicable or persecutory and do not immediately dismiss the situation as fantasy, projection, wish fulfilment or an attempt of the client to meet their needs through such ways, unless other factors corroborate these theories. In his work *'On Personal Power'* (1986) Rogers says: *'The non rational concerns of the client are given a full hearing and...are empathically understood, as a necessary and deeply meaningful inner journey.'* Endeavour then, to accept the fact that the client may have psychic ability, particularly if this is a belief that can be found challenging and hard to handle from the counsellor's own view of the world.
- Consider use of creative therapies and two chair work to enable the client to gain different perspectives on what is happening in a safe way and how they would communicate with the entity (or the projected part of themselves) if they could.
- Reflect realistically, however, and use careful assessment when considering the possibility of any mental or physical health condition that may be a cause, contributory trigger or factor. Use of medication or drugs

can also be a foundation for various disturbances in perception so there can be a need to make careful enquiries. Many people have experiences which may be described as beyond the usual spectrum of 'normality' or which may be labelled as psychotic episodes but without meeting the full criteria for a psychotic mental health condition.

- Be aware of what I would call the 'lies and limitations' of myth, fiction, media, film and stereotyping when it comes to potential 'quick fix answers' like exorcism, spiritual healing or any rituals deemed to be curative. In her work on trauma, Herman literally talks of exorcism and a desire for catharsis. We can see the symbolic links with haunting in her comments when she says: *'It is understandable for both patient and therapist to wish for a magic transformation, a purging of the evil (of the trauma). Psychotherapy, however, does not get rid of the trauma. The goal of recounting the trauma story is integration, not exorcism.'* Allow the client to take the lead on exploring the options surrounding many such matters and offer support for decisions or experiments the client may make, unless potentially harmful to the client or others.

- Own and explore my personal anxieties and perhaps the wider universal terror around death. Similarly, individual and collective unease around the possible existence and meaning of supernatural entities. Be aware of both my own and the client's issues around the very human hope and desire for an afterlife, for 'something more than this.'

- Bear in mind the potential of a client's fear of rejection. They may have been used to coping alone. They coped before they entered therapy. Being haunted can be a lonely experience when no-one else can see what they see, or hear what they hear. Witnessing, validation, sharing experiences and provision of support can be achieved through safe and appropriate counselling interventions. Shame may well be present, particularly if the client has endeavoured not only to hide their experiences but also their explanations for such events. Dr Marriot raises that social considerations and comparisons to other people may well be having an impact on the individual resulting in a state of *'hiding, denial and pretence…which might suggest that they have not experienced professional or personal relationships that were conducive to sharing important aspects of their lives.'* Learn to tolerate and be open to the unknown. In their work on recovering memories of childhood sexual abuse, Pope and Brown (1996) also make suggestions that seem to fit with our model of working with a haunted client. They posit that: *'Both client and therapist need room for ambivalence and confusion. Both must tolerate doubt, ambiguity and uncertainty.'* They advise therapists to adopt a stance of *'Rethinking, keep an open mind, avoid premature cognitive commitment'* and to resist the urge to rescue by *'using techniques that appear to move toward quicker and more absolute certainty.'* Resist the urge to blame the client for

that which is hard to understand and that leaves the counsellor with no resolution. The counsellor should not contribute to the client's problem.
- Provide appropriate containment and boundaries to manage both my own and the client's sense of bewilderment, unease and lack of safety about what is happening. Together we may be holding something that may not even have defined boundaries or the clarity between life and death unless we hold a firm religious or spiritual faith. There may be more to the universe than we have previously considered. Thus I need to contain the tension between the 'common' sense and the 'non' sense. Be aware of the opportunity for growth, learning and personal development. In his recent research paper Dr Marriot reiterates that: *'The presence of this thread can perhaps inspire hope within clinicians that positive therapeutic interventions conceptualise their own states of both current being and potential futures.'* He further raises that these experiences and issues for the client will be impacting their *'core sense of identity'* and *'their sense of self in the world.'* Such opportunities for personal growth can be opened up through a sensitive and open-minded approach offered by the therapist. In turn the therapist himself is afforded with a valuable opportunity to continue to learn.
- Simultaneously I would need to be aware of the limits of my own competence when dealing with such cases. Know when to refer.
- To summarise, maintain the focus on the client, not on their ghost. From a relational model Rogers himself said, *'The individual and not the problem is the focus.'* The presenting problem may not be the real underlying issue. Pope and Brown advise us to *'Develop a working hypothesis about causality.'* In other words actively consider the issue of 'Why now, why this and why this person?'

I became aware of one further need. Whether there is an afterlife or not, whether there are ghosts or not and whether these have anything to do with people who have already passed away, I feel that I have discovered a respect for people who have died. I would endeavour to maintain this stance, alongside my respect for my living clients.

It is notable that many of these ideas have been taken from models aimed to work with post traumatic stress and moving on from abuse. Van der Kolk, McFarlane and Wiesaeth (1996) state that: *'The key element of the psychotherapy of people with PTSD is the integration of the alien, the unacceptable, the terrifying, the incomprehensible: the trauma must come to be personalised as an integrated aspect of one's personal history.'* So whether Steve will ever believe in ghosts or not, whether he will ever enter therapy or not, it may be that in accepting that he has had some sort of illogical experience in his life and to be able to 'integrate' this without remaining unduly disturbed by it, may be all that we can hope for.

Freud is famously rumoured to have said that *'Sometimes a cigar is just a cigar.'* On occasion, maybe, a ghost has to be interpreted as simply what it seems to be - a ghost.

Where To From Here? Supernatural Evolution

'We are the children of God,' Sybil insisted defensively. 'Evolution, after all, is only a hypothesis.'
From 'Sybil' by Flora Rheta Schreiber.

On an optimistic note, mental health awareness and development of appropriate treatments continues to grow. As I write, the publication of DSM 5 is pending. In February 2010, I felt encouraged when I discovered an online paper by Dr Vaughan Bell, who has made a response to the draft publication of this significant mental health 'Bible.' He notes some changes and revisions in this latest version which appear positive, firstly observing that dissociative and somatoform disorders have now been entirely *'De-Freuded'* and that ironically *'American psychiatry presumably wishes to finally put the old Viennese ghost to rest.'* We can hope, therefore that people who suffer from conversion disorders or hallucinogenic and other 'out of the ordinary' symptoms can now be freed up from the 'hysteria' label that has persecuted them and minimised their distress for centuries. Secondly, Dr Bell raises that DSM is moving away from a recommendation to diagnose certain people as being 'at risk' of psychosis along with the automatic prescription of anti psychotic medication, which may unnerve many patients who may never actually become psychotic. Bell suggests that such a diagnosis of psychosis: *'Might pathologise lots of eccentric but perfectly functional people. Research has shown that about ten percent of Joe Public have higher levels of hallucinations and delusion-like ideas than the average psychotic inpatient but are rarely bothered by their experiences. In other words, lots and I mean lots, of people have unusual experiences – hearing voices, magical ideas, expansive moments – that never cause them any problems, but these people would now be diagnosed with a form of not-quite-mental-illness.'* With this less rigid approach, it seems that people such as Steve, along with voice hearers, psychics and 'hauntees' may find themselves off the severely mentally disordered hook or at least, with more of a borderline than a full diagnosis if they do become immersed in mental health services.

To this end, Bell raises that DSM 5 is likely to include a new term of *'Psychosis Risk Disorder'* which he describes as a *'Something's-a-bit-strange-but-you're-not-completely-mad state, where people might have hallucinations, delusion-like ideas and disorganised thoughts, but not to the extent that they are completely disabled by them.'* This may of course, come as further relief to psychics and hauntees alike, or anyone who simply seems to live in a personal reality that does not fit in with the general norms and expectations of society. It may also help to prevent the automatic labelling of psychosis and perhaps often resulting unnecessary treatments for such people, as we observed in part three.

With this growth and evolution in psychiatric diagnostic criteria of course comes the need for therapists to continue to enable their own understanding and learning about any 'supernatural' cases presenting in therapy. Additionally we need to own and be open to what we do not yet know, so let us examine some of these themes further.

As person centred therapists are aware, Carl Rogers advocates a natural urge for humans to *'become their potentialities.'* The client ultimately knows best and will evolve and change during therapy, given the right conditions. Rogers uses the famous image of the potato left in the dark which will instinctively become aware of the direction of the light and will naturally grow towards it. Psychic healer Ashworth adds that *'...the truth is not static and it must continue to unfold into new realisations or none of us would evolve.'* He continues with the theme of 'becoming' by telling us that *'...we often fail to identify fully with what and who we are becoming, because of the gradual unfoldment.'*

George Malley, in the film *'Phenomenon'*, is being persuaded by members of the medical profession to have his tumour – and his brain – given up to science to aid research. He resists, stating that he would rather have a brain tumour than any paranormal experience causing his condition – because it is something within, rather than external to us. George sees the possibility of what the human brain is capable of and the amazing phenomena it can experience. He says: *'I think I am what everybody can be....I'm the possibility.'* He goes on to explain *'What I'm talking about is the human spirit, that's the challenge, that's the voyage, that's the expedition.'* For George, it is the evolution of the brain that is significant and a cause for the excitement and joy of possibility, not the suggestion of any triggering external supernatural source.

So humans have potential for growth but where does this sit with religious faith? Religions vary but essentially seem to hold the same basic premise, that God, the Supreme Being or whichever deity or growthful 'light' is the focus of a particular faith. He/She/It/They holds a far greater knowledge than the living human being and will only reveal this greater knowledge in time. Let us consider Mormonism once more, since this is the faith which has been pertinent to this story. Mormons believe essentially that human beings have the potential to become like God – who can also be perceived as a super being, possibly from outer space and who, like us, maintains a physical body. Mormons see the possibility of growth and discovery for human beings and are not advocates to a belief where everyone must 'know his place' and remain subservient. For Mormons, God currently knows best and people can become 'better.' In this faith, science and religion seem to tie up quite neatly together and an evolutionary process can be interpreted from this belief. Article nine of the Mormon doctrine states that: *'We believe all that God has revealed, all that He does now reveal and we believe that He will yet reveal many great and important things pertaining to the Kingdom of God'* (2009). There is a sense of future and the potential for change in this part of the doctrine. Whilst we can strive to be Godlike, only God manages the whole, bigger picture.

Robert Buckman argues from an evolutionary point of view that as our factual knowledge of the universe grows, a need for a belief in God and superstition shrinks. It seems to me, however, that even if traditional religions are becoming less popular and church populations diminish, there still seems to be a universal fascination for the supernatural. It may be that we still hold an inherent need for the unknown; for something 'bigger' than ourselves. Otherwise all we are left with is a sense of 'Is this it? I can't get out of life alive if this is all there is…'

As we have explored earlier, from a supernatural viewpoint, Paul Roland argues that the brain operates on a low frequency and he likens this to seeing an image on a photograph but glancing at the picture we are not overly aware of the series of dots that make up that image. The universe, therefore, operates on a higher frequency. He goes on to argue that the existence of discarnate spirits and our growing awareness of their presence forms part of a natural evolutionary process. He explains that our awareness of what he interprets as a quite natural phenomenon is being 'drip fed' gradually by our experiences - through listening to the narratives from others and gathering the 'evidence' (or 'dots') displayed to us by psychics and mediums to gain a bigger picture. He claims clearly that as human beings we all possess a sixth sense which affords us with a sensitivity to the *'more subtle forces and presence around us and not something abnormal or supernatural.'* So the argument lies in the fact that this is entirely a natural process for all of us and not something to be unduly worried about. Roland confirms: *'There is, therefore, an evolutionary aspect to the whole theory of the existence of the supernatural which indicates that at some point human beings will be able to accept the broader reality of ghosts as readily as we accept what we can easily perceive more solidly through our other five senses.'*

There are indications that in the meantime some people will go on to become active mediums, psychics or spiritualists who are able to form a bridge between the grounded 'reality' of our world - that we can perceive with our senses - and the next. Many of these individuals are born with the ability to communicate with the dead. Others may develop it later, or have the skills thrust upon them – perhaps even as a result of transition or trauma, which links in with the themes presented in part one. Ordinary mortals tend not to tune into our sixth sense; however, as we fear disturbing the perceived and comfortable reality in which most of us prefer to operate in our daily lives. Personally I can identify with this. Despite developing a slight interest in the occult some twenty years ago and having acquired a few ineffective 'skills' with palmistry and tarot which are now long forgotten, I am adamant now that I do not want to see a ghost, nor sense that it is likely that I ever will. I consider myself to be a person grounded in material reality. I think I need this belief particularly at the present time in order to provide some sort of anchor to my partner Steve. I am aware, however, that I could be stating the latter fact as a defence. I do not wish to disturb my sense of reality on this particular issue. But I could change in time.

One source of contemporary fictional writing has resonated with me, particularly when we consider the above quote and the likelihood that in time, ghosts could be explained. In *'The Curious Incident of the Dog in the Night-time'* (2004) Mark Haddon details some experiences of his character Christopher Boone, a teenager with Asperger's Syndrome who views the world from what others without the condition may view as 'unusual' and unique. On the subject of ghosts, Christopher, who is highly mathematically gifted, puts his faith in science and he says: *'Lots of things are mysteries. But that doesn't mean there isn't an answer to them. It's just that scientists haven't found the answer yet.'* He goes on to say: *'Eventually scientists will go on to discover something that explains ghosts, just like they discovered electricity which explained lightening, and it might be something about people's brains, or something about the earth's magnetic field, or it might be some new force altogether. And then ghosts won't be mysteries. They will be like electricity and rainbows and non-stick frying pans.'*

Whether we consider the issue of the supernatural therapeutically, spiritually, scientifically, or from a more conventionally religious viewpoint, each message seems to be illustrating the same belief – that we don't know yet, but we are gaining clues and we are learning. Whichever way I tilt the mirror, any definitive answers remain obscure. I have, however, certainly come to a strong realisation during the course of my research that some people could be psychic. Additionally, whether I believe in ghosts or not, I have learned that as so many thousands of people over the centuries have encountered supernatural phenomena, to disregard or to dismiss such experiences would be foolish. Ghosts are an evolutionary process and one day we may understand what 'causes' them. In the meantime we have yet to arrive near a full awareness and explanation that will satisfy the sceptics and the scientists. Whichever way we view it, we can summarise the evolution of our increasing awareness as human beings discovering supernatural phenomena by returning to these famous words of Carl Rogers: *'We are in the Process of Becoming.'*

On the Unknown

'A patient is confronted by the unknown in the therapist, whom he seeks to know in order to lessen the anxiety of being in the presence of someone who remains unknown.' From 'Learning from the Patient' by Patrick Casement.

Until this point of having 'become' arrives, however, we must learn to tolerate the unknown. In mystical terms Owens and spiritualists like him raise that destination is less significant than the journey, that *'The mystical mind is comfortable living with mystery, knowing that sometimes you just need to be – to surrender to divine guidance and not figure anything out'* and that *'The mortal mind tends to get us stuck in life by refusing to live in mystery, by always wanting to have the answer now.'* As I approach the conclusion of this piece of autobiographical study, I do, however, remain aware of the needs of my 'mortal mind,' that I and the readers of this book desire an answer and we want it now. As with many books, mysteries or otherwise, it may be that an ending, an explanation, some sense of neatness and importantly, of resolution is quite naturally expected. An expectation that somewhere along the journey, John will be revealed as mine and Steve's shared *'electricity, rainbow or non stick frying pan'* our newly discovered 'fact.' Maybe Steve is finally diagnosed with a physical or mental health condition, or there is a satisfactory investigation which illuminates conditions within the workplace which have caused some form of mass hallucination. Or we may even learn that such a person who fits John's identity actually existed as a living person and he is a returning discarnate entity. Or that somehow we keep searching and we find that religion or science thrust a meaning into our lives that provides an answer that we can hold onto; thereby justifying this full and sound sharing of the situation, which will enhance the knowledge and understanding of the reader. Explained, the situation described is terminated and our lives become peaceful, happy ever after. And there is a meaning within the story.

At this point in my life, at the time of writing this, I can provide none of the satisfaction or comfort of these things. Whether we gain any explanation from traditional or spiritualist faith, from science, from a combination of the two, or from neither, all I can do is what so many therapists are challenged with on a daily basis in our work – the fact that so often we have to remain with not knowing and we end with no real conclusions. This toleration of anxiety caused by not knowing is discussed by psychoanalyst Melanie Klein, who maintained that fear, dread and anxiety in babies is linked with a basic terror of annihilation. Knowledge occurs in the here and now and we cannot, as a rule, know the future, although it seems spiritualists may challenge this from time to time. Fear of the unknown triggers anxiety and the intolerableness of this state is avoided, denied, rationalised or explained through factual understanding.

Psychoanalyst Wilfred Bion (cited in Casement) urges us as therapists to: *'Discard your memory; discard the future tense of your desire; forget them both, both what you knew and what you want, to leave space for a new idea. A thought, an idea unclaimed, may be floating around the room searching for a home. Amongst these may be one of your own which seems to turn up from your insides, or one from outside yourself.....'* Bion himself moved from a scientific to a more mystical approach over his career, advocating the need to *'dismantle prior ways of thinking,'* recognise the intellect as potentially restrictive and being open to growthful change whilst the therapist needs to *'abandon the desire to cure.'* For us as therapists, not being able to make accurate interpretations, but to wait for the knowledge to emerge from the client, perhaps fits in with the image of the ghost that is floating around the room and which cannot be labelled or defined as understandable fact. Whether this 'ghost' is revealed as Steve reacting to an external phenomenon or as a process embedded as part of his inner psyche, it may be that this process is similar to being with our clients and waiting for them to achieve their personal insights during their therapeutic encounters.

I am aware that over the years I have had a need, quite naturally for a log of ideas, guesses, theorising and discussion about John. I have required and collected different viewpoints and interpretations in order to make my own sense of what has been happening. Many psychoanalytic therapists for example, may maintain that Steve's situation has been caused by a trauma in childhood, possibly pre verbal and possibly linked with a molestation in a public toilet by a man in uniform. This may have caused scratching down the right side of his face and this emotional and psychosomatic trauma is being continually re-activated through the trigger of a more recent life transition. They may stick to this hypothesis through thick and thin. Considering the evidence I presented in part one, I may even have travelled this therapeutic road myself and thereby substantiate the view that all hauntings are products of the mind and not the results of external supernatural phenomena. It is highly unlikely, however, that this event of physical or sexual abuse actually occurred. Whilst Steve finds this interpretation intriguing he also finds it reasonably amusing.

Nevertheless, in order for counselling to work we do require underpinning theoretical models. Casement agrees and cites the importance of theory in order to support the counsellor's need to *'bear the strain'* and *'moderate the helplessness of not knowing'* which *'includes a capacity to tolerate feeling ignorant or incompetent.'* He also quotes Freud who said *'And thus a store of ideas is created, born from man's need to make his helplessness tolerable'* (1994).

In order for life to work, therefore, as in therapy we need theory and I have been interested to witness how easily this has been offered, by Steve's co-workers, by our friends, through contact with religious and psychic 'experts' and through my own research.

Who learns from whom? It seems that the instinct is for the living to seek out knowledge and enlightenment from the dead and we give away our power relatively easily through flight owing to the emotions of shock and fear upon an unexpected encounter with a ghost. Even in controlled environments in which souls of the dead are actively sought out for communication, for example though mediums, the dialogue tends to centre around requesting whether the dead have any 'messages' for the living. Surely then, this indicates that the dead have a higher power, a richness of experience and can impart wisdom regarding the future, the nature of the afterlife and hold the absolute truth to various other questions that the living may wish to pose to them. It seems, however, that there is an alternative possibility, which according to Jung is that it may be the dead who are seeking knowledge from the living. It follows that if souls only know their own absolute truths at the point of death, they therefore seek further knowledge from living beings. This may include, as we have already seen, the discovery that they have actually died.

Steve told me that the not understanding, more so than his initial terror and lack of control in the situation is what lingers most of all as his own particular difficulty. We also discussed the specific issue of death anxiety – and the unknowns of death itself. Whilst all human beings eat, defecate, copulate and die, the boundaries and procedures around the first three can be blurred, as eating disordered or celibate individuals make up their own rules. Death, however, is certain, an absolute one death per person. What do we fear most about death? The answers vary not only in accordance with life experience but also perhaps partly depending upon age. I was in my early forties when I encountered our entity and this coincides with a tendency at this age to reflect on mortality generally. I am now on the downward descent, fully aware of entering the second half of my life. For me death triggers anxiety of travelling into the unknown. For Steve, now at over sixty years of age, death anxiety is different. For him death is about life's footprint. His fears are around a sense of not having been alive at all, not having done anything that mattered, made a difference or moved anything on. He acknowledges a need to be remembered, even to be a 'hero' which to me again hints at a sense of his thwarted potential and perhaps a flawed desire to be 'special'. When asked what being a hero would mean to him, however, he told me he doesn't know any further. It is OK not to know. Sometimes, knowing itself is not without its problems. Haaken agrees that knowing is an issue, that *'Sometimes, knowing is anxiety provoking because it unsettles prior beliefs, ideals or self perceptions.'* If we were also to consider therapy from a phenomenological orientation, a quest for knowledge is actively avoided. Practitioners such as Wilberg (2008) explain that: *'Phenomenological thinking promotes uncertainty. For counselling students, trainers and practitioners, this place of "not knowing" can be both challenging and liberating.'* Additionally Wilberg raises that *'Phenomenology is the science of the phenomenon. A phenomenon is a perception or experience as it is without explanation.'* Clearly the phenomenon of our ghost story provides rich material for the phenomenologist. Wilberg also includes an observation of that eminent therapist: *'Yalom certainly stresses we should both be fellow travellers neither knowing the path.'* I guess death is the only certainty, but what, if anything, happens beyond death remains fundamentally unknown unless one holds an absolute spiritual or religious faith.

I noticed that the psychologist and prolific writer Irvin Yalom, referred to in Wilberg's article and now approaching eighty years of age, has been writing quite recently about the reality of facing his own death. When interviewed in *'Therapy Today'* in May 2008, he discussed his pending book entitled *'The Ripple Effect.'* When asked what in particular frightens him about his own death, Yalom quotes philosopher Epicurus: *'Where death is, I am not.'* Epicurus posits that nothing is to be feared from death if the soul perishes and there is no afterlife: *'Why fear death when we can never perceive it?'* Yalom goes on to explain further that in his view, *'There won't be any me there to feel terror, sadness, grief, deprivation. My consciousness will be extinguished, the switch flicked off, lights out.'* He likens death to the state before birth, that of *'non being',* a comforting *'oblivion.'* Yalom's argument lies in the fact that *'Epicurus is saying that indeed we won't be there, that we won't know when it happens because death and 'I' can never co-exist. Because we are dead, we don't know that we are dead, and in that case, what is there to fear?'* Here I can truly access the full horror of the state of the stuck phantom, the soul who is trapped between life and death, either holding knowledge of their own death or otherwise and continuing to experience the relentless residue of emotion. It seems that neither Epicurus nor Yalom appear to have taken this into account. Yalom, does, however, perceive his own impact - immortality if you like - rather as I do, by passing things on to others. If not through children, then through clients, or through writing books, even organ transplants. These are the 'ripples' – the effects we pass on to others as a continual process. Whilst Steve's fear is that his ripples will be indiscernible, my own is anxiety about what lies beyond the water.

From my personal viewpoint, the presence of ghosts, like the ripples of life itself, is a process and not a destination or a result. If we were to achieve absolute knowledge and certainty about the supernatural we could hold a definitive answer to the possibility of life after death, the reasoning behind why certain people seem to possess a sixth sense and the purpose of returning or discarnate spirits. We will have arrived.

PART FIVE

THE END OF THE RAINBOW

Encounters 2009

'And the more I see - the more I know
The more I know – the less I understand' From 'The Changingman' by Paul Weller & Brendan Lynch.

Let us pick up Steve's story again.

So how was he doing? Was there a pot of gold at the end of his particular rainbow? Or was there merely a patch of mud in which he remained stuck? Sadly, it seemed to me during the year 2009 that it was the latter.

In February 2009, ghostly matters once more came to a head. For some weeks reports of the fire doors opening and closing by themselves began to filter through. Steve, psychically closed down, however, was unaffected. Then, one night, John appeared, standing right behind him. *'Help me,'* he said. *'Help me, help me.'* The same, sad refrain. *'Help.'*

He followed Steve around for the rest of the night. Steve was badly scarred in the face, bloody and distressed, he had had enough. His endeavours to close down had failed him and not only that, but on this particular night, he was alone in his perceptions of John. To escalate matters further, the team leader Michael, had now left. Unfortunately a new manager, Simon, had been disbelieving and unempathic to Steve's experiences on the night shift. Steve says of the events on this night that: **'It's like going crazy because no-one else sees it. It's only me that sees it and he was actually following me around completely and I was thinking surely somebody can see him – surely somebody's got a feel of him or something. I actually stopped whilst there was a group of people nearby and he was quite close to me. I was thinking – please look and see if you can see him but they just turned around and started talking to me as if nothing was going on. Even though others had seen things and sensed things – bits of legs and arms – this was private to me. It was more like he was telling me that "I** *need you alone to do something about something." I remember getting badly scarred and going down to Simon and him saying, "You'd better go and sit down in the canteen for ten minutes," and so I went and sat in the canteen as per normal because that's what all the team leaders have let me do. I don't know if instructions have come down from higher levels – you know, something like "When Steve gets like this you need to leave him alone for five minutes." So I went into the canteen and Simon followed me in after a few minutes and asked, "How are you?" I said,"Well, I don't know - do you know anything?" and he said "I don't know anything and I don't want to know, I don't believe it." And I'd got this really bad scar on my face and you know I was too kind of like built up with all this anxiety with this thing following me around that I don't feel I could have said anything to him and I'd have lost my temper or I don't know, so I just looked at him thinking, what does he mean he doesn't believe me, is he saying I'm a liar or he doesn't believe in ghosts – if he doesn't believe in ghosts then where does he think this mark's coming from? Hundreds of things went through my brain at the same time and he says – I can't remember exactly how he said it - but he almost said, "I want you back in the workplace in ten minutes or I'm afraid you'll have to go home if you can't carry on." So after a couple of minutes after he'd gone I just phoned him up and said, "I'm going home Simon" and I went. And that was it because I just didn't want to face him – I didn't want to face him and I didn't want to face the trauma of what was going off in the place. You know I was fought on two levels there.'*

Steve's defensiveness, sense of isolation and lonely rage is evident here. Despite the fact that his colleagues had previously encountered sensations, gained a sense of John through hearing voices and seeing disembodied parts of him – or so they have claimed – on this occasion Steve was alone in being able to see the apparition. John had clearly latched onto Steve and Steve only.

To escalate the distress of the issue further, the new manager had come onto the night shift and had informed Steve that he was not believed. Perhaps the fundamental mistake that this manager made was to tell Steve that he was a liar, rather than to go down the more sensitive route of saying he did not believe the situation – that he did not believe in ghosts. He could, however, have risked acknowledging that some odd situation was occurring. This would have perhaps been considerably more acceptable to Steve.

'Ghost' events escalated thick and fast once more during and following the month of February and I again subsequently became more emotional and prolific in the writing of my diary:

17 February 2009: *Steve badly scarred last night and bleeding. Very low mood which continued for some time. His colleague Hassan sensed 'someone rushing down the aisle' (well away from Steve) and then the carousels began shaking. At* this moment Steve got 'hit.' This resulted in the deepest gouging and grazing of his face to date. We then went to the pub for dinner. This pub is close to the crematorium and a funeral party was present, which often occurs. Steve is quiet and grows quieter. Suddenly he says: 'I think I am a medium.' He has been watching an elderly woman in the funeral party and realises that he is the only person who can see her. She disappears after three or four minutes. She was not dressed in black and seemed to be travelling from group to group but was being ignored by everyone. Steve feels cold and shakes. I did not dare approach anyone to ask who had died. In the cold light of common sense later on, Steve and I discuss the possibility of him having seen another ghost and we attempt to explain the woman's presence logically. The verdict on that incident remains open.

Speaking some months after the event, Steve remains confused about this incident. He says: **'In retrospect I'm thinking was I heightened with the thought of seeing ghosts and actually this little lady was probably looking for somebody and I kind of drew the conclusion that she may be a ghost. I don't know – I've never come to any kind of arrangement in my head to say that was real or that was false. I think with my heightened sense it could be either. It could have been me being a fool or it could have been me being a medium. I don't know. I don't really care to tell you the truth. It's like, I don't want it so if it happened, it happened – it may have been something, it may not have been and I think it may not have been – it may have been a living person I just projected onto.'**

I wrote: *That same night at work, Steve must have been 'open.' John is standing behind him. 'Help me' he says. Steve weeps. John follows him all night. No-one else can see John. This is the last straw. Steve changes to the morning shift.*

As a result, Steve finally changed shifts in March and began to work in the early mornings. There are upwards of eighty people who work this shift and the energy is very different. No-one has reported anything untoward. Steve settled in and so worked unmolested for a couple of months. He describes this experience as follows: **'Being a night shift worker, it took about a week to get used to it and after a time I kind of enjoyed it. I think I brought my work ethics on to days and the team leaders - more of them on this shift – kind of left me alone and I really got on with my job. There was nothing else for me to do. I didn't know anyone hardly and I thought, Well, this is new I just got on with it and I had team leaders coming up to me at the end of the some of the shifts and saying, "Thanks Steve, for putting that work in," because it was noticed that I had worked hard all the time.'**

For me, although I was aware that the presenting problem clearly still existed, I was now feeling confident that through changing his shift Steve had found a way to combat the abuse and work on his responses to it in a healthy way. Also by making this change he would be having a break from his ongoing anxiety. Rothschild says, *'It is not possible to resolve trauma when a client lives in an unsafe and/or traumatising environment.'* The logical response is to leave the environment, or to build up one's defences further, which may not ultimately be helpful to an individual. Steve achieved the build up of defences initially by employing the closing down rituals passed onto him by the Mormons. It had become obvious that the experience that causes the physical and psychological trauma for Steve continued to be present and without his defences being employed would continue to traumatise him whilst he remained in the unsafe environment. During this time it also felt important for me to support him in an environmental sense at home.

I had fully reclaimed my space in my home and I could once more walk around at night in the dark, in confidence. I cleared my attic of long forgotten books and paraphernalia on the occult – tarot, palmistry, astrology and other themes which interested me and which I had collected over twenty years ago. If Steve needed to close down his psychic ability, then I would make sure I would do all I could to assist him in this. Whilst in one sense I was closing down on a practical level, I was feeling more fully open in another – I was becoming open to the possibility of the existence of supernatural forces. Instead of saying 'I don't believe,' I moved into an 'I don't know and it's OK not to know' position. I had been learning and I was continuing to learn. I was shocked when his 'closing down' defences failed him and he was compelled to move to a day shift. All was peaceful there for a while until mid March:

19 March 2009: *Steve by now has changed to the morning shift. Steve was hit and marked for the first time on the morning shift. 'It' has followed him – and found him.*

Steve pondered: **'I think my thoughts were around if it happens on days, where do I go? What happens to me – what protection is there for me? And if it happens in front of everybody, do I freak people out – what do I do? And I said to Kate if it happens to me what do I do? And she said, "Well, come straight off the floor and come into the offices and I can sit you down and talk to you for ten minutes until you've settled down." I think it was her wanting for it not to get to a situation on days as well as on nights.'**

When it happened on the morning shift, I had mixed feelings really. It was like, Oh my God, it can happen to me anywhere. And also kind of like a situation where you think, there must be something here for it to happen during the day as well. I was standing receiving goods as they were coming in and there must have been about twelve or sixteen people standing around me and therefore it was not possible I could have done these things to myself. And people have recognised that I got hit and when I got hit the first time I went and told the team leader – that day it was Ricky who used to be on nights a long time ago before all of this happened and he asked me "Are you alright Steve?" and I said, "I've been hit," and he replied, "I can see you have, you'd better go" and I just walked off the shop floor, so I don't

think anybody really noticed. I think all the team leaders know about it because I think they have a meeting during the day and I think things are told to them. So there again I have this kind of stigma that says they talk about it and I wonder what have they said – Steve gets this mark or Steve's acting a prat or, you know, beware of Steve. I don't know what the message was – but Ricky was kind of – for want of a better word – gentle with it, kind of a gentleman – "OK Steve I can see you've been hit" – kind of "I'm really sorry, you get yourself off the shop floor, see to yourself, you know."

26 March 2009: 10.30am – the same day and time as last week, Steve is marked.
End of April 2009: Steve has had another conversation with the Mormons who have informed him that since the closing down ritual is not working, he has to change tactic. John has apparently latched on too heavily to be fully shut out. Since John has attached to Steve, only Steve can help implement change in the situation. This means that Steve has to face John alone. His task is to calm John down and to help him find peace. If John is angry then Steve is to walk away. The angry part (the demon) should not be engaged with. What makes a client change I wonder? How long does an individual need to suffer and endure before they finally seek help?

Steve observes: **'The conversation was about how it's really impossible to close down because people come to me and say "I've felt this," and ask, "Are you OK Steve?" Because this is happening around me and it's very hard to shut myself down when people want to know if I'm OK or are talking about, you know, have you heard about this happening or have you heard about that happening. So when I spoke to one of the Mormons he was realising, this is not going to work, because obviously you can't close down as other people are involved as well. He told me to say to it, "In the name of Jesus Christ, go" and by that command he should go. I told him "Well, I've already done that" – so obviously being religious, probably self righteous – I don't know – but what he then told me is that I don't command the amount of physical strength that is leant to me by the priesthood so therefore I cannot banish him – I don't have that power. And because they can't come into the warehouse because we never know when he's going to hit, they'd have to follow me around. It needs that priesthood to say "I banish you from this place" so they can't help. The only way you can help is by me saying to it "Well, how can I help you, what do you want, how do you feel?" And I said to the Mormons, "Yes, OK, that's fine, but you're saying that I don't get afraid or I'm not scared or I'm not jumpy or you know it's very hard to find your tongue in front of something that scares the hell out of you." So therefore it's like "Calm down Steve – talk to this thing."**
"OK, I'll try it again".'

18 May 2009: *Steve is back on nights following a two month break on the morning shift. Unfortunately he was not able to remain on this shift permanently at that time. So far, there is no sign of the 'bogeyman' on nights as Steve called him today. Steve's attitude has changed and he is ready for some contact and to take some positive action. Steve is frustrated. 'Where is he when I'm ready to face him and send him away?' he asks. He is opened up but the uncooperative entity has dispersed.*

Steve added: **'I think it was bravado really, I don't know - if he did appear what would I have done? But it was like – people welcomed me back onto the night shift and were asking me what happens if things occur and I think I was saying to them – if I remember rightly –"Look I'm ready for this, I need to confront him, I've been told to confront him and that's what I'm going to do." So it was like pushing myself forward saying, "I can do this," and telling people - so therefore if it happens then I've got to do it because I've told everybody I've got to do it.'**

I wrote: *The team leader, Simon, attempts to put Steve on disciplinary for the last two occasions of being off sick (times Steve has to leave or take time out to tend to his physical wound and to deal with his emotional state following attacks). Steve relishes the challenge and has his witnesses lined up – about a dozen of them including Russell, Tom, Andrew, Hassan, Lizzie, Paula, Bernie and Nathaniel. These people have all been affected strongly over the years and in particular during Steve's absence owing to working the morning shift. Colleagues reported seeing disembodied parts of a man, encountered cobwebs, heard voices and screams and felt the 'chills.' A handful of other colleagues feel cold spots and cobwebs. The remaining third of the team appear to have been unaffected.*

Whilst I am aware of feeling quite vitriolic towards management, the new young manager's viewpoint is understandable. Coming onto nights with no knowledge of the culture, the recent history or the impact of events or personalities of the team, in Steve he is faced with an older, perhaps quite intimidating individual who is displaying signs of:

- Psychic ability, which is easier for the sceptic to choose to disbelieve.
- Mental ill health, possibly one reason he is giving Steve a wide berth as far as possible.
- Malingering, lying or a manipulation of the system which is counterproductive and therefore makes it necessary to proceed with standard managerial actions and disciplinary systems.

Faced with these options, I was aware at one point of feeling quite sorry for Simon in fact. The attempt at holding a disciplinary case was dropped.

15 June 2009: *Thunderstorm tonight before Steve left for work. He told me that next day that the electrics at work had repeatedly malfunctioned. It seems that* there may be a sense that John is building up to making his presence felt in the same way as the static in the air.

17 June 2009: *Last night Steve and his colleague Russell witnessed a row of carousels moving independently. Steve was then marked heavily in the face. Colleagues saw his head flip back violently as he was hit. He was determined not to allow the sensation of despair take over this time.*

As for me right now, I am fine. If Steve is alright, then so am I. It is interesting to observe the transactional analytic position of 'You're OK, I'm OK' into which I have moved after all of these years of listening to what my partner is experiencing. I noted at this point that my diary becomes very matter of fact, reporting events as if they were day to day occurrences of no greater import than the recordings of any other diary, kept for any reason. I felt at this point that human beings do indeed sooner or later have a power to integrate more or less any experience – even the completely inexplicable ones.

2 July 2009: *Last night I attended an audience with psychic Sally Morgan; an event which I recorded further in part three, included when I discussed the work of mediums. Following on from this audience, I was feeling emotionally tense and edgy. During that night at work, Steve is pushed violently in the back and marked in the face. He is really mad! Steve seems to be reacting angrily now, rather than with a depressive response. The manager again is unsupportive, which of course, may be fuelling Steve's frustration.*

8 July 2009: *Steve is marked.*

16 July 2009: *Steve and I travel to the Greek island of Kephalonia on holiday. During a tour of the island we visit the monastery of the patron Saint, St Gerasimos. This site houses the remains of the Saint himself and his body is paraded annually through the town according to common tradition. The church is crowded and Steve and I stand at the back once we enter. A ceremony is taking place at the front and we move a little closer. The sarcophagus containing the body of the Saint is unlocked by the priest. At this moment Steve is not OK. He goes extremely cold (although the temperature is in the forties) and he feels a strong sensation of cobwebs all over his face. I'm holding his hand and I sense him freezing and see the goose bumps on his flesh. We leave. Steve then goes back in alone – the place is still full of Greeks taking part in the service and tourists watching. Near the body of the Saint, the same thing happens. Steve's reactions are physical, fortunately he is not left battling with any emotional residue, once we leave again, he feels fine.*

I just can't take him anywhere…

Steve said later of the incident: **'I don't know what to make of that. That was so weird. I do believe that I've got kind of whatever, a tinge of, or something like – sending a sense out to these things that are around me - and I just get a sense of my "being" not wanting it. Therefore I get really cold although in Greece it was really hot and I was really warm. How can you have goose** *bumps in the nineties, it's just not possible. I knew I wasn't going to get depressed because it wasn't in the same kind of context as in somebody who obviously died in a way that was bad. This was an apparent saint who had died in a way that he had masterminded his deeds and his death in a way that he wanted to, I think. But the way John died that I'm contending with at the workplace, and all that with the marks, despair and stuff - perhaps I'm in a real parallel situation - well that's the situation that I'm getting. I just felt really, really cold as if this saint guy was reaching out to me. A sense of something coming out, filling the room and making me cold was the sense that I got. That was weird. I think that was the part when I realised that actually, if I wanted to work at being a medium, I think I could go to wherever – a spiritualist church or college or whatever and see what they say and see how they structure a class or how they structure a situation where you can actually become a medium. Not that I believe in it or I don't believe in it – I just think when you're going to these places it's constructed to say that you are that – it's part of their job – that's what they are getting paid for, to say to those people sitting on the seats that you can do this. The reason I don't go is that I don't think I'd get anything out of it because I'm so kind of a non believer in all this. It's like saying well, you don't really know – you don't really know what you're doing and you don't know what I'm doing in the sense of you never know anything truly - and if what is being said is being said as a truth to something to build you up into a sense of the knowledge. I think your mind can play tricks on you to make you think that you can be a medium or that you need to be a medium. I just get a sense of nobody can really train you or tell you to heighten your senses. It's all within you – if you want to do it then let go.'*

So it may be that Steve could use a natural ability if he chooses to but he remains sceptical and unwilling. I am aware of the disappointment cited by my psychic friend Rose and others that he does not choose this path. It may be that the shock has simply been too much for him to want to develop any skills further and who can blame him? He has been 'sledge hammered' in the way Owens describes here: *'How readily you open your mind to the divine presence is up to you. Depending on how hardhearted you are, the Gods may use either a gentle push or a sledge hammer to get your attention.'* Anything to do with 'Gods' or not, this supernatural entity is literally physically hammering the living to gain attention.

25 July 2009: *First night back at work for Steve following our holiday and he is marked in the face. Apparently, whilst we were away, a new experience occurred for a worker who has not so far been affected, his colleague Gus. Gus was hit by a tote – a very heavy object – which was thrown at him violently through the air. Throughout the night fire doors were opening and closing unaided. The lights* went out. It was clearly a very active night. Steve has worked out that nearly two thirds of the night shift have now been affected in some way and to varying extents.

11 August 2009: Steve was away on a course for the past week and returned for his first night back last night. Apparently things had been very active during his absence. Lights malfunctioning and fusing, heavy totes moving and even upending and three colleagues had heard screaming. They could not detect whether these screams were male or female. Several had refused to work in specific areas owing to an escalating sense of acute fear.

Steve said: **'I mean if all that doesn't prove there is something in that place, then what more do you want, what more proof does the management want?'**

12 August 2009: Steve is hit hard – to the extent that he is pushed into the clothing bins. His face is only faintly marked the next morning as it healed up quickly. He has negotiated working on the ground floor from now on – if he were to be pushed and fall from one of the open plan upper floors, he could be killed. Steve is angry and has now started to seriously consider leaving the job. He is not OK and now, I am not OK.

I am reminded of the claims of many psychics and ghost hunters that spirits cannot hurt the living. I think they are wrong. For example spiritual psychologist Dr Edith Fiore informs us that: *'Usually it's not possible for spirits to move heavy objects, but at times they are able to manipulate small ones…Don't be frightened if you see something levitate or move. It may be an entity trying to catch your attention. Some are desperately seeking help. They need to have you know that they are there.'* Moreover Roland also seeks to negate an image of spectres being anything other than well intentioned towards us when he questions: *'…whether we can shrug off the negative image we have of ghosts as malevolent entities created by centuries of superstition and lurid horror fiction and instead accept them simply as discarnate personalities on the other side of life.'*

I don't think this thing is so passive. I feel like we are living within a horror story and that if there are such things as ghosts, then at least some of them have the potential to commit murder.

Steve provided this comment on the escalation of violence and his view of spirit behaviour: **'Yes, it was changing a bit – it was more urgent – to make me do something. It's kind of like saying "You're not helping at all, therefore I'm angry with you." I can never understand being told that ghosts cannot hurt you. I mean, something that is in a situation where somebody's angry with you, no matter what kind of situation it is, then there's some way of getting at you. That's the way I felt. And in a psychic way – talking about mediums – is it only me that's getting this? Don't a lot of mediums get attacked by malevolent beings or something? That's part of the reason I don't want to do it. All they're saying is they're getting in touch with some sort of - I** don't know – some sort of spirit guide who is often a spiritual Indian who takes them travelling or talks to them and they're really nice people. I'm sorry but when you die you are not always nice are you?'

21 August 2009: We are on holiday in the Lake District and whilst we are there we visit Muncaster Castle. We had not realised that this is one of the most haunted places in England. 'This is the most haunted room in the castle,' our audio guide informs us when we are in one of the bedrooms. 'Leave now if you feel strange, uncomfortable or become scared.' For Steve, not a thing happens. Psychic my arse.

11 September 2009: Back at work, Steve is marked in the face. He doesn't see any apparition. I am aware at this point once more of how much I have integrated this experience. I seem to have stopped feeling much. I am not angry, I am not frightened, or even particularly curious any more. I feel concerned for Steve but that is about it.

13 September 2009: Last night Steve was marked. He sees John for the first time since returning from the morning shift. 'Help me,' says John. Steve feels a malevolent presence. Steve swings between depression and rage. He resolves to try and record John on his mobile phone.

19 September 2009: Gus hears footsteps when working alone in T86. Everyone senses that John is around. Steve goes cold and is hit. He has asked permission to take his mobile phone into the warehouse to try and capture an image of John. He takes out the phone and attempts to take a picture. Steve feels a surge of vibrating energy sweep through the phone he holds in his hand. The phone cracks right across its face and dies. Eighty pounds worth of phone is completely destroyed.

Steve told me later: **'Well, I thought with it being taped, if I can get some sort of movement, if it's a blur or something that moves – because my phone has got a video function in it – I thought well, here is a real opportunity. I can remember feeling that he's around me and I'd just taken my phone out to kind of get it all ready in case something happens and I can't really remember what kind of feeling it was – all I can remember is it going "crack" and I looked at it, it had gone, the front had cracked all the way round. I felt like, oh shit, I've broken my phone, but I think at the time, prior to this me and Lou had both become insensitive towards it because it had become a fairly regular occurrence – it happens to us, we were used to it so its like saying that was a good opportunity missed because he didn't want my phone, so he's cracked it. I thought afterwards he knew about my tape recording as well because he said, "Switch it off." There's a voice that says "Switch it off" on the tape so therefore, when I analyse it afterwards he probably felt like "I told him to switch it off, so now I'm going to break it" I don't know. In those days when he was alive he couldn't know what a fucking mobile phone was – it's a different kind of reality to**

him. Anyway it just cracked and I don't know what cracked it but I don't know what made that cross the priest gave me burn either. So I don't know what it was. It certainly wasn't me.'

1 October 2009: The work colleagues are starting to talk about the possibility of going to the papers. They are frustrated and want the situation to change.

In front of a group of the annual intake of agency workers who he was training, Steve was badly marked in the face last night and shoved violently against fellow trainer, Gus. By now, we had been given the phone number from Rose of a medium and psychic trainer who is an 'expert' in the field of paranormal studies. Steve needs someone to talk to. The medium is empathic and reassuring but quickly dismisses 'ghosts' in the sense that concurs with my research so far. He tells Steve that Claudia's take on the haunting is mistaken and that psychics tend to dramatise and illustrate supernatural occurrences. Perceptions of paranormal happenings are in fact concerned with recorded events (and not people) and Steve is picking up these activities owing to being 'sensitive' to it all. He did in fact cite the example of legions of Roman soldiers playing out their march through time and space. It seems that this once again concurs with the Stone Tape theory which I briefly explored in part two. It also seems that over the centuries a sufficient number of people have seen enough of these types of events for such occurrences to become collectively described as 'ghosts.' This therefore has over time provided adequate 'evidence' for many believers that there is such a thing as a ghost. Some of these ghosts are products generated by the mind. Perhaps some are not.

It puzzles me then, why this expert did not go on to explain how Steve can actually interact with John? John can clearly see Steve, or at least, sense Steve's presence (or essence). It even makes me wonder whether Steve is haunting John, you never know. Nor did Steve remember to mention the demonic screaming he had captured on the audio tape. It would have been interesting to discover his thoughts on this piece of hard 'evidence.'

The psychic expert seemed to be interested in Steve's physical marks, which he referred to as 'stigmata.' His additional reasoning about the case included his perception that this is indeed a 'haunting;' but nothing to do with any deceased person. God would not, apparently allow anyone – the essence of any deceased person - to suffer and wander the earth. Once more the idea appears to be that spirits all return to the warm, safe fluffiness of spirit land – where it seems, unconditional love reigns. Ultimately, Steve needs to 'stand his ground' and to 'close down' which is of course, advice he has been given before from other sources. He needs to be able to say 'I don't want this.' Life transitions and religious blueprints are also significant in opening up an individual's awareness to the spiritual world.

Now tell us something we don't bloody know.

I feel furious when we discuss all this later. I wrote: *It feels to me like although it sounded like a supportive conversation, it was still crap. I am furious with religion, spirituality and with secular viewpoints. All trying to fit Steve into their own theories. Thinking about my own journey through the 'haunting' from naively* thinking Steve had fallen asleep, to psychic essences to mental health explanations, what conclusions am I left with? NOTHING FUCKING HELPS, that's what.

Steve's opinion was as follows: **'I think talking to somebody other than those who work in the place – it was helpful just to talk to somebody who wasn't even in the room. He was on the phone so I couldn't look at his expressions, I couldn't see anything – it was just talking to him and he had a nice pleasant voice as well – plummy – so it was like me listening to his plummy voice but in retrospect, you can't cram everything into one conversation so it was like – well, I don't know if I purposely kept things away from him because I didn't want to express exactly what was going off for me to a complete stranger. I really don't know but it was kind of like unhelpful and when I told Lou I was still up with the fact I'd talked to somebody outside of all of this and I felt happy about it but then Lou pointed out things and I was thinking yeah, what a load of bollocks. It doesn't help and this person only goes on what he feels or what he knows and nobody knows. I kind of realised nobody fucking knows what's what. It's a reality that nobody knows about. Nobody. There's no clues to it. There's nobody said, I've actually spoken to a ghost. I mean, I'm saying I have, but I don't know if I have – because I don't know what it is. But he knows nothing about it, I'm sorry, as high as he is – he doesn't know anything really.'**

7 October 2009: *Steve marked, objects are thrown violently at him and he is pushed over, all in front of others. He explodes in rage at the managers. Steve by now has firmly concluded that he is being haunted in the sense that something malevolent is out to harm him. This is nothing to do with 'conventional' spiritual or psychic stuff. It's out to get him. Paranoia? Mental breakdown? Demonic harm?*

I don't know whether I can take much more of this. I become tearful. I begin to question whether I can continue in the relationship. Is any relationship worth this much stress and trouble? But this is only a fleeting thought.

14 October 2009: *The manager, Simon, has now left. I don't think he can take any more of the night shift, especially with the threat of publicity looming. A new manager has arrived, a woman I will call Stephanie. Steve is hit and marked in front of her. As a result of witnessing this, she discloses to Steve she too has some psychic ability and an interest in spiritual matters. All this since being a kid. They go together to the first aid office to mop up Steve's wounds. Paula happens to be there. Suddenly the door slams on them and all three of them go very cold. Stephanie feels an entity behind her – literally breathing down her neck. She feels the breath of him on her hair. 'He's here' she says. They all feel him. Steve has a sense of being believed and supported once more.*

Steve said: **'I think everybody's got to have a tinge of some sort of reality to the other side – the spiritual side or whatever – when its like Simon who just solidly like a stupid little kid** *believes in everything that he sees and everything he believes in is locked in his head. But when you get somebody who says, I've experienced things like that and I've done that, I think collectively it becomes a lot stronger and again Paula feels the same way – she's a religious person and she feels as if she's got some sort of connection to the other side. And I think with me being in the room as well knowing that I – that there's things happening to me – I think the whole force of us together actually kind of made him come into the room and I thought about it before and I'm thinking collectively there's three of us. If I remember before I met Tom some time ago and we had that really cold spell, the one that thrilled us right to our bones, well, he's the same – he can pick it up as well so he's got an open mind. I think anybody with an open mind does actually feel it, does actually get a tinge of John as well. I think that's why there's only about, up to a point, a third of the team who really feels him strongly because I think they're open and another third get hints. A lot of the others are closed and I think that's the difference. And when somebody's really open and I know Stephanie says she's really open to it, then collectively I think it's a big force and I think he's drawn to that big force and I think that he entered the room because we were all three of us kind of apprehensive of him coming in and showing himself. I'm going back to the fact that she saw that mark on my face – she'd heard about it but she'd never seen it. So she was thrilled that it actually happened straight in front of her. It was like "Oh my God," you know "It's true, this does happen to you," because she saw it running round my face – my face was OK then it just opened up. She could see the mark swelling up and everything. I think she was thrilled to know because it's like, because she believes in something like that, it was proof to her that there's something like that as well and she picked up on it because of it – it's positive to her thoughts and to her knowledge of what was happening around.'*

21 October 2009: *Steve faintly marked last night.*

23 October 2009: *I do some more research. What else can I do? I've shifted once more into a need to be doing something practical. I look up Charles Bonnet Syndrome. This occurs when people with visual deterioration perceive hallucinations, anything from lines and patterns to full landscapes and people, but is usually of a peaceful nature. Such experiences, however, are visual, not auditory. This leads me onto Alice in Wonderland Syndrome. This comprises distorted perceptions of the body, a bit like when Steve felt his hands to be bigger when he was ill and Sally Morgan's perception of her fingers to be 'like sausages.' The marks on his face are real, however. I look up stigmata, the top medium who Steve spoke to recently holding a particular fascination with this. These marks need to mirror the wounds of Jesus on the cross. So another dead end here. Once* more I go through schizophrenia and all its types with a fine tooth comb. I look up delusions, I look up dementia. I check out personality disorders once more. My copy of DSM 4 is becoming well thumbed. I seek, but nothing fits. What are we missing? What am I defending myself against finding?

If I were to answer that honestly, I would now say that I am defending myself against the knowledge that there is more to reality than the material world in which I live; that there is more to the universe than meets the sensory perceptions. That science and mental health has its place but is not the be all and end all. That some of the issues we term as 'supernatural' form an evolving learning process. Darrin Owens posits that the mystical mind is linked with love and the mortal mind is linked with fear. He says: *'The mortal mind is stuck in the world of the physical senses; the mystical mind operates apart from your sensory perceptions. In a psycho-spiritual sense, the mystical mind allows you unlimited impressions and intuitions and infuses you with the divine. It's responsible for those 'a-ha' moments when you know you have been downloaded with wisdom, when you finally get it.'* Over these past few years I have not achieved an 'A-ha' moment, but the seeds of wider possibilities are certainly sown. Whether Steve has been opened up to the 'divine' also remains open for question. For him there was no real cognitive development in terms of any alteration in his beliefs. His personal learning, he told me later, was around realising his potential and capacity for surviving unexpected severe depressed feelings that seemed to emerge from nowhere. He said: **'In some way it was good for me; I had never felt like that before, not even when my parents died. I learned that I could move through it. Fight my way out of it. I experienced myself surviving. As for the ghost, well, it was what it was.'**

Before I go on to end, it is important to be aware of one final fact which is significant in this story. Steve had been training some agency workers, employed for the winter. Among these was a young, hard working woman who I will call Maria. Maria had formed something of a bond of trust with Steve and a few weeks earlier had appeared extremely distressed. When Steve had asked her what the matter was, she had confided in him that she was pregnant with her second child. She and her husband wanted this baby; however, owing to medical difficulties she was experiencing with her own health, but not that of the foetus - she had been advised to terminate the pregnancy. She was currently in a position when she had to consider her options. Only Steve and some of the management team knew of her condition and the reason for her low mood.

Then this is what happened on **4 November 2009.** Steve came home from his shift at about 6.15am and told me that it was all over. The ghost had been vanquished. I was in bed at the time and the room was in darkness. *'My face,'* said Steve, *'is the worst it has ever been, I am covered in scratches, please don't freak out.'* I allowed the light to filter into the room as Steve told me gradually about the night's experiences. With the coming of the daylight I could see that scratches were indeed covering his face, which was extremely well marked and bloody in places. I would need to take a photograph later. Steve's encounters with John over night had been lengthy and communicative. Such powerful and continual contact with him had escalated the markings and they were especially severe. Steve also felt sore and was aching all over his body as if he had been badly beaten up. Again I wonder if these injuries were consistent with those inflicted on John's brother Dan, presumably caused by John himself or whether this is what John suffered in his death?

John had followed Steve around all night at work, appearing directly behind him at times. No-one else could see him. This included Steve's trusted friend Lizzie, who at one point, had John standing behind her chair. Sometimes the colleagues had had feelings, cold spots, objects thrown at them, but sometimes they did not. This time, however, it felt that Steve, as the main conduit, was entirely alone with the ghost.

Then came the pivotal moment. John indicated Steve's pregnant colleague, Maria. *'That's my daughter,'* he said, *'Tell her not to have an abortion. Tell her I'm sorry.'* Shocked, Steve felt protective of Maria and told a couple of the male colleagues to ensure that they were keeping an eye on her in the work area where she was located. Exhausted from the amount of contact and the physical pain, Steve had been sent by an empathic manager to sit in the canteen for a while. He had time to think things through and seize an opportunity. He had something of a revelation and he asked Maria to help him. Although she had not worked for the company for long, she had been aware of the marks repeating on Steve's face and the 'strange thing' that he had had to deal with for the best part of four years. On instinct, Steve asked her to go and encounter John with him. *'But I'm scared,'* she said. Understandably, she was feeling fearful of either the ghost, or of the somewhat bizarre behaviour of her colleague. *'You won't see anything,'* said Steve. With some persuasion they went together to T86, the 'powerhouse' of Steve's sightings. Here is sited the clothes for baby girls. John was standing at the end of the gangway. Steve had his arm around Maria. *'John, I've brought your daughter and she forgives you,'* said Steve. Speaking, from her viewpoint, into the thin air, Maria added *'I forgive you, father.'* John smiled at them both and turned to leave. And then that was that.

Steve explains: **'What it felt like – wow - it was such a powerful night, I was being hit all over the place. It was like having a fight with Mike Tyson all the time and my face was becoming bloody raw, like in ribbons. But I wasn't bothered because I knew that something was going to happen and I kept going from chamber to chamber and people were asking me "What's wrong with you?" and I was saying "I don't know – something's going to happen" I feel something really harmful is going to happen and that's how I felt. I went to the desk and saw the team leader and she asked me,"What's wrong Steve?" and I said, "I don't know – there's something..." and I frightened quite a number of people and I told the team leader that I couldn't stand still,** something is going to happen, I don't know what it is, something urgent is happening. And she saw my face and my face at that point was about half covered and she said "My God, you've been hit all over the place" I said, "I know, it's coming to a head and I don't know what's going to happen." Then, going from chamber to chamber I came across Maria and all of a sudden I saw him – John - standing right next to her and he was saying "That's my daughter." I thought, "Fucking hell, please don't let anything happen to Maria," so I went up to two other people and said, "Look, stay with her and let nothing happen." They were really freaked out but I said, "Just stay with her." And I left because I thought he would follow me rather than stay with Maria, which he did.

Then I went back to her but left again - I just could not stand still - I was like, what do I do, where do I go? I know something's going to happen. I was going to people saying "Look, please stay safe, just stay safe" and everybody that believed me was freaked out and everybody who didn't believe me thought "Fucking idiot." And I went down to another team leader who told me to sit down and have a drink but before I even sat down I thought fucking hell, what an opportunity, he thinks she's his daughter, I'll just go and get her, take her to him and say "She's sorry," and see if it works and I went and talked to Maria and convinced her – she was OK with it because she knew the history of the problem that this character had – his daughter being pregnant and I'd said "He thinks that you're his daughter – don't ask me why, he just thinks it. Would you do this?" And she said "Yes, but I'm really frightened." I said, "Don't worry, if anything's going to happen, it's going to happen to me, it's not going to happen to you." By which time I knew it wasn't going to happen to her, my face was red raw then and she looked at my face and went "Oh fucking hell, what will happen to me?" I said, "Don't worry, it's only going to happen to me."

We went down to the most powerful place there was, T86 and there he was, stood right at the bottom. I said to Maria "Can you see him?" She said, "No, I can't see a thing." I said, "Don't worry, he's right at the bottom," and I put my arm round her and she walked with me and I thought "This person thinks I'm crazy." You know I can remember thinking – 'If she can't see him, then this person, Maria, thinks I'm crazy, she must do.' But she didn't! And I said to John, "This is your daughter and she wants to say she's sorry," and I just nudged Maria a little bit and she said, "I forgive you father." And he gave such a radiant smile, such a kind of like...oh....and like I say, it's like tilting a mirror - and he's gone. He just smiled and turned the mirror and from then on, I knew, I just knew, we'd got him. I knew that he'd gone.

I hadn't banished him, I'd just made him happy. And he's gone. I don't think ever I could banish him because his strength was more powerful than anything I'd know, so there was no way I was going to banish him. But I wanted to make him happy and he went and I don't know – please don't let him start up again!

It's a remarkable story but it actually happened over a period of nearly four years so therefore I didn't know Maria was going to be there at the end of it. I didn't know she was going to have all of these problems with her pregnancy. But that's exactly what was needed at the time. It was like the story going for four years until it actually happened and it actually happened on that date and he was as strong as he's ever been. You know, my face, was marked all over so therefore it was a different night, it was a very strong night, I felt the urgency and I knew, I knew that something was going to happen. I thought it was going to be bad, but it turned out to be good because he was happy and turned away and I think all it wanted was that pinnacle time that said, "This can end here." And it did.

As for the possibility of a demon coming through at the same time, well, I don't know and I'll never know about that will I? I mean it just felt nasty. People have said that it's an entity coming through of a spirit and there's argument for and against about all that, but honestly I don't know what I saw, I don't know what the truth is about all that has happened.'

So what are we left with? Let us assume that all of that time ago, when Steve himself ascertained John's history with his daughter becoming pregnant by Dan and being thrown out of home by her father, is what actually happened. If you like, the accurate version of this ghost story. Clearly Steve, holding the essence of Dan had been mistaken for John's brother. Maria, pregnant, has the essence of his daughter, who John regretted throwing out of the house prior to his sudden death. All of these people possibly linked through reincarnation. Or just through coincidence. We will never truly know. The essence of John, finally recognising that he is forgiven, can perhaps move on to the place where he should be. Steve doesn't think John will be back. Again, this is something we do not know. But this book has to end sometime and I do wonder whether I may have attained my 'neat' ending after all.

Steve and I both felt very moved. Steve had spent a night of laughter, tears, relief and no emotional ill effects of despair. He felt resolved. My own tears leaked out as he told me the story before I had to get up to start my day's work as a counsellor, listening to the life stories of others. Maria was given a big thank you for her help, random as it was but given willingly in a state of bewilderment and under the most peculiar of circumstances. Certainly, some explanation and processing needed to go ahead between her and Steve about the strange events and the task that was asked of her. It is likely that Steve will be leaving his job in the next year or so. In the meantime, let us hope that his remaining time there is peaceful and free from supernatural activity. His face had virtually completely healed up over night. It was pointless to take a photograph. This was my final diary entry:

End of 2009: *The ghost has gone. The carousels and cranes remain still. No smells, no cobwebs, no voices and no danger of Steve being pursued or molested physically and psychologically. He has reclaimed all areas of the warehouse including the dreaded T86 which may of course have been a logical place from which to haunt owing to the clothing for babies and connections with pregnancy. Now, the only inhabitants of the warehouse, at least visible to the naked eye, are the workers.*

Whether Steve and I will ever fully 'believe' in ghosts or not, we know that these events have occurred and have been part of our history. As time moves on and the events of that November night recede, our energies become focussed on other matters and life continues peacefully. It becomes more of a challenge for Steve and me to even imagine that all of this actually happened. But we know that it did.

This is the story of a 'supernatural survivor' who was haunted by just one ghost, but one was enough.

Final Thoughts

Is psychic ability a blessing or a curse? I guess it depends on your perspective. My personal journey has been around learning to live with a new partner who, it seems, may have discovered a degree of psychic ability. Steve clearly doesn't want to enrich or utilise this ability and therefore chooses the road of endeavouring to close it all down. Or, if not psychic, he has been unfortunate enough to have become the subject of a haunting by an entity that attached itself to him, needing attention and resolution through forgiveness. Or perhaps this was a malicious entity motivated by harm and was actually nothing to do with any deceased person, whether dealing with unfinished business or offering unconditional love from a realm beyond life. Or possibly more than one entity had entered the space, from another dimension, certainly one element at least appearing to be 'demonic.'

Whatever the case, Steve and I have to adjust to this new found discovery in a way perhaps similar to learning of a diagnosis of physical or mental illness or any other change in personal circumstances that is going to affect a relationship. We need to own and stay open to this learning in order to survive. As we know, when one partner becomes a therapist, with all the change that introspection brings, this can be a challenge for the remaining uninitiated partner. It is of course, also a challenge for a person to enter therapy. Either way, change is inevitable and the impact on close attachments needs to be borne in mind. Therapist Michael Jacobs typifies this research when he tells us that: *'Counselling and therapy sometimes leads to the splitting of partnerships; but it is regrettable when therapy so concentrates upon the client that it does not also help the client to recognise the needs of his or her partner'* (1995). For new psychics, or maybe for those people who are receiving spiritual healing, the challenges are clearly just as extreme. Ashworth himself advises that: *'A healing awakening can bring with it a great upheaval on the domestic front and I have seen very many cases where one partner is going through healing or spiritual evolution which results in the break up of the relationship.'* Ashworth's own first marriage failed on account of his new found psychic abilities. There have been times, albeit only fleeting thoughts, when I have wondered if I could continue with my relationship, given how much distress the haunting has caused. For me it became obvious that whether a person is the focus of a haunting, particularly a long term violent experience like Steve's, or whether the individual discovers a psychic ability which has life changing implications, there will be a degree of stress involved, which may even escalate into some symptoms of trauma for the affected person.

Whilst I have detailed the facts around the haunting of my partner which occurred over the last few years, considering the situation cognitively and experientially, offering perspectives from fictional literature, film, autobiography and case studies from my therapeutic work in addition to research on neurological function and the origins of supernatural belief, this book of course, has in many ways been about me. Ask me again if I believe in ghosts and the short answer is still 'no.' The longer answer is 'Read this book.' I cannot deny the experiences I've had which lead me to believe that this particular ghost existed, attacking Steve on and off over a three or four year period with results I clearly witnessed. It is noticeable how I have changed and challenged my own perceptions and beliefs around supernatural phenomena, journeying from a reasonably firmly held belief that supernatural experiences can be the result of underlying trauma, neurological dysfunction or underlying mental health issues and were all a result of projections and hallucinations originating within the mind. As I continued with my observations, interpretations, speculations and emotional experiencing of the phenomena with which I was being presented, however, it seems apparent during the progress of my writing that I was becoming more open minded about supernatural occurrences, psychic awareness and the fact that I was learning to hold challenging experiences. My resulting discomfort, which I now feel I have successfully integrated – comprises a sense that I know what I know and am open to what I don't know. This of course, impacts on my work as a therapist and provides material for further growth for myself and for me to work more effectively with any of my clients who are impacted by psychic or supernatural issues.

Of course, Steve is my partner and I need to be aware that to have treated him as a client was not possible. I needed to own the fact that however much I may read, watch and research, becoming involved in conversations with therapists, psychics and clients along the way over the past few years, I have needed to hold and to own my defences. The horror of having a partner who is being haunted is insurmountable. My sense has been that there is something wrong with him. He could be ill, he could be dying. He could be insane. He could be psychic, he could be crazy, he could be a liar. He could be acting out something from his history; he could be fearful of something in the future. I have no real idea. I have needed to cope. I have needed to intellectualise, to explore, to feel and to search for my own conclusions, such as they are. I have needed to feel; my rage, helplessness, fear, grandiosity, vulnerability and bewilderment. I have been aware at times of my over identification with Steve, of my confluence, my extreme reactions, my urge to continually rescue and probably lots of other responses that readers of this book picked up as I went along. To be honest, my main defence immediately upon finishing my writing initially comprised a protective response of *'I don't really care what anyone thinks.'* From this, over the months, especially as 26 March 2010, the fourth anniversary of John's first appearance came and went peacefully, myself and Steve have moved into a position of full integration. We speak of what happened occasionally, but we are no longer living it.

For me essentially, what I also needed for myself over the years was to write. Hopefully, by doing this I have offered here a chance for discussion, speculation and interest in my story. I also recognise the opportunity for readers to demonstrate reactions of scepticism, disbelief, disregard and even disgust. Ultimately, however, like any of my clients opening up in therapy, all I can do is to tell you what happened, as honestly as I can, and how it felt.

AFTERWORD

Following a peaceful period of time which lasted about seven months, the experiences suddenly began to re-occur. During the summer months of 2010 Steve was persecuted several times and he endured the familiar scarring to his face. Interestingly, many of these incidents occurred in the canteen when members of the night shift team were on their break. People surrounding Steve when he was 'hit' reported feeling very nauseous and understandably, 'freaked out.' Elsewhere, Steve also again had sight and communication with the apparition which once more caused a significant level of confusion and distress for both of us. I have chosen not to record any more of these occurrences. Whilst this narrative of events is concluded, it appears that the situation itself is bound to continue whilst Steve remains present in the warehouse. Whether the events are natural forces or supernatural in origin, the priority now is physical and mental survival. Bearing this in mind as I write these final lines, Steve is contemplating leaving his employment.

'He came back, but he is already a ghost, a dead man. You can't kill a ghost can you?' (Swift 2004)

Louisa Marsh
December 2010

BIBLIOGRAPHY

Ackroyd, P (1991) *Dickens* London, Minerva

Ashworth, D (2001) *Dancing With the Devil: Survival for Healers and Therapists,* Bath, Crucible

Assagioli, R (1993) Psychosynthesis, *A Manual of Principles and Techniques* London, Aquarian/Thorsons

Bass, E & Davis, L (1988) *The Courage To Heal. A Guide For Women Survivors of Child Sexual Abuse* USA, Cedar

Beauregard M & O'Leary D (2007) *The Spiritual Brain: A Neuroscientist's Case for the Existence of the Soul* New York, HarperCollins Publishers

Bell, V (2010) *The draft of the new 'psychiatric bible is published* Mind Hacks www.mindhacks.com/blog/2010

Bernheim KF & Lewine RJ (1979) *Schizophrenia, Symptoms, Causes, Treatments* London, Norton & Co

Bion, W (1974) *Brazilian Lectures 1* Rio de Janeiro: Imago Editora

Bion, W (1980) *Bion in New York and Sao Paulo* Ed F Bion. Perthshire: Clunie Press

Boadella (1987) *Life Streams. An Introduction To Biosynthesis* London, Routledge & Kegan Paul

Bond, T (2002) *Naked Narrative: Real Research?* CPR June 2002 Vol 2 no. 2

Briere, JN (1992) *Child Abuse Trauma. Theory and Treatment Of Lasting Effects* London, Sage Publications

Broadbent, DE (1958) *Perception and Communication* London Pergomon Press

Bronte, E (1976) *Wuthering Heights* Middlesex, Penguin Books

Buckman, R (2002*) Can We Be Good Without God? Biology, Behaviour and the Need to Believe* New York, Prometheus Books

Casement, P (1994) *On Learning From the Patient* London, Routledge

Charles, D (2003) *Real Feelings* CPJ October 2003 Vol 14 no. 8

Courtois, CA (1988) *Healing the Incest Wound* New York, WW Norton & Company

Coward, Noel (1941) *Blithe Spirit: An Improbable Farce* London Samuel French Ltd

Cushway and Sewall (1992) *Counselling with Dreams and Nightmares* London, Sage Publications

Dahl, R (1974) *Charlie and the Chocolate Factory* Middlesex, Puffin Books

Dahl, R (1996) *James and the Giant Peach,* London, Penguin Books

Dahl, R (1988) *Matilda* London, Penguin Books

Dawkins, R (2006) *The God Delusion* London, Bantam Press

Dean, J (1998) *Multiple Personalities* www.geocities.com/Athens/Froum/5212/multiper.htm

De Salvo, L (1989) *Virginia Woolf: The Impact Of Childhood Sexual Abuse On Her Life And Work* London, The Women's Press

Dickens, C (1985) *The Christmas Books Volume 1, A Christmas Carol/The Chimes* London Penguin Books

Dickens,C (1997) *The Signal Man* from *Best Ghost Stories* Hertfordshire Wordsworth Editions Ltd

Dickens, C (1983) *Dombey and Son* Middlesex, Penguin Books

Dickens, C (1985) *Hard Time,* Middlesex, Penguin Books

Dickens, C (1983) *Our Mutual Friend* Middlesex, Penguin Books

DSM III Diagnostic and Statistical Manuel of Mental Disorders (1980) Third Edition Washington, American Psychiatric Association

DSM IV Diagnostic and Statistical Manuel of Mental Disorders (2005) Fourth Edition Washington, American Psychiatric Association

Finkelhor, D & Browne, A (1986) *A Sourcebook On Child Sexual Abuse* California, US, Sage Publications

Fiore, E (1987) *The Unquiet Dead: A Psychologist Treats Spirit Possession* New York, Ballentine Books

Fordham F (1964) *An Introduction to Jung's Psychology* Middlesex, Penguin Books

Foskett, J (2003) *Is Religion Counselling's Last Taboo?* CPJ October 2003 Vol 14 no. 8

Fraser, S (1989) *My Father's House, A Memoir Of Incest and Of Healing* London, Virago Press Ltd

Freud, S (1962) The Aetiology of Hysteria *The Standard Edition of the Complete Psychological Works of Sigmund Freud.* Vol 3 London, Hogarth Press

Gallagher, Dr V (1991) *Becoming Whole Again* Florida, TAB Books

Ganaway, GK (1989) *Narrative Truth: Clarifying the Role of Extraneous Trauma in the Etiology of MPD and its Variants* Dissociation 2 no 4:209

Gil, E (1990) *United We Stand. A Book For People With Multiple Personalities* USA Launch Press

Goleman, D (1997) *Vital Lies, Simple Truths. The Psychology Of Self Deception* London, Bloomsbury

Gurney, E, Myers, F & Podmore, F (1886) *Phantasms of the Living* Society for Psychical Research, London, Trubner & Co

Haaken, J (1998) *Pillar Of Salt. Gender, Memory and the Perils of Looking Back* London, Free Association Books

Haddon, M (2004) *The Curious Incident of the Dog in the Night-time* London Vintage Books

Hall, L & Lloyd S (1993) *Surviving Child Sexual Abuse. A Handbook For Helping Women Challenge Their Past* London The Falmer Press, 2nd edition

Hartmann, E (1987) *The Nightmare: The Psychology and Biology of Terrifying Dreams* New York, Basic Books

Herman, JL, (1992) *Trauma and Recovery* New York Basic Books

Hines, T (2003) *Pseudoscience and the Paranormal* New York, Prometheus Books

Hurt, S (1998) *Am I Not A Person?* Nottingham, The Word Factory

Jacobs, M (1995) *The Presenting Past* Buckingham, Open University Press

Jones-Wood, C (1998) Information from Oakwood Associates Consultancy on *Dissociative Identity Disorder*

Jung, C (1989) *Memories, Dreams, Reflections* London, Collins, Routledge & Kegan Paul

Karr-Morse R and Wiley MS (1997) *Ghosts From the Nursery: Tracing the Roots of Violence* New York, The Atlantic Monthly Press

Keyes, M (2007) *Anybody Out There?* London, Penguin Books

Knight, M (2008) *Touched By Evil* London, Hodder & Stoughton

Lee, P (2007) *Science, Not Superstition: The Nature of Ghosts* www.paullee.com/ghosts/sns.html

Le Bon, G *Crowd: A Study of the Popular Mind* Cited in Buckman (2002)

Maltz, W (1991) *The Sexual Healing Journey. A Guide For Survivors Of Sexual Abuse* New York, Harper Collins

Marriot, M (2008) *Personal religious or spiritual beliefs, and the experience of hearing voices, having strong beliefs, or other experiences affecting mental well-being and general functioning* Michael.marriot@nottsshc.nhs.uk

Miller, A (1984) *The Crucible* Middlesex, Penguin Books

Morgan, S (2008) *My Psychic Life* London, Penguin Books

Nesbit, E (2000) *The Railway Children* London, Carlton Books

Newberg A, D'Aquili E, Rause V *Why God Won't Go Away: Brain Science and the Biology of Belief* (2001) New York Ballentine Books

Ogden, T H (1992) *Projective Identification and Psychotherapeutic Technique* London, Maresfield Library

Owen, W (1984) *Strange Meeting*, in *First World War Poetry* ed by J Silkin, Middlesex, Penguin Books

Owens, Darrin (2006) *Reader of Hearts: The Life and Teachings of a Reluctant Psychic* California, New World Library

Parsons, M (2001) *Psychic Reality, Negation and the Analytic Setting* in *The Dead Mother: The Work of Andre Green* Ed G Kohon London, Routledge

Pennacchia, YM (1994) *Healing the Whole, The Diary Of An Incest Survivor* London, Cassell

Pope, KS & Brown, LS (1996) *Recovered Memories of Abuse, Assessment, Therapy, Forensics* Washington DC, American psychological Association

Rogers, C (1995) *On Becoming A Person* London, Constable

Rogers, C (1986) *Carl Rogers on Personal Power* London, Constable

Roland, P (2007) *The Complete Book of Ghosts: A Fascinating Exploration of the Spirit World, From Apparitions to Haunted Places* London Arturus Publishing Limited

Romme, Prof. M & Escher, S (1993) *Accepting Voices* London, Mind Publications

Rose, S (1999) Psychological Trauma: A Historical Perspective *Counselling, The Journal of the British Association for Counselling* Vol 10 no. 2 139-141

Rosenfeld, H (1971) *Problems of Psychosis* eds P Doucet and C Laurin Amsterdam Excerpta Medica

Rothschild, B (2000) The *Body Remembers: The Psychophysiology of Trauma and Trauma Treatment* New York, London Norton & Company

Rowling, JK (1999) *Harry Potter and the Prisoner of Azkaban* New York Scholastic Inc

Sanford, LT (1991) *Strong At The Broken Places* London, Virago Press

Schreiber, FR (1974) *Sybil: The Classic True Story of a Woman Possessed by Sixteen Personalities* New York Grand Central Publishing

Sebold A (2002) *The Lovely Bones* London Picador

Selwyn Margaret (1994) *The Awakening Year: An Exploration in Gestalt Psychotherapy* London Tudor

Shakespeare, W (1981) *Hamlet* Middlesex, Penguin Books

Shakespeare, W (1981) *Macbeth* Middlesex, Penguin Books

Smedley, T (2007) *How to Make a Ghost Redundant* People Management Journal (CIPD) Vol 13 no. 22

Smith, M (1993) *Ritual Abuse - What It Is, Why It Happens, How To Help* New York, Harper Collins

Smith, P (1993) *Childhood, Sexual Abuse, Sexuality, Pregnancy and Birthing* New Zealand, Inside Out Books

Stephenson, P (2002) *Billy* London HarperCollins

Stokes, D (1980) *Voices In My Ear: The Autobiography of a Medium* London Futura Publications

Thigpen CH and Cleckley HM (1957) *The Three Faces of Eve* London, Secker & Warburg

The Living Bible (1977) East Sussex, Coverdale

Tolstoy, L (1983) *Anna Karenin* Middlesex, Penguin Books

Townsend, M (2007) *Magnetic Hallucinations* ASSAP www.assap.org

Townsend, M (2007) *Recording Ghosts ('stone tape theory')* ASSAP www.assap.org

Troops for Truddi Chase (1987) *When Rabbit Howls* London, Sidgwick & Jackson

Van der Hart O, Nijenhuis ERS, Steele K (2006) *The Haunted Self: Structural Dissociation and the Treatment of Chronic Tramatization* New York W W Norton & Company

Van Derbur, M (2004) *Miss America By Day: Lessons Learned from Ultimate Betrayals and Unconditional Love* Denver Colorado, Oak Hill Ridge Press

Van der Kolk, B, McFarlane, A & Weisaeth, L (1996) *Traumatic Stress: The Effects of Overwhelming Experience on Mind, Body and Society* http://trauma-pages.com/vanderk3.htm

Venerable Raine, N (1998) *After Silence: Rape and My Journey Back* New York, Crown Publishers Inc

Walker, Alice (2000) *The Color Purple* London, The Women's Press

Wilberg, G (2008) *The Joy of Not Knowing* Therapy Today September 2008 Vol 19 no. 7

Williams, MJ (1991) *Healing Hidden Memories* Florida, Health Communication Inc.

Williams, V (2003) Religion, *Counselling & Psychotherapy – Complementary or Controversial?* CPJ August 2003 Vol 14 no 7

Yalom, I (2008) *The Ripple Effect* Therapy Today May 2008 Vol 19 no. 4

FILM & TELEVISION

Am I Normal? Spirituality 28/4/08 BBC 2
Between The Lines: Railways in Film and Fiction (2009) BBC 2
Brief Encounter (1945) D: David Lean
Britain's Most Haunted (2002) Living TV
Carrie (1973) D: Brian De Palma
Casper the Friendly Ghost (1995) D: Brad Silberling
Dallas (Series 1985/86) CBS
Dr Who: Blink (2007) Series 3 9/6/07 BBC 1

The Enemies of Reason (2007) 13/8/07 Channel 4
The Entity (1983) D: Sidney J Furie
The Exorcist (1973) D: William Friedkin
Ghost (1990) D: Jerry Zucker
Ghostbusters (1984) D: Ivan Reitman
Ghost Hunters (2004) 6/10/04 Syfy
Ghost Whisperer (2005) 23/09/05 CBS
The Life of Brian (1979) D: Terry Jones
Medium (2005) 3/1/05 NBC
The Others (2001) D: Alejandro Amenabar
Phenomenon (1996) D: Jon Turteltaub
Poppy Shakespeare (2008) D: Benjamin Ross Channel 4
Scooby Doo (1969-1976) Hanna-Barbera Productions
The Shining (1980) D: Stanley Kubrick
The Sixth Sense (1999) D: M Night Shyamalan
The Truman Show (1998) D: Peter Weir
Truly Madly Deeply (1991) D: Anthony Minghella
Unexplained Mysteries: When Ghosts Attack (2007) 1/11/03 CBS
What Lies Beneath (2000) D: Robert Zemeckis

ADDITIONAL INTERNET RESOURCES

www.assap.org (2007)
www.cdnn.info/news/industry/i050120.html (2007)
www.ghostvillage.com (2007)
www.intervoiceonline.org (2008)
www.mormonwiki.com/Articles_of_Faith (2009)
www.news-medical.net (2007)
www.nightterrors.org (2007)
www.paranormaldatabase.com (2007)
www.sleepeducation.com (2007)
www.smalltownghosts.com/stg1/McPike.html (2007)
www.spr.ac.uk (2008)
www.geocities.com/eel (2007)
www.survivalafterdeath.org (2007)
www.wikipedia.org (2007)
www.yourghoststories.com (2007)

Lightning Source UK Ltd.
Milton Keynes UK
UKOW030906181111

182224UK00001B/9/P